Canadian	International	Prime Ministers	
	1899 • Canadian volunteers fight in the Boer War	**1896–1911** • Wilfrid Laurier (Liberal)	**1900**
	1903 • Alaska boundary dispute		
1905 • Alberta and Saskatchewan become provinces			**1905**
	1914 • First World War begins		**1910**
	1918 • First World War ends	**1911–1920** • Robert Borden (Conservative)	
1914 • War Measures Act	• Spanish flu pandemic		
	1919 • Paris Peace Conference		**1915**
	• Treaty of Versailles		
1917 • Halifax explosion	• League of Nations established	**1920–1921** • Arthur Meighen (Conservative)	
• Conscription crisis	1922 • Chanak Crisis		**1920**
• Khaki election	• Mussolini comes to power in Italy	**1921–1926**	
1919 • Winnipeg General Strike	1923 • Halibut Treaty	• William Lyon Mackenzie King (Liberal)	
1926 • King-Byng Crisis	1928 • Joseph Stalin gains control of the Soviet Union	**1926 (3 months)** • Arthur Meighen (Conservative)	**1925**
• Imperial Conference leads to Balfour Report	1929 • Stock market crash	**1926–1930** • William Lyon Mackenzie King (Liberal)	
1927 • Old-age pensions introduced	• Depression begins		
	1933 • Adolph Hitler comes to power in Germany	**1930–1935** • R.B. Bennett (Conservative)	**1930**
1931 • Statute of Westminster	• Franklin Roosevelt introduces economic "new deal" in the U.S.		
1932 • Co-operative Commonwealth Federation (CCF) founded	1936 • Spanish Civil war begins	**1935–1948** • William Lyon Mackenzie King (Liberal)	**1935**
• Federal relief camps established	1938 • *Kristallnacht* in Germany		
1935 • On-to-Ottawa Trek	1939 • Second World War begins		
1936 • CBC created	1941 • Japan bombs Pearl Harbor		
1937 • Rowell-Sirois Report	1944 • D-Day		**1940**
1939 • British Commonwealth Air Training Plan begins	• UN sets up World Bank and International Monetary Fund		
1940 • National Resources Mobilization Act	1945 • U.S. drops atomic bombs on Hiroshima and Nagasaki, Japan		**1945**
1942 • Canadians vote in favour of conscription	• Second World War ends	**1948–1957** • Louis St. Laurent (Liberal)	
1949 • Newfoundland joins Canada	• United Nations created		
	1948 • Universal Declaration of Human Rights		**1950**
1951 • Massey Report	1949 • NATO formed		
	• Geneva Convention		
	1950 • Korean War begins		
	1953 • Korean War ends		**1955**
	1955 • Warsaw Pact formed		
	1956 • Suez crisis	**1957–1963** • John Diefenbaker (Conservative)	
	1958 • U.S. and Canada sign NORAD agreement		

THINK HISTORY

CANADIAN HISTORY SINCE 1914

Michael Cranny

Garvin Moles

PEARSON

Feedback on this publication can be sent to editorialfeedback@pearsoned.com

Pearson Canada Inc.
26 Prince Andrew Place
Don Mills, ON   M3C 2T8
Customer Service: 1-800-361-6128

1 2 3 4 5   TC   19 18 17 16 15
Printed and bound in Canada

Publisher: Susan Cox
Senior Marketing Specialist: Barbara Mlotek
Managing Editor: Lee Ensor
Project Manager: Adrianna Edwards, Focus Strategic Communications, Inc.
Developmental Editors: Jessica Pegis, Cara James, Tricia Carmichael, Sheila Fletcher, Christel Kleitsch, Caroline Kloss, Martha Malic
Production Editors: Allana Barron, Christine Higdon, Marie Kocher, Lisa Santilli
Editorial Assistant: Kayla Sippel
Project Managers, Editorial: Adrianna Edwards, Ron Edwards, Focus Strategic Communications, Inc.
Copy Editors: Kathleen ffolliott, Francine Geraci
Proofreader: Francine Geraci
Fact Checker: Tracy Westell, Christine Higdon
Indexer: Ron Edwards, Focus Strategic Communications, Inc.
Photo Researcher and Permissions Editor: Danny Meldung/Photo Affairs, Inc
Manager, Project Management K–12: Alison Dale
Project Manager, Production: Jon Maxfield
Cover Design, Interior Design: Alex Li
Composition: ArtPlus Ltd.
Vice-President, Publishing: Mark Cobham

ISBN: 978-0-13-415161-8

ACKNOWLEDGEMENTS

Contributing Writers

Allan Hux

Mike Clare
Kevin Reed
Paula Waatainen

Jenise Boland
Mike Denos
Rob Lewis
Holly Mair
Janet Ruest
Glen Thielman

Reviewers

Anthony Asturi   Trillium Lakelands District School Board
Michael Burgess   Peel District School Board
Mike Clare   Faculty of Education
                        University of Ontario Institute of Technology
Ian Duncan   Halton District School Board
Allan Hux   Acting President, Ontario History, Humanities
                        & Social Sciences Consultants' Association
                        (OHHSSCA)
Desiree Ludin   Peel District School Board
Chris Valentine   Simcoe District School Board
Paula Waatainen   West Vancouver School District
Jeff Young   Trillium Lakelands District School Board

First Nations, Métis, and Inuit Content Reviewers

Dean Cunningham   Faculty of Education
                        Simon Fraser University
Robert Leavitt   Professor Emeritus of Education
                        University of New Brunswick
Kevin Reed   Limestone District School Board

Bias Consultant

Sherida Sherry Hassanali   Mount Saint Vincent University

CONTENTS

CONTENTS

Inquiry in history is similar to detective work. Historians search for evidence that gives us insight into the life and times of people living in the past. "The past" includes everything that happened; "history" is an account created by people as they investigate what happened in the past.

Historians are very interested in **primary source evidence**, which is created by people living at the time of the events. Historians, journalists, and other observers look back into the past and construct their own interpretations of a certain event, person, or movement. They analyze, review, and summarize primary sources. These accounts are called **secondary sources**.

Examples of Primary Source Evidence		Examples of Secondary Source Evidence	
• letters	• diaries	• biographies	• documentaries
• photographs	• physical artefacts	• journal articles	
• oral tradition	• newspapers of the time	• textbooks	

With the introduction of electronic communications, many people were worried about the loss of primary source evidence. They were afraid that the words, ideas, and images carried by the telegraph, telephone, and Internet would be lost. With the revelations of Edward Snowden, an ex-CIA agent who leaked government information, it appears that many people's communications have been captured by government agencies and others. Will computer hard drives and computer servers be the archives for the historians of the future? Does material ever disappear from the Internet?

Through various activities in *Think History*, you will have the opportunity to learn about historical inquiry and to search for and review many sources. You will be expected to construct your own interpretations about certain events and people using relevant evidence from the past. When new evidence is found, students of history need to adjust their interpretations and conclusions. There is not one single, absolute interpretation of an event in the past. The diagram of the historical inquiry process on the next page is designed to help you be aware of the process and feel comfortable applying it.

Historical Inquiry Process

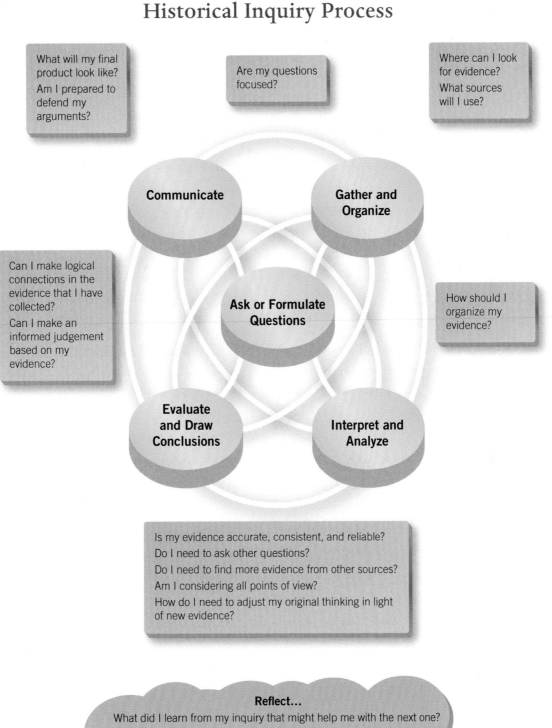

What will my final product look like?

Am I prepared to defend my arguments?

Are my questions focused?

Where can I look for evidence?
What sources will I use?

Communicate

Gather and Organize

Can I make logical connections in the evidence that I have collected?

Can I make an informed judgement based on my evidence?

Ask or Formulate Questions

How should I organize my evidence?

Evaluate and Draw Conclusions

Interpret and Analyze

Is my evidence accurate, consistent, and reliable?
Do I need to ask other questions?
Do I need to find more evidence from other sources?
Am I considering all points of view?
How do I need to adjust my original thinking in light of new evidence?

Reflect...
What did I learn from my inquiry that might help me with the next one?
How did my inquiry help me better understand _____?
What advice could I offer someone else doing a similar inquiry?

What Is Historical Thinking?

Historical thinking is much more than memorizing names and dates. When you use historical thinking concepts, you think about how events in the past have shaped our world today. There are six concepts that we can use to guide our historical thinking.

Historical Significance

Is a person, group, event, or development historically significant? Ask:

- Did it **result in change**? If so, was the change:
  - **Lasting**, or did the situation reverse itself?
  - **Profound**, having great impact?
  - **Widespread**, affecting a large number of people?
- Is it **revealing**? Does it shed light on a bigger issue or what life was like?

For example, if you are asked to write about three events leading to the First World War, asking these questions could help you narrow down your search.

Significance varies over time. The importance of issues changes over time, so the significance of those issues changes as well. Significance is also something determined by those who write or tell the narratives of history. They are individuals with their own opinions, making decisions on what to leave out and what to leave in.

Continuity and Change

Change is always happening, both quickly and slowly, both positive and negative. However, there are also things that stay the same. For example, the neighbourhood you live in may have changed greatly over time, or not at all. It may have changed slowly for twenty years and then quickly in the last ten.

Some ways to make sense of continuity and change would be to:

- Build a **timeline**, or a sequence of events
- Look for **turning points**, or moments when there is a noticeable change
- Look for evidence that there has been **progress** or **decline** over a period of time
- Organize your study by deciding on what time periods you will be comparing

Cause and Consequence

What brings about change? Historical events can have more than one cause. There can be **direct** causes (an Irish family decides to immigrate to Canada in 1850 because of the potato famine) and **indirect** causes (the same family is completely dependent on that crop for different political and social reasons, spanning decades). After the event happens, there are consequences—noticeable changes that can be either **short-term** (the potato famine reduced the Irish population by 25 percent) or **long-term** (the loss of many Irish speakers made English the language of the majority in Ireland for the first time).

When looking at cause and consequence, we can try to determine:

- What is significant? What is not?
- What were the actions of the people or groups involved?
- What were the conditions that helped lead to change?
- What were the **intended** and **unintended** consequences?
- What if that had not happened?
- How might things have been different?

Historical Perspectives

We see the world in a very different way than people did in the past. When studying events in the past, we try to infer how people felt at the time by examining evidence. We need to avoid **presentism**, which means that we look at events in the past based only on how we see the world in the present. When considering historical perspectives, you should:

- Think about how **historical context** may have influenced the perspective of a person or group. If we accept that things change over time, we must understand that people's feelings and beliefs will also change.
- Compare the perspectives of different people or groups on the same issue. They may have lived at different times, in different places, or under different conditions.

The Ethical Dimension

When we examine any period in history, it's natural to have questions about the ethics of the people, laws, or events of that time. Were they **fair**? Were they **honest**? People in the past cannot be excused for their actions, but we should examine those actions within the **context** of that time and place. Some guidelines to help tackle the ethical dimensions of the past are:

- Realize that people who create the historical narratives in our textbooks, documentaries, and museum displays hold their own ethical stances. Sometimes they do so openly and explicitly, but other times it may only be implied.
- When making an ethical judgment about past actions, consider the historical context. Be cautious about imposing our current sense of right and wrong.

Evidence

Historians make **interpretations** based on evidence such as primary sources. Two major types of primary sources include **accounts** (such as an eyewitness testimony about an event) and **traces** (something left behind from the past that we can examine, such as a store catalogue, a death certificate, or a photograph).

The Atari Graveyard

In April 2014, a team of archaeologists, a documentary film crew, city representatives, and hundreds of onlookers gathered at the landfill outside of the town of Alamogordo, New Mexico to look for evidence of an event that for years had been dismissed by many as an urban legend.

Between September 22 and 24, 1983, Atari Inc., an American video game company, had quietly disposed of thousands of returned or unsold video games and other "e-waste" in the landfill. Eyewitnesses told stories over the years of seeing the dumping. Some had even taken games home from the landfill before they were buried. Articles about the disposal appeared in the local newspaper and the *New York Times* in 1983. The city of Alamogordo eventually protested the dump, which had been authorized by the landfill operators but not city council. Still, as the years passed, many of these stories were dismissed as untrue.

However, the search in 2014 proved that these stories were at least partly true. The most famous game found buried in Alamogordo was *E.T., the Extra-Terrestrial,* also called "the worst video game ever made." In November 2014, the City of Alamogordo began selling copies of the unearthed Atari games online. In that same month, a boxed copy of the *E.T.* game cartridge sold for $1537 on eBay.

E.T., the Extra-Terrestrial and its destruction are considered a turning point in the gaming industry. Not long after the failure of the videogame in 1983, revenues in the industry dropped dramatically. Some thought the videogame industry would not recover. This was proven not to be the case as Nintendo (DS and Wii), and later other companies such as Sony (PlayStation) and Microsoft (Xbox), took over the market.

Using the six historical thinking concepts, generate a list of questions that you might ask about the Atari Graveyard story. Which of the historical thinking concepts would be the most interesting starting point for research into this story?

Evidence

- Why did many people think the story was an urban legend instead of being true?
- Should seeing the concrete evidence of the materials in the site have been required to verify the story, or should other evidence, such as eyewitness accounts, have been enough?

Historical Significance

- Was the failure of the E.T. videogame and its impact on Atari a turning point in the gaming industry?
- What do the video games of the early 1980s reveal to us about the culture of North America during that period?

Ethical Dimension

- What does this story tell us about of how companies deal with "end-of-lifecycle" products? Was it ethical for Atari just to bury these surplus and damaged goods in a city landfill?
- How much should this example influence our opinions of corporate policies today?

Continuity and Change

- How has the video game industry changed since the early 1980s, and how has it remained the same?
- What factors have influenced changes in video games?

Evidence

Historical Significance

HISTORICAL THINKING

Ethical Dimension

Continuity and Change

Historical Perspectives

Cause and Consequence

Historical Perspectives

- How are the perspectives of this story potentially different for the people involved (e.g., Atari, game collectors, Alamogordo citizens, and so on)?
- How might people today view the dumping of e-waste into a landfill differently than how it was viewed in the early 1980s?

Cause and Consequence

- How important a cause was the E.T. videogame to the collapse of Atari and the gaming industry in North America? How important were the other causes?
- What were the consequences of this disposal? Which were intended and which were unintended?

©1982 ATARI

UNIT

1

Canada, 1914–1929

During the first three decades of the 20th century, many events, trends, and themes shaped Canada and its diverse population. International recognition, domestic changes, acts of intolerance, and economic hardships forced many Canadians to ask hard questions about who they were and what they valued. The tragedy and triumph of the First World War saw Canada begin to come of age as an independent nation while still a proud and valued Dominion within the British Empire.

At the turn of the century, Canada was looking for immigrants. Many came to work in the cities and on the Prairies, where free land was offered.

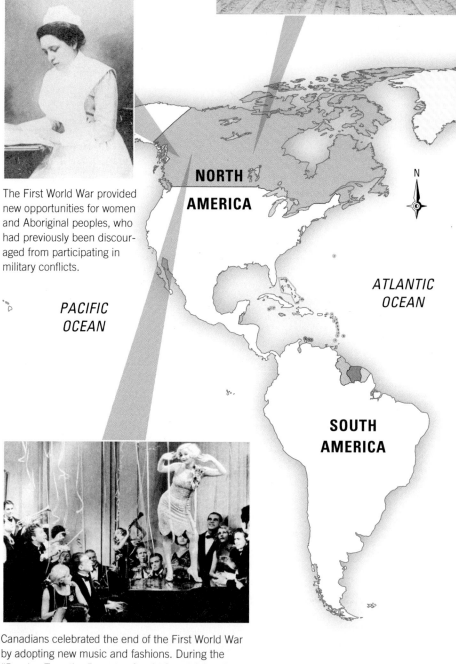

The First World War provided new opportunities for women and Aboriginal peoples, who had previously been discouraged from participating in military conflicts.

Canadians celebrated the end of the First World War by adopting new music and fashions. During the "Roaring Twenties," women fought for social and legal equality, labour unrest gave rise to the formation of unions, and Canada strengthened its status as an autonomous nation.

The First World War had a profound impact on Canada. On the battlefield, Canadian troops fought well as a united force and began to see themselves less as British Empire colonials and more as citizens of an independent country.

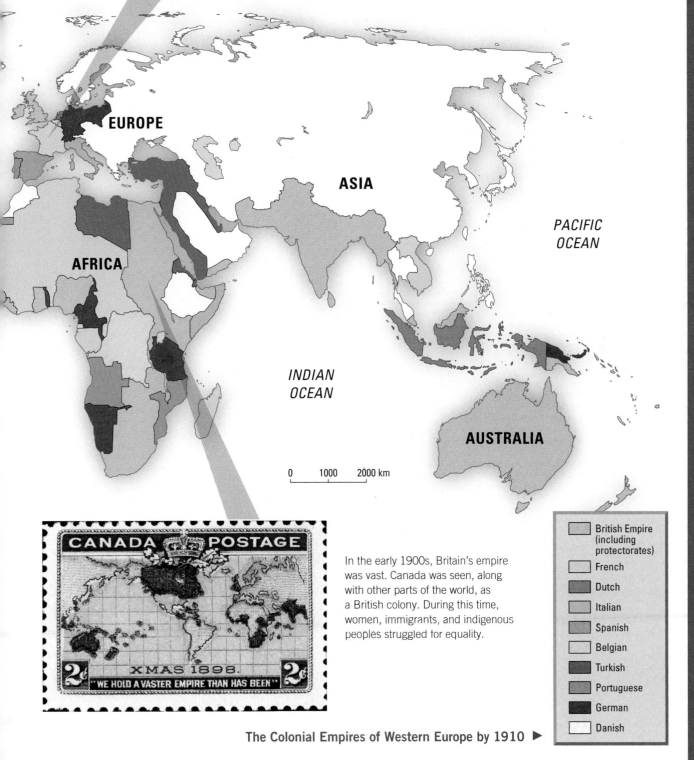

EUROPE

ASIA

PACIFIC OCEAN

AFRICA

INDIAN OCEAN

AUSTRALIA

0   1000   2000 km

In the early 1900s, Britain's empire was vast. Canada was seen, along with other parts of the world, as a British colony. During this time, women, immigrants, and indigenous peoples struggled for equality.

CANADA POSTAGE

XMAS 1898.
"WE HOLD A VASTER EMPIRE THAN HAS BEEN"

British Empire (including protectorates)

French

Dutch

Italian

Spanish

Belgian

Turkish

Portuguese

German

Danish

The Colonial Empires of Western Europe by 1910 ▶

©P

1

A Different Nation: Canada Enters the Twentieth Century

? INVESTIGATE

Social, Economic, and Political Context

- How did technology impact Canada's economy during this period?

- What impact did industrial development have on the nation?

- How did women influence Canadian society in the early 1900s?

Communities, Conflict, and Cooperation

- What attitudes did many Canadians have toward minorities?

- What steps did the government take to control immigration to Canada?

Identity, Citizenship, and Heritage

- What was Canada's relationship to Britain in the early 20th century?

- What challenges did Aboriginal peoples face in the early 1900s?

- Why were the attitudes of English- and French-speaking Canadians different regarding Britain?

A parade on Granville Street in Vancouver in 1914

Continuity and Change Why do people celebrate certain dates, such as the beginning of a new century or a new millennium? How did people in your family celebrate the beginning of the 21st century and the new millennium in 2000?

TIMELINE

1896

Wilfrid Laurier becomes prime minister of Canada

Klondike gold rush begins

1899

Canadian volunteers fight in the Boer War in South Africa

1903

Alaska boundary dispute settled between the United States and Canada

1905

Alberta and Saskatchewan become provinces

1906

Tom Longboat, an Onondaga from the Six Nations Reserve near Brantford, Ontario, wins the Boston Marathon

CHAPTER FOCUS QUESTION

What defined Canada in the early 1900s, and what attitudes and expectations did Canadians have for the century ahead?

On a cool October evening in 1904, a tall, dignified man stood in front of a crowd in Toronto's Massey Hall. He was Wilfrid Laurier, Canada's prime minister. Laurier stepped to the podium that night and presented a bold vision of Canada for the new century:

> Let me tell you, my fellow countrymen, that the twentieth century shall be the century of Canada and of Canadian development. For the next seventy-five years, nay for the next one hundred years, Canada shall be the star towards which all men who love progress and freedom shall come.
>
> –*Wilfrid Laurier*, **Toronto Globe**, *October 15, 1904*

What was Canada like at the beginning of the 20th century when Laurier made his bold prediction? Manitoba, Ontario, and Québec were much smaller than they are today. Newfoundland was still a self-governing colony, and the territory of Nunavut had not yet been created. The census of 1911 reveals that Canada's population was only 7.2 million, less than a quarter of what it was by the end of the century.

People's attitudes about good manners and behaviour in general, the role of women, national identity, minorities, and Aboriginal peoples were also different then. In this regard, Canada fit the claim that "the past is like a foreign country; they do things differently there." In our study of history, it is important to try to see the world through the eyes of Canadians at that time. This will help us understand why they took the actions that they did.

HISTORICAL THINKING

- Evidence
- Historical Significance
- Ethical Dimension
- Continuity and Change
- Historical Perspectives
- Cause and Consequence

KEY TERMS

prohibition
suffragist
imperialists
nationalists
autonomy
head tax
Indian Act
reserves
residential schools
assimilation

? HISTORICAL INQUIRY

Gather and Organize

What does this picture from Vancouver tell us about Canada in 1914? Why are pictures an important piece of historical evidence, and what do they add to a newspaper story? Why might they be more important for us than for the people in 1914?

1908
Anne of Green Gables is published

1909
First airplane flight in Canada

1911
Laurier era ends

Robert Borden elected prime minister

1912
RMS *Titanic* sinks off coast of Newfoundland

1914
Passengers on the *Komagata Maru* are refused landing in Vancouver

First World War begins

- How did women influence Canadian society in the early 1900s?

GO ONLINE

The WCTU stood for many of the social standards we have today. Read about their beliefs and values at Historica Canada.

Society and Manners

By the early 20th century, most Canadians lived on farms or in small villages, yet morals and manners of the day were set by a minority of middle- and upper-class Anglophones. These people were greatly influenced by the attitudes of **Victorian** England. This period—named after Queen Victoria, who was the British monarch from 1837 to 1901—was known for its appearance of moral strictness. Families were expected to attend church regularly; they supported Britain and the monarchy; and they believed in honour, virtue, and duty. It was an age in which right and wrong, good and evil, seemed clear; they were not seen as issues that needed discussion or debate.

There was little tolerance for those who did not obey the law, and the application of the law could be quite harsh. At the time, the death penalty was the sentence for murder. Most convictions, however, were for crimes against people's property. Drunkenness was a close second.

Women of the Era

In the early 1900s, the Woman's Christian Temperance Union (WCTU), founded in the 1870s, was still actively campaigning for **prohibition**. These women saw alcohol as the cause of many of society's problems. They also supported women's right to vote. With the vote, women believed they could influence the government to address social problems of the day, such as child labour, pollution, and poverty. Nellie McClung was a well-known **suffragist** who, together with other women, campaigned for women's rights (see Chapter 3).

Since moral codes of behaviour were strict and well-defined, the courtship of young, middle-class ladies was a formal affair under the watchful eyes of their families and community. Once married, women had few rights over property or children, and divorce was rare. Women were not considered persons under the law—unless they committed a crime. Even a woman's salary was legally the property of her husband. Women who worked outside the home, usually before marriage, were employed mainly as servants or factory workers. Some women were teachers and nurses; a few even became doctors.

FIGURE 1–1
Woman's Christian Temperance Union convention in Calgary, 1911

Interpret and Analyze
What class of women do you think this photograph represents? Why would these women be concerned about society's problems? What Calgary women are missing from this photograph?

Arts and Leisure

As Canada started to become more urbanized, its literature and art became more sentimental, expressing a preference for rural life, simple values, and happy endings. In 1908, Lucy Maud Montgomery published the much-loved novel *Anne of Green Gables*, a rural romance set in Prince Edward Island. Stephen Leacock gently mocked small-town Ontario life in his humorous *Sunshine Sketches of a Little Town* (1912). Ernest Thompson Seton wrote moving stories about animals. Pauline Johnson, daughter of a Mohawk chief and his English wife, read poems about her Mohawk heritage to packed halls. Ontario painter Homer Watson gained international recognition with his farm scenes. In Québec, Ozias Leduc painted religious works and landscapes filled with a sense of spirituality. In British Columbia, Emily Carr explored the landscapes and peoples of the West Coast through painting and writing.

For leisure, Canadians enjoyed outdoor activities, such as running, cycling, and rowing. In the summer, trips to the beach were popular despite confining "bathing costumes." In the winter, tobogganing was a must.

Still a British Nation

At the beginning of the 20th century, some of Britain's colonies, including Canada, had their own governments but still depended on Britain to resolve disputes with other countries. The British government often made decisions that did not have Canada's best interests in mind.

The Alaska Boundary Dispute

The dispute was over the exact border of the Alaskan "panhandle," a strip of land running down the Pacific Coast between British Columbia and Alaska. Of particular concern was the question of ownership of a fjord called the Lynn Canal. This waterway provided access to the Yukon, where gold had been discovered in 1896. In a speech, Prime Minister Laurier reflected on the relations between Canada and the United States:

> I have often regretted... that we are living beside a great neighbour who, I believe I can say without being deemed unfriendly to them, are very grasping in their national actions and who are determined on every occasion to get the best in any agreement....
> –Wilfrid Laurier, October 23, 1903

In 1903, the matter was finally settled. The British, weary from fighting the Dutch for territory in South Africa during the Boer War, and unwilling to become involved in another international conflict, determined that the Lynn Canal was part of Alaska, not B.C. Many Canadians were angered by this decision, believing Britain had sold out Canada's interests to keep peace with the U.S.

KEY TERMS

Victorian of or pertaining to the reign of Queen Victoria; also someone who shares the values of that period

prohibition the banning of the sale and consumption of alcohol

suffragist a person who advocates that women should have the right to vote

HISTORICAL INQUIRY

Communicate

Select one of the painters on this page, and do an Internet search to view a few of his or her paintings online. Choose one painting and write about how it reflects life at that time.

- What was Canada's relationship to Britain in the early 20th century?

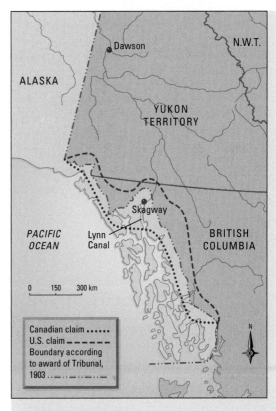

FIGURE 1–2 The Alaska boundary dispute

Interpret and Analyze From the map, explain how the Canadian claim would have allowed easier access to Dawson.

KEY TERMS

imperialists people who support imperialism, the policy of one nation acquiring, controlling, or dominating another

Canadiens French descendants of the original settlers of New France

nationalists people who have a strong attachment to their culture or nation

autonomy the power to govern oneself and make one's own decisions

homesteaders newcomers who claimed and settled land

ethnocentric the belief that one's own culture is superior, and that other cultures should be judged by its values

head tax the fee that Chinese immigrants were required to pay after 1885 in order to enter Canada

French-Canadian Nationalists

While unhappy with Britain's decision regarding the Alaska boundary, most English-speaking Canadians were proud to be British subjects, and they shared Britain's dreams of expanding the British Empire. These **imperialists** had eagerly supported Britain in the Boer War in 1899.

French-speaking Canadians, however, did not share this enthusiasm for the British Empire. They were the descendants of people who had settled New France more than 200 years earlier, and they saw themselves as **Canadiens** rather than British subjects. French Canadians tended to be **nationalists**, believing that Canada should have **autonomy** and be totally independent from Britain. For example, nationalist leader Henri Bourassa resigned from Laurier's Cabinet when Laurier agreed to send volunteers to fight with the British in South Africa during the Boer War. Bourassa's stand against Canada's involvement in Britain's wars became an even bigger issue during the First World War.

Language rights was another issue that divided French-speaking and English-speaking Canadians. After a bitter dispute, French Canadians first lost the right to French-language instruction in Manitoba except under certain circumstances. Saskatchewan and Alberta declared themselves to be "English only" at their founding in 1905. Henri Bourassa voiced the concerns of many French Canadians when he suggested that Canadiens might not have any reason to stay in Canada if their rights as a minority were not protected, as the people of Québec had believed they would be at the time of Confederation.

? HISTORICAL INQUIRY

Interpret and Analyze

How does the map of the world on the Canada postage stamp compare to maps of the world in your school atlas or on the Internet? Why might this map be interpreted as both nationalist and imperialist by Canadians before World War I?

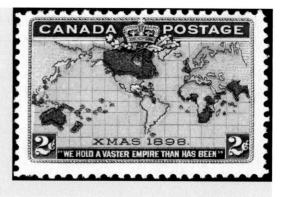

FIGURE 1–3 This postage stamp shows the extent of the British Empire in 1898.

Interpret and Analyze The British Empire was the biggest of the European empires that controlled much of the land and people of the world. What does the expression "the sun never sets on the British Empire" mean?

CHECKPOINT

1. **Historical Perspectives** Imagine you could go back to the Canada of 1914. What attitudes would you find most difficult to deal with? Why? What specific social values do you hold that would conflict with those commonly held in 1914?

2. Describe the situation of women in Canada in the years before the First World War.

3. Explain why some Canadians did not share enthusiasm for Canada's ties to Britain. Do you think their objections were justified? Explain.

Canada's Changing Population

After becoming prime minister in 1896, Laurier realized that for Canada to prosper, it needed more people, especially in the West. His government launched an advertising campaign to attract immigrants to Canada. It circulated posters in the United States and northern and eastern Europe promoting the Prairies as the "Last Best West" to distinguish it from the American West, where land was becoming limited and more expensive. These efforts resulted in a significant increase in immigration.

Entry into Canada was easy if you were reasonably healthy and had funds to establish yourself. The federal government offered immigrants willing to farm the Prairies 160 acres (65 hectares) of land for only $10. These **homesteaders**, as they were called, had three years to build a house and begin cultivating the land. The loneliness and harsh conditions of life on the Prairies prompted some to move to urban centres.

Not Everyone Is Welcomed

Some Canadians did not welcome changes to Canada's ethnic composition. Many French-speaking Canadians were concerned that the new immigrants would outnumber the Francophone population. Most Canadians were **ethnocentric**, believing their own race or group was superior, and therefore they disliked "outsiders." As a result, many newcomers to Canada experienced discrimination.

Eastern Europeans, particularly the Ukrainians and Polish people who settled the Prairies, were targets of ethnic prejudice. Their language and customs were unfamiliar to Canadians, who often ridiculed these people.

Many Chinese, Japanese, and South Asian immigrants settled in British Columbia. They, too, suffered from discrimination and racism. R.B. Bennett, a future prime minister, reflected popular prejudice when he declared in 1907, "British Columbia must remain a white man's country." As long as Asian immigrants did work that other Canadians considered too unpleasant—such as hauling coal, packing fish, and washing dishes—their cheap labour was generally accepted. But when Canadian workers began to fear that Asian immigrants would compete against them for other jobs, they joined in denouncing them.

The federal government tried to limit immigration from Asia in 1885 by introducing the Chinese Immigration Act. Under this Act, every Chinese immigrant to Canada had to pay a **head tax** of $50 upon arrival. In 1907, an angry mob of 9000 people smashed windows and destroyed signs on stores owned by Chinese and Japanese immigrants in Vancouver. This race riot resulted in severe restrictions on Japanese immigration. A year later, there was a virtual ban on East Indian immigration.

- What attitudes did many Canadians have toward minorities?
- What steps did the government take to control immigration to Canada?

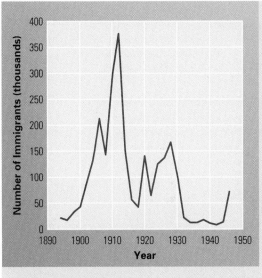

FIGURE 1–4 Immigrants to Canada, 1894–1946

FIGURE 1–5 Today many Canadian communities are multicultural, as shown on this street in Toronto.

Continuity and Change How has Canada modified its immigration policy since 1914, and how has the country benefited from its growing ethnic diversity?

- What challenges did Aboriginal peoples face in the early 1900s?

KEY TERMS

Indian Act an Act created to regulate the lives of the First Nations of Canada

reserves land set aside by the government for the use of First Nations

residential schools government-authorized schools, run by the churches, in which Aboriginal children lived apart from their families and were educated in Canadian culture

assimilation adoption of the customs and language of another cultural group so that the original culture disappears

GO ONLINE • • • • • • • • • • • • • • • •

The last residential school closed in 1996. Research and find out more about Canada's residential schools.

Cultural Extinction?

As thousands of immigrants settled into the western provinces, Aboriginal peoples found themselves more and more displaced. Their lives were regulated by the **Indian Act** passed in 1876. By the 1880s, most Aboriginal peoples of the Prairies were living on **reserves**. The main purpose of reserves was to free up land for settlers and immigrants from Europe, and to avoid the violent clashes that had taken place between Aboriginal peoples and settlers in the United States.

On the reserves, Aboriginal people were encouraged to take up farming instead of traditional hunting. But their attempts to adapt to farming were hindered by several factors. The soil on the reserves was often unsuitable for crops. They traded their land for equipment and livestock, but were given hand tools and animals ill-suited for plowing. Even when Aboriginal farmers managed to harvest crops, efforts to sell them were often hindered by government agents who would deny them the passes they needed to leave the reserve and market their crops. As a result, many Aboriginal people experienced hunger.

Loss of land was not the only problem Aboriginal peoples faced. The Canadian government established **residential schools** in an attempt to force Aboriginal children to set aside their identity and traditions and become part of the dominant culture. Children were taken from their communities by Indian agents, police, or priests and sent to schools hundreds of kilometres away. The overcrowded dormitories, unsanitary conditions, and lack of medical care caused tuberculosis and other diseases to spread quickly. Many students were physically and sexually abused. They were punished for speaking their language, forbidden to practise their culture, and denied contact with their families.

Residential schools, reserves, and enforced farming were all part of the federal government's policy of **assimilation**, which was intended to make Aboriginal peoples abandon their traditions and adopt a European way of life. This policy had been in place since 1871, and by the early 1900s the populations of Aboriginal peoples were declining. By 1913, an article in *Maclean's* magazine claimed that "the white man of Canada... is slowly, steadily and surely absorbing his red brother." Aboriginal peoples did not agree. Their struggle to establish land claims and reclaim their culture was just beginning.

FIGURE 1–6 An Aboriginal man plowing land on a reserve

Cause and Consequence Why would some Aboriginal people take up farming? What would they need to transition from hunters to farmers? Who was pressing them to make these changes?

CHECKPOINT

1. Despite their poor treatment in Canada, immigrants kept coming. Explain the factors that attracted immigrants to Canada.

2. Why were many English- and French-Canadian people upset by the changes to Canada's ethnic composition?

3. What were the steps taken in British Columbia to restrict Asian immigration?

4. How were the policies of the federal government designed to assimilate Canada's Aboriginal peoples?

©P

Canadians tend to think that sport is fair to all athletes of ability, and that excellence alone is the key to success and acceptance. In fact, racism has always been a problem in sport. Many must overcome the barrier to participation it creates.

Tom Longboat, one of Canada's greatest distance runners, endured intense racism in spite of his almost legendary prowess. At the time, newspapers regularly used racist language to describe the origins of non-white Canadians, and called Longboat "Heap Big Chief" and other names. However, he was admired and acclaimed in Toronto and elsewhere. He is one of Canada's greatest sports heroes—yet today, many Canadians know nothing of him.

Tom Longboat's nickname was Wildfire. He was Onondaga, born on Six Nations Reserve near Brantford, Ontario in 1887. Like most children on the reserve, Longboat was sent to a residential school.

He hated the school and its harsh discipline so much that he ran away.

From the beginning, Longboat's running ability distinguished him. As an unknown, he won the Hamilton Bay long-distance race in 1906 and the famous Boston Marathon in 1907, setting a world record in the process.

Tom Longboat had to endure racism, even from his admirers. Fame did not protect him from insults but he seems to have weathered them. After a dispute with his manager, he took control of his career and continued to win important races, although many doubted his ability to succeed. He retired a success in 1913. He made a great deal of money from athletics, but unlucky investments left him nearly broke.

In 1916, Tom Longboat joined the Canadian army and became a "runner," taking messages back and forth through the trench systems. He was wounded several times and, on one occasion, was reported to have been killed in action. After the war, he worked for the city of Toronto, eventually retiring to the Six Nations Reserve, the place of his birth.

Tom Longboat is a member of the Canadian Sports Hall of Fame and the Indian Hall of Fame. The Tom Longboat Awards remind Aboriginal athletes to follow in the tradition of one of the greatest runners in the world. In 1999, Canada Post issued a commemorative stamp in his honour.

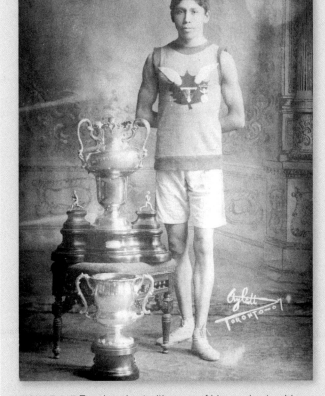

FIGURE 1–7 Tom Longboat with some of his running trophies
Historical Significance Why was it important to have good publicity in the early years of the 20th century?

1. Describe how Tom Longboat's career as a professional athlete might be different today compared to the early 1900s. What additional sources of income would he be able to access today?

2. What personal qualities do you think might have helped Longboat deal with and overcome racism?

3. How was Tom Longboat recognized for his achievements, and how is his memory celebrated and remembered?

4. If Tom Longboat were selected for the Canadian Olympic or PanAm Games, what government support would he receive as an elite athlete, and how might this experience enhance his future athletic career?

Throughout this textbook, you will be presented with many points of view about historical events. You are not expected to agree with these points of view, but to use them to come to your own conclusions. The following guidelines will help you in analyzing historical information.

Dealing with Evidence

There are two main categories of evidence: primary and secondary. Primary sources are created at the time of an event. Eyewitness accounts are the most obvious primary sources. These are often found in diaries, government documents, photographs, newspaper articles, and political cartoons. Secondary sources are created after the event, often describing or analyzing it. The perspective of time may provide a more balanced analysis in these sources.

Understanding Bias

When you interpret evidence, you cannot help but see it through personal biases. Similarly, primary and secondary sources carry the authors' personal views. Having a bias is not necessarily wrong. It is important, however, to be aware of biases when you analyze evidence. These might include political, racial, religious, ethnic, gender, or economic biases.

Reliability and Credibility

When you read a document, it is important to determine how reliable it is as a source of information. Ask yourself questions such as:

- Who is the author? Was he or she close to the event?
- Why might the author have recorded the event?
- What were the author's information sources?
- What are the author's biases or points of view?
- What was the purpose of the document, and who was the intended audience?

Photographs should also be examined closely when they are used as a historical piece of information. The reader should ask: Who took the photograph? How was the photograph to be used? Sources of information must also be credible, that is, they must be accurate and record the truth. One way to determine the accuracy of a source is to see whether the information is supported by other sources. The following sources offer information about immigrants to Canada in the years before the First World War.

Source 1

Rank	Nationality	Number of People	% of Total Immigration
1	U.K.	150 542	37.4
2	U.S.	139 009	34.5
3	Russian	18 623	4.6
4	Ukrainian	17 420	4.3
5	Italian	16 601	4.1
6	Polish	9945	2.5
7	Chinese	7445	1.9
8	Jewish*	7387	1.8
9	German	4938	1.2
10	Bulgarian	4616	1.1
	Other	25 903	6.4
Total		**402 429**	**99.8**

–Canada Year Book, *1914*

FIGURE 1–8 Immigrants to Canada in 1913

*Today, Judaism is properly thought of as a religion, a culture, a nationality, or all three.

Source 2

A historian describes the attraction Canada had for farmers from Eastern Europe:

In the mountain trenches of Galicia... the furrows of the strip farms ran to the very edges of houses. No wonder that... pamphlets (promoting Canada) were so successful. Across the oceans lay a promised land where 160 acres [65 hectares] of fertile soil could be had for the asking. Thus was initiated a great emigration of Poles and Ukrainians from Austria-Hungary.

–Pierre Berton, **The Promised Land**

Source 3

FIGURE 1–9 Galicians from Eastern Europe at an immigration shed in Québec City

Source 4

Conditions in the slums as described by J.S. Woodsworth, a minister and social activist, in a letter to a Winnipeg newspaper in 1913:

> *Let me tell you of one little foreign girl. She lives in a room.... Her father has no work.... The place is incredibly filthy. The little girl has been ill for months—all that time living on the bed in which three or four persons must sleep and which also serves the purpose of table and chairs. For weeks this little girl has had an itch which has spread to the children of the surrounding rooms. She has torn the flesh on her arms and legs into great sores which have become poisoned.*
>
> *–J.S. Woodsworth*

Interpret and Analyze

1. Classify each of the sources as primary or secondary. Explain your choices.

2. How reliable might the statistics in Source 1 be? What are some possible reasons for inaccuracies in population statistics?

3. Make a list of information about immigrants that can be found by examining Source 3. What questions would you ask to determine how reliable this photograph is as a historical source? Given the advances in digital technology, are photographs today more or less reliable than those taken 100 years ago? Explain.

4. How reliable is Source 4? What does it tell us about Winnipeg in 1913?

5. Use all four sources to create a picture of Canadian immigration at this time. List some additional sources that might help you to get a more complete picture of the subject.

Urbanization

While thousands of immigrants were settling farms on the Prairies, thousands more were moving to towns and cities. Some immigrant groups, particularly Jewish people, who were not allowed to own land in Europe, chose urban life, which was more familiar to them. For others, living in large communities without having to do back-breaking farm work was appealing. Canada's economy was in transition and the rise in manufacturing meant more job opportunities in urban centres. The population of Canada's western cities exploded in the early 1900s. For example, Winnipeg expanded from 42 340 people in 1901 to 136 035 people in 1911. It optimistically called itself the "Chicago of the North."

The growing cities were filled with contrasts between the wealthy and the poor. The rich lived in luxury. They usually had servants; their houses were lit by electricity, warmed by central hot water heating, and had running water. Across town, the working class lived in shacks and overcrowded tenements. Low wages forced women and children to take jobs and work long hours to support their families. Restrictions on child labour were few and seldom enforced. Lack of clean water and proper sewers, together with pollution from neighbouring industries, caused widespread health problems. Pneumonia, diphtheria, tuberculosis, and typhoid were common in poorer districts. Still, people flocked to the cities, attracted by jobs as well as by cultural and social opportunities unavailable in rural Canada.

GO ONLINE
Read more about poverty in Canada in the 1900s at CBC Learning.

HISTORICAL INQUIRY

Formulate Questions

What questions would you ask the people who live in these two different houses if you could meet them?

FIGURE 1–10 Left: Wealthy home in Toronto, circa 1910; right: One-room home in Winnipeg, 1912

Interpret and Analyze Find evidence in these photographs of the contrasts between rich and poor as described in the text. Which photograph do you think most people would associate with the time period? Why?

Innovations
Farther and Faster

While not exactly an information highway by today's standards, the pace of change in communications in Canada in the years before the First World War seemed amazing. Radio messages could be sent over oceans, telephones connected people in cities, and Canadians were experimenting with new and faster ways to travel from place to place.

The telephone Invented in the 1870s, the telephone was increasingly popular in the early 1900s. People had to share lines and go through an operator to make a call.

Wireless communication Italian-born Guglielmo Marconi invented the wireless telegraph, receiving the first wireless radio message sent across the ocean in 1901, at Signal Hill in Newfoundland.

The Father of Radio Québec-born inventor Reginald Fessenden has been called Canada's greatest forgotten inventor. He made the first broadcast of music and voice in 1906. Fessenden was later called the Father of Radio.

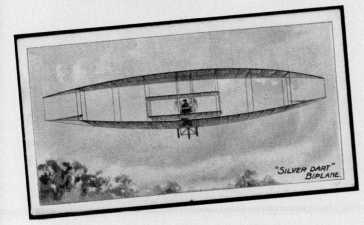

"SILVER DART" BIPLANE.

The bicycle craze Bicycles were the new craze at the turn of the century, when one in 12 people owned a bicycle. Bicycles liberated women from restrictive clothing and from chaperones, even though they were often criticized for riding.

Air travel The Wright Brothers made the first airplane flight in the United States in 1903. In Canada, Alexander Graham Bell and Douglas McCurdy developed the Silver Dart, a gasoline-powered biplane.

- How did technology impact Canada's economy during this period?
- What impact did industrial development have on the nation?

? HISTORICAL INQUIRY

Gather and Organize

What were three key sectors in the Canadian economy between 1900 and 1914? How has this changed in the present day? What were working conditions like for people in these three sectors in 1914? How do they compare today?

GO ONLINE

Canadian ingenuity affected more than just cars and communications in the early 1900s. Research other technologies invented in that time.

An Economy Transformed

From its earliest days as a young British colony, Canada was known for its abundance of natural resources. The export of timber, wheat, and minerals was an important part of Canada's economy. Canada's export industries also benefited from cheap shipping costs across the Atlantic Ocean. As well, the opening of the Panama Canal in 1914 created a shorter shipping route for Canadian products from the West Coast en route to Europe. Mining also contributed to the economic boom in the early 1900s. Prospectors and investors flocked to the Yukon and British Columbia after gold was discovered near the Klondike River in 1896. On the East Coast, many found work in Nova Scotia's new coal mines and steel mills.

The Manufacturing Industry

In the late 1800s, electric power was becoming more widely available with wood- and coal-burning steam engines. In the early 1900s, **hydroelectric power** stations were built to provide power to Canada's factories. The arrival of electricity in factories was an enormous boost to Canada's industrial growth. With electric power, bigger and better machines could be used to produce many more goods. This **industrialization** created more jobs in manufacturing. Much of the small manufacturing sector was tied to processing resources or providing tools and equipment for farms and homes. Few people could foresee that the rising popularity of automobiles would change the economy of southern Ontario and the way in which Canadians lived and worked.

With jobs came an increase in the demand for consumer goods. Canada Dry, Shredded Wheat, Palmolive soap, Heinz ketchup, and other brands became familiar to Canadian shoppers, along with the first five-cent chocolate bar. In 1913, more than 300 000 telephones were in use in Canada, and more and more automobiles were appearing on Canadian streets. By 1914, wireless radios were used on board many ships, following their much-publicized role in the rescue of passengers on the ill-fated RMS *Titanic* in 1912.

FIGURE 1–11 The 1908 McLaughlin-Buick sold for $1400, which was beyond the reach of most Canadians.

Continuity and Change What recent developments in transportation and communication are comparable to the impact of the automobile in the first decades of the 20th century? Explain.

Corporate Giants

Corporations grew larger during this period of industrial expansion. Huge companies, such as Maple Leaf Milling, which produced flours and packaged cereals, Massey-Harris—destined to become the largest producer of agricultural equipment in the British Empire—and Imperial Oil controlled much of industry. With little competition, employers could set high prices for the goods they produced and pay low wages to their workers. Some workers began to form **trade unions** to press for better pay, reduced hours of work, and better safety conditions. When employers refused to give in to union demands, some unions went on strike. Most employers opposed union demands. As a result, strikes could get violent and, in some cases, the police and military were called in to break up the protests. For example, in 1913, coal miners in Nanaimo were involved in a bitter strike that lasted more than two years. The miners were striking over unsafe working conditions and low pay, while the Western Fuel Company, to keep wages low, was trying to stop the workers from forming a union. Eventually, the Canadian government sent in troops to bring the situation under control. They arrested 39 people and broke the strike.

Financial speculation caused by the boom of the previous two decades saw many businesses expand quickly, but by 1910, a series of bank failures led to a collapse in the stock market. By 1914, Canada was in a **recession** after almost two decades of rapid growth. Industries cut back on production, and many workers became unemployed. On the Prairies, most farmers were planting a new, higher-yielding wheat, but the boom was over—the international demand for wheat was down because there was too much of it on the market being sold at rock-bottom prices.

KEY TERMS

hydroelectric power electricity produced from the energy of falling water

industrialization change in production systems to large-scale mechanized factories

trade union a group of workers who unite to achieve common goals in discussions with owners and management of businesses and industries

recession a decline in the economy, resulting in lower levels of employment and production

GO ONLINE

In the 1900s, Canadian department stores Eaton's and Simpsons were fierce competitors, and families often had exclusive loyalty to just one merchant. Learn more about these companies and what happened to them at the Canadian Museum of History.

FIGURE 1–12 Workers at the Robert Simpson Company mail-order office, 1909. Mail-order companies became a popular and practical way for many Canadians to shop, comparable to online shopping today (inset).

Continuity and Change How does the mail order business in the 1900s compare with online shopping today? Consider advertising to customers, order-taking, payment, and delivery. How much has the business changed?

CHECKPOINT

1. Describe the contrasts between rich and poor in cities during this period.

2. What technological changes were taking place in Canada prior to the First World War?

3. Why did employers and unions have stormy relations in these years?

4. Which groups of people do you think benefited the most from industrialization? Explain your response.

CHAPTER FOCUS QUESTION   What defined Canada in the early 1900s, and what attitudes and expectations did Canadians have for the century ahead?

In the two decades before the First World War, Canada experienced remarkable changes. Wilfrid Laurier skilfully guided Canada through 15 years of prosperity, as well as political and social upheaval. Immigration transformed Canada into a truly transcontinental nation with growing cities and industries. Agriculture and manufacturing prospered. New technologies changed social and cultural habits. However, not all Canadians were part of the new positive outlook. Aboriginal peoples, immigrants, women, and workers struggled for their rights. By 1914, Canada was beginning to resemble the country we live in today.

Historical Perspectives

1. **a)** Many factors affect a person's perspective. The boxed list includes those that generally have a significant influence on one's perspective. Add any factors not included that you feel are relevant to your situation. Rank the factors in the chart according to the importance they have in determining your perspective (one being the greatest influence).

    b) What effect do you think your background has on the way you view Canada today?

    c) People living in Canada in the two decades before the First World War had many different perspectives. Use the organizer to summarize how people in each of the groups might have viewed their place in Canada. Include one or more reasons why they would have had that perspective.

Factors Determining One's Perspective	Ranking
Age	
Gender	
Ethnicity	
Religious or philosophical beliefs	
Education	
Worldview	
Family income/parents' occupations	
Place of residence	
Places you have visited or lived	

Groups	Perspective of Canada Before the War	Evidence
Aboriginal peoples		
English Canadians		
French Canadians		
European immigrants		
Asian immigrants		
Women		
Industrialists		
Workers		

Knowledge and Understanding

2. From what you know of Canadian history before 1913 and from what you have learned in this chapter, how was the French-Canadian view of Canada different from the English-Canadian view? What issues were viewed differently by these two groups?

3. Use information in this chapter to discuss the interactions between the Canadian government and immigrants such as Chinese people.

4. Public hearings on the treatment of Canada's Aboriginal peoples in residential schools were held. What was the goal of the Truth and Reconciliation Commission? Would you recommend the same process for other groups? Why or why not?

5. Historians look for turning points in history, marking the change from one era to another. Many see the First World War as the end of an era and the beginning of the modern age. What recent event would you choose as a turning point in Canadian or world history? Explain your choice.

Apply Your Thinking

6. Using the groups from the organizer on page 18, list both the positive and the negative impacts of the various changes that were taking place in Canada at the start of the 20th century. Write a paragraph stating which group gained the most and which group lost the most as a consequence of these changes.

Communicate

7. Choose three new technologies from today that you think will have as great an impact as did those described in this chapter. Support your choices with at least two reasons. Create art work, if you wish, to accompany your reasons.

8. Examine the following quotation from Mary Prokop, whose parents moved to Alberta from Ukraine in 1900. What does this document say about some immigrants' experience of Canada at that time? How accurate is this description of these conditions? How do you know?

With the help of friends, my father had built a log cabin with a lean-to shed or barn against it.... That first winter was the very hardest mother had ever experienced...at least in the old country, though food was scarce, they had always been warm. Here they were cold and isolated in the unfinished house for the entire winter.

–*Quoted in* **First Wave of Ukrainian Immigration to Canada, 1891–1914**

HISTORICAL INQUIRY

Evaluate and Draw Conclusions

9. Read through the statistics and information about Canada in Figure 1–13. Select the four changes that you think were most significant to Canada's emerging autonomy and explain your choices.

	1914	2015
Population	8 million	35.5 million
National Anthem	God Save the King	O Canada
Nationality	British	Canadian
Flag	Union Jack	Maple Leaf
Governor General	Duke of Connaught (British)	Rt. Hon. David Johnston (Canadian)
Foreign Affairs	British Foreign Office	Canadian Dept. of Foreign Affairs
Final Court of Appeal	Judicial Committee of the Privy Council	Supreme Court of Canada

House of Commons	221 MPs (all male)
	   133 Conservative
	   86 Liberal
		308 MPs (77 women)
		   163 Conservative Party of Canada
		   96 New Democratic Party
		   35 Liberal Party of Canada
		   7 Independent
		   2 Bloc Québécois
		   2 Green Party of Canada
		   2 Forces et Démocratie

Senate	87 Senators (all male)	105 Senators (33 women)
Eligible Voters	1 820 742	23 677 639
Prime Minister	Robert Borden, Conservative	Stephen Harper, Conservative

FIGURE 1–13 Canada's population and government in 1914 and 2015

2 Trial by Fire: Canada Enters World War One

Social, Economic, and Political Context

- What effect did the War Measures Act have on the legal rights of Canadians?
- What effect did the war have on the role of women?
- What was the war's impact on the home front?

Communities, Conflict, and Cooperation

- How did Canada get involved in the First World War?
- How did the nature of warfare and technology contribute to a war of attrition?
- What were conditions like for men in the trenches?
- Describe Canada's military role in the First World War.

Identity, Citizenship, and Heritage

- How did Canada's contribution on the battlefield affect Canadian identity?
- What impact did conscription have on Canadian unity?
- What challenges did Aboriginal soldiers face during the war and upon their return home?
- What factors contributed to Canada's emerging autonomy?

Canadian soldiers fighting in the First World War are shown returning from Vimy Ridge, France, in this May 1917 photo.

Historical Significance Why are the soldiers celebrating their return from Vimy Ridge? Not everyone cheers after a battle. Who is missing from this photo?

TIMELINE

1914
Archduke Franz Ferdinand assassinated in Sarajevo
Germany invades Belgium and France
Britain declares war on Germany; Canada automatically at war
War Measures Act passed in Canada

1915
Canadian troops exposed to poisonous gas at the Battle of Ypres

1916
Canadians suffer heavy losses in the Battle of the Somme
Women in Manitoba, Saskatchewan, and Alberta gain the right to vote in provincial elections

CHAPTER FOCUS QUESTION

What consequences did Canada's participation in the First World War have for Canadian society and its status as a nation?

HISTORICAL THINKING

Evidence

Historical Significance

Ethical Dimension

Continuity and Change

Historical Perspectives

Cause and Consequence

When the First World War began in 1914, few believed it would last very long. Many young people in Canada and elsewhere saw the war as an exciting chance for travel, adventure, and glory. Most were afraid that the conflict would be over before they could get into the action. To them, signing up for war was a romantic idea and a way to honour the British Empire:

> *These young men were the cream of Canada's youth and chivalry, all volunteers, all willing to face the great adventure for King and country, for freedom and civilization. No conscripts were they, but freemen, glad ... to demonstrate Canada's loyalty and to make some return to England for the civil and religious liberty we had enjoyed under the protection of her flag....*
> –*George Sterling Ryerson*, **Looking Backward, 1924**

"The Great War," however, was a far different reality than this romantic vision. It was modern, industrialized warfare on a vast scale. The "war to end all wars" claimed the lives of more than 8 million soldiers, cost almost $350 billion, and changed the map of Europe. What could cause such a devastating international conflict? Why was the war so long and terrible, and what were the long-term consequences of the war for our nation? To answer these questions, we must understand the historical forces at work in Canada and around the world at the time—in particular, nationalism, imperialism, and militarism.

KEY TERMS

imperialism
militarism
Triple Alliance
Triple Entente
nationalism
profiteering
War Measures Act
enemy alien
internment camp
no man's land
Western Front
war of attrition
convoy
Victory Bonds
honour rationing
propaganda
conscription
khaki election
Hundred Days Campaign

? HISTORICAL INQUIRY

Formulate Questions

Individually or in pairs, make a list of the nine headings in this chapter. Then change each of them into a question. Which historical thinking concept do you think will be addressed in each section?

1917

Canadian troops battle at Passchendaele

Canadian troops capture Vimy Ridge

Women in Ontario and British Columbia gain the right to vote in provincial elections

Wartime Elections Act gives federal vote to women related to servicemen

Borden re-elected as head of Union Government

Conscription introduced in Canada

Halifax devastated by an explosion

Income tax introduced as a temporary measure

1918

Conscription begins

Armistice declared on Europe's Western Front

Most Canadian women win the right to vote in federal elections

KEY TERMS

alliance a union or agreement among groups working toward a common goal

imperialism the policy of one nation acquiring, controlling, or dominating another country or region

militarism a nation's policy of enlisting, training, equipping, and maintaining armed forces ready for war

Slavic relating to peoples in eastern, southeastern, and central Europe, including Russians, Serbians, Croatians, Poles, Czechs, and so forth

Causes of the First World War

What caused the First World War? There is no simple answer. At the beginning of the 20th century, several factors pushed the world to the brink of war. Industrialization drove the Great Powers—Britain, France, Germany, Italy, Austria-Hungary, and Russia—to expand their territories. As they sought more land, resources, and influence, they also tried to protect their territory by building up their military resources and creating **alliances**. Meanwhile, the nations colonized by the Great Powers struggled to keep their independence. These power struggles created tension around the world, and one event, as you will read about later, triggered the First World War.

Imperialism and the Age of Empires

Why were the Great Powers so prepared to engage in war? Since the 15th century, several European nations had been aggressively expanding their territory (see map on pages 2–3). Powerful countries practised **imperialism** by establishing colonies all over the world to create empires. They exploited the land and resources of the weaker nations they controlled. Massive industrialization in the 19th century fuelled the Great Powers' desire to expand their domains, giving them access to more raw materials and creating new markets for their manufactured goods. Africa—with its wealth of gold, diamonds, ivory, agricultural land, and other resources—became the last frontier for colonizers in the late 1800s. European empires aggressively pursued their interests in Africa, often competing for the same territory.

At the beginning of the 20th century, Germany was struggling to establish itself as an imperial power. Its colonies in Africa were not as economically or strategically advantageous as the areas controlled by Britain. Germany's leaders wanted their country to have its own "place in the sun" and to extend its sphere of influence. Germany's aggressive pursuit of this goal brought it into conflict with other imperial powers, in particular Britain and France.

HE WONT BE HAPPY TILL HE GETS IT

FIGURE 2–1 This cartoon postcard was used by the British as part of their propaganda campaign against Kaiser Wilhelm II of Germany during the First World War.

Evaluate and Draw Conclusions What is the message of this cartoon?

Increasing Militarism

Imperialism brought crisis after crisis, fostering distrust and tension among the Great Powers. As they expanded their empires, the Great Powers developed their military resources to protect their interests and intimidate each other. They glamorized their armed forces, and the size of their armies and navies became essential to national prestige. They embraced **militarism** and saw war as an acceptable way to resolve conflicts and achieve their goals. Militarism was a constant threat to peace in the years leading up to the First World War.

©P

By the beginning of the 20th century, Britain had established the largest navy in the world to protect its vast empire. Germany's desire to be a major power in Europe drove it to build up its military resources to match Britain's naval strength. In response, Britain dramatically increased the size of its navy and built the HMS *Dreadnought*, the largest and fastest battleship in the world. Germany in turn built more ships, including dreadnoughts of its own. It also increased the size of its army and its reserve of weapons. This buildup of military resources forced France—who had long-standing grudges with Germany—to arm itself in a desperate attempt to maintain the balance of power. This arms race increased international tensions, and by 1914 Europe had become an armed camp.

FIGURE 2–2 Ships such as the British warship HMS *Dreadnought*, launched in 1906, were heavily armoured to protect them from enemy fire.

The Role of the Balkans

As the Great Powers struggled to expand their colonies around the world, they also fought over limited resources in Europe. Of particular interest were the Balkans, a cultural and geographic region on the Adriatic Sea in southeastern Europe. Three different empires—Russia, Austria-Hungary, and the Ottoman—wanted to control this area.

- Russia's approach was to promote Pan-Slavism, the idea of uniting the **Slavic** peoples of the Balkans. Russia hoped that supporting these nations would allow it access to the region's warm-water ports. This was extremely important to Russia as most of its ports were frozen in winter, limiting its ability to import and export goods.

- Austria-Hungary saw Pan-Slavism as a threat to its power. Several of the nations under its control were Slavic and located in the Balkans, including Slovenia and Croatia. Austria-Hungary feared that it would lose its grip on its territory if these peoples united.

- For more than 500 years, the Ottoman Empire had controlled the Balkans and southeastern Europe, as well as areas of northern Africa since 1517. But this empire was crumbling by the beginning of the 20th century. It had already lost its hold of the Balkans and feared losing even more territory.

? HISTORICAL INQUIRY

Evaluate and Draw Conclusions

What makes HMS *Dreadnought* historically significant? How prominent was this ship? What were the consequences of its construction? Why is it remembered today?

Historical Significance

FIGURE 2–3 Imperial struggles in the Balkans

KEY TERMS

Triple Alliance the alliance of Germany, Austria-Hungary, and Italy prior to the First World War

Triple Entente the alliance of France, Britain, and Russia prior to the First World War

nationalism devotion to and support of one's culture and nation, sometimes resulting in the promotion of independence

Black Hand a terrorist group of Bosnian Serbs that was determined to free Bosnia from Austria-Hungary

The False Security of Alliances

These intense rivalries in Europe resulted in a rush to make or join alliances. By the early 1900s, all the Great Powers in Europe were in alliances with other countries, promising to support one another if they were attacked.

- The **Triple Alliance** was made up of Germany, Austria-Hungary, and Italy. However, when the war broke out in 1914, Italy did not follow the Triple Alliance into battle. Instead it joined the war in 1915 on the side of the Triple Entente.

- The **Triple Entente** (also known as the Allies) consisted of France, Britain, and Russia.

These countries hoped that forming alliances would reduce the threat of war, but it proved to have the opposite effect. Alliances made it easier for a country to be drawn into war. Because members pledged to protect one another, if any one of them was involved in a conflict, its allies would automatically have to fight as well. As you will see, one dramatic event was all it took to drag the whole of Europe into war.

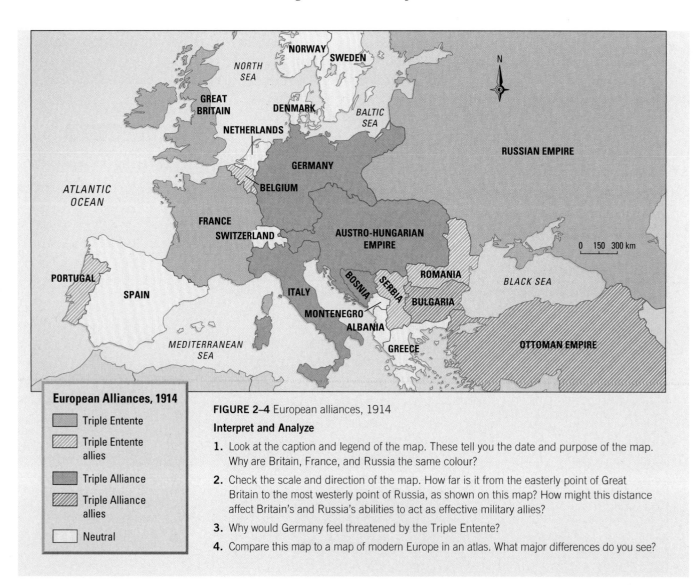

European Alliances, 1914
- Triple Entente
- Triple Entente allies
- Triple Alliance
- Triple Alliance allies
- Neutral

FIGURE 2–4 European alliances, 1914

Interpret and Analyze

1. Look at the caption and legend of the map. These tell you the date and purpose of the map. Why are Britain, France, and Russia the same colour?

2. Check the scale and direction of the map. How far is it from the easterly point of Great Britain to the most westerly point of Russia, as shown on this map? How might this distance affect Britain's and Russia's abilities to act as effective military allies?

3. Why would Germany feel threatened by the Triple Entente?

4. Compare this map to a map of modern Europe in an atlas. What major differences do you see?

The Threat of Nationalism

As the Great Powers sought to expand their empires, they paid little attention to the interests of the nations they colonized. They practised their own type of **nationalism**, showing great pride in and patriotism for their mother country. But another type of nationalism—an intense loyalty toward and desire to preserve one's own cultural identity, language, and traditions—simmered in the colonized countries.

The Balkans were a hotbed of nationalism. Some of the countries in the area were newly created while others regained independence as the Ottoman Empire disintegrated. The Austro-Hungarian Empire also controlled several Slavic nations that wanted independence and rebelled against Austrian rule. Bosnia, in particular, was highly contested as Serbia wanted to include this territory within its borders. Some Bosnian Serbs formed the **Black Hand**, a group willing to fight for their nationalistic goals. They wanted to unite the Slavic peoples to form "Greater Serbia." To Austro-Hungarian imperialists, Serbian nationalism was a deadly idea that had to be crushed at all costs.

A Chain Reaction

In 1914, to demonstrate its imperial rule, the Austro-Hungarian Empire sent its crown prince, Archduke Franz Ferdinand, to Bosnia's capital of Sarajevo. His visit gave the Black Hand an opportunity to strike back at the Empire, whom they viewed as an invader. As the archduke's procession made its way through the city, a Black Hand member, Gavrilo Princip, shot and killed Archduke Ferdinand and his wife.

HISTORICAL INQUIRY

Evaluate and Draw Conclusions

Why are the three "isms" discussed in this chapter—nationalism, imperialism, and militarism—considered "long-term causes" of World War I?

• How did Canada get involved in the First World War?

FIGURE 2–5 Archduke Franz Ferdinand and Duchess Sophie, moments before they were assassinated on June 28, 1914

This assassination triggered a chain reaction that started the First World War. Austria-Hungary blamed Serbia for the assassination. As part of the agreement of the Triple Alliance, Kaiser Wilhelm II of Germany offered Austria-Hungary a "blank cheque," promising to support them even if they went to war. When Serbia refused to submit to an ultimatum from Austria-Hungary, the Empire declared war. This caused Russia to mobilize its troops to defend Serbia as part of its promotion of Pan-Slavism. Germany responded with its own mobilization. This prompted Britain to put its navy on alert and France to mobilize its army. When Germany violated the neutrality of Belgium in order to attack France, Britain declared war on Germany to protect its ally. Canada, as part of the British Empire, automatically went to war, too. Gradually, the conflict drew in more and more countries around the world.

TIMELINE

Timeline to War, 1914

June 28   Franz Ferdinand and his wife Sophie are assassinated in Sarajevo, Bosnia.

July 6   Germany promises Austria-Hungary a "blank cheque" to support any military action in Serbia.

July 23   Austria-Hungary delivers an ultimatum to Serbia, threatening severe consequences:
- Serbia must dismiss all anti-Austrian teachers, government workers, and army officers.
- Austrian officials will be allowed to enter Serbia to investigate the assassination.
- Serbia must cooperate with the Austrian investigation.

July 26   Russia begins to mobilize its armed forces in anticipation of war.

July 28   Austria-Hungary rejects Serbia's partial acceptance of its demands and declares war.

July 31
- Russia announces its general mobilization.
- Austria-Hungary and Germany demand that Russia stop mobilizing; Russia ignores this command.
- France agrees to respect Belgium's neutrality, but Germany refuses.

August 1   Germany declares war on Russia.

August 3   Germany declares war on France.

August 4
- Germany invades Belgium and Luxembourg to attack France.
- Britain declares war on Germany.
- Canada is automatically at war as part of the British Empire.

HISTORICAL INQUIRY

Evaluate and Draw Conclusions

Why are the events on this 1914 timeline considered the "short-term causes" of World War I?

CHECKPOINT

1. **Historical Significance** List the causes and contributing factors that resulted in the outbreak of war and then select the three you think are most important. Justify your choices.

2. Imagine you are the prime minister of Canada. Compose a letter to the prime minister of Britain explaining why you do, or do not, support an alliance between Britain, Russia, and France.

3. Write a well-reasoned argument for the following proposition: "The First World War was unnecessary and could have been prevented."

©P

Political cartoons are a useful source of information about historical or current issues. They simplify an issue by portraying political personalities or events in an exaggerated way and using symbols to represent ideas. In this way, they are a very effective means of convincing a reader to see an issue in a specific way. But the perspective about the issue presented in a political cartoon is often extreme and harshly critical. Political cartoons represent political figures as caricatures, exaggerating their physical and personality traits for comic effect. Political cartoons often use stereotypes to emphasize their message. They also employ analogy to compare people or events to other things that the audience will relate to and understand. While these devices help convey perspectives on historical events or current issues, you need to be aware of the biases and prejudices that may taint political cartoons when you interpret them.

Steps to Interpreting Political Cartoons

1. Read the text and look closely at the drawing.

2. Identify the central issue or event in the cartoon.

3. Identify the devices used by the cartoonist (caricature, analogy, words, symbols, stereotypes, sizing, etc.).

4. Identify the biases of the cartoonist by examining the devices used.

5. Interpret the cartoon.

THE CHAIN OF FRIENDSHIP

FIGURE 2–6 The Chain of Friendship. This British cartoon appeared in some Canadian newspapers at the outbreak of war. It highlights some of the main causes of the First World War by representing the European countries in 1914 as different characters.

Evaluate and Draw Conclusions

1. Identify the countries represented by the child and the adult who is picking on him. Why is one country shown as a child?

2. The cartoon uses caricatures of speech and clothing to identify European countries. Identify Germany, Britain, France, and Russia. Explain your choice in each case.

3. Use the cartoon to make a list of the countries on either side of the conflict. Compare your list to the map in Figure 2–4.

4. What is the meaning of the title of the cartoon? Could it be interpreted as an ironic or sarcastic title? Explain.

5. If you added Canada to the "Chain of Friendship," where would it appear and what size would it be? Explain your design.

Canada's Response to the War

Communicate

What did the statement "most English-speaking Canadians were of British origin" mean? Why do you think Aboriginal, African, and Japanese Canadians were not welcome in the Canadian army in 1914?

Although Canada had become a political union in 1867, Britain still controlled the foreign policy of all its dominions. This meant that when Britain declared war on Germany, Canada was automatically at war, along with the rest of the British Empire.

Mobilizing the Forces

In 1914, most English-speaking Canadians were of British origin, and they supported the war out of a strong patriotic feeling for Britain and the Empire. One Toronto newspaper captured the excitement of the time:

> *Cheer after cheer from the crowds of people who had waited long and anxiously for the announcement of Great Britain's position in the present conflict in Europe greeted the news that the Mother Country had declared war against Germany. Groups of men sang "Rule Britannia," others joined in singing "God Save the King"; some showed their sense of the seriousness of the situation by singing "Onward Christian Soldiers"....*
>
> –Toronto Mail and Empire, *August 5, 1914*

FIGURE 2–7 At the start of the First World War, crowds gathered in St. Thomas, Ontario, in 1914 to cheer the soldiers on their way.

Gather Evidence How did public attitudes change as the war dragged on over four years and casualties mounted?

Wilfrid Laurier, the leader of the Liberals and a French Canadian, joined English Canadians in pledging support for Britain and the Empire. Laurier stated, "It is our duty to let Great Britain know and to let the friends and foes of Great Britain know that there is in Canada but one mind and one heart and that all Canadians are behind the Mother Country."

Prime Minister Borden initially offered Britain 25 000 troops, but more than 30 000 volunteers from across Canada signed up within a month. Many felt the patriotic urge to defend their "mother country." A lot of people volunteered because they believed that the war would be over by Christmas. Others signed up because they were unemployed and the war meant a chance to escape financial hardships at home.

Not all Canadians who wanted to volunteer were welcome. Women were considered too frail and too emotional to partake in battle, so they were encouraged to stay at home and support the soldiers. Women who did join the services worked as nurses and ambulance drivers behind the front lines. Initially, the Canadian forces did not accept Aboriginal peoples and were reluctant to take African and Japanese Canadians. Volunteers from these groups managed to overcome such racist attitudes to join, but few were promoted. Such discrimination did not prevent these recruits from serving their country well (see Case Study, page 44).

Rank	Daily Rate
Major-General	$20.00
Colonel	$6.00
Major	$4.00
Captain	$3.00
Lieutenant	$2.00
Sergeant	$1.35
Corporal	$1.05
Private	$1.00

FIGURE 2–8 Canadian Army rates of pay, 1917

©P

A National Identity Emerges

Canada had to prepare for war. When Canada joined the war, its army swelled from 3000 to more than 30 000 soldiers. The enormous task of training and supplying the troops with clothing and munitions went to Sam Hughes, the Minister of Militia. Camp Valcartier in Québec was built in only four weeks to house and train Canada's soldiers. After basic training that lasted only four months, 32 000 enthusiastic, but ill-prepared, Canadian and Newfoundland troops set sail for England.

Before the war, Canada was a patchwork of regions. Few transportation and communication connections existed, and travel across the country was difficult. Regions had little contact with one another; people lived their lives close to home. Wartime training changed that. Young men from all over the country came together to train, first at Valcartier, then at bases in England. As they gathered and worked together, they began to develop a national sense of Canadian identity. In the words of one Canadian soldier:

> We were in Witley Camp [in England] and right alongside us was a battalion from French Canada. We didn't speak much French and they didn't speak much English, but they were the finest sports you ever saw.... You met people from Nova Scotia, or from Prince Edward Island, clean through to British Columbia.
>
> –Ben Wagner

The army formed by these volunteers was known as the Canadian Expeditionary Force (CEF). When the CEF arrived in England, British commanders assumed that, as a colonial army, the CEF would be integrated into the larger, more experienced British units. For much of the war, however, the CEF maintained its independence and fought as a separate unit, which contributed greatly to a growing sense of national identity and autonomy.

- What factors contributed to Canada's emerging autonomy?

GO ONLINE
While the war broke down many barriers between ethnocultural groups, African Canadian, Asian, and Aboriginal recruits often suffered racism. Read more online.

GO ONLINE
Twenty-five thousand soldiers of the First Canadian Contingent trained in Valcartier, Québec. Research and learn more about wartime training.

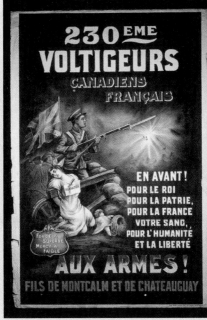

FIGURE 2–9 Colourful recruiting posters with urgent messages for volunteers appeared across Canada.

Evaluate and Draw Conclusions
Compare these two posters. What methods does each one use to appeal to different language and cultural groups? What image of war does each one present?

Deciding How to Finance the War

- What was the war's impact on the home front?

Initially, Ottawa planned to raise money for the war by borrowing from Britain. Later, when Britain needed all its capital for its own military, Canada borrowed from the United States. Most Canadians did not think they should be taxed for the war. Some even wondered if the war would lead to the collapse of the economy, as many pre-war construction contracts were cancelled and workers were laid off.

FIGURE 2–10 The 38th Battalion, Machine Gun Section, Ottawa, Ontario, 1915

Soon, however, the demand for war supplies resulted in a rapid economic expansion. **Artillery** shells, in particular, were in high demand. Sam Hughes created the Shell Committee to oversee the manufacture of artillery shells. Canada provided a large portion of Britain's shells. But Hughes was a poor administrator and the Ministry of Militia soon became bogged down in inefficiency and war **profiteering**. While he insisted on using Canadian manufacturers, troops were often supplied with equipment that was inappropriate or of poor quality. By mid-1915, contracts worth about $170 million had been signed with wealthy businessmen, but only $5.5 million in shells had actually been made. Some of the shells were of such poor quality that they exploded before being fired, killing the gun crews.

The War Measures Act

- What effect did the War Measures Act have on the legal rights of Canadians?

To meet the demands of war, Prime Minister Borden introduced the **War Measures Act** in 1914. The Act gave the government the authority to do everything necessary "for the security, defence, peace, order, and welfare of Canada." For the first time, the federal government could intervene directly in the economy to control transportation, manufacturing, trade, and agricultural production. The government also had the power to limit the freedom of Canadians. It could censor mail. It suspended *habeas corpus*, which meant that police could detain people without laying charges. Anyone suspected of being an **"enemy alien"** or a threat to the government could be imprisoned, or **deported**, or both. Recent immigrants from Germany and the Austro-Hungarian Empire were treated particularly harshly under this Act. Approximately 100 000 of them had to carry special identity cards and report regularly to registration officers. More than 8500 people were held in isolation in **internment camps**. These policies fostered nationalism and prejudice in Canada, and led to attacks on German-owned clubs and businesses.

CHECKPOINT

1. Examine the quotation on page 28. What does this document say about the attitude of people in Canada toward Britain at this time? How does the quotation on page 29 demonstrate a growing feeling of Canadian identity among Canadian troops?

2. What prevented women and other groups from participating in the war?

3. Why did the government feel the need to control the economy, transportation, and trade after war was declared? Was this a genuine need? Explain.

4. List the rights and freedoms suspended by the War Measures Act.

5. Explain why there was such enthusiasm for the war when it began.

The War on Land

Germany's **Schlieffen Plan**, developed years before the First World War began, was a bold strategy for a two-front war. Germany believed it could fend off Russia in the east while it defeated France in the west with a lightning-speed massive attack. The timetable left little room for error. German armies needed to drive through Belgium and swing south to capture Paris within a few weeks. Once this was accomplished, Germany could turn its attention to Russia. The Schlieffen Plan made two critical assumptions:

- It would take Russia time to mobilize its huge army. But Russia's forces were already on the move when Germany declared war.

- Britain would remain neutral. The plan relied on the fact that in the past, Britain had not become involved in disputes between countries in Europe. But, as part of the Triple Entente, Britain had promised to defend France if it was attacked. Also, all the Great Powers had promised not to attack Belgium, so Britain felt compelled to enter the war when Germany did just that.

The Reality of the Schlieffen Plan

The Schlieffen Plan almost worked. By August 1914, German troops were only 50 kilometres from Paris. But German leaders had made some changes that weakened the original plan. They pulled troops from the west to reinforce their defences in the east. The soldiers were exhausted by the pace of their attack through Belgium and into France. The Allies were able to rally and stop Germany's advance at the Battle of the Marne in September 1914, making a quick German victory impossible. Instead, the German army dug a defensive line of trenches along the river Somme and into Belgium. To counter this, British and French troops dug their own system of trenches to face them. Eventually a vast network of trenches stretched from the English Channel to the Swiss border. Between the trenches of the two enemies lay **no man's land**, a terrible waste-land of corpses, barbed wire, and mud. By Christmas 1914, armies protected by trenches that ran through northern France and Belgium on the **Western Front** were locked in a stalemate. With millions of soldiers on each side, neither Britain and France nor the Germans were able to advance, and no one was prepared to retreat.

KEY TERMS

artillery large guns used to fire shells

profiteering making a profit by raising prices on needed goods or producing poor-quality materials

War Measures Act an Act that gives the federal government emergency powers during wartime, including the right to detain people without laying charges

habeas corpus the right of a detained person to be brought before a judge or other official to decide whether the detention is lawful

enemy alien a national living in a country that is at war with his/her homeland

deport to send back to one's country of origin

internment camp a government-run camp where people who are considered a threat are detained

Schlieffen Plan Germany's plan to stage a two-front war with Russia in the east and France in the west

no man's land the area between the trenches of two opposing forces

Western Front the area of fighting in western Europe during the First World War, characterized by trench warfare and inconclusive battles with heavy casualties on both sides

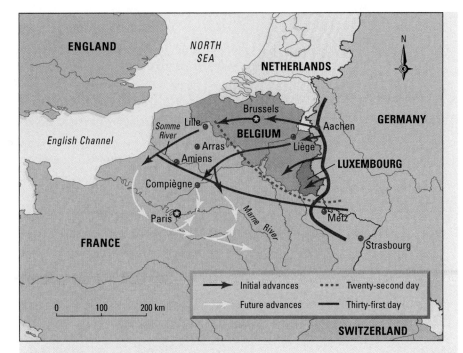

FIGURE 2–11 The Schlieffen Plan

Life in the Trenches

No soldier could have been prepared for the horrible conditions of trench warfare. Trenches were cold and damp in the winter and often flooded in the heavy rains of northern France and Belgium. Muddy trenches became stinking cesspools, overrun by rats. Men spent weeks in the trenches without washing, which allowed disease to spread. Soldiers' clothes were infested with lice, and many men developed trench foot, a painful condition that caused their feet to swell and turn black. Many of the wounded were left to die in no man's land because rescue attempts were too dangerous. Mental exhaustion also took its toll. Men were in constant fear for their lives, either from deadly sniper fire or from exploding shells. One soldier reported:

The air is full of shells... the small ones whistling and shrieking and the heaviest falling silently, followed by a terrific explosion which perforates even the padded eardrums, so that a thin trickle of blood down the neck bears witness that the man is stricken stone-deaf. The solid ground rocks like an express [train] at full speed, and the only comparison possible is to a volcano in eruption with incessant shudder of earthworks and pelting hail of rocks.

–*Quoted in* Toronto Globe, *April 15, 1916*

FIGURE 2–12 Many Canadian soldiers lost their lives in the trenches and suffered psychological disorders and nervous breakdowns.

Gather and Organize What can you tell about life in the trenches from this photograph? How might these conditions have contributed to psychological problems?

- What were conditions like for men in the trenches?

- How did the nature of warfare and technology contribute to a war of attrition?

KEY TERM

war of attrition a military strategy based on exhausting the enemy's manpower and resources before yours are exhausted, usually involving great losses on both sides

New Technology and the War

New technologies developed at the beginning of the 20th century changed the way wars were fought. In earlier wars, foot soldiers, supported by cavalry (soldiers on horses), tried to outmanoeuvre the enemy to take control of the battlefield. By 1914, however, new weapons were so powerful and deadly that it was suicidal to charge across open ground. Machine guns fired at unprecedented speed; massive artillery attacks killed thousands. Airplanes, invented only a decade before the war began, flew over the battlefields to pinpoint the enemy's location and movements and were later equipped with machine guns and bombs.

Although soldiers were using modern weapons on the battlefield, many of their commanders failed to understand how the new technologies demanded new tactics. Over the next three years, generals stubbornly engaged in a **war of attrition**, each side repeatedly attacking the other until one was completely exhausted and unable to continue. To attack the enemy, soldiers were ordered "over the top," meaning they had to leave the relative safety of the trenches to face the horror of no man's land. Hundreds of thousands of soldiers on all sides were slaughtered as they were mowed down by machine guns. These weapons kept either side from advancing, which was the main reason for the stalemate on the Western Front. Later in the war, armoured tanks were used to protect soldiers as they advanced across the battlefield. Tanks could break through the protective wall of barbed wire in front of trenches. By 1918, the trench system was itself obsolete.

Major Canadian Battles

The first division of the Canadian Expeditionary Force (CEF) arrived in France in February 1915. These forces soon became involved in combat along the Western Front, including decisive battles in France and Belgium at Ypres, the Somme, Vimy Ridge, and Passchendaele.

- Describe Canada's military role in the First World War.

- How did Canada's contribution on the battlefield affect Canadian identity?

The Second Battle of Ypres

Some of the bloodiest battles of the early war were fought in and around the Belgian town of Ypres. On April 22, 1915, French and Canadian troops were blinded, burned, or killed when the Germans used chlorine gas, a tactic that had been outlawed by international agreement since 1907. As the clouds of gas drifted low across the battlefield, soldiers tried to escape from the deadly fumes. Many suffocated or choked to death. One soldier described the scene as follows:

> *[We noticed] a strange new smell.... A queer brownish-yellow haze was blowing in from the north. Our eyes smarted. Breathing became unpleasant and throats raw.... Some fell and choked, and writhed and frothed on the ground.... It was the gas.*
> **–Canada and the Battle of Vimy Ridge, *1992***

Despite the Germans' use of poison gas, the battle continued for a month, but neither side gained much advantage. More than 6000 Canadians were killed, wounded, or captured holding their ground until reinforcements arrived.

One of the doctors serving with the Canada Corps was Lieutenant Colonel John McCrae, who wrote the famous poem "In Flanders Fields" to commemorate Canadians serving at the Second Battle of Ypres. It is said that he wrote the poem in about 20 minutes, but tossed it aside because he was dissatisfied with it. The story goes that a soldier later found it and convinced him to send it to a popular British magazine. The first verse of this famous poem is reprinted below:

> *In Flanders fields the poppies blow*
> *Between the crosses, row on row,*
> *That mark our place; and in the sky*
> *The larks, still bravely singing, fly*
> *Scarce heard amid the guns below.*

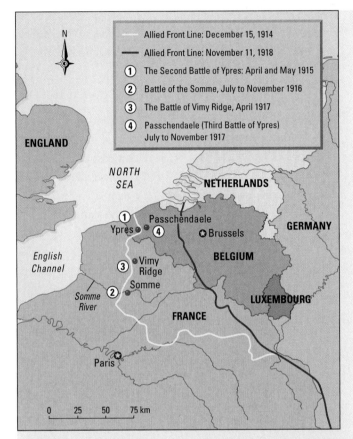

FIGURE 2–13 Map showing the Western Front and major battles

Map legend:
- Allied Front Line: December 15, 1914
- Allied Front Line: November 11, 1918
1. The Second Battle of Ypres: April and May 1915
2. Battle of the Somme, July to November 1916
3. The Battle of Vimy Ridge, April 1917
4. Passchendaele (Third Battle of Ypres) July to November 1917

FIGURE 2–14 The Belgian town of Ypres in 1917 showing the massive destruction caused by the war

I past the worse fighting here since the war started, we took all kinds of prisonners but God we lost heavy, all my camarades killed or wounded.... dear wife it is worse than hell, the ground is covered for miles with dead corpses all over.... pray for me dear wife I need it very bad.... as long as I leave I'll remember it.

–Francis Xavier Maheux, September 20, 1916

Note: The quotation above contains spelling and punctuation errors. It has been reproduced as it was originally written.

FIGURE 2–15 The Canadian National Vimy Memorial in France commemorates Canadian soldiers who were killed during the First World War.

Historical Significance Why did Canada build the Vimy War Memorial, and what is its significance for Canadian identity? How is the Vimy War Memorial commemorated in the Canadian War Museum?

What If...

Imagine that Canada had lost at Vimy Ridge. How might that have affected Canadian identity?

The Battle of the Somme

In July 1916, the Allies launched a massive attack against a line of German trenches near the Somme River in France. The attack failed because

- The Allies shelled the German lines for days before the attack began, but the shells did not destroy the Germans' defences or the barbed wire around their trenches.

- The commanders used tactics that, though previously successful, proved to be useless in trench warfare. Troops were ordered to march across open fields, and wave upon wave of men were shot down by German machine guns.

- Despite heavy losses on the first day of battle—including nearly 58 000 British troops—the attack continued.

The battle lasted five months and the Allies captured only 13 kilometres of land. Both sides suffered heavy losses. There were more than 1.25 million **casualties**, with almost 24 000 Canadians among them. The Royal Newfoundland Regiment alone lost approximately 90 percent of its men, and every officer was either wounded or killed. Most soldiers were badly shaken by the slaughter.

Despite their heavy losses, Canadian troops distinguished themselves during the Battle of the Somme and were brought in to lead assaults in several major battles over the course of the war.

The Battle of Vimy Ridge

In 1914, the Germans took control of Vimy Ridge, a key position near the Somme. This vantage point gave a clear view of the surrounding countryside, supply routes, and enemy positions. For more than two years, both French and British forces tried to capture the ridge but were unsuccessful.

Late in 1916, Canadian troops were chosen to lead a new assault on Vimy Ridge. Lieutenant-General Julian Byng, a popular British officer (later appointed a governor general of Canada; see Chapter 3), carefully planned the attack. His troops trained and rehearsed until Byng decided they were ready. In preparation for the attack, artillery bombarded German positions for more than a month. Meanwhile, sappers (army engineers) built tunnels to secretly move troops closer to the ridge. On April 9, 1917, Canadian troops moved into position. The Canadian Corps followed their plan of attack and in less than two hours they had taken their first objective. On April 10, they captured Hill 145, the highest point on the ridge. By April 12 they had taken "the pimple," the last German position.

It was a stunning victory. The Canadians had gained more ground, taken more prisoners, and captured more artillery than any previous British offensive in the entire war. Although the cost was high—more than 3500 men were killed and another 7000 wounded—the losses were significantly lower than in any previous Allied offensive. Byng's meticulous planning and training, and Canadian professionalism and bravery, had paid off. The Battle of Vimy Ridge marked the first time that Canadian divisions attacked together. Their success gave them a sense of national pride and the reputation of being an elite fighting force.

Passchendaele

Byng was promoted for his role at Vimy. His replacement was a Canadian, General Arthur Currie, a former realtor from Victoria, British Columbia. As the first Canadian appointed to command Canada's troops, Currie brought an increasingly independent Canadian point of view to the British war effort. Although he was a disciplined leader open to new strategies, Currie still took orders from Field Marshall Sir Douglas Haig. In October 1917, Currie and the CEF were asked to break through German lines and retake the town of Passchendaele in

FIGURE 2–16 Passchendaele; soldiers and horses sometimes drowned in the mud-filled craters which could be more than 30 metres wide.

Belgium. Haig's earlier assault on Passchendaele had left massive shell craters, which the heavy autumn rains turned into a muddy bog. Currie warned that casualties would be high, but Haig overruled him. Currie was right. The Canadians captured Passchendaele, but the "victory" resulted in more than 200 000 casualties on each side, including more than 15 000 Canadians. The Allies had gained only seven or eight kilometres, and the Germans soon recaptured the town.

Women on the Western Front

More than 2800 women served during the First World War. They were part of the Royal Canadian Army Medical Corps and worked on hospital ships, in overseas hospitals, and in field ambulance units on the battlefields. Many were killed or injured by artillery fire, bombs, and poison gas.

FIGURE 2–17 Edith Anderson, of the Six Nations Grand River Reserve, cared for wounded soldiers in France.

CHECKPOINT

1. What was the Schlieffen Plan, and why did its failure result in a stalemate on the Western Front?

2. **Ethical Dimension** Discuss whether chemical weapons should be allowed in warfare.

3. The use of gas as a weapon was outlawed by the 1907 Hague Convention. What is the point of an international agreement if, when the time comes, countries do whatever they wish?

4. Make a list of conditions at the front that might have contributed to psychological damage. Use the information on pages 31–35 to gather information.

5. The First World War quickly changed from a war of movement to a stalemate. Create a two-column chart listing the weapons and strategies that favoured the defence and the offence. Rank the items in importance in each list.

Innovations
War Technology

During the First World War, transportation and weapons technology developed rapidly as nations dedicated their resources to the war effort. The result was an industrial war with more casualties than had ever been experienced.

A new type of warfare The machine gun was largely responsible for changing the way wars were fought. Its ability to fire about 400–500 rounds per minute made it an effective defensive weapon. The water-cooled Vickers gun was capable of sustained fire. Both sides lined their trenches with hundreds of machine guns, making infantry attacks across no man's land futile and forcing leaders to develop new strategies.

Lighter than air Dirigibles (inflatable airships) were developed in the late 1800s. Germany's Ferdinand von Zeppelin built huge, rigid dirigibles that were filled with a lighter-than-air gas, such as hydrogen, and propelled by an engine suspended underneath. Germany, France, and Italy used dirigibles for scouting and bombing missions during the First World War.

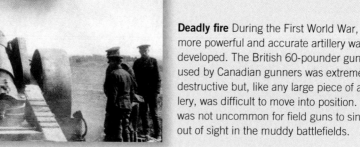

Deadly fire During the First World War, more powerful and accurate artillery was developed. The British 60-pounder gun used by Canadian gunners was extremely destructive but, like any large piece of artillery, was difficult to move into position. It was not uncommon for field guns to sink out of sight in the muddy battlefields.

Warfare in the air Planes were first used to scout enemy positions. Later in the war, pilots would throw grenades at enemy planes or shoot at them with hand-held guns. Eventually, machine guns were added to planes and both sides engaged in aerial dogfights. Aircraft design improved rapidly, but it was still an age of no-parachutes and new pilots. Notice the undercarriage on this fighter plane following a heavy-handed landing.

The silent enemy Although the United States and Britain did much of the work developing early submarines, Germany used them the most. Their U-boats (from Unterseeboot, or "undersea boat") were armed with torpedoes that could sink large ships. Germany used its submarines to attack the convoys of merchant ships and freighters that carried supplies to Britain in the hopes of starving the British into submission. This German mine-laying U-boat was captured by the British.

New armour The British developed tanks to shelter soldiers from gunfire while crossing no man's land and to drive through the barbed wire that lined the trenches. In doing so, tanks solved the problems of trench warfare. They were first used during the Battle of the Somme to break through the German lines.

Chemical warfare Germany was the first to use poison gas on the battlefield, releasing clouds of chlorine gas at Ypres in 1915. The gas blinded soldiers and attacked their respiratory systems. Early in the war, the only defence against poison gas was rags soaked in water or urine. Then simple cloth chemical-soaked hoods were tried, as in this photograph of a soldier wearing an HP helmet. Later, anti-gas respirators, or gas masks, made poison gas a less effective weapon.

- Describe Canada's military role in the First World War.

KEY TERMS

biplane an airplane with two sets of wings, one on top of the body and one underneath

reconnaissance military search or exploration

sharpshooter a person skilled in shooting

dogfight aerial duel between aircraft

ace a fighter pilot who has shot down five enemy aircraft

GO ONLINE

Research and find out more about Canada's flying aces during the First World War.

The War in the Air

During the First World War, airplanes were still a new invention and being a pilot was very dangerous. Thousands of air crew and pilots were killed in training and due to mechanical failure. The average life expectancy of a pilot in 1917 could be measured in weeks. Parachutes were not introduced until late in the war.

At the beginning of the war, pilots flew alone in **biplanes** doing aerial **reconnaissance**, photographing and reporting on enemy troop movements. Soon, however, pilots on both sides were armed, dropping bombs on the enemy below and firing guns at each other in the air. Fighter pilots had to be **sharpshooters** with nerves of steel and lots of luck. Aerial **dogfights** were spectacular scenes as pilots used elaborate spins and rolls to avoid enemy planes and stay out of their line of fire.

Air Aces

When a pilot could prove that he had shot down five enemy aircraft, he became an **ace**. Although Canada did not have its own air force (Canadians who wanted to be pilots had to join the British Royal Flying Corps), it produced a number of aces. Among them were Billy Bishop, Ray Collishaw, Billy Barker, Wilfrid "Wop" May, and Roy Brown. Some historians credit Brown with shooting down the German flying ace Manfred von Richthofen, who was known as the Red Baron. Because air aces became heroes in their homelands, they were often withdrawn from active duty overseas to promote fundraising and recruitment at home.

FIGURE 2–18 A pair of Canada's ace pilots: Nanaimo's Raymond Collishaw (left) (60 victories) and Arthur Whealy (27 victories). Many air aces were Canadian even though Canada supplied only a quarter of Britain's pilots.

Evaluate and Draw Conclusions Why would valuable pilots be pulled from active service to promote the war effort at home? Why were they good for promotion? How do you think they felt about recruiting after they saw so many of their friends killed in battle?

Canada's top air ace in the First World War was William Avery "Billy" Bishop, from Owen Sound, Ontario. His record was impressive. He shot down 72 planes, the second highest number of "kills" in the war (Germany's Red Baron had 80). Bishop was the first Canadian pilot to be awarded the Victoria Cross, Britain's most prestigious medal for bravery. He became the toast of Canada because of his success, and toured to promote the war effort and help sell Victory Bonds. In the following passage from his diary, he describes some of his daring adventures:

> He dived for about 600 feet [180 metres] and flattened out. I followed him and opened fire at forty to fifty yards [35 to 45 metres] range, firing forty to fifty rounds. A group of tracers ("visible bullets") went into the fuselage and centre section, one being seen entering immediately behind the pilot's seat and one seemed to hit himself. The machine then fell out of control in a spinning nose-dive. I dived after him firing....

> I must say that seeing an enemy going down in flames is a source of great satisfaction. The moment you see the fire break out you know that nothing in the world can save the man, or men, in the doomed machine.

But the life of this Canadian legend was less glamorous than it appeared. In a letter home to his wife, Margaret, he wrote:

> I am thoroughly downcast tonight.... Sometimes all of this awful fighting makes you wonder if you have a right to call yourself human. My honey, I am so sick of it all, the killing, the war. All I want is home and you.
>
> –Billy Bishop

In warfare, society's norms are put on hold, as soldiers are often expected to kill, and in some cases are glorified for their number of kills. Many soldiers, past and present, suffer emotional trauma after experiencing the atrocities of war and have difficulty adjusting when they return home. At the time of the First World War, soldiers' battle stress was called shell shock or battle fatigue. It is currently identified as post-traumatic stress disorder.

1. Bishop's diary is his personal account of what happened. His "kill" total has sometimes been questioned because his deeds were not always witnessed. Explain why you think Bishop was given credit for the "kills." Is the diary a primary source? Evaluate it as a historical source.

2. Using the two sources presented here, identify Bishop's personal reactions to killing in warfare. What might account for his conflicting feelings?

3. Bishop most likely killed the pilots he shot down. He needed courage and nerve to do what he did. What do you think the effect of the war would be on someone like Bishop?

4. Do you think soldiers today are encouraged to count "kills"? Why or why not?

5. Are there times when killing is not justified in the heat of battle? Explain.

FIGURE 2–19 A stamp commemorates Canadian air ace Billy Bishop.

- Describe Canada's military role in the First World War.

KEY TERMS

allegiance loyalty or faithfulness

merchant marine civilian ships and sailors that transported food, weapons, and munitions

convoy a group of ships travelling together protected by an armed force

Victory Bonds bonds issued by the Canadian government to support the war effort

honour rationing a civilian effort to consume less and conserve supplies on the home front

income tax a tax on personal income

corporate tax a tax charged to businesses based on their total revenues

The War at Sea

When war broke out between Britain and Germany, leaders expected that huge battles would be fought at sea. As part of the growing militarism in the years before the war, Britain asked Canada to help contribute to its naval forces. In 1910, Prime Minister Wilfrid Laurier introduced the Naval Service Act, which authorized the building of Canadian warships. The ships would be under Canadian control but could be turned over to Britain if war broke out. Many French Canadians felt that Canada should not automatically support Britain in war. This created tensions with English Canadians, most of whom felt they owed Britain their **allegiance**.

During the war, Britain relied heavily on its own navy to protect the freighters that brought supplies and troops to the Western Front. While Canada's navy was small and unable to contribute much to the war effort, Canada's **merchant marine** played a significant role in the war by doing the dangerous work of ferrying munitions and food to Britain. Although not officially members of the armed forces, many merchant marines lost their lives when their ships were attacked crossing the Atlantic.

Submarine Warfare

Although Germany could not match Britain's navy in size and strength, its U-boat was a dangerous weapon because it could travel under water without being detected. Equipped with torpedoes, U-boats took their toll on Allied warships and merchant ships. Eventually the Allies developed the **convoy** system to help protect their ships from the German U-boats. Freighters travelled together and were defended by armed destroyers. The Allies also developed an underwater listening device that helped them locate and destroy U-boats. Both of these advances helped to greatly reduce the threat of German submarines.

Germany's aggressive use of submarines also contributed to the United States entering the war in 1917. In 1915, a German U-boat sank the *Lusitania*, a British passenger liner, killing close to 1200 passengers. Among the dead were Canadian and American civilians. In February 1917, Germany announced that U-boats would sink any ship within the war zone around Britain—including ships that were not from Allied countries. German leaders believed that this move would put a stranglehold on Britain and help end the war. But this threat also made American ships targets and encouraged the United States to enter the war on the side of the Allies on April 2, 1917.

FIGURE 2–20 Illustration of the sinking of the *Lusitania*

Cause and Consequence Countries at war usually avoided civilian targets like passenger ships. For several years, Germany had been careful to target Allied ships and not to sink ships from neutral countries like the United States. Why did Germany decide to attack passenger ships like the *Lusitania*?

©P

The Home Front

- What was the war's impact on the home front?

Canada and many of its citizens were committed to supporting the war effort. Prime Minister Borden replaced Sam Hughes's Shell Committee with the more efficient Imperial Munitions Board, and munitions factories started building ships and airplanes as well as shells. The production and export of Canadian goods reached record highs. Resources such as lumber, nickel, copper, and lead were in high demand. Canadian farmers produced as much wheat and beef as they could to feed the troops overseas. This demand for Canadian goods helped its economy boom during the war.

Most of what Canada produced was exported to Europe, so many goods became scarce within Canada, which caused prices to rise. Some Canadian businesses made enormous profits from the inflated prices. Workers became increasingly frustrated by government controls that kept wages low yet allowed prices to rise. Workers' demands for higher wages and better working conditions became a major issue after the war.

What Was It Worth?

Year	Forest Products	Mineral Products	Agricultural Products	Animal Products
1911	$12.0	$6.7	$61.4	$40.6
1912	$11.0	$5.6	$81.8	$36.9
1913	$10.1	$12.1	$106.5	$30.3
1914	$10.6	$16.0	$146.2	$26.7
1915	$9.9	$12.2	$95.8	$38.2
1916	$14.1	$12.4	$196.8	$67.8
1917	$14.9	$15.5	$266.2	$93.3
1918	$4.5	$14.0	$403.5	$112.2

FIGURE 2–21 Value of exports from Canada to Britain during the First World War (in millions). Notice how the value of goods rose dramatically, especially in certain sectors.

Interpret and Analyze In which year were Canadian exports to Britain the highest? How significant were the increases in 1916? Why did some exports decrease in 1918?

Supporting the War Effort

By 1918, the war effort was costing Canada about $2.5 million daily. The government launched several initiatives to cover these costs.

- Canadians were urged to buy **Victory Bonds**. The government raised close to $2 billion through these bonds, which Canadians could cash in for a profit when the war was over.

- **Honour rationing** was introduced to help combat shortages on the home front. Canadians used less butter and sugar, and the government introduced "Meatless Fridays" and "Fuel-less Sundays" to conserve supplies.

- In 1917, the Canadian government introduced **income tax**—a measure that was supposed to be temporary. Affluent individuals and families had to pay a tax of between 1 and 15 percent of their income.

- A **corporate tax** was also introduced, charging businesses four percent of their revenues. Many Canadians thought this was too low, considering the profits some companies made during the war.

Despite these efforts, the government still did not raise enough money to cover the costs of the war effort. It had to borrow money from other countries, in particular the United States, to pay its debts.

FIGURE 2–22 This poster, showing a Canadian nurse, reminded the public of Edith Cavell, a British nurse who was executed by the Germans in 1915 for helping Allied soldiers escape German-occupied countries. The names on the poster represent German atrocities.

Interpret and Analyze What is the purpose of this poster, and why may it be considered propaganda?

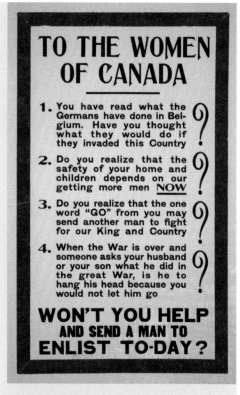

FIGURE 2–23 This recruiting poster was aimed at Canadian wives and mothers.

Interpret and Analyze Why do you think a war poster targeted women? How effectively does this poster communicate its message to its intended audience? Explain.

• What effect did the war have on the role of women?

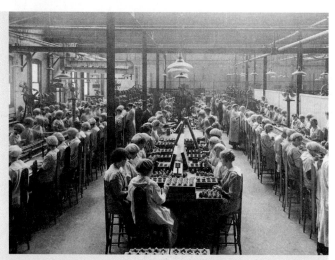

FIGURE 2–24 Munitions assembly, Verdun, Québec. About 35 000 Canadian women worked in munitions factories where shells were manufactured, and thousands more drove delivery trucks.

Getting the Message Out

During the First World War, Canadians were bombarded with **propaganda**. It was everywhere: films, magazine articles, radio programs, political speeches, and posters. Appealing to their sense of patriotism, propaganda encouraged people to join the army, buy Victory Bonds, use less fuel, eat less meat, and support the government. Some of the campaigns used social pressure to encourage men to join the army, contributing to the fact that the majority of Canadians who served in the First World War were volunteers.

Propaganda often distorted the truth. The number of Allied soldiers killed or wounded was minimized, while enemy casualties were exaggerated. British commanders were praised even as they continued to waste lives in futile attacks. When Germany invaded Belgium in 1914, refugees who escaped to England told horrible stories about the invasion. Writers used these stories to portray German troops as barbarians intent on destroying the civilized world. While this propaganda was intended to recruit soldiers, it also fuelled prejudice on the home front. Many Canadian citizens were treated as enemy aliens, subjected to harsh restrictions by the government and violent attacks by angry citizens.

Women and the War

Before 1914, middle-class women had few options for working outside the home. Some became nurses or teachers. Others were employed as domestic servants or worked at low-skill, low-paying jobs in food and clothing industries. During the war, increased industrial production created a demand for labour. Women were hired for all types of work, from operating fishing boats to working on farms. One Toronto woman who worked filling artillery shells described her motivation on the job as follows:

> There was everybody, every single class.... [W]e began to realize that we were all sisters under the skin.... [T]here's nothing that draws people together more than mutual trouble.... [W]e felt, "The boys are doing that for us, what are we doing for them?" You just rolled up your sleeves and you didn't care how tired you were or anything else.
>
> –Tapestry of War, *1992*

As much as this work was valued, it was not universally accepted. Because women earned about 50 percent of the value of men's wages, some feared their cheap labour would undercut the earnings of men after the war.

©P

Suffrage Is Granted to Women

Without women's efforts on the home front, Canada's wartime economy would have collapsed. But when the war ended, most employers assumed that women would return to work in their homes. Many women believed that their contribution to the war effort should allow them to make decisions about how their country was run. During the 1915 provincial election in Manitoba, one of the Liberal Party's campaign promises was to give women the right to vote. They kept their promise, and Manitoban women received this right in January 1916. Thanks to the efforts of suffragists across the country, women in other provinces soon won the right to vote as well. Alberta and Saskatchewan followed Manitoba's example later in 1916, with Ontario and British Columbia following in 1917. In 1918, women were granted the right to vote in federal elections, with the exception of Aboriginal and immigrant women. Since 1917, only women in the armed forces and women related to servicemen had been allowed to vote in a federal election (see page 46).

(see page 46)

KEY TERM

propaganda information, usually produced by governments, presented in such a way as to inspire and spread particular beliefs or opinions

The Halifax Explosion

During the war, Halifax, Nova Scotia was a valuable base for refuelling and repairing Allied warships. It was also the chief departure point for soldiers and supplies headed to Europe. The harbour was extremely busy, but there was little traffic control and collisions were frequent.

On December 6, 1917, the SS *Mont Blanc*, a French munitions vessel carrying more than 2500 tonnes of explosives, was accidentally hit by another ship. The collision caused a fire and an explosion so powerful that it devastated Halifax's harbour and levelled much of the city. More than 2000 people were killed, another 9000 were injured, and thousands were left homeless by the explosion and the fires it caused.

FIGURE 2–25 Halifax Harbour after the explosion in 1917

Historical Significance Do you think the Halifax explosion might have made people think differently about the war? Explain.

CHECKPOINT

1. How was propaganda used during the war? Discuss whether it is appropriate to manipulate information for patriotic purposes during war. Find examples of government propaganda in the wars that Canada has participated in during the 21st century.

2. List specific military contributions made by Canada.

3. Explain how women contributed to the war effort, and describe how their status in Canadian society changed as a result.

4. What contributions did Canadians on the home front make to the war effort?

5. The suffragists had excellent reasons for granting women the right to vote. How do you think the war helped them win this right? Why were some women still excluded?

6. The Halifax explosion was so powerful that parts of the ships landed kilometres away. Why might ships loaded with explosives and other munitions be permitted in a harbour so near a city?

case study

- What challenges did Aboriginal soldiers face during the war and upon their return home?

Aboriginal Peoples and the First World War

Canada's Aboriginal peoples contributed greatly to the war effort, both by giving money to the cause and by volunteering. This was despite the fact that Aboriginal peoples still faced racism, poverty, and assimilation in Canada. In fact, at the start of the war, the government actively discouraged Aboriginal peoples from enlisting. Why, then, did they take part in the conflict?

Many Aboriginal people felt strongly about their relationship with the British Crown, with which they had signed important agreements. Some were descended from Loyalists who had fought for Britain in the American Revolution and in the War of 1812. Other young Aboriginal men saw the war as a chance for both adventure and employment.

More than 4000 Aboriginal people served in the First World War, including nurse Edith Anderson, from the Six Nations, and Boston Marathon winner Tom Longboat, an Onondaga. Francis Pegahmagabow, an Ojibwe from the Shawanaga First Nation, enlisted in 1914. He is now recognized as one of Canada's most highly decorated Aboriginal soldiers and most effective sniper.

By the end of the war Aboriginal soldiers had proven themselves on the battlefield. Several became officers, and others were platoon leaders and instructors. Around 50 were decorated for bravery and for their victories in battle. Métis soldier Henry Norwest and Inuit Lance-Corporal John Shiwak were also recognized as highly effective snipers. Lieutenant Oliver Martin, from the Grand River Reserve, became a pilot in the Royal Flying Corps.

When they returned home, many Aboriginal soldiers hoped that their achievements and bravery would also be recognized outside of the armed forces. They had travelled overseas and had proven their skills and bravery. Many expected to be treated the same as other veterans, because they had been treated as equals during the war. However, they soon found that not much had changed at home. Although able to vote while serving overseas, they lost that right once they returned to Canada. While some received veterans' benefits such as land and money, many more did not. They were also still bound under the Indian Act.

Some Aboriginal veterans, such as Francis Pegahmagabow, became more politically active

Portrait by Irma Coucill. Courtesy of the Woodland Cultural Centre.

FIGURE 2–26 Francis Pegahmagabow won his Military Medal for bravery at Passchendaele.

FIGURE 2–27 National Aboriginal Veterans Monument in Ottawa

Interpret and Analyze What do you think the various elements of the monument symbolize?

GO ONLINE

Find out more about the National Aboriginal Veterans Monument and its inscription.

because of their experiences during and after the war. Pegahmagabow became the chief of the Parry Island Band in 1921. As a chief and later as a band councillor, he fought for the rights of his people. Veteran Frederick Onondeyoh Loft, whom you will read more about in Chapter 3, organized the League of Indians of Canada. Many other veterans wrote to the government asking for equal rights. One veteran wrote that it was unfair to be ignored by the country they had fought for.

Thinking It Through

1. What motivated Aboriginal peoples to enlist in the First World War? What experiences might have helped them to excel on the battlefield?

2. Learn more about the conditions Aboriginal veterans faced when they returned to Canada. Has anything changed since then? What brought about those changes?

The Conscription Crisis

By 1917, thousands of Canadian men had been killed and many thousands more had been seriously wounded. Many men were working in essential industries at home to support the war effort, so there were not enough volunteers to replenish the Canadian forces in Europe.

When the war began, Prime Minister Borden promised there would be no **conscription**, or compulsory enlistment, for military service. But when Borden learned how many men were needed to win the battle at Vimy Ridge, he saw that Canada would have to send more troops to Europe. In 1917, Borden introduced the **Military Service Act**, which made enlistment compulsory. At first, the Act allowed exemptions for the disabled, the clergy, those with essential jobs or special skills, and **conscientious objectors** who opposed the war based on religious grounds. Conscription turned out to be a very controversial and emotional issue that divided the country and left lasting scars.

Opposition in Québec

While Canada had a high overall rate of volunteers, recruitment was uneven across the country, with the lowest levels in Québec. Many French Canadians were farmers and were needed at home. The majority of them did not feel a patriotic connection to either Britain or France because their ancestors had come to Canada generations before. They saw the Military Service Act as a means of forcing them to fight in a distant war that had no connection to them. Relations between Francophones and Anglophones were also strained because French language rights had been lost in many schools outside Québec. When Francophone men did volunteer, there was little effort to keep them together and few officers spoke French. This did little to encourage French Canadians to volunteer to fight overseas and made them feel like second-class citizens on the home front.

Québec nationalist Henri Bourassa was one of the most outspoken critics of conscription. Bourassa believed that the country had lost enough men and spent enough money on a war that had little to do with Canada. Spending more money and sending more troops would bankrupt the country and put a strain on Canada's agricultural and industrial production. He argued that a weakened economy would eventually threaten Canada's political independence. He also believed that conscription would bitterly divide the nation by aggravating tensions between Francophones and Anglophones. Bourassa was right. Violent clashes erupted in Québec between people protesting conscription and those who supported the war.

- What was the war's impact on the home front?

KEY TERMS

conscription forced enlistment in the armed forces of all fit men of certain ages

Military Service Act a 1917 Act that made conscription compulsory for all Canadian men between the ages of 20 and 45, calling up the younger men first

conscientious objector a person who opposes war for religious or moral reasons

- What impact did conscription have on Canadian unity?

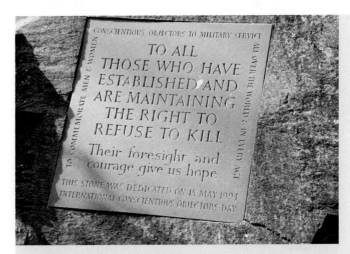

FIGURE 2–28 Stone dedicated to conscientious objectors; thousands of conscientious objectors from the United States took refuge in Canada in the early 1970s to avoid fighting in the Vietnam War (see Chapter 7). They were termed "draft dodgers" (those who wanted to avoid mandatory conscription) or "deserters" (those who abandoned military posts without permission).

Historical Perspectives What is your opinion of conscientious objectors? If you were drafted, how would you respond?

KEY TERMS

Military Voters Act an Act that allowed men and women serving overseas to vote

Wartime Elections Act an Act that gave the vote to Canadian women related to servicemen, but cancelled the vote for conscientious objectors and immigrants from enemy countries

khaki election the name given to the 1917 federal election because of Borden's efforts to win the military vote

Union Government the coalition government formed by Conservatives and some Liberals and independents that governed Canada from 1917 to 1920

HISTORICAL INQUIRY

Gather and Organize

Consider how and why many industrial workers, prairie farmers, industry owners, women married to soldiers, enlisted soldiers, potential conscripts, French Canadians, English Canadians with families in Britain, and conscientious objectors had different perspectives in the 1917 federal election. Create a Venn diagram to show which of the nine groups had similar perspectives.

The Labour Movement

By and large, Canadian industrial workers felt they were already contributing to the war effort and did not want to give up their jobs to fight in Europe. Farmers, especially on the Prairies, also opposed conscription because they needed their sons to work the farm at home, not fight a war in Europe. Between 1914 and 1918, only one-sixth of the Canadian Expeditionary Force were farmers.

Borden's government, which did not want to alienate rural voters, initially agreed to exempt farm workers from military service. However, because of rising casualties in Europe, he cancelled the exemption in 1918, igniting protests among farmers across the country. As things would turn out, a genuine shortage of farm workers ensued, and young children and women were pressed into unpaid service as workers. The Canadian Food Board fashioned an organization known as "Soldiers of the Soil" to appeal to adolescent boys. The group was run as a mock military unit, and once the young men had completed their agricultural tour of duty, they would be "honourably discharged." Women farmers were known as "farmerettes." Thousands of women were eventually recruited to pick fruit in Ontario's Niagara Region.

The Khaki Election of 1917

To try to strengthen his position on conscription, Borden asked Wilfrid Laurier and the Liberals to join his Conservatives to form a union or coalition government. But Laurier was firmly against conscription, believing the "law of the land... declares that no man in Canada shall be subjected to compulsory military service except to repel invasions or for the defence of Canada...."

Failing to get the Liberal leader's support, Borden passed two pieces of legislation to try to ensure he would win an election. He introduced the **Military Voters Act**, which allowed men and women serving overseas to vote. He also passed the **Wartime Elections Act**, which gave the vote to all Canadian women related to servicemen, but cancelled the vote for all conscientious objectors and immigrants who had come from enemy countries in the last 15 years. The 1917 election became known as the **khaki election** because of these attempts to win the support of people serving during the war.

Before the election, Borden was able to sway some Liberals and independents who favoured conscription to join him in forming a wartime **Union Government**. In addition, the Liberals lost much support outside Québec because of Laurier's position on conscription. As a result, the Union Government won the majority of votes in the 1917 election.

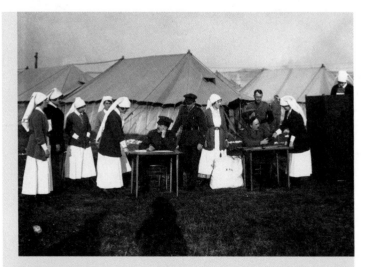

FIGURE 2–29 Prime Minister Borden gave Canadian men and women serving overseas the right to vote in the federal election of 1917. For the women in this photograph, it was their first time voting in a federal election.

Conscription Divides the Country

The Union Government won the election with strong support from the armed forces and women, but the anger and resentment stirred up by the conscription debate did not subside. In Québec, people continued to demonstrate against conscription even after the election. Crowds in Montréal marched through the streets shouting "À bas Borden" ("down with Borden"). Canadian troops were pelted with rotten vegetables and stones when they taunted French Canadians for refusing to enlist. Tensions finally erupted at anti-conscription riots in Québec City during the Easter weekend of 1918. On April 1, four demonstrators were shot and killed by soldiers. Ten soldiers were wounded over that weekend as well.

Nevertheless, conscription took place. Of the 401 882 men across Canada who were called up, only 125 000 were enlisted and about 25 000 conscripted soldiers reached France before the end of the war.

	Union Government (Borden)	Liberals (Laurier)
Atlantic Canada	21	10
Québec	3	62
Ontario	74	8
Western Canada	55	2
Total	153	82

FIGURE 2–30 Results of the 1917 election by region; number of seats in Parliament

Interpret and Analyze Find evidence to support the view that the 1917 election divided the country.

HISTORICAL THINKING · **Ethical Dimension**

Conscription Around the World, 2011

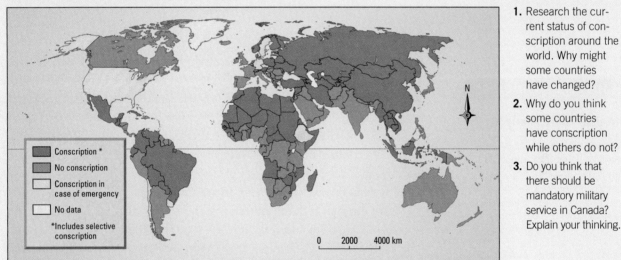

Conscription *
No conscription
Conscription in case of emergency
No data
*Includes selective conscription

N

0   2000   4000 km

FIGURE 2–31 Mandatory military service in countries around the world in 2011

1. Research the current status of conscription around the world. Why might some countries have changed?

2. Why do you think some countries have conscription while others do not?

3. Do you think that there should be mandatory military service in Canada? Explain your thinking.

CHECKPOINT

1. Why did Prime Minister Borden believe that conscription was necessary? Who was opposed to conscription and why?

2. Write a letter to the editor of the *Toronto Star* from Henri Bourassa explaining why conscription was not good for the country.

3. In pairs, create small election posters for the khaki election. Aim your advertising at two of the following groups: soldiers, women, French Canadians, or English Canadians.

4. Why do you think Borden did not allow conscientious objectors or recent Canadian immigrants from enemy countries to vote in the 1917 election? Why did he not give the vote to all women in 1917?

5. By 1917, Canadian soldiers were being used as "shock" troops, leading the attacks in battles. Imagine you are in the position of Robert Borden. Make a list of pros and cons for sending more troops.

abdicate to give up a position of authority

socialist a believer in a political and economic system in which the means of production and distribution in a country are publicly owned and controlled for the benefit of all members of society

Central Powers the German Empire, the Austro-Hungarian Empire, the Ottoman Empire, and the Kingdom of Bulgaria

Hundred Days Campaign the final Allied offensive against the Central Powers on the Western Front, from August 8 to November 11, 1918

armistice an agreement by warring parties to end hostilities

The End of the War

After three long years in a stalemate on the Western Front, two important events in the spring of 1917 changed the direction of the war. Like the other members of the Triple Entente, Russia dedicated its resources to the war. Thousands of soldiers died fighting along the Eastern Front. At home, supplies and food were limited and prices soared. People became increasingly frustrated, and a series of revolutions forced Czar Nicholas to **abdicate** in March of 1917. The Provisional Government was formed, but the Russian people were still dissatisfied with it and the war. In October 1917, **socialist** revolutionaries, called Bolsheviks (the Russian Social-Democratic Workers' Party), overthrew the Provisional Government, promising the war-weary public "peace and bread." They began negotiating with the **Central Powers** to end the war.

While Russia's internal politics weakened the Allies on the Eastern Front, another important event of early 1917 shifted power on the Western Front. The United States, still angered by the sinking of neutral ships such as the *Lusitania*, learned that Germany promised to support Mexico if it attacked the United States. On April 2, 1917, the United States declared war on Germany. In eight months, American soldiers reached the Western Front.

The Hundred Days Campaign

On March 3, 1918, Russia and the Central Powers signed the Treaty of Brest-Litovsk. This truce on the Eastern Front freed German troops to fight on the Western Front. Germany knew that it needed a quick victory before American troops reached France. In a desperate offensive beginning in March 1918, the German army struck at weak points in the Allies' lines and drove deep into France. Positions that had been won at great cost in lives, including Ypres, the Somme, and Passchendaele, were lost within weeks. By the summer of 1918, the new front line was only 75 kilometres from Paris.

With the arrival of the Americans, the Allies rallied and were able to stop the German advance. In August 1918, the Allies launched a series of attacks that came to be known as the **Hundred Days Campaign**. Canada's offensives were among the most successful of all the Allied forces during this campaign. Canadian troops, under the disciplined command of General Currie, broke through German lines and won important battles at Arras, Cambrai, and Valenciennes.

The Central Powers Collapse

Their final offensive in France and the battles of the Hundred Days Campaign exhausted the Germans and the rest of the Central Powers. They had no reserves and could not continue without fresh troops, food, and supplies. The Central Powers collapsed one by one. In November 1918, the German Kaiser abdicated and fled to Holland and Austria-Hungary agreed to a cease-fire. An **armistice**, or truce to end the war, on the Western Front was finally signed in a railway car in France at 5:00 a.m. on November 11, 1918. The war was to stop at 11:00 a.m. This corresponds to the date and time of our modern-day Remembrance Day ceremonies.

HISTORICAL INQUIRY

Interpret and Analyze

Compare the historical significance of the Battle of Vimy Ridge and the Hundred Days Campaign for the Canadian army and the country. Consider military and political importance, the impact on the peace conference, and Canadian identity.

counter points

Did the war have positive or negative consequences for Canada?

The First World War brought profound changes to Canada. It changed the way we see ourselves as a nation. Canadian troops fought well as a united force and their victories at Vimy Ridge and Passchendaele distinguished them as disciplined and courageous fighters. The need for war supplies stimulated the economy, resulting in major growth in Canadian industry. Most women won the right to vote for the first time. The First World War marked Canada's coming of age as it moved from a collection of disparate communities to a nation united by a sense of pride and identity. Canada gained international status by participating at the Paris Peace Conference in 1919, and Canadians began to see themselves less as colonials in the British Empire and more as citizens of an independent country. According to Canadian historian George Woodcock,

> ...the emergence of Canada... as a nation among nations within the broader world context, caused people to think less of what divided them than of what united them. They shared a single, if immense, geographical terrain, a common histori- cal tradition in which their various pasts inter- mingled of necessity, and an identity in which the sense of being colonial—and therefore being linked irrevocably to a land far away—metamor- phosed into a sense of being Canadian.
>
> —George Woodcock

A Country Divided

However, it was also argued that the war had a nega- tive effect on the solidarity of Canada. The issue of conscription and the bitterness of the debate between Anglophones and Francophones have never been com- pletely forgotten. Those who spoke out against conscrip- tion were accused of being unpatriotic and labelled cowards. Such accusations isolated many French Canadians from a government that had broken its prom- ise not to impose conscription. The War Measures Act also caused problems in many communities where immi- grants from Eastern European countries suffered racial discrimination even after the war. Aboriginal leaders, who

hoped their peoples' contributions to the war would ensure them a better situation, were disappointed. If anything, Canadian society was more discriminatory than ever.

The Cost of War

The losses both at home and throughout the world were staggering. Approximately 13 million people were killed during the First World War, and millions more were psychologically or physically wounded. The economic costs of the war in destruction and lost productivity were enormous. Between 1914 and 1918, Canada sent many millions of dollars worth of materials overseas, creating a debt that took decades to pay off. Some historians challenge the idea that the First World War marked Canada's coming of age. Historian Jonathan Vance asks, "How could a war that saw the deaths of 60 000 Canadians and the wounding of 170 000 others become a constructive force in the nation's history?" Vance believes that Canada's "coming of age" was a myth that developed during the 1920s and 1930s to transform the horrors of the war into a more positive experience. The maturity myth was meant to help heal the coun- try, Vance says, because believing in it meant wartime losses had served a real purpose for Canada.

Thinking It Through

1. Define "coming of age." How did the First World War help bring about Canada's "coming of age"?

2. Make a study tool on the theme of Canadian unity and the consequences of the First World War. Which events enhanced Canadian unity and which diminished it?

3. You and a partner have been chosen to be on a panel to discuss the impact of the First World War on Canada's development. One of you will defend George Woodcock's position, the other, that of Jonathan Vance. Prepare your arguments and present them to the class for further discussion. Be sure to refer to specific groups of people in your answer, such as women, the Aboriginal peoples, soldiers, and so forth.

CHAPTER FOCUS QUESTION   What consequences did Canada's participation in the First World War have for Canadian society and its status as a nation?

The First World War influenced many events throughout the 20th century. It was also Canada's "baptism of fire" and helped create a Canadian identity. Before the war, Canada was generally seen as part of the British Empire, and many Canadians identified with Britain as much as they did with Canada. The First World War changed that. Men from across the country trained together and then fought together far from home. Canadian troops proved themselves at Ypres, Vimy Ridge and other battles, and Canada won a place at the peace table at the end of the war. But the war also exposed a deep divide in the land: the different goals and aspirations of French and English Canadians were dramatically at odds, as the conscription crisis of 1917 had shown. On the positive side, women, working in factories and fields and doing jobs formerly reserved for men, saw their roles in society differently as a result. In 1917, women voted for the first time in a federal election. Although the cost in lives was great, the First World War helped transform Canada into a modern industrial nation with international standing.

Continuity and Change

1. Complete the following organizer to show how Canada changed over the course of the First World War. To what degree do you consider the First World War a major turning point in the history of Canada?

	August 1914	November 1918
Relations with Britain		
Status of women		
Feelings of national identity		
Role of government		
French–English relations		

Knowledge and Understanding

2. Create an annotated timeline showing steps to Canadian autonomy. Start at 1914 and add dates to the timeline as you progress through each chapter. Provide the date and name of the event, and explain how the event contributed to Canadian autonomy.

3. Create a bubble diagram, or flow diagram, around the assassination of Crown Prince Franz Ferdinand in Sarajevo. Link events that led up to the assassination and what resulted from it. Try to show cause and result where possible.

4. How did the revolution in Russia and the U.S. declaration of war against Germany influence the outcome of the First World War?

5. In a small group, discuss the following: Without the support received from the home front, Canadian soldiers would not have been as successful on the battlefields of Europe. Write down your group's responses so you can share with the rest of the class.

6. Review the descriptions of technology and trench warfare. In a letter home from a First World War nurse or soldier, explain why you think so many soldiers are being killed or wounded. When you have finished your letter, bracket any parts that the wartime censors would have "inked out" of your letter.

7. Write a paragraph explaining the concept of total war. Provide specific examples from Canada during the First World War.

Apply Your Thinking

8. In a small group, discuss the wartime internment and monitoring of "enemy aliens." Record your thoughts on display paper and present the results of your discussion to the class. In what ways was the treatment of these immigrants unjust? Do you think immigrants could be treated this way today in a similar situation? Can you think of modern parallels?

9. Use the organizer you developed in the Chapter Focus section to help you answer the following:

   • Assess Canada's contributions to the First World War. Provide specific examples of Canadian contributions and evaluate how important that contribution was to the war effort.

   • Explain the social, political, and economic impacts of the war on Canada.

Cause and Consequence

10. How did each of the technologies in the War Technology feature on pages 36–37 help to change the nature of war in the early 20th century?

Communicate

11. You have the opportunity to accompany either Robert Borden or Henri Bourassa during the weeks when conscription was a national issue. Write a series of blogs on your experience. Be sure to mention the Wartime Elections Act, the Military Service Act, and the election of 1917.

? HISTORICAL INQUIRY

Evaluate and Draw Conclusions

12. Primary sources give us glimpses into what people of a certain period were thinking about, and into the issues that were important to them. At the beginning of the war, being part of the British Empire meant that Canada almost automatically went to war when Britain was threatened by a powerful enemy. Most Canadians of British origin accepted this but feared that Canadians would lose their identity by being put into British army units to fight as "British" soldiers. Consider this excerpt from a 1916 letter to Prime Minister Robert Borden from his Minister of Militia, Sam Hughes:

I do recall my visit to... Britain in the autumn of 1914. I did expect... that I would have been permitted to exercise some "control and direction" over our gallant Canadian boys... But there had evidently been some communication... that "control and direction" of this magnificent Force should be under the British government direct. The then Mr. George Perley, Acting High Commissioner, implied such in the following words; — "You do not pretend surely to have anything to do with the Canadian soldiers in Britain."

–Excerpt from letter, November 1, 1916

As you read through the excerpt, consider the following questions.

• What surprised Hughes on his 1914 visit?

• What was the heart of the issue for Hughes and other Canadians?

• Knowing what you know about Sam Hughes, why do you think he would call the first Canadian volunteers a "magnificent force"?

• How important was it to Canadian identity that Canadians fight as part of their own army?

3

Canada and the Post-War Years: The Roaring Twenties

❓ INVESTIGATE

Social, Economic, and Political Context

- How did Canada participate in World War One peace treaties?
- Why were many ordinary Canadians dissatisfied after the war, and what was their response?
- How did Canada's economy change after World War One?
- How did regionalism affect Canadian unity?

Communities, Conflict, and Cooperation

- Why was the League of Nations formed?
- How did Canada increase its independence after World War One ended?
- Why was communism seen as a threat in Canada?

Identity, Citizenship, and Heritage

- How was Canadian identity expressed during the 1920s?
- What groups in Canada were marginalized in the 1920s?
- How did Aboriginal people struggle to maintain their identity?
- How did women attempt to achieve equality in Canadian society?

A flapper dances on a piano during the 1920s "Jazz Age."

Cause and Consequence Why would some people be ready to party in the 1920s? What did they have to celebrate? What were they eager to forget? At this time, the United States and some Canadian municipalities still prohibited the production, sale, and consumption of alcoholic beverages. Why were some citizens prepared to break this law?

TIMELINE

1919

Winnipeg General Strike gives voice to post-war dissatisfaction

League of Nations established, with Canada as an independent member

1921

Minority government elected

Agnes Macphail becomes first woman elected to Parliament

Frederick Banting and Charles Best discover insulin

1922

Prime Minister Mackenzie King refuses to send troops to support Britain during the Chanak Crisis

1923

Mackenzie King signs the Halibut Treaty with the United States and refuses to let Britain sign

Foster Hewitt gives play-by-play for first radio broadcast of a Canadian hockey game

CHAPTER FOCUS QUESTION

How did Canada adjust to political, social, and economic changes following the First World War?

HISTORICAL THINKING

Evidence · Historical Significance · Continuity and Change · Cause and Consequence · Historical Perspectives · Ethical Dimension

The 1920s are generally thought of as a decade of prosperity, fun, and wild living. To some extent this was true. The end of the war released an emotional flood of relief. Prompted by the horror and exhaustion of war, young people in particular tried to sweep away the remnants of the old world. This was the "Jazz Age." Bold new music, shocking fashions, and crazy fads quickly spread across the United States and into Canada.

This 1927 editorial from *Canadian Homes and Gardens* may give a false picture of what life was really like for most women, but it certainly catches the optimism of the age:

> *There is a certain magic to housekeeping these days—the magic of electricity—over which I confess I never cease to marvel. Your modern housewife leaves the dishes within a machine, pops the dinner into an oven, laundry into a washer, and jumps into a roadster [car] with never a thought except for... the round of golf which she is away to enjoy for an afternoon. She returns to find the washing done, her china and crystal sparkle, a six course dinner is ready for serving.*
>
> –Canadian Homes and Gardens, *May 1927*

Life did improve for many people in the 1920s. For many more, however, the prosperity of the decade was merely an illusion. Life continued as before, filled with discrimination, poverty, and lack of political power.

KEY TERMS

War Guilt Clause
communism
Winnipeg General Strike
collective bargaining
Persons Case
Famous Five
Canadian Constitution
regionalism
minority government
Old Age Pension Act
Chanak Crisis
Halibut Treaty
King-Byng Crisis
Imperial Conference
Balfour Report
Statute of Westminster
Great Depression

1924
Revised Red Ensign approved for use on Canadian government buildings abroad

1926
King-Byng Crisis illustrates Canada's need for autonomy from Britain

Imperial Conference leads to the Balfour Report and the Statute of Westminster, making Canada independent within the Commonwealth

1927
Federal government introduces old-age pensions; first government-run assistance program in Canada

1929
Persons Case opens way for Canadian women to be appointed to the Senate

Stock market crashes

Canada's Emerging Autonomy

- How did Canada participate in World War One peace treaties?

What If...

Imagine Canada had not been given a separate seat at the Paris Peace Conference. How might that have affected Canadian autonomy?

After signing the armistice, the leaders of the Allies and the other countries that won the war met in Paris in 1919 to discuss the terms of a peace agreement. The **Paris Peace Conference** lasted for six months and resulted in a number of treaties that defined new borders and compensation for losses suffered during the war. More than 30 countries attended the conference, each with their own agenda. Germany and its allies were not allowed to participate. Russia, which had already negotiated the Treaty of Brest-Litovsk with Germany in 1918, was not invited.

	Dead	Wounded	Missing	Total
Canada	57	150	unknown	207
Britain	659	2032	359	3050
France	1359	4200	362	5921
Germany	1600	4065	103	5768
Russia	1700	5000	unknown	6700
Austria-Hungary	922	3600	855	5377
United States	58	190	14	262

FIGURE 3–1 Approximate* number of military casualties of the First World War (in thousands)

* Although precise casualty numbers for the First World War are not available, these numbers can be considered a reliable estimate of the casualties incurred by these countries.

Participating in Peace

The Paris Peace Conference marked an important moment in Canada's emerging autonomy from Britain. Because Canada had contributed so much to the war and its soldiers had fought under Canadian leaders on the battlefields, Prime Minister Borden demanded Canada have its own seat at the conference. U.S. President Woodrow Wilson opposed Canada's participation. He thought that Britain should vote on behalf of the British Empire and that a separate vote for Canada was really just another vote for Britain. But British Prime Minister Lloyd George reminded Wilson that Canada had fought longer and supplied more troops than other countries. In the end, Canada won a seat at the conference and Borden insisted that he be included among those leaders who signed the **Treaty of Versailles**. For the first time, Canada gained international recognition as an independent nation.

The Treaty of Versailles

One of the treaties that came out of the Paris Peace Conference was the Treaty of Versailles. This document laid out the terms of peace between Germany and the Allies. Initially, U.S. President Wilson proposed a 14-point plan for "just and lasting peace" that emphasized forgiveness and future international cooperation. But some Allied leaders wanted to shame Germany and make it pay for the damage their countries had suffered during the war.

FIGURE 3–2 Leaders from around the world gathered in Versailles, outside of Paris, to negotiate a peace agreement, which became known as the Treaty of Versailles.

©P

In the end, the Treaty of Versailles included the following terms:

- Germany had to agree to a **War Guilt Clause**, meaning that it had to accept sole responsibility for causing the war.
- Germany's territory would be reduced. Alsace-Lorraine would be returned to France. Rhineland, on the west bank of the Rhine River, would remain part of Germany but would be demilitarized. Some of Germany's land would be given to Poland so it would have a corridor to the sea. Germany also had to give up control of its colonies.
- Germany had to pay war reparations totalling approximately $30 billion.
- The German army was to be restricted to 100 000 men. Germany also had to surrender its navy—including its U-boats—and much of its merchant fleet. It was not allowed to have an air force.
- Austria and Germany were forbidden to unite.

The Treaty of Versailles was signed on June 28, 1919. Naturally, Germany was reluctant to agree to such punishing terms, but it submitted because the Allies threatened to resume fighting. The reparation terms were particularly harsh. Like other European countries, Germany's economy was in ruins after the war and it could not make full reparation payments. Under the Treaty of Versailles, different ethnic and cultural groups were combined to create new nations, which left many people without a homeland. This meant that the feelings of nationalism that helped fuel the war were still unresolved. Many historians believe that, instead of lasting peace, the treaty brought the certainty of renewed war. Even British Prime Minister Lloyd George later found the terms too harsh. He observed that, "We shall have to fight another war all over again in 25 years at three times the cost."

KEY TERM

Paris Peace Conference a meeting in Paris in 1919 to discuss the terms of a peace agreement after the First World War

Treaty of Versailles one of the treaties that ended the First World War; it imposed strict sanctions on Germany

War Guilt Clause an article in the Treaty of Versailles that made Germany responsible for starting the First World War

HISTORICAL INQUIRY

Gather and Organize

Compare the map below with the map of Europe on page 24. Describe the changes in national borders, then list the names of the new countries created.

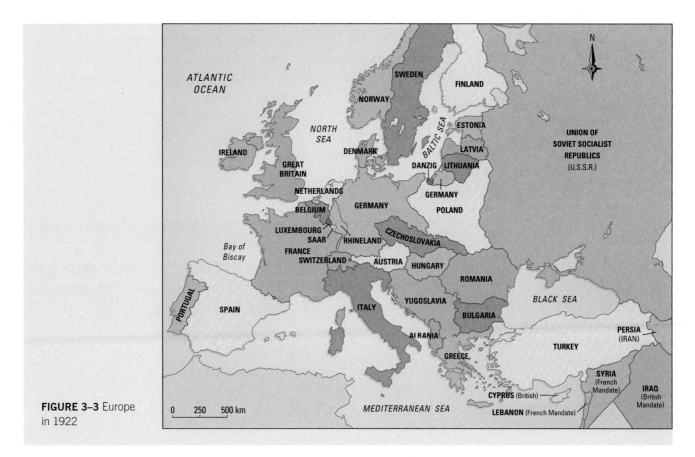

FIGURE 3–3 Europe in 1922

- Why was the League of Nations formed?

Prime Minister
Robert Laird Borden

- born 1854, Grand Pré, Nova Scotia
- teacher, lawyer
- first elected to Commons in 1896
- prime minister 1911–1920

Domestic Record

- passed the War Measures Act (1914) during the First World War
- introduced income tax as a "temporary" measure in 1917
- made conscription mandatory in 1917 by passing the Military Service Act
- won the 1917 khaki election by passing the Military Voters Act and the Wartime Elections Act
- sent federal troops to break up the Winnipeg General Strike (1919)

International Record

- led the Canadian delegation at the Paris Peace Conference in 1919
- fought to allow Canada to sign the Treaty of Versailles
- won Canada a place in the League of Nations
- was lead author of Resolution IX at the Imperial War Conference (1917), arguing that Canada deserved recognition as an autonomous nation

The League of Nations

The Treaty of Versailles included the formation of the League of Nations. The League was Woodrow Wilson's brainchild—as the idea of international cooperation was one of the most important elements of his 14-point plan for lasting peace. The League was based on the principle of collective security. If one member came under attack, all members united against the aggressor, much as the forging of alliances hoped to accomplish at the beginning of the war. As part of his struggle to be included in the Paris Peace Conference, Prime Minister Borden also won the right for Canada to become a member of the newly formed League. The League's 42 founding nations first met in Paris on January 16, 1920.

The idea of a League of Nations was not welcomed by everyone. Britain and France had doubts about it and wanted the freedom to pursue their imperialist ambitions. But their leaders realized that Wilson's proposal had propaganda value, so they agreed to the basic concept, at least in principle. Smaller nations, always concerned about becoming victims of the great powers, eagerly looked forward to a new era of peace. Ironically, the United States refused to join the League. Wilson had powerful opponents who rejected the principle of collective security, which would involve the U.S. in world affairs.

The League's Limitations

In many ways, the League of Nations proved to be a more idealistic vision than a practical solution to world problems. The refusal of the United States to join the League greatly undermined its effectiveness to resolve disputes in the years after the First World War. It required the nations of the world to cooperate with one another, which was not something they had done very well in the past. The League could punish an aggressive nation by imposing economic sanctions against it, thus restricting trade with the offending nation. But the League did not have a military force of its own to impose its decisions on aggressor nations. Nor was it easy to impose sanctions.

CHECKPOINT

1. After comparing Figure 2–4 and Figure 3–3 (on pages 24 and 55), identify which countries that existed in 1914 gained land because of the Treaty of Versailles. Which countries lost land? Why might the creation of many new, small countries create some instability in Europe?

2. With a partner, prepare briefing notes for the Canadian delegation to the Paris Peace Conference. Emphasize Canada's status as a nation, its contributions to the war, and the costs of the war to Canada.

3. Research the terms of the Treaty of Versailles. Make a PMI chart on the treaty's terms and their possible consequences.

©P

Canada After the War

• How did Aboriginal people struggle to maintain their identity?

After four long years of fighting, Canadian soldiers were finally on their way home. Most returned to Canada in early 1919 only to find that there were no steady pensions for veterans, no special medical services for those wounded in the war, and above all, few jobs. To make matters worse, many employers had grown rich during the war. The veterans had made the sacrifices, but it seemed that others were reaping the rewards.

Aboriginal soldiers returning to Canada faced even greater disappointments. During the war, they benefited from some of the social changes that took place, including gaining the right to vote under the Military Voters Act. Aboriginal peoples also believed that their contributions to the war effort would be acknowledged. But they found that nothing had changed. They still faced prejudice, and Aboriginal soldiers received even less support and fewer opportunities than other veterans after the war. They were denied many veterans' benefits and settlement packages, which included land and money, and lost the right to vote.

Flu Pandemic of 1918–1919

During the winter of 1918 to 1919, a deadly influenza virus (called Spanish Flu) swept across Europe, killing millions. Many returning soldiers carried the virus to North America. Young people were especially susceptible to the virus, which caused the deaths of an estimated 21 million people worldwide, more than the war itself. From 1918 to 1920, approximately 50 000 Canadians died during the epidemic. Many small Aboriginal communities were almost wiped out. Schools and public places were closed for months in an effort to stop the spread of the virus, and in some communities, people were required to wear breathing masks in public.

FIGURE 3–4 After the devastation of the First World War, conditions were right for the flu virus to spread rapidly.

FASTFORWARD

Worldwide Pandemics

When an infectious disease spreads rapidly across a continent or the whole world, it is called a pandemic. The World Health Organization (WHO) is an agency of the United Nations that coordinates international efforts to monitor outbreaks of infectious diseases. It has three criteria to determine whether a flu outbreak is a pandemic:

- It is a new flu germ to which humans do not have immunity.
- Infected people can become very ill or even die.
- It is contagious and spreads easily.

Pandemics have affected humans throughout history. Today, pandemics can spread more rapidly due to increased mobility of the global population. The SARS outbreak of 2003 demonstrated how air travel could help spread disease across continents. H1N1, or Swine Flu, which was first identified in Mexico in 2008, rapidly spread around the globe. H1N1 is a very similar strain to the Spanish Flu, which caused the pandemic of 1918 that killed millions. The Ebola virus, spread by direct contact with bodily fluids such as blood, causes a severe, often fatal, illness. The most recent outbreak of Ebola (2014-2015) has killed more than 11 000 people. Since late 2003, H5N1, or avian (bird) flu, has killed fewer than 400 people, but some experts believe it could be the cause of the next pandemic.

- Why were many ordinary Canadians dissatisfied after the war, and what was their response?

FIGURE 3–5 English translation of a 1919 Russian Communist publication

Interpret and Analyze What do you think the chains represent? What message is being conveyed?

KEY TERMS

inflation the rise in prices for goods and services that increases the cost of living and triggers demand for higher wages

communism a social and economic theory that property, production, and distribution of goods and services should be owned by the public, and the labour force organized for the benefit of all members of society

branch plants factories, offices, or other operations set up in Canada but owned or controlled by U.S. or other foreign companies

tariffs taxes on imported goods

primary industry an industry that deals with the extraction or collection of raw materials, such as mining or forestry

secondary industry an industry that deals with manufacturing or construction

An Uneasy Adjustment

In November 1918, Canadians celebrated the end of the First World War. Soldiers returned home to find that there were few support services for them, and few jobs. Many Canadians who had jobs were also dissatisfied. During the war, workers had reluctantly agreed to lower wages as part of their patriotic duty. After the war, **inflation** made life difficult for many people because wages no longer covered the cost of rent and food. Workers demanded more money, and confrontation with employers was inevitable.

The Rise of Organized Labour

At the end of the First World War, many people around the world were dissatisfied with governments and the disparity between rich and poor. As you read in Chapter 2, the Bolsheviks established a communist regime during the violent 1917 Russian Revolution. Under **communism**, all the means of production (such as factories and farms) and distribution (transportation and stores) are publicly owned. There is no private or individual ownership of business or land. The Bolsheviks encouraged workers around the world to join this revolution. Communism never gained widespread support in Canada, but the ideas of these revolutionaries inspired workers in Canada to try to improve working conditions.

One Big Union and General Strikes

Workers' demands for higher wages, better working conditions, and the right to join unions resulted in numerous strikes across Canada. Many strikes were long, bitter disputes. Standoffs between workers and employers, for example, led to four years of labour wars in Eastern Canada. Whole communities in the Maritimes depended on a single employer for jobs: the British Empire Steel Corporation. When demand for wartime industries declined after the war, the company tried to save costs by reducing wages. The workers responded by reducing their output and striking. When the strikes turned violent, the company looked for support from provincial police and federal troops. In 1926, a Royal Commission criticized the labour practices of the British Empire Steel Corporation, but the Commission's findings did little to ease suffering and poverty in the Maritimes.

There were also many strikes over wages and working conditions in western Canada. Some western union leaders were more socialist in their policies, believing as the Bolsheviks did, that ordinary people should be more involved in government. At the Western Labour Conference in March 1919, union leaders from Western Canada founded One Big Union (OBU), which would represent all Canadian workers. The OBU's goal was to help workers gain more control of industry and government through peaceful means. The main weapon would be the general strike, a walkout by all employed workers.

Canada's Changing Economy

● How did Canada's economy change after World War One?

Canada began the 1920s in a state of economic depression. By the middle of the decade, however, the economy started to improve. Wheat remained an important export for Canada, but there was also enormous growth in manufacturing and in the extraction of natural resources. The demand for Canadian pulp and paper grew, and new mills were built in several provinces. Mining also boomed. Record amounts of lead, zinc, silver, and copper were produced for export. These minerals were used to produce consumer goods such as home appliances. The expanding forest and mining industries increased demand for hydroelectric power and several new hydro-generating stations were constructed to provide Canadian industries with cheap energy.

The United States Invests in Canada's Economy

Before the war, Canada traded mainly with Britain. After the war, Britain was deeply in debt, and the United States emerged as the world's economic leader. During the 1920s, American investment in Canada increased. American companies invested in pulp and paper mills and mines across Canada. The majority of these resources were then exported to the U.S. For example, almost 75 percent of the newsprint produced in Canada was exported to the U.S. Most of the metals mined in Canada were used in American-made products, such as cars and radios.

American Ownership of Canadian Businesses

Rather than lend money to Canadian businesses the way the British had, most American investors preferred to set up **branch plants**. By manufacturing cars in Canada for the Canadian market, American car makers avoided having to pay Canadian **tariffs**. By the end of the 1920s, the Canadian auto industry had been taken over by the "Big Three" American automobile companies—General Motors, Ford, and Chrysler. American companies also owned a large proportion of Canada's oil business, nearly half the machinery and chemical industries, and more than half the rubber and electrical companies.

Many Canadians were so pleased with American investment that they did not question the long-term consequences. It was true that the United States enriched Canada's economy by extracting or harvesting raw materials (**primary industries**), but these materials were transported to the U.S. for processing and manufacturing (**secondary industries**). It was the American economy that benefited most from this development.

❓ HISTORICAL INQUIRY

Communicate

Why did business and industry leaders on the one hand and workers and union leaders on the other have such different perspectives on the way the economy should work after World War I? What were the demands of business owners and of the workers? How did the political and economic beliefs of capitalists, socialists, and communists complicate the situation in Canada? Write an essay to communicate your opinion, arguments, and conclusions.

FIGURE 3–6 Forestry continues to be big business in Ontario. This primary industry is worth an estimated $10 billion in revenue per year.

The Winnipeg General Strike: Labour Unrest or Communist Conspiracy?

In 1919, the labour movement grew across Canada. Workers formed trade unions in many different industries. These groups usually demanded higher pay, better working conditions, and an eight-hour workday. Scores of workers took action by walking off the job. It is said that more workdays were lost to strikes and lockouts in 1919 than in any other year in Canadian history.

Post-war tensions between labour and business boiled over in Winnipeg, at that time the financial centre of Western Canada and its largest city. The city's metal and building trades workers demanded higher wages, a shorter workweek, and the right to **collective bargaining**, which would allow union leaders to negotiate with employers on behalf of the union members. Labour and management negotiated for months. Finally, in May 1919, negotiations broke down and the Winnipeg Trades and Labour Council voted for a general strike. Up to 30 000 people walked off the job, crippling the city.

The strike closed factories and retail stores. Many people sympathized with the striking workers and joined their strike, including firefighters and postal workers. There were no streetcars or deliveries of bread or milk, and no telephone or telegraph services. Winnipeg was paralyzed. The Strike Committee, which coordinated the strike, bargained with employers and allowed essential food items to be delivered. Opponents of the strike felt that this showed that the strikers were running Winnipeg, instead of the legally elected civic government.

Not everyone sympathized with the strikers. Many people in Canada worried that the formation of trade unions might lead to the same violent uprisings that happened in Russia. The **Red Scare** contributed to an anti-communist sentiment that made people nervous about unions. In response to the strike, business leaders, politicians, and industrialists formed the Citizens' Committee of 1000. The committee saw the union leaders as part of a communist conspiracy to overthrow the government. They urged Winnipeg's leaders to restore order. The city responded by firing the entire police force, who sympathized with the strikers, and replacing them with a special force to contain the strike. The mayor of Winnipeg also had many civic workers and the strike leaders arrested.

FIGURE 3–7 Strikers attacked this streetcar as it moved through the crowd because it was operated by the Citizens' Committee of 1000.

The federal government decided to intervene because it feared that the disruption and protest could spread to other cities. It changed the Criminal Code so that foreign-born union leaders—and anyone whom it believed was trying to start a revolution—could be arrested and deported without trial. The federal government also sent troops to Winnipeg to try to restore order.

On June 21, strikers held a parade to protest the mayor's actions. The parade turned violent when the Royal North-West Mounted Police and the city's special force, armed with clubs and pistols, charged the crowd. In the resulting clash, one striker died, 30 were injured, and scores were arrested. This event became known as **Bloody Saturday**. Defeated, the strikers returned to work after a 43-day protest.

What did the strike achieve? In the short run, the union movement suffered a setback. Seven of the arrested leaders were convicted of conspiracy to overthrow the government

* Why was communism seen as a threat in Canada?

and served between two months and two years in prison. Many striking workers were not rehired; others were taken back only if they signed contracts vowing not to join a union. Distrust and divisions between the working class and businesses grew deeper.

In the long run, the verdict is less clear. A Royal Commission set up to examine the strike found that the workers' grievances were valid. Gradually, much of what they fought for was achieved. Some of those involved in the strike took up political positions in which they could work toward social reform. For example, J.S. Woodsworth (a well-known social reformer who was arrested during the strike) went on to found the Co-operative Commonwealth Federation (see Chapter 4), which later became the New Democratic Party.

Thinking It Through

1. **Historical Perspectives** Why did business and industry leaders on the one hand and workers and union leaders on the other have such different perspectives on the way the economy should work after World War I? Explain your response.

2. Write a newspaper headline to explain the reaction of the Citizens' Committee of 1000 to the Winnipeg General Strike. Remember the attitudes and values of the times.

3. Write a letter to the editor of a newspaper to explain why you think the Winnipeg strikers were, or were not, justified in their actions.

KEY TERMS

Winnipeg General Strike massive strike by workers in Winnipeg in 1919

collective bargaining negotiation of a contract between unions and management regarding such things as wages and working conditions

Red Scare the fear that communism would spread to Canada

Bloody Saturday June 21, 1919, when the Royal North-West Mounted Police charged a crowd of protesters during the Winnipeg General Strike

GO ONLINE
J.S. Woodsworth used the conditions he saw as motivation to make a difference in politics. Learn more about J.S. Woodsworth and his accomplishments and contributions to Canada's social safety net.

WORKERS' LIBERTY BOND

This is to Certify that the Bearer

S. J. Farmer

N⁰ 1492

HAS CONTRIBUTED THE FACE VALUE OF THIS BOND TO THE

Workers' Defence Fund

AND HAS THEREBY ASSISTED IN THE "FIGHT FOR LIBERTY" OF THE WORKERS ARRESTED FOR LOYALTY TO THE COMMON CAUSE OF LABOR.

ISSUED BY THE WORKERS' DEFENCE FUND, WINNIPEG, MAN.

DATE, NOVEMBER 15th, 1919.

ROBT. GILL, Chairman.   JAMES LAW, Secretary.

FIGURE 3–8 Canadians were able to show their support for the strikers in Winnipeg by buying bonds to assist in the "fight for liberty." The Workers' Defence Fund used the bonds to help pay for the legal costs of those arrested.

Evaluate and Draw Conclusions
Why do you think some non-union Canadians would sympathize with the strikers and buy these bonds?

FIGURE 3–9 This young woman with a liquor flask in her garter reflected the carefree attitude toward alcohol that was at odds with those who supported prohibition.

Interpret and Analyze In what ways would this young woman have outraged the older generation? What comparisons can you make with the attitudes of young and old today?

Illegal Alcohol and Prohibition

There was one product that Canada exported in large quantities to the United States: illegal alcohol. Although organizations such as the Woman's Christian Temperance Union succeeded in bringing about prohibition during the First World War, alcohol was still available for those with money. People could get it as a "tonic" from a doctor, or from a "bootlegger"—someone who made or sold alcohol illegally. By 1920, the provincial governments had to admit that prohibition was not working: it was too unpopular with most Canadians. From 1921 on, most provincial governments regulated the sale of alcohol rather than ban it. In a series of **plebiscites**, Canadians eventually adopted government-controlled liquor outlets.

In the United States, prohibition continued until 1933. Canadians took advantage of this golden opportunity to supply the U.S. with illegal liquor. Rum-running—smuggling alcohol into the U.S.—became a dangerous but profitable business. Ships from ports in the Maritimes and Québec, speedboats from Ontario, cars and trucks from the Prairie provinces, and salmon trawlers from British Columbia transported alcohol to the U.S. as fast as they could. Although it was dangerous, rum-running was extremely profitable. Many Canadians tolerated rum-runners and admired how they flouted the U.S. authorities. Canadian governments seemed content to close their eyes to the practice.

CHECKPOINT

1. Why did many women support prohibition? Why was prohibition not a very successful solution to the problem of alcohol abuse?

2. Explain the terms *communism*, *general strike*, and *collective bargaining*.

3. **a)** What were the consequences for Canada of the 1917 Communist (Bolshevik) Revolution in Russia on Canada?

   b) Why was the One Big Union seen as a threat?

4. **Historical Perspectives** Review the concept of perspective and understanding bias in Building Your Inquiry Skills—Analyzing Evidence: Primary and Secondary Sources (pages 12 to 13). In a two-column organizer, list reasons why the views from the following two newspaper sources would differ.

Source 1

...this is not a strike at all, in the ordinary sense of the term—it is a revolution. It is a serious attempt to overturn British institutions in this Western country and to supplant them with the Russian Bolshevik system of Soviet rule....

–**Winnipeg Citizen**, *May 17, 1919*

Source 2

It must be remembered that [Winnipeg] is a city of only 200 000, and that 35 000 persons are on strike. Thus it will be seen that the strikers and their relatives must represent at least 50 per cent of the population. In the numerical sense, therefore, it cannot be said that the average citizen is against the strike... there is no soviet [revolutionary council]. There is little or no terrorism.

–**Toronto Star**, *May 23, 1919*

©P

The Roaring Twenties

The upswing in the economy meant that many Canadians could afford more luxuries and leisure time. The decade became known as the "Roaring Twenties," reflecting the general feeling of indulgence. The misery of the First World War was over and people enjoyed the new forms of entertainment that were available. The "flapper" look dominated women's fashion. "Bobbed" hair, hemlines above the knees, and silk stockings outraged the older generations. Young people also scandalized their parents with dances such as the Charleston, the Shimmy, and the Turkey Trot.

- How was Canadian identity expressed during the 1920s?

KEY TERM

plebiscite a direct vote by electors on an issue of public importance; the outcome of the vote may not be binding on the government

Increased Mobility

In the 1920s, the automobile was beginning to change the landscape of the country. The invention of the assembly line in 1913 by Henry Ford meant that cars could be mass produced inexpensively and quickly. The most popular automobile was the Model T Ford. By the late 1920s, 50 percent of Canadian homes had an automobile. Its popularity prompted more and better roads to be built, making it easier for people to travel.

Aviation expanded rapidly in the years after the war. Airplanes helped to make the rugged coast of British Columbia and Canada's remote northern regions more accessible. Many veteran pilots became "bush pilots" who flew geologists and prospectors into remote areas to explore mining opportunities. Wilfrid "Wop" May was one of the best-known bush pilots who became famous for his daring exploits. In 1929, he and another young pilot tackled dangerous flights from Edmonton to help save the people of Fort Vermilion from a contagious outbreak by delivering serum. May's most famous adventure was his participation in the RCMP hunt for Albert Johnson, the "Mad Trapper" of Rat River. May's flight made Canadian history due to the duration of the chase and because it was the first time two-way radios and aircraft were used in pursuit of a criminal.

FIGURE 3–10 Jack Bowen, Frank Riddell, and Wilfrid "Wop" May (far right)

Improved Communications

By the 1920s, the telephone had become a standard household appliance. Telephone lines were shared by many neighbours, which meant anyone could listen in on your conversation. Widespread use of the radio began to break down the isolation between far-flung communities. It soon became a necessity, bringing news as well as popular culture and entertainment into Canadian homes across the country. The radio was a revolutionary development. Smaller Canadian stations, however, soon found it difficult to compete with bigger, more powerful stations from the United States. By the end of the 1920s, nearly 300 000 Canadians were tuning in to American stations for their news and entertainment. Canada would move to introduce legislation to ensure Canadian content, which you will learn about in Chapter 6.

GO ONLINE

Some say "Wop" May shot down the infamous Red Baron. Learn more about Wop May online.

Canadian Inventions and Inventors

During the 1920s, Canadians witnessed rapid changes in technology. Many innovations occurred in household appliances, and inventors from Québec made surviving the Canadian winter a little easier.

An alternative to the snow shovel Born in Québec, Arthur Sicard responded to Canadian winters by inventing the snow blower in 1925. The difficulty of travelling on snowy roads in early automobiles led him to find a way to efficiently remove snow. He adapted a four-wheel-drive truck to carry a snow-scooping section and a snow blower that would clear and throw snow up to 30 metres away from the truck.

A vehicle of necessity Armand Bombardier of Valcourt, Québec, was only 15 years old when he developed the snowmobile in 1922. Over the next few years, he improved on the first machine and designed vehicles that could travel on snow-covered roads. His invention helped people in rural and remote areas of Canada overcome the isolation of winter.

A medical breakthrough In 1921–1922, Frederick Banting, assisted by Charles Best, discovered insulin. This discovery continues to help millions of people suffering from diabetes. In 1923, Banting shared the Nobel Prize in Physiology or Medicine.

Rogers hits the airwaves In 1925, Edward Rogers of Toronto invented the world's first alternating current (AC) radio tube, replacing the noisy, battery-operated model. The AC radio tube allowed radios to be powered by ordinary household electric current. In 1927, he launched the world's first all-electric radio station, called Canada's First Rogers Batteryless (CFRB). In 1931, he was granted Canada's first television licence.

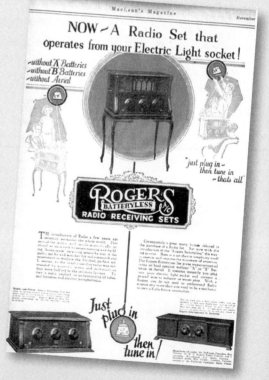

©P

A New Culture Emerges

With the Roaring Twenties and new-found prosperity, people sought out different forms of entertainment. Canada began to find its voice as a nation with a distinct culture. As a result, several new forms of distinctly Canadian art and entertainment emerged in the 1920s.

Moving Pictures

Soon radio entertainment was rivalled by moving pictures—the movies. At first, movies were silent. An orchestra or piano player would provide sound effects to accompany the silent screen, while subtitles conveyed the messages and dialogue. The "talkies" arrived in 1927 with comedians such as Laurel and Hardy and the Marx Brothers.

Movies about Canada were made here during the early days, but Canadian-made films could not compete with productions from the big studios in the United States. Eventually Hollywood came to dominate the industry. In the absence of a home-grown industry, many Canadian actors, writers, and technicians were drawn to the glitter and glamour of Hollywood. Many were very successful. Movie star Mary Pickford, born in Toronto, became known as "America's Sweetheart."

FIGURE 3–11 The Mounties as a symbol of Canada were a favourite topic with Hollywood. In true Hollywood style, the Mounties always caught the villain and got the girl.

Evaluate and Draw Conclusions What stereotypes are used in this photo to portray the RCMP? Do these stereotypes still hold for the Mounties today?

GO ONLINE
The Group of Seven is a source of Canadian pride. Find out more about this group of artists and their work.

New Art

The increased American influence on Canada's culture coincided with the development of a new Canadian art movement. In 1920, the **Group of Seven** held an exhibition in Toronto that broke with traditional Canadian art. These painters were in tune with the new post-war national confidence. Rather than imitate realistic classical styles, members of the group sought to interpret Canada's rugged landscape as they saw it, using broad, bold strokes and brilliant colours. Although criticized by some critics in the early years as the school of "hot mush" painting, the Group of Seven had gained wide acceptance by the end of the 1920s.

FIGURE 3–12 Stamp commemorating the Group of Seven

New Words

The emerging sense of independence and identity was also reflected in Canadian literature. The political magazine *Canadian Forum* first appeared in 1920. Political debates and works of Canadian poets and writers appeared regularly on its pages. As well, *Maclean's* magazine published Canadian stories and articles from across the country, being careful to use only Canadian spellings. Canadian novelists R.J.C. Stead, F.P. Grove, Martha Ostenso, and Morley Callaghan wrote novels about Canadians and their experiences. And poets A.J. Smith and Frank Scott wrote passionately about Canada and Canadian issues. Yet Canadian magazines and writers found it difficult to compete with American magazines and books.

Sports as Popular Entertainment

The thirst for entertainment led to tremendous interest in spectator sports. Hockey came into Canadian homes across the country when sportswriter Foster Hewitt made the first play-by-play radio broadcast in 1923. Canadian athletes also succeeded on the international stage, including two notable athletes who excelled in several sports. Lionel Conacher was a baseball player, a star at lacrosse, a football player, and an NHL all-star. Nicknamed the "Big Train," Conacher was known for his power, stamina, and speed. One day in 1922, he hit a triple in the last inning of a baseball game to win the championship for his team and then later the same day he scored four times and assisted once in lacrosse, bringing victory to that team as well. Fanny "Bobbie" Rosenfeld is one of Canada's greatest female athletes. She was a star at basketball, softball, hockey, and tennis, as well as track and field. In the 1928 Olympic Games in Amsterdam, she won a gold and a silver medal for Canada, becoming a national hero and the best-known Canadian woman of her time.

FIGURE 3–13 Bobbie Rosenfeld (number 677). At the Amsterdam Olympics, Rosenfeld won a silver medal in the 100-m dash and a gold in the women's relay team. She was at one time the joint holder of the world record for the 100-yard [91-metre] dash, which she ran in 11 seconds.

CHECKPOINT

1. What evidence is there that the 1920s were the beginning of the modern "consumer age"?

2. **a)** Which innovations made the 1920s a period of great change in communications?

   b) Beside each development, make short notes on how the change affected Canadian society.

   c) **Continuity and Change** How did these technological developments make Canada a "smaller" country?

3. How did new technology contribute to the spread of American popular culture in Canada?

4. What does the interest in professional sports tell you about leisure time and the standard of living for Canadians in this period?

5. Compare and contrast Bobbie Rosenfeld's and Lionel Conacher's achievements as athletes with those of popular sports heroes of today. How would you account for the differences?

As technology was transforming lives at the turn of the 20th century, so too was the camera transforming the art world. Photographs could record history, but art was challenged to go beyond. New styles were evolving to help artists express the mood of the location and event, not just physical appearance—a style known as *modernism*.

In Canada, the Group of Seven wanted to develop its own distinctive expression of location. To achieve this goal and to articulate the national feeling, the Group turned to the land for inspiration.

In 1913, Lawren Harris and J.E.H. MacDonald, two of the founding members of the Group, attended an art show in Buffalo that showcased contemporary Scandinavian artists. For Harris and MacDonald, the show proved exactly what they were trying to do—create a national style. In the Scandinavian paintings, they saw the same massing and simplifying of shapes and colours the Group had been experimenting with.

The war interrupted the Group's early efforts but once it ended, the artists emerged with an even greater awareness of independence and a determination to express a unique Canadian identity. With renewed energy, they set out to capture and represent the moods and strength of the land. As Harris once said, "to realize how far this country of Canada was different in character, atmosphere, moods, and spirit from Europe and the old land... It had to be seen, lived with, and painted with complete devotion to its own character, life, spirit, before it yield its secrets."

1. The Group of Seven artists saw their technique as new and modern. Do you think it reflected the changes that were happening in Canada in the 1920s? Or do you think the style was a continuation of an older Canada? In your response consider changes in technology, social values, urbanism vs. rural Canada, and the experience of war.

2. Has the Group prevented new styles of painting from becoming popular in contemporary Canada? What new artists have become as famous as the Group of Seven? Consider Alex Colville, Mary Pratt, Norval Morrisseau, William Kurelek, Anne Savage, and others.

FIGURE 3–14 *Lake Superior, c. 1924,* by Lawren S. Harris

• What groups in Canada were marginalized in the 1920s?

Left Out

Not everyone benefited from the social and economic changes of the Roaring Twenties. Many Canadians still battled discrimination, lack of political representation, and poverty.

The Role of Women

In the 1920s, hopes were high for reforms in health, education, and the working conditions for women and children. Women were gaining more control of their lives and were taking on roles traditionally held by men, such as factory workers, politicians, and even sports stars. Despite these gains, women still faced many social and political restrictions.

Women's Social Status

The main role of women was as wives and mothers. Married women were expected to stay at home and raise a family. Single women had limited career opportunities. They could be nurses or teachers, but these jobs paid very poorly. A few women became doctors, lawyers, professors, or engineers, but most women who worked in business or industry held jobs as secretaries, telephone operators, or sales clerks. Women usually earned much less than men for doing the same job.

• How did women attempt to achieve equality in Canadian society?

Political Reform

Although most women had won the right to vote in federal elections in 1918, only four women ran for office during the 1921 election. Only one, Agnes Macphail, won her seat. Macphail was the only woman in the House of Commons until 1935. The four Western provinces elected nine women to their legislatures, but the federal and provincial governments remained firmly male dominated. Although progress for women at the political level was slow, they made gains in social reform. In 1921, the very first maternity leave legislation was passed; however, it only applied to women in British Columbia and only permitted six weeks of leave. Four years later, the federal divorce law was changed to allow women to obtain a divorce on the same grounds as men.

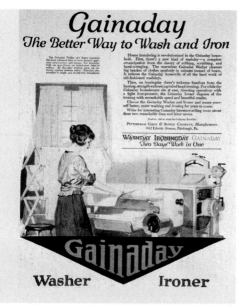

FIGURE 3–15 New labour-saving devices—such as the washing machine, refrigerator, vacuum cleaner, and electric iron—became more affordable to middle-class women. But this often meant that women were expected to maintain higher standards of cleanliness in the home.

©P

The Persons Case

The **Persons Case** of 1929 brought the issue of women participating in politics to a head. Emily Murphy, a well-known suffragist, was appointed a magistrate in Alberta. Her appointment was challenged on the basis that only "persons" could hold this office under the BNA Act, and that women were not "persons" in the eyes of the law. The Supreme Court of Alberta ruled that Murphy did, indeed, have the right to be a judge, but the matter did not stop there. Emily Murphy and four other women activists, known as the **Famous Five**, challenged Prime Minister Mackenzie King to appoint a woman senator and to clarify the definition of "persons." In April 1928, the Supreme Court of Canada decided that women were not "persons" under the **Canadian Constitution**. Murphy and her associates appealed to the Judicial Committee of the Privy Council in Britain. On October 18, 1929, the Judicial Committee declared its support for the women:

> *[The exclusion] of women from all public offices is a relic of days more barbarous than ours.... To those who would ask why the word "person" should include females, the obvious answer is, why should it not?*
> —*Privy Council Judgement, October 18, 1929*

Following the decision, Henrietta Muir Edwards wrote:

> *Personally I do not care whether or not women ever sit in the Senate, but we fought for the privilege for them to do so. We sought to establish the personal individuality of women and this decision is the announcement of our victory. It has been an uphill fight.*
> —*Quoted in* **A Harvest to Reap: A History of Prairie Women,** *1976*

The struggle for equality was far from won. The economic upheaval of the next decade would threaten the Famous Five's hard-earned gains.

FIGURE 3–16 The Famous Five were Nellie McClung, suffrage activist and writer; Emily Murphy, writer and the first female magistrate in the British Empire; Irene Parlby, the first female cabinet minister in Alberta history; former Alberta MLA Louise McKinney; and Henrietta Muir Edwards, who helped found the National Council of Women of Canada and the Victorian Order of Nurses.

Interpret and Analyze How do the backgrounds of the Famous Five represent the changing roles of women in the early 20th century?

Aboriginal Peoples: The Struggle to Preserve an Identity

Aboriginal peoples saw little of the good life in the 1920s. While the last treaties were signed in 1923 with the Chippewa and Mississauga First Nations (the Williams Treaties), they did little to advance the cause of Aboriginal rights. The treaties covered 22 000 square kilometres of land in southern and central Ontario. In return for giving up the land—as well as the right to hunt, fish, and trap on it—the Chippewa and Mississauga received a cash settlement.

Aboriginal veterans returning from the battlefields of Europe also found that their contribution to the war effort did little to change their situation at home. Aboriginal peoples were still not classified as "persons" under the law. They could not vote in provincial or federal elections. In British Columbia, Aboriginal people did not win the right to vote in provincial elections until 1949. It was not until 1960 that all Aboriginal peoples across Canada could vote in federal elections.

A Policy of Assimilation

The government continued to use residential schools in an attempt to assimilate Aboriginal children. First Nations peoples were instructed by the government to replace traditional or family leaders with graduates of residential schools. This practice often divided the community between those who supported traditional leaders and those who sought to replace them.

FIGURE 3–17 In 1920, attendance at residential schools was compulsory. Instruction was in English and children were not allowed to speak their first language, at the risk of being severely punished. These students pose in front of the Brandon Indian Residential School in Brandon, Manitoba.

Interpret and Analyze Use the diagram on page 78 in Building Your Inquiry Skills: Establishing Cause, Effect, and Consequences to create a cause-and-consequence diagram dealing with residential schools.

Cause and Consequence

In the early 1920s, First Nations peoples in British Columbia challenged the federal and provincial governments by fighting for the right to hold potlatches, an important cultural ceremony among certain peoples of the Pacific Coast. At this ceremony, births, deaths, marriages, and other significant events were recorded in the oral tradition. Potlatches involved families and even entire villages and were a way to show publicly any change in status—such as marriages, births, or deaths—or to redistribute wealth in the form of gifts.

The government viewed potlatch ceremonies as an obstacle to assimilation. The practice was forbidden in 1884. The ban was vigorously enforced after the First World War when the Kwagiulth people decided to hold several potlatch ceremonies in 1921. The provincial government arrested the chiefs responsible, and many were sentenced to jail terms. The ban on the potlatch was not lifted until 1951.

Frederick Onondeyoh Loft and the League of Indians of Canada

Though they did not have the same rights as other Canadians, thousands of First Nations, Métis, and Inuit men and women enlisted and fought during World War One. When they returned home, they did not receive the same benefits as other soldiers. Frederick Onondeyoh Loft, a Mohawk from Six Nations, was determined to fight such injustices.

In 1919, Loft formed the League of Indians of Canada to protect the rights and well-being of all First Nations people. He was concerned about a number of issues. Not only were Aboriginal veterans not receiving benefits, they also did not qualify for loans to start farming their reserve land. In contrast, non-Aboriginal veterans were receiving land and farming implements from the government. The Canadian government also dispersed nearly 34 500 hectares of "surplus" reserve land to non-Aboriginal veterans during the 1920s. As president of the League, Loft worked tirelessly to build support for the organization across Canada, and to protect the rights of individuals and communities. But the Department of Indian Affairs saw him as a troublemaker and blocked his efforts, even trying to remove his **status.**

While the League failed to become a national force, some First Nations, especially in the West, formed provincial organizations. It was not until 1970 that Loft's dream of a national First Nations organization became a reality.

The Road to Self-Determination

In addition to residential schools, Aboriginal peoples also fought against the federal government's use of **enfranchisement** to try to enforce assimilation. In 1920, the Indian Act was changed to allow the government to enfranchise people without their consent. This meant that the government could take away a person's Indian status and land. Aboriginal peoples resisted the government's policy of involuntary enfranchisement and it was given up two years later. But Aboriginal women who married men who were not status Indians were still forced to give up their Indian status.

Cayuga Chief Deskaheh (Levi General), a leader of the Six Nations Council of the Iroquois Confederacy, took the issue of Aboriginal **self-determination** to the League of Nations in 1923. He wanted international recognition of the Six Nations as an independent state and to end ties with Canada and the Indian Act. The Six Nations would have their own laws, financing, employees, and police. In a radio talk in 1925, Deskaheh explained the rationale behind the Six Nations' fight for self-determination. Britain blocked Deskaheh's efforts for the League of Nations to hear the Six Nations' claims. Self-determination for Aboriginal peoples in Canada is still an issue today.

> This story comes straight from Deskaheh, one of the chiefs of the Cayugas. I am the speaker of the Council of the Six Nations, the oldest League of Nations now existing. It was founded by Hiawatha. It is a League which is still alive and intends, as best it can, to defend the rights of the Iroquois to live under their own laws in their own little countries now left to them, to worship their Great Spirit in their own way, and to enjoy the rights which are as surely theirs as the white man's rights are his own.
>
> –*Chief Deskaheh*

FIGURE 3–18 The Ku Klux Klan, founded in the southern United States, promoted fanatical racial and religious hatred against non-Protestants and non-whites. In the 1920s, the Klan established short-lived local branches in Canada.

Evaluate and Draw Conclusions What does the existence of the Ku Klux Klan in Canada say about the attitudes of the time?

HISTORICAL INQUIRY

Interpret and Analyze

How were women, First Nations, and African Canadians treated in the 1920s? What institutions did they turn to for support, and what success did they have in the 1920s?

African Canadians: Undisguised Racism

The Canadian government discouraged the entry of African Americans into Canada during the heyday of immigration before the First World War. Those who managed to move to Canada faced blatant discrimination. In Nova Scotia, the Education Act of 1918 allowed separate schools for "Blacks" and "Europeans," a policy that remained unchanged until 1954. Racial segregation was openly practised and, in some instances, supported by the courts. For example, in 1921, the Superior Court of Québec ruled in favour of racially segregated seating in Montréal theatres.

There were also instances of tolerance. In 1919, the Brotherhood of Railway Employees accepted African Canadian porters as members. In 1924, Edmonton City Council refused to support an attempt to ban African Canadians from public parks and swimming pools.

Immigrants

After the First World War, the Canadian government adopted immigration restrictions, giving preference to applicants from Britain and the United States. Some Canadians wanted restrictions on immigration for personal reasons, and others welcomed immigrants because they would work for low wages in jobs that Canadian workers did not want. Labour groups, however, supported the restrictions because unions saw the willingness of some immigrants to work long hours for low wages as "unfair competition."

Restrictions on Asian immigrants were particularly severe. In 1923, the federal government passed a law that virtually excluded Chinese immigrants to Canada until 1947 (see Chapter 1). A Canada–Japan agreement in the 1920s restricted immigration from Japan to 150 servants and labourers per year.

In 1925, as the economy improved, the government relaxed restrictions on immigration. Thousands of immigrants landed monthly at Canada's ports looking for jobs and security. Many were forced to work in terrible conditions for pitiful wages.

CHECKPOINT

1. **Historical Perspectives** What does it mean to be a "person" in a legal sense? How did the idea of not being a person affect women, Aboriginal peoples, and visible minorities?

2. What was the attitude toward women in positions of authority in Canada during the 1920s?

3. Give examples to show that the federal government was pursuing a policy of cultural assimilation of—or discrimination against—Aboriginal peoples.

   What responses show that Aboriginal peoples were prepared to defend their rights?

4. With a partner, list the issues and criticisms faced by women in the 1920s and women of today. Which are most similar and most different?

5. How were African Canadians treated in Canada during the early 20th century?

6. Which groups supported immigration and which did not? Explain.

©P

A Renewed Challenge to Canadian Unity: Regionalism

- How did regionalism affect Canadian unity?

After the war, **regionalism**, or the concern of the various regions of the country with their own local problems, became more pronounced in Canadian politics.

The Maritimes and Newfoundland

During the 1920s, the Maritime provinces (Nova Scotia, New Brunswick, and Prince Edward Island—Newfoundland was not part of Canada until 1949) found that their influence in national politics was declining. The population in the Maritimes was small, which meant it had fewer seats in Parliament. Some businesses and banks moved to Ontario and Québec, while others suffered because their products (such as coal) were no longer in demand. Prominent business and political leaders formed the Maritime Rights movement and urged politicians to promote policies that would benefit the Maritimes.

Rural Ontario and the Prairies

Other regional challenges came from farmers in rural Ontario and on the Prairies. They were frustrated by the National Policy of 1878 that placed tariffs or duties on foreign goods imported into Canada. These tariffs made foreign goods more expensive, encouraging people to buy goods produced in Canada. Western farmers in Manitoba, Saskatchewan, and Alberta felt alienated by this policy because they had no such protection. They were forced to buy Canadian-made machinery, but their agricultural products were sold on the open world market. Farmers wanted **free trade**, abolishing tariffs and allowing them to buy cheaper American-made machinery. They also wanted lower freight rates and storage fees.

When neither the Liberals nor the Conservatives met their demands, farmers formed their own political parties. By the early 1920s, Ontario and the Prairie provinces had all elected members of United Farmers' parties to their legislatures. In some provinces, these parties formed the government. In 1920, the federal Progressive Party was created, led by Thomas Crerar, a former Minister of Agriculture in Robert Borden's Union Government. The Progressive Party wanted a new National Policy based on free trade and public ownership of the railways.

KEY TERMS

regionalism a concern for the affairs of one's own region over those of one's country

free trade trade between countries without tariffs, export subsidies, or other government intervention

FIGURE 3–19 In 2001, Manitoban farmers demanded more financial aid from the government by driving their vehicles to the legislature in a national day of protest.

Continuity and Change How effective do you think this protest was in getting support for the farmers? In what ways was this protest the same as and different from protests of the 1920s?

HISTORICAL INQUIRY

Interpret and Analyze

How did farmers and workers express their discontent after World War I?

Québec

The economic boom in the 1920s, and Québec's proximity to the United States, led to rapid growth in many Québec industries. Cheap labour and vast forests resulted in the expansion of the province's pulp and paper industry to feed the U.S.'s demand for newsprint. Increased manufacturing in Canada and the U.S. during this decade helped to expand Québec's mining industries. To provide power to its growing industries, Québec took advantage of the hydro-electric potential of its many rivers. The abundant hydroelectric resources attracted the aluminum industry, and the Aluminum Company of Canada opened several plants.

As Québec's industries expanded, so did its desire to protect its own interests. Hostility to the Conservative Party because of conscription and language rights helped the Liberals sweep all 65 seats in Québec in the 1921 federal election. Provincial politics were dominated from 1920 to 1936 by Premier Louis-Alexandre Taschereau's Liberal Party.

Western Interests

For most of the 1920s, British Columbia was led by Liberal John Oliver, who often attacked the federal government for favouring the interests of Eastern Canada. B.C.'s growing economic strength during the 1920s meant its politicians had a stronger voice in federal politics. The products of B.C.'s forests and mines were in demand. Communities grew around the new pulp and paper mills and mines. After the war, the port of Vancouver began to benefit from the Panama Canal that had opened in 1914. More importantly, Pacific Coast ports could challenge Eastern Canada's dominance in shipping Western grain. Premier Oliver went to Ottawa three times to demand railway freight rates be reduced, a fight he won each time. As a result, annual shipments of grain from B.C. ports increased throughout the 1920s. By the end of the decade, 40 percent of Canada's grain was exported through B.C.

FIGURE 3–20 Cow East and West

Interpret and Analyze What point is being made by the cartoon? How effective is the cartoon in explaining its message? Why?

Canadians Choose a New Government

Regionalism and the Progressive Party greatly influenced the results of the 1921 federal election, effectively upsetting the balance of power between the Liberals and Conservatives.

In the 1921 election, both the Liberals and the Conservatives had new leaders. William Lyon Mackenzie King was chosen to lead the Liberals in 1919. He had a reputation as a reformer and was an authority on social and economic issues. Arthur Meighen, a brilliant debater and long-standing Member of Parliament, was chosen to replace Borden as the leader of the Conservatives. He then also became prime minister. While King always tried to find the middle path that would offend the fewest people, Meighen believed in principles over compromise and did not care who might be offended by his stand on issues. Meighen's hard line alienated many groups before the election. His involvement in creating the Conscription Act and the new electoral laws of 1917 meant he had little support in Québec. His harsh treatment of the leaders of the Winnipeg General Strike also provoked the hostility of the labour movement.

The Progressive Party's election platform was based on their proposed National Policy, calling for free trade and to **nationalize** the railways. In the election, the Progressives managed to win an astonishing 64 seats, mostly in Western Canada. This made it the second largest party in Parliament, giving the Liberals a **minority government**. Because they were not the majority, the Liberals needed the support of some of the opposition members to pass legislation.

Despite its initial success, the Progressive Party did not last very long. However, it was influential in bringing about changes to Canada's social policy. In 1926, for example, King was challenged by the Progressives to set up an old age pension. The **Old Age Pension Act** was passed in 1927. The Act was an acknowledgement that government had a role to play in providing a network of social services for its citizens. The Progressive Party lost public support in the 1925 and 1926 elections, and it eventually dissolved. But it did manage to change Canadian politics by helping to create Canada's first minority government.

Prime Minister
Arthur Meighen

- born 1874, Anderson, Ontario
- lawyer
- first elected to Commons in 1908
- prime minister 1920–1921, June–September 1926

Domestic Record

- helped write and pass the Military Service Act and Wartime Elections Act
- created the Canadian National Railways in 1919 by nationalizing several transportation companies
- played a prominent role in ending the Winnipeg General Strike in 1919
- formed a minority government during the King-Byng Crisis in 1926

International Record

- successfully argued against an Anglo-Japanese alliance at the 1921 Imperial Conference

FIGURE 3–21 In a 1920 speech, Arthur Meighen said, "Thousands of people are mentally chasing rainbows, striving for the unattainable, anxious to better their lot and seemingly unwilling to do it in the old-fashioned way by honest intelligent effort. Dangerous doctrines taught by dangerous men, enemies of the State, poison and pollute the air...."

Interpret and Analyze What groups was Meighen referring to? How would they have reacted to his speech?

CHECKPOINT

1. List the concerns expressed by each region during the 1920s: Maritimes; Québec; Prairies and rural Ontario; Western Canada. To what extent were the concerns resolved?

2. Why was the Progressive Party so successful during the 1921 election? What impact did this have on the federal government from 1921 to 1926?

Prime Minister
William Lyon Mackenzie King

- born 1874, Berlin (Kitchener), Ontario
- author, editor, journalist, lawyer
- first elected to Commons in 1908
- prime minister 1921–1926, 1926–1930, 1935–1948

Domestic Record

● created the Industrial Disputes Investigation Act in 1907

● helped create Canada's first old-age pension program in 1927

● fought for Canadian autonomy during the King-Byng Crisis (1926) and in signing the Halibut Treaty with the United States (1923)

● appointed Cairine Wilson as the first woman senator in 1930

● commissioned the Rowell-Sirois Report of 1937

● introduced unemployment insurance in 1940

● held national plebiscite on conscription in 1942

● passed the Family Allowance Act in 1945

● helped create the Canadian Citizenship Act in 1947, which was the first statute to define Canada's people as Canadians

● longest-serving prime minister in Canadian history

International Record

● defended Canada's autonomy during the Chanak Crisis (1922)

● helped create the definition of Dominion status at the Imperial Conference of 1926

● insisted that Parliament decide if Canada would become involved in international conflicts

● successfully led Canada through the Second World War

Canada's Growing Independence

After the First World War, Prime Minister Borden took a number of important steps that raised Canada's profile internationally, including participating in the Paris Peace Conference and signing the Treaty of Versailles (see Chapter 2). Mackenzie King, once he became prime minister, continued to push for greater independence from Britain.

The Chanak Crisis

In 1922, Mackenzie King refused Britain's call for support when British occupation troops were threatened by nationalist Turks during the **Chanak Crisis**. Chanak was a Turkish port controlled by Britain as a condition of one of the treaties signed at the Paris Peace Conference. If Turkey regained this port, it would have clear access to Europe through the Black Sea to the Mediterranean. Britain saw this as a threat and sent a telegram to King, asking him to send Canadian troops to support the Empire. Instead of automatically granting Britain's request, King brought the issue to Parliament. By the time the issue was debated in the House of Commons, the crisis in Turkey had passed. The Chanak Crisis marked the first time that Canada did not automatically support the British Empire in war.

The Halibut Treaty

The following year, Canada negotiated a treaty with the United States to protect halibut along the coasts of British Columbia and Alaska. Mackenzie King insisted that Canada be allowed to sign the **Halibut Treaty** without the signature of a British representative. Britain wanted to maintain its imperial right to sign international agreements on Canada's behalf. When Britain tried to pressure King into letting their representative sign the treaty, King insisted that it was a matter between Canada and the U.S. He threatened to set up an independent Canadian representative in Washington, and Britain backed down. The Halibut Treaty was the first treaty negotiated and signed independently by the Canadian government.

The King-Byng Crisis

In 1926, Mackenzie King publicly challenged Britain over the role of the **governor general** and Britain's influence on Canada's internal politics in what became known as the **King-Byng Crisis**. During the election of 1926, King was able to avoid a scandal that erupted (see page 77) and appeal to nationalist sentiments. He claimed that it was undemocratic for the governor general, an official appointed by Britain, to refuse to take the advice of the prime minister, who was elected by Canadians. Since the King-Byng crisis, no governor general has acted against the wishes of an elected prime minister.

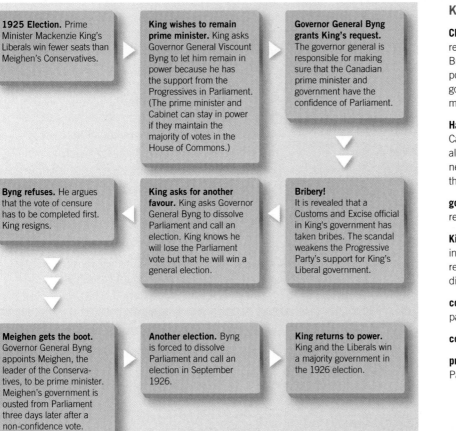

1925 Election. Prime Minister Mackenzie King's Liberals win fewer seats than Meighen's Conservatives.	King wishes to remain prime minister. King asks Governor General Viscount Byng to let him remain in power because he has the support from the Progressives in Parliament. (The prime minister and Cabinet can stay in power if they maintain the majority of votes in the House of Commons.)	Governor General Byng grants King's request. The governor general is responsible for making sure that the Canadian prime minister and government have the confidence of Parliament.
Byng refuses. He argues that the vote of censure has to be completed first. King resigns.	King asks for another favour. King asks Governor General Byng to dissolve Parliament and call an election. King knows he will lose the Parliament vote but that he will win a general election.	Bribery! It is revealed that a Customs and Excise official in King's government has taken bribes. The scandal weakens the Progressive Party's support for King's Liberal government.
Meighen gets the boot. Governor General Byng appoints Meighen, the leader of the Conservatives, to be prime minister. Meighen's government is ousted from Parliament three days later after a non-confidence vote.	Another election. Byng is forced to dissolve Parliament and call an election in September 1926.	King returns to power. King and the Liberals win a majority government in the 1926 election.

FIGURE 3–22 After the King-Byng Crisis, King gained national support by claiming it was undemocratic for the governor general, a British representative, to go against the wishes of a prime minister elected by Canadians.

KEY TERMS

Chanak Crisis the Canadian government's refusal in 1922, led by King, to support British troops in defending the Turkish port of Chanak; the first time the Canadian government did not support the British military

Halibut Treaty a 1923 treaty between Canada and the U.S. to protect halibut along the Pacific Coast; the first treaty negotiated and signed independently by the Canadian government

governor general the person who represents the British crown in Canada

King-Byng Crisis a situation that occurred in 1926 when Governor General Byng refused Prime Minister King's request to dissolve Parliament and call an election

coalition a formal alliance of political parties

confidence in politics, it means support

prorogue to postpone or suspend, as in Parliament

FASTFORWARD

King-Byng Revisited?

In 2008, Prime Minister Stephen Harper faced a crisis similar to that of Mackenzie King in 1926. The three opposition parties (Liberal, New Democrat, and Bloc Québécois) were dissatisfied with the minority Conservative government's financial policies and formed a **coalition** to oust the government. They asked Parliament to hold a non-**confidence** vote against Harper's government. Before the vote took place, Harper asked Governor General Michaëlle Jean to **prorogue**, or suspend, Parliament for a month so the government could bring in a new financial policy. Governor General Jean agreed. During the month Parliament was suspended, Harper managed to convince the Liberal leader to accept the Conservatives' new financial plan and support them in the non-confidence vote. With the Liberals' support in Parliament, Harper's Conservative government stayed in power.

FIGURE 3–23 This cartoon shows the three opposition leaders, Stéphane Dion, Gilles Duceppe, and Jack Layton, pointing at Stephen Harper.

Interpret and Analyze How would you have advised Governor General Jean regarding Harper's request to suspend Parliament?

How many times have you been asked to discuss the causes of an event on an exam? As you probably know, it is much easier to describe *what*, *where*, and *when* an event happened than to explain *why* it happened. For example, there is no disagreement that the First World War (what) began in Europe (where) in 1914 (when). Explaining the causes, effects, and consequences of the war is not so straightforward. Was one country more responsible than others? Why did countries declare war? What future events resulted from the decisions made at the Paris Peace Conference?

Events in history are the result of many other events that directly or indirectly caused that incident to happen. This is called causality. Understanding causality helps us to see the relationship between one event (the cause) and another event (the effect). The effect then leads to long-term results or consequences that in turn lead to more effects (see Figure 3–24). Some of the results of the First World War still affect us today. For example, the location of boundaries in the Balkans, and in Middle East countries such as Iraq, established by the treaties of 1919, are still a source of conflict today. Historians (and geographers) use cause-effect-consequences organizers to explain change.

People often have different perspectives and worldviews. Few people will understand events in exactly the same way. They will explain the causes, effects, and consequences of an event in different ways, and their differing viewpoints will often lead them to different conclusions about the same event.

You will find examples of cause and effect throughout this textbook. Issues related to history, politics, human rights, economics, and identity all raise questions about cause-effect-consequence relationships. How did Canada's status in the British Empire change in the early 20th century? What impact did the atrocities in the Second World War have on the development of human rights legislation? How did the Quiet Revolution affect Canadian identity?

Evaluate and Draw Conclusions

1. Referring to Figure 3–24, create a cause-effect-consequences organizer for the Winnipeg General Strike.

2. How do Canadians feel about their American neighbours today, and how determined do you think they are to maintain and develop their own culture and identity?

3. Note the immediate and longer-term effects of closer relations between Canada and the United States in the 1920s.

4. Record the effects of discrimination on one or more of the following groups during the 1920s: Aboriginal peoples, African Canadians, or immigrants.

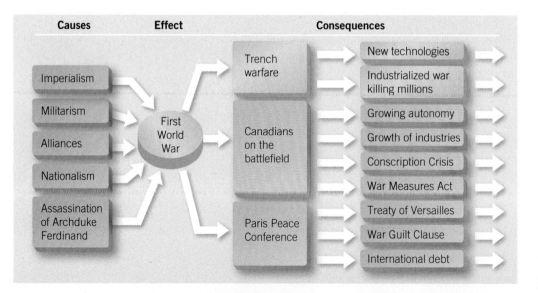

FIGURE 3–24
Cause-effect-consequences organizer for the First World War

Causes	Effect	Consequences
Imperialism		New technologies
Militarism		Industrialized war killing millions
Alliances	First World War	Trench warfare
Nationalism	Canadians on the battlefield	Growing autonomy
Assassination of Archduke Ferdinand	Paris Peace Conference	Growth of industries
		Conscription Crisis
		War Measures Act
		Treaty of Versailles
		War Guilt Clause
		International debt

The Imperial Conference and the Balfour Report

It was at the **Imperial Conference** of 1926 that Canada made the greatest progress toward changing its legal dependence on Britain. At this conference, the dominions of the British Empire (Canada, Australia, New Zealand, South Africa, and the Irish Free State) requested formal recognition of their autonomy, the freedom to govern themselves. A special committee under the leadership of Lord Balfour, a respected British politician, examined the request. The committee's findings, published as the **Balfour Report**, supported the dominions' position:

> ...[We] refer to the group of self-governing communities composed of... Britain and the Dominions. Their position and mutual relation may be readily defined. They are autonomous communities within the British Empire, equal in status, in no way subordinate one to another in any aspect of their domestic or external affairs, though united by a common allegiance to the Crown....
>
> —Summary of Proceedings at the Imperial Conference, 1926

The Statute of Westminster

The recommendations of the Balfour Report became law in 1931, when the **Statute of Westminster** was passed by the British government. This statute formally turned the British Empire into the **British Commonwealth**. The commonwealth countries were considered free and equal states that shared an allegiance to the British Crown. Canada was now a country equal in status with Britain and could make its own laws. There were, however, two remaining restrictions on Canada's independence. Canada's constitution, the British North America Act (BNA Act), remained in Britain because the Canadian federal and provincial governments could not agree on an **amending formula**, the procedure for changing the Act. As well, the Judicial Committee of the Privy Council, a court of final appeal for Canadians, resided in Britain until 1949.

KEY TERMS

Imperial Conference a meeting of the leaders of the countries in the British Empire

Balfour Report the conclusions of the 1926 Imperial Conference that acknowledged Canada as an autonomous community within the British Empire

Statute of Westminster the law that changed the British Empire into the British Commonwealth; all commonwealth countries to be considered equal in status with Britain and able to make their own laws

British Commonwealth an association of nations that were formerly colonies of the British Empire

amending formula the process by which changes can legally be made to the Canadian Constitution

CHECKPOINT

1. **Historical Significance** What was the historical significance of each of the following for Canada: Chanak Crisis, Halibut Treaty, Statute of Westminster?

2. How was King able to turn an election defeat in 1925 into an election victory?

3. Explain the challenges faced by minority governments.

4. **Continuity and Change** Review the Fast Forward. Which elements of the King-Byng Crisis and Harper's prorogation of Parliament are the same? What is the key difference between the two events?

5. What restrictions to Canadian autonomy remained after the Statute of Westminster was passed?

- How did Canada increase its independence after World War One ended?

Was Canada more or less independent by the end of the 1920s?

While Canada gained greater political independence from Britain in the 1920s, it developed much closer economic and cultural ties to the United States. In 1922, U.S. investment in Canada topped that of Britain's investment for the first time. By 1930, 61 percent of foreign investment in Canada was from the U.S. During the same period, close to a million Canadians moved to the U.S. in search of better jobs and higher pay.

Despite a growing cultural industry in Canada, most Canadians listened to American radio stations, watched Hollywood films, and drove American-designed Model T Fords. Even Canadian sports teams were being bought up by U.S. interests. The National Hockey League became Americanized as smaller Canadian cities were unable to compete following the inclusion of U.S. teams.

One historian described the close ties between Canada and the United States in the 1920s:

> ...in the immediate aftermath of the war, the United States had a... depression and Canada had a... depression too. Coal strikes broke out in the United States; coal strikes broke out in Canada. The United States embarked on Prohibition; so... did almost all the provinces of Canada. The United States spawned the Prohibition gangster; Canada spawned the Prohibition rum-runner to keep him supplied.
>
> –Ralph Allen, **Ordeal By Fire: Canada, 1910–1945**

Year	Britain %	U.S. %	Other %
1910	77	19	4
1918	60	36	4
1920	53	44	3
1922	47	50	3
1925	41	56	3
1926	44	53	3
1930	36	61	3

FIGURE 3–25 Percent of foreign investment in Canada

Interpret and Analyze In what year did U.S. investment in Canada overtake that of Britain? What are some reasons that might account for this change?

A Separate Identity

Had the U.S. simply replaced Britain in controlling Canada's development? On the one hand, Canada's economy was very dependent on that of the U.S. Canada was also awash in American popular culture. But it is hard to say how much the exposure to American entertainment diminished Canadian identity in the 1920s. For example, the people of Québec remained relatively untouched by the influence of American culture in Canada. A different language and a protective church helped to ensure that most French Canadians remained beyond American influence.

On the other hand, concern about American cultural and economic domination made Canadians determined to protect their identity. A Royal Commission in 1928 recommended that the government regulate private radio to ensure Canadian content. Although Canadians benefited from having a larger, more prosperous neighbour to the south, they never showed interest in becoming part of the U.S. J.A. Stephenson, a British correspondent in Canada during the 1920s, observed:

> The people of Canada are imbued with... a passion to maintain their own separate identity. They cherish the rooted belief that they enjoy in their existing political and social order certain manifest advantages over their neighbours.
>
> –Quoted in **Contemporary Review**, October 1931

Thinking It Through

1. In Vancouver in 1923, U.S. President Warren Harding made the following statement about the interdependence of Canada and the U.S: "We think the same thoughts, live the same lives, and cherish the same aspirations...." Do you think many Canadians would have agreed with Harding? Why or why not?

2. Write a letter to the editor of a newspaper, explaining why you agree or disagree with President Harding's statement. Give examples of Canada's dependence or independence to support your argument.

The Stock Market Crash

In the latter half of the 1920s, the North American economy was booming, and Canadians were optimistic about the future. Like the United States, Canada had watched its industrial base expand during the war. It was now poised to overtake Europe, along with the United States, as an industrial leader.

However, as you will see in the next chapter, the prosperity soon came crashing to an end. On Tuesday, October 29, 1929, the New York Stock Exchange collapsed. On that day, prices of all stocks fell dramatically. The order to traders was to "Sell, sell, sell!" More than 16 million shares changed hands, but prices continued to fall. Everyone knew a disaster had occurred. As you will read in the next chapter, the stock market crash marked a shift from the prosperity of the 1920s to the crushing poverty of the **Great Depression** of the 1930s.

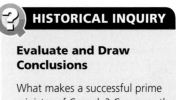

FIGURE 3–26 Front page of Toronto's *The Globe* just days before the stock market crash

Interpret and Analyze How does this front page show the different opinions on the state of the stock market prior to the crash? What words express concern? Confidence?

CHAPTER FOCUS QUESTION   How did Canada adjust to political, social, and economic changes following the First World War?

Canadians in the 1920s began to develop a distinct sense of identity from Britain. Events and developments following the First World War at times encouraged and at other times hindered this trend.

1. **a)** Complete the organizer below, gathering examples of events from the chapter that helped in the growth of a Canadian identity and examples of events that worked against developing an identity.

    b) Which of the examples do you think had the greatest impact on the growing sense of Canadian identity? Which examples most hindered the growth of a Canadian identity? Give reasons for your choices.

    c) How many of the examples affect your sense of identity as a Canadian today? Explain.

    d) Pretend you are in a foreign country and are mistaken for an American by someone you meet. How would you explain the difference? What makes us Canadian?

Events helping to promote a Canadian identity

GROWING SENSE OF CANADIAN IDENTITY

Events hindering the growth of a Canadian identity

Knowledge and Understanding

2. Continue the annotated timeline begun in Chapter 2 showing steps to Canadian autonomy. Review the events that are covered in the chapter. Write the name and date of each event on the timeline and explain how the event contributed to Canadian independence.

3. List the advantages and disadvantages of foreign investment and branch plants in Canada. Use your list to determine whether the positive impacts of foreign investment outweigh the negative impacts.

4. What do the immigration policy, Aboriginal policy, and treatment of African Canadians reveal about the attitudes and values of Canadian authorities in the 1920s?

5. What current political parties offer a change from traditional parties? How effective are these alternative parties at influencing government policy?

Historical Significance

6. What was the historical significance of the King-Byng Crisis?

Apply Your Thinking

7. Outline the historical significance of the contributions of Emily Murphy and Frederick Onondeyoh Loft. Consider their actions and the consequences of those actions today.

8. Compare the struggle of women and Aboriginal peoples during the 1920s. In your opinion, which group was more successful in the short term and long term? Provide specific evidence to support your opinion.

9. Rank the following from most to least important for their impact on Canada's independence. Provide information to support your ranking.

   Chanak Crisis
   Halibut Treaty
   King-Byng Crisis
   1926 Imperial Conference
   Balfour Report
   Statute of Westminster

10. Debate: Prime Minister Mackenzie King did more for Canadian autonomy than any other Canadian prime minister.

Communicate

11. Discuss with a partner why the 1920s are described as the "Roaring Twenties." Do you agree with the name? Explain your answer. If you do not agree, decide on another name.

❓ HISTORICAL INQUIRY

Evaluate and Draw Conclusions

12. What point is the cartoon in Figure 3–27 making about Canadian identity? WASP stands for White Anglo-Saxon Protestants and refers to Canadians of British descent. United Empire Loyalists fought for Britain during the American Revolution and, after the war, settled in what is now Canada.

FIGURE 3–27

Chapter 3 ■ Canada and the Post-War Years: The Roaring Twenties 83

Thinking It Through

Use this study guide to continue synthesizing your learning about Canada's history between 1914 and 1929. As you work through the following steps, refer back to the focus questions for chapters in this unit to help you review your understanding.

STEP 1 Unpacking Knowledge

Use a chart to collate and summarize important events, key terms, important persons, and concepts you studied in Chapters 1, 2, and 3.

Chapter 1	Chapter 2	Chapter 3
A Different Nation: Canada Enters the Twentieth Century	Trial by Fire: Canada Enters World War One	Canada and the Post-War Years: The Roaring Twenties

STEP 2 Organizing Your Understanding

Historical Significance

Using the information you gathered in Step 1, create a chart like the one shown below to help you organize your questions. Use the examples given here to guide you.

Sample Questions	Event/Person/Date/Key Term	Historical Significance
What steps did Canada take to become an autonomous nation?		
What was Canada's role in the First World War? How did the war affect developments in Canada?		
How were labour and the economy affected by events immediately after World War One?		
What is regionalism, and how was it expressed in Canada between 1914 and 1929?		

©P

STEP 3 Making Connections

Use the information you gathered and organized in Steps 1 and 2 to help you think about how persons, events, policies, social trends, and other things you have learned about the history of Canada between 1914 and 1929 might be connected. Discuss these connections in a group or with a partner.

Complete a mind map around **one** of the following:

- Society, Economy, and Politics
- Community, Conflict, and Cooperation
- Identity, Citizenship, and Heritage

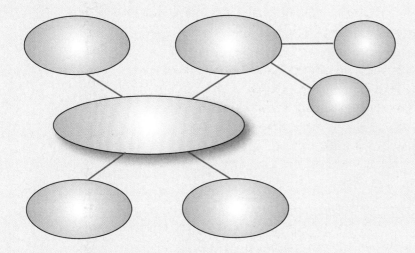

STEP 4 Applying Your Skills

Historical Perspectives

Evidence

This painting from 1919 is called *The Battle of Vimy Ridge*. Examine the image. What does the image show? What can examining this single image tell you about the battle? What important features of the Battle of Vimy Ridge are can you *not* learn from it?

Explain why the image is important evidence yet cannot be considered a complete body of evidence about the battle. Make a list of other pieces of evidence that would help you and others understand this important event. Provide a brief rationale for each item you include.

▲ **SOURCE 1:** *The Battle of Vimy Ridge,* Richard Jack, 1919. The Battle of Vimy Ridge took place in France in April 1917.

STEP 4 continued

Historical Perspectives

Evidence

This shot of Bloor and Dundas streets in Toronto was taken in 1926 at the height of the Roaring Twenties. What evidence can you find that shows the city's prosperity during this period? Make two or three generalizations about the lives of the people in the cars. What might they be thinking, hoping, or aspiring to? Describe what you think you would see if the camera were able to pan 360 degrees.

◄ **SOURCE 2:** Bloor and Dundas Streets in Toronto in 1926

Founded in 1891, Massey-Harris grew to be the largest manufacturer of agricultural machinery in the British Empire. The company sold products such as tractors and combines throughout Canada, the United States, and Europe. What factors combined to make this company so successful in the early part of the 19th century?

▲ **SOURCE 3:** A farmer in Alberta uses a horse-drawn Massey-Harris binder in 1911.

STEP 5 Thinking Critically

Evidence

Ethical Dimension

Conservative Party Platform, 1927
Resolution on Immigration

Read the recommendations on immigration made by the Conservative Party in 1927 and answer the following questions:

- In what ways is this public pronouncement racist?
- Who is favoured in this statement of policy?
- Who might take issue with Item 7? Why?
- Do an Internet search for current government policy on immigration. How has it changed since 1927? Are there any similarities? Explain.
- Whom might they be planning to exclude with item 8?

That Canada adopt an aggressive system of immigration based upon selective principle and with that end in view efforts be directed to:

1. *Repatriation of Canadians.*

2. *Securing a larger percentage of British settlers.*

3. *Taking full advantage of the assistance tendered by the British Government to promote Empire settlement.*

4. *Making arrangements ... to ensure proper training of the youth of the British Isles as agriculturalists to better qualify them as Canadian settlers.*

5. *That in the selection and settlement of immigrants a sane classification and distribution should be made, taking into consideration the immigrant's previous occupation and adaptability and that in such distribution the needs of all provinces be given the fullest consideration.*

6. *That in selecting new immigrants, relatives of present citizens of Canada should receive favourable consideration.*

7. *That special concessions be granted to Canadians to enable them to settle our vacant lands.*

8. *That such races be excluded as are not capable of ready assimilation.*

Source: Reid, Stewart, McNaught, Kenneth, and Crowe, Harry S. 1959.
A Source-book of Canadian History. *Toronto: Longmans, p. 413.*

Canada, 1929–1945

Canada was tested again during the 1930s and the Second World War. The legacy of World War One was the Great Depression and another more devastating global conflict. The boom of the 1920s hid, temporarily, deep economic problems created by the war and helped bring Adolf Hitler and other dictators to power. Canadians suffered during the Great Depression. Canada went to war to stop Hitler and other aggressors bent on world domination. These two crises shaped Canadian identity in new and unexpected ways.

The Great Depression was a decade of hardship and despair that highlighted weaknesses in the Canadian and global economies. As people struggled to survive, tensions divided the country—notably, between immigrants and non-immigrants, men and women, and Western and Central Canada.

PACIFIC
OCEAN

ATLANTIC
OCEAN

N

The atrocities of the Second World War were sometimes used to appeal to Canadian nationalism. As the war continued, Canadians became less tolerant of immigrants, in particular, "enemy aliens." Japanese Canadians were one of the groups targeted and were sent to internment camps in British Columbia. Many Japanese-Canadian families were separated and most lost all their possessions.

The Great Depression closed factories and threw thousands of people out of work. Many "took to the rails," travelling great distances looking for non-existent jobs. Governments had few programs to deal with the unemployed and the destitute, often using the police to force people to move on.

The Second World War was total war. All citizens were expected to play their part, and warring governments deliberately targeted civilian populations. Germany was first, using bombers to level cities, pounding them into submission. Bomber attacks on London and other British cities were intended to weaken morale.

PACIFIC OCEAN

INDIAN OCEAN

0   1000   2000 km

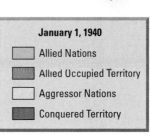

The global economic crisis of the 1930s gave rise to totalitarian dictators who promised easy solutions to create a better life for citizens. Adolf Hitler's imperialistic aggressions led to the Second World War, during which Canadians fought for the first time as an independent nation. Other dictators arose in Italy, Spain, and Japan.

January 1, 1940

Allied Nations

Allied Occupied Territory

Aggressor Nations

Conquered Territory

©P

4

Decade of Despair: Canada in the Great Depression

? INVESTIGATE

Social, Economic, and Political Context

- What were the causes of the Great Depression?

- What were the effects of the Great Depression on Canadians?

- How did governments in Canada respond to the Great Depression?

- How did Canadians use politics to try to solve the problem of the Depression?

- How did the Great Depression affect women?

Communities, Conflict, and Cooperation

- What were the effects of the Great Depression on the global community?

- Why did the Great Depression cause conflict within Canadian society and elsewhere?

Identity, Citizenship, and Heritage

- How were Aboriginal people treated during the 1930s?

- How did minority groups fare during the Depression?

The Fehrs, a destitute family from Saskatoon, Saskatchewan, are shown in this 1934 photo. The children ranged in age from three months to ten years.

Gather Evidence Why would a severe economic downturn—a depression—be hard on a large family like the Fehrs? Why do you think the 1930s were known as the Great Depression or the Dirty Thirties? What questions would you like to ask Abraham and Elizabeth Fehr and their four oldest children?

TIMELINE

1929

New York Stock Exchange crashes on Wall Street

1930

Severe drought devastates the Prairies (1930–1937)

R.B. Bennett becomes prime minister

1931

City dwellers outnumber rural population in Canada

1932

Co-operative Commonwealth Federation (CCF) established

Federal relief camps established

1933

Unemployment hits highest level

Hitler comes to power in Germany

CHAPTER FOCUS QUESTION

What were the causes and consequences of, and responses to, the Great Depression?

James Gray was a young man at the beginning of the Depression. This account of his family's struggle to survive those difficult years is a vivid picture of the hardships endured by ordinary Canadians in the bleakest decade of the 20th century:

> *For two months, half a million farm people huddled around stoves and thought only of keeping warm. If food supplies ran low, they ate less. Only when fuel reached the vanished point would they venture to town for a load of relief coal.... Winter ended with a thaw... and presently we were into summer which was much worse.... There was no escape from the heat and wind and dust of the summer of 1936.... From Calgary to Winnipeg there was almost nothing but dust, in a bowl that extended clear down to Texas. Within the bowl was stifling heat, as if someone had left all the furnace doors open and the blowers on.*
>
> –James Gray, **The Winter Years**, 1976

For most Canadians, the 1930s was a decade of despair. In this chapter, you will learn about the causes, effects, and government's response to the Great Depression.

KEY TERMS

depression
supply and demand
prosperity
recovery
On-to-Ottawa Trek
Regina Riot
New Deal
laissez-faire
welfare state
Co-operative Commonwealth Federation (CCF)
capitalism
Regina Manifesto
Social Credit Party
Union nationale
Québec nationalism
equalization payments

1935
On-to-Ottawa Trek
Mackenzie King becomes prime minister

1936
Canadian Broadcasting Corporation established
J.M. Keynes publishes *General Theory of Employment, Interest and Money*

1937
Royal Commission on Dominion-Provincial Relations created

1939
Second World War begins

• What were the causes of the Great Depression?

KEY TERMS

depression a long period of severe economic and social hardship, massive unemployment, and suffering

market economy an economic system in which individuals produce goods and prices are determined by supply and demand

mixed economy an economic system in which both individuals and the government produce and sell goods

supply and demand the quantity of a product that is available and the market's desire for that product; the price of the product varies based on supply and demand

prosperity in the economic cycle, the period of economic growth and expansion

recovery in the economic cycle, the period following a recession during which the value of goods and services rises

credit the ability or power to obtain goods before paying for them

overproduction more goods being produced than being sold; leads to a decrease in production, which leads to increased unemployment

protectionism a system of using tariffs to raise the price of imported goods in order to protect domestic producers

Causes of the Great Depression

The end of the prosperity of the 1920s came as a surprise to many Canadians. The stock market crash on October 29, 1929 marked the beginning of a recession, which progressed to a decade-long **depression** in Canada and around the world. Prior to examining the causes of the Great Depression and what was happening in the economy at the time, a basic knowledge of economic principles is necessary.

FIGURE 4–1 People flood the streets of New York after the stock market crash.

Basic Economic Principles

In a **market economy**, or free enterprise system, the means of production—factories, machinery, and land—are owned by individuals, not the government. Individuals decide what types of goods and services they produce and the prices for their products. People are free to buy what they like from whomever they choose. Canada has a **mixed economy**, meaning that the government has some involvement in the economy, including the creation of government-owned industries (for example, Canadian National Railways), limitations on workers' rights to strike, and subsidies to support certain industries.

In a market or mixed economy, production and prices are determined by **supply and demand**. Supply refers to how much of a product is available. Demand refers to how much people want that product. Usually, when the supply of a product is low, demand makes the price higher; when there is a great supply, the price is lower. For example, at the beginning of the 1920s, a shortage of wheat as a result of the First World War led to a higher price for Canadian wheat. As other countries began producing wheat after the war, increased supply lowered wheat prices.

Market economies regularly go through cycles of growth and decline (see Figure 4–2). Expansion in many economic activities results in a period of **prosperity**. This eventually is followed by a slowdown in the economy, called a recession. If the slowdown is longer and more severe, it is called a depression. **Recovery** is when the economy begins to grow again.

Overproduction

During the 1920s, many industries in Canada expanded as demand for their goods was high. Consumers had been lured by all kinds of products—from toasters to cars—which companies eventually persuaded them to buy on **credit**. But when the economy slowed down, many companies faced **overproduction** as they produced more goods than they sold. At first, manufacturers lowered prices and stockpiled goods. Eventually, they cut back and produced fewer goods. This decrease in production led to layoffs in factories, which meant people could not afford to buy consumer goods or even pay their bills, so sales slowed down even more.

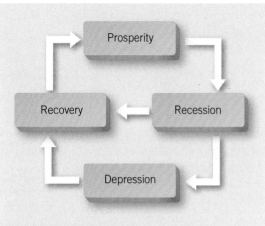

FIGURE 4–2 In the economic cycle, market economies have ups and downs.

Evaluate and Draw Conclusions How would governments try to alter this cycle? Provide specific examples.

Economic Dependence on Exports

The Great Depression exposed a major weakness in the Canadian economy: its heavy dependence on the export of primary resources. Two exports in particular—wheat from the Prairie provinces, and newsprint from British Columbia, Ontario, and Québec—made Canada extremely vulnerable to changes in world markets. Eighty percent of Canada's production on farms, and in forests and mines, was exported.

In the early 1920s, wheat farmers in Canada and the United States produced record quantities of crops and sold them at record prices. But as more countries, including Argentina and Australia, produced wheat crops, there was more competition on the international market. Wheat was being overproduced and the price of wheat began to fall. As international sales decreased, farmers' incomes dropped. Soon, many were unable to meet their mortgage and loan payments.

GO ONLINE •
Find out more about how fish, vegetables, and other foods were often used in place of money during the Great Depression.

Tariffs and U.S. Protectionism

Canada's economy was hit particularly hard because of its close ties to the U.S. economy. The United States had become Canada's biggest trading partner and largest investor. Consequently, when the U.S. economy "crashed," Canada's economy was bound to feel the consequences.

Since the United States did not need raw materials from other countries, it imposed high tariffs on foreign goods. These tariffs were meant to protect the U.S. domestic market by making foreign items, such as Canadian wheat, more expensive. However, this **protectionism** led other countries to impose their own tariffs in response to the United States' actions. Tariffs caused a slowdown in world trade as opportunities for export shrank. Canadian exports decreased substantially as the U.S. and other countries stopped buying Canadian products.

reparations compensation from a defeated enemy for damages caused by war

speculation buying shares "on margin" with the expectation that the value of the shares will increase enough to pay back the loan and make a profit

Black Tuesday October 29, 1929, when the New York Stock Exchange collapsed

Debt from World War One

The United States lent several countries money during and after the First World War. Many of these countries relied on trade with the U.S. to raise money to pay these debts. But as protectionism grew, international trade decreased and several countries were unable to pay back the loans. Britain and France in particular relied on German **reparations** to pay their war debts. After the First World War, Germany's economy was in ruins. The enormous reparations it was obligated to pay Britain and France under the Treaty of Versailles further stunted its ability to recover (see Chapter 3). Because Germany could not make its reparation payments, Britain and France in turn could not pay their war debts. The war debt placed a particular burden on Newfoundland and Labrador, where jobs were scarce, and there were many veterans looking for work.

Reckless Speculation and the Stock Market Crash of 1929

Business was booming in the early 1920s. Companies wanted to expand, and in order to raise money, they would issue shares (or stocks). Investors bought these shares believing that the company would do well and the value of the stocks would rise. Between 1922 and 1926, Canadian companies issued $700 million worth of new shares.

During the 1920s, many investors were buying "on margin." This meant buying shares with only a 10 percent down payment, assuming that when the prices of the stocks increased the remaining 90 percent would be paid. This process is called **speculation**. Loans for stocks were easy to obtain, and high demand had driven the price of stocks up beyond their real value.

When some investors started selling their stocks in order to cash in on high profits, others rushed to follow their lead. As a result, stock prices fell. People panicked and began to sell off huge volumes of stocks, making prices drop even further. On **Black Tuesday**, October 29, 1929, the New York Stock Exchange collapsed, followed by the Toronto and Montréal stock exchanges.

Falling Off the Economic Edge

The consequences of the stock market crash were devastating. Investors who had borrowed heavily to buy shares went bankrupt in a single day. While few Canadians actually invested in stocks, the crash affected millions of people. Many companies cut back on production or closed their doors when the prices of their goods dropped. More and more people lost their jobs and could not find work. Without jobs, they could no longer afford to buy such items as cars, radios, or telephones. Without customers, the people who worked in the factories producing these goods also lost their jobs. Within a year, millions of Canadians were out of work.

	1928–1929 Average Income per Person	1933 Average Income per Person	Percentage Decrease
Canada	471	247	48
Saskatchewan	478	135	72
Alberta	548	212	61
Manitoba	466	240	49
British Columbia	594	314	47
Prince Edward Island	278	154	45
Ontario	549	310	44
Québec	391	220	44
New Brunswick	292	180	39
Nova Scotia	322	207	36

FIGURE 4–3 Average per person income, 1928/1929 and 1933. Note that these numbers represent the average Canadian. Many Canadians fell well below this average and many had no income at all.

Interpret and Analyze Which province do you think was hardest hit by the Depression? Explain.

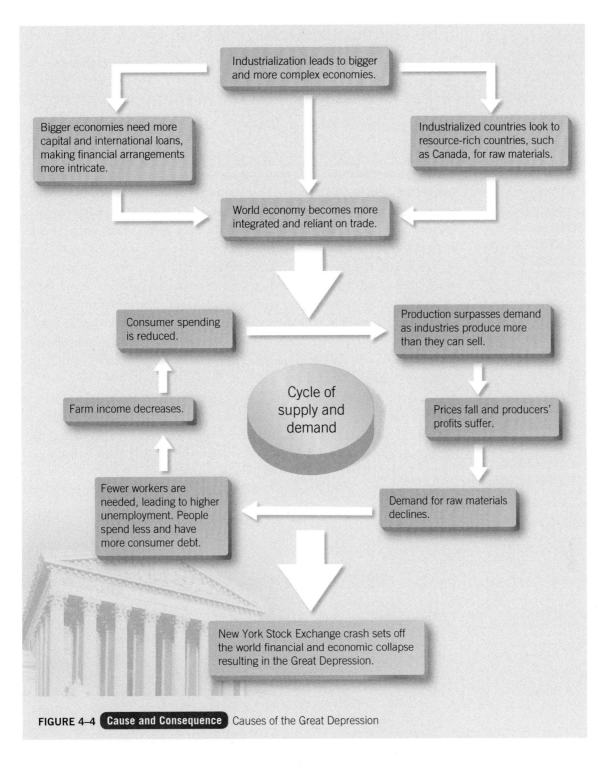

FIGURE 4–4 `Cause and Consequence` Causes of the Great Depression

The diagram shows the following flow:

- Industrialization leads to bigger and more complex economies.
- Bigger economies need more capital and international loans, making financial arrangements more intricate.
- Industrialized countries look to resource-rich countries, such as Canada, for raw materials.
- World economy becomes more integrated and reliant on trade.
- Consumer spending is reduced.
- Production surpasses demand as industries produce more than they can sell.
- Farm income decreases.

Cycle of supply and demand

- Prices fall and producers' profits suffer.
- Fewer workers are needed, leading to higher unemployment. People spend less and have more consumer debt.
- Demand for raw materials declines.
- New York Stock Exchange crash sets off the world financial and economic collapse resulting in the Great Depression.

CHECKPOINT

1. `Cause and Consequence`

   a) What factors contributed to the Depression?

   b) Explain how a reduction in consumer spending can result in a slowdown in the economy.

2. Why was the Depression so severe in Canada?

3. Explain why Canada's close economic ties to the U.S. contributed to the Depression.

4. Why were so many people able to invest in the stock market?

● What were the effects of
the Great Depression on
Canadians?

The Desperate Years: Making Ends Meet

The Depression affected the entire country, but conditions in the Prairie provinces were particularly severe.

Drought on the Prairies

In the boom years of the early 1920s, many farmers planted wheat to take advantage of world demand and rising prices. But one-crop farming takes its toll on the land. Farmers replaced native grasses with wheat crops, which used up nutrients in the soil. Just after the economic crash in 1929, the Prairies were hit by a disastrous drought that lasted almost eight years. Many farmers could not grow crops and families struggled to survive.

As the drought deepened, the winds began. Millions of hectares of fertile topsoil—dried up by the drought and overfarming—blew away. By mid-spring of 1931, there were almost constant dust storms. Dust sifted in everywhere. It piled in little drifts on windowsills, and got into cupboards and closets. In a bad windstorm, people could not see the other side of the street. The semi-arid area in southern Alberta and Saskatchewan, known as Palliser's Triangle, was hit especially hard.

As if this were not enough, a plague of grasshoppers descended on the Prairies. They stalled trains and buses and clogged car radiators. The insects effectively wiped out any crops that farmers on the Prairies managed to grow during the drought. This combination of events devastated many farms and forced thousands of families to abandon their land.

KEY TERM

pogey relief payments by a government, sometimes in the form of vouchers for food and other essentials

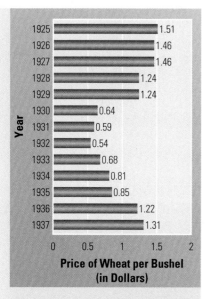

FIGURE 4–5 Wheat prices dropped to the lowest level in more than a century in 1932.

Cause and Consequence Construct a cause-effect-consequence diagram (see Chapter 3, page 78) to explain the impact of wheat prices on Prairie farmers in the 1930s.

FIGURE 4–6 Windstorms such as this one turned the Prairies, already suffering from years of drought, into a dust bowl during the Depression years. Overcultivation of fields and poor land-use practices prior to the 1930s contributed to the erosion of the soil.

Unemployment

As the Depression deepened, more and more factories and businesses closed their doors and people lost their jobs. In a population of more than 11 million, only about 300 000 Canadians earned enough money to pay income tax in 1939. At that time, married people earning more than $2000 and single people earning more than $1000 paid tax. People were evicted from their homes because they could not afford to pay rent. The loss of a job also meant the loss of respect, as this man explained:

> *I never so much as stole a dime, a loaf of bread, a gallon of gas, but in those days I was treated like a criminal. By the twist in some men's minds, men in high places, it became a criminal act just to be poor, and this percolated down through the whole structure until it reached the town cop or railway bull and if you were without a job, on the roads, wandering, you automatically became a criminal.*
>
> *–Quoted in* **Ten Lost Years**, 1997

FIGURE 4–7 Unemployed men of all ages line up at a soup kitchen in Port Arthur, Ontario.

Collecting Pogey

Thousands existed on "**pogey**," government relief payments given to those who did not have an alternative source of income, similar to welfare today. The government did not make getting relief easy. The payments were purposely kept low—$60 per month in Calgary to $19 per month in Halifax for a family of five—to encourage people to look for work rather than depend on the payments. People had to wait in line for hours and then publicly declare their financial failure. They also had to swear that they did not own anything of value and prove that they were being evicted from their home. If the applicants met these requirements, they received vouchers that could be exchanged for food and other essentials. The vouchers were never enough to cover expenses, and getting them was a humiliating experience.

Private charities helped by providing used clothing and meals, while soup kitchens were set up to help the hungry and homeless. For some people, the hardships were too much to bear. One Winnipeg man came home to discover that his wife, who had been living on relief, had drowned their son, strangled their daughter, and poisoned herself. The note she left said, "I owe the drugstore forty-four cents. Farewell."

FASTFORWARD

Permanent Food Banks

In 2014, Food Banks Canada helped more than 800 000 Canadians in an average month. Between 2008 and 2014, there was a 25 percent increase in the number of Canadians using food banks. The two largest groups accessing food banks are those living on social assistance and those with low-paying jobs.

While some food banks are government funded, most rely on the generosity of Canadians. People donate money, food, clothing, and their time. Their contributions are an example of active citizenship and help to support the less fortunate. What do permanent food banks reveal about the Canadian economy and the lives of many Canadians?

Riding the Rails

By the winter of 1933, more than one quarter of Canada's workforce was unemployed. The country was filled with young, jobless, homeless men drifting from one place to another, looking for work. These **transients** travelled across the country by "hopping" freight trains. Some men even rode on the roof or clung to the rods underneath the train.

After "riding the rails," the men would stay a day or two in the many shantytowns that had sprung up in and around cities. These sprawling shantytowns were often referred to as "jungles." Sydney Hutcheson, a young unemployed man in the summer of 1932, recalls what life was like during these years:

FIGURE 4–8 As the Depression grew worse, more and more people found themselves destitute and out of work.

> ...I made Kamloops my headquarters as there were hundreds of men in the jungles on the north side of the Thompson River right across from town.... I made three round trips across Canada that summer by boxcar.... I carried my packsack with a change of clothes, razor, a five pound pail and a collapsible frying pan that a man made for me in the jungles in Kamloops in exchange for a pair of socks. I also had a little food with me at all times such as bacon ends, flour, salt, baking powder and anything else I could get my hands on.
>
> –Sydney Hutcheson, **Depression Stories, 1976**

The Disadvantaged

Canadians who had difficulty earning a decent wage when times were good suffered even more during the Depression. Even with emergency assistance payments, there was discrimination. City families received more than country families because it was assumed that country families had livestock and a big garden. Some groups of people, including immigrants, Aboriginal peoples, and women, were particularly disadvantaged.

New Canadians

The Canadian government had previously supported immigration because it served the economic interests of Canada. During the Depression, however, immigrants were viewed with hostility when they competed for scarce jobs. Many immigrants who were already employed lost their jobs because they had been the last to be hired. By 1935, more than 28 000 immigrants were deported from Canada.

- How did minority groups fare during the Depression?

? HISTORICAL INQUIRY

Evaluate and Draw Conclusions

Examine Figures 4–7 and 4–8, as well as Sydney Hutcheson's story on this page. How do you think men felt when they had been unemployed for years and had to line up at soup kitchens for a meal? Have you ever volunteered at a soup kitchen or an out-of-the-cold program in your community? Could governments in Canada replace food banks and social assistance and provide a minimum income for everyone?

©P

The Chinese population in Vancouver suffered greatly. Already at a disadvantage due to immigration policies and social prejudice, many Chinese people did not qualify for relief payments. By 1932, many were starving.

> By [1932] destitute Chinese men, most of them elderly, were begging in the street.... The first... Chinese deaths from starvation finally forced the provincial government to show some concern. It funded the Anglican Church Mission's soup kitchen..., but it expected a Chinese to be fed at half of what it cost to feed a white man on relief. Some destitute Chinese said they'd rather starve than accept relief.
>
> –*Denise Chong*, **The Concubine's Children, 1994**

● How were A
  treated duri

KEY TERMS

transient an unem
moves from place to place in search
of work

anti-Semitism discrimination or hostility
toward Jewish people

Jewish people in particular were targeted and they faced blatant **anti-Semitism**. Many professions were closed to them; employers often posted signs forbidding them to apply. Across Canada, many clubs, organizations, and resorts barred Jewish people. These barriers made it particularly difficult for Jewish people to make ends meet during the Depression.

FIGURE 4–9 In the 1930s, many establishments barred Jewish people by posting signs such as this.

Interpret and Analyze What message would this sign give to Jewish families in Canada?

Aboriginal Peoples

Aboriginal families on relief were given only $5 a month, compared to the $19–$60 received by non-Aboriginals. They were expected to live off the land, even though conditions on the reserves were so poor that they had been unable to do so for decades. The government continued to take lands from the reserves, further limiting Aboriginal peoples' resources. In one particular case, the government transferred land from the Squamish Capilano Indian Reserve to the company that was building the Lions Gate Bridge without consulting or compensating the First Nation. While visiting Canada in 1939, King George VI and his wife Queen Elizabeth drove over the completed bridge to honour it. A request by the Squamish First Nation that the Royals stop, receive gifts, and meet Mary Agnes Capilano was ignored. Later they were assured that "Their Majesties took particular pains to acknowledge the homage of their Indian subjects, and that in passing them the rate of speed was considerably lowered."

Faces of Despair: Women in the 1930s

In the 1930s, the primary responsibility of women was seen to be the maintenance of the home and family. Most women were expected to get married and leave the labour force as soon as they could. There were a limited number of jobs considered acceptable for middle-class women. Most were clerical, "pink collar" sector jobs for which women earned 60 percent of men's wages. The garment industry, involving long hours of piece work, was one of the few occupations open to minority and working-class white women.

During the Depression, many women who did have jobs were forced into unwanted retirement and married women were fired from their jobs. Most were told that these measures were taken to provide jobs for men supporting families. But Agnes Macphail, the first female Member of Parliament in the House of Commons, claimed that in taking employment, women were doing what they could to ensure the survival of themselves and their families.

Most families suffering economic hardship relied heavily on women's capacity to find ways to cut household costs. They gave up commercially prepared foods and kept bees to cut down on sugar costs, expanded gardens, and picked wild berries. They found ways to reuse everything, such as transforming old coats into quilts. Flour bags were particularly useful, as this mother recalled: "You'd take an empty sack of flour... give it a good wash and bleach out the lettering... cut two holes for the arms and one at the top for the neck.... You had a dress for a nine-year-old girl."

For women on the Prairies, the dust bowl added another problem on washday:

I could never get my laundry white. I'd try and try. The children's things, the curtains and the sheets, why they all looked as grey as that sky out there. I'd work my fingers to the bone scrubbing.... We were lucky to have a deep well and good water but even down that well... the water came up with dirt and dust in it.... The wind blew that dust all the time. It never stopped.

–Ten Lost Years, 1997

FIGURE 4–10 The poster on the left encouraged women to come to Canada in the 1920s. The photograph on the right shows the great deal of physical labour required on washday, particularly the constant hauling of water from a well (most homes did not have running water) and the tiring scrubbing on a washboard.

Interpret and Analyze Compare and contrast the depictions of a farm woman's life in these images. Think of a present-day example where the media's portrayal of a situation differs from reality.

- How did the Great Depres
  affect women?

Suffragist Nellie McClung lamented the effect of constant work on women:

On the farms before electricity and labour saving devices lightened their loads, women's work obsessed them. Their hours were endless.... Many broke under the strain and died, and their places were filled without undue delay. Some man's sister or sister-in-law came from Ontario to take the dead woman's place.

–The Stream Runs Fast, 2007

Pregnancy and the young offspring it brought added to the household's difficulties. Counselling abortion or providing it, and the advertisement and sale of birth control devices, were offences under the Criminal Code, yet couples managed to have fewer children as the Depression deepened. The general fertility rate (the annual number of births per 1000 women) went from 128 in 1921 to 99 in 1931 and to 89 by the end of the decade.

Many single and married women in desperation wrote to Prime Minister Bennett. Barbara Harris, a young woman from Moose Jaw, explained her difficult situation:

Dear Sir-
I am 19 yrs. of age Mr. Bennett, but it really is impossible for me to get work. I haven't got any shoes to wear & no coat & so I haven't any home or any relatives here, Im all alone as it were. Now I tho't perhaps you could help me a little.... Here... it just seems impossible to get relief unless you go & work for your board & room & I can't work like that as I need clothes so badly. It's even a fact that not only haven't a coat to wear but I haven't any stockings either. Mr. Bennett if you could just help me out a little bit I would be very pleased & would appreciate it very much & would you kindly give me an answer.

–The Wretched of Canada, 1971

Note: The last two quotations on this page contain spelling and punctuation errors. They have been reproduced as they were originally written.

A young mother from Manitoba described her dilemma:

Dear Sir-
I am a young mother of two small children a girl (6) and a boy (4) now in worst of hard times an accident happend, my girl was playing & fell and cut her face very badley, so out off this got a blood poison in her face, she's in hospital now. Just at present I have no money to pay the doctor or fare for the train to go and see her.... Now Mr. Bennett what I want to say is if you can lend me some money for a period of 3 or 4 months when my cows will come fresh I'll turn you the money, everybody here is broke and no where to get.... So please lend me some money... and a couple of dollars wouldn't mean as much as one cent means to me. I'd make you a mortgage for horses and cattle.

–The Wretched of Canada, 1971

Bennett responded to many of these women by sending them $2–$4 of his own money. This was a lot of money at the time, considering that government relief was $10–$15 a month. Despite this aid, women and their families suffered greatly during the Depression.

Thinking It Through

1. What were the social attitudes toward women during the 1930s? What were the objections to women working during the Depression?

2. Evaluate the impact of the Depression on married women compared to married men, and on single women compared to single men.

3. Make a list of three to five lessons that we should learn from the difficulties faced by women and families during the Depression. Share your list.

4. How might many women have felt about their life in the 1930s when they reflected on the high expectations promised by the media in the 1920s? Review the images on pages 52, 62, 65, 66, 68, and 69.

The Plight of Women

For women, there were few jobs other than domestic work, which paid just a few dollars a week. Some critics believed working women actually contributed to the Depression. Médéric Martin, a former mayor of Montréal, summed up the attitude of many toward working women:

> *Wouldn't national life be happier, saner, safer if a great many of these men [the unemployed] could be given work now being done by women, even if it meant that these women would have to sacrifice their financial independence? Go home to be supported by father, husband, or brother as they were in the old pre-feministic days?*
>
> –Chatelaine, *September 1933*

Most unemployed single women did not qualify for government relief and had to rely on charities to get by. In Vancouver, women's groups such as the Women's Labour League campaigned for more support. As a result, the city provided milk for babies, clothing allowances for women and children, and medical care for pregnant women during the Depression.

The Fortunate Minority

While the majority of people suffered during the Depression, wealthy Canadians with secure jobs noticed little change in their lifestyle. Gray Miller, for example, earned $25 000 a year as chief executive officer of Imperial Tobacco. In contrast, clerks in the company's United Cigar Store earned only $1300 a year working 54 hours a week. As **deflation** led to falling prices, money was worth more and the living conditions for those with secure jobs improved. A young reporter who was paid only $15 a week found that he could live well. Saturday night dances at a local hotel were easily affordable. "For two dollars a couple, a three-course dinner was served with full valet service at tables arranged in cabaret style around a magnificent ballroom." For the majority of Canadians, however, this lifestyle was an impossible dream.

[Margin glossary]

...site of inflation, defla-... ...curs when the price of goods and services falls

majority government a government in which the ruling party has more seats in the House of Commons than all other parties combined

---

? HISTORICAL INQUIRY

Gather and Organize

What would be some key sources on the lives of children, teens, women, and men in the Great Depression? Where would you find them? What questions could you ask about these sources? How would you record your research and compare your information from different sources and on different parts of the country?

CHECKPOINT

1. What part of Canada was hardest hit by the Depression? Explain.

2. **a)** What seemed to be the government's attitude toward people who had lost their jobs? Why do you think this was the case? Do you think this attitude exists today toward the unemployed?

   b) Compare the possible attitudes of people who received social assistance in the 1930s and those who receive assistance today.

3. What did people have to do to qualify for "pogey"? Why do you think people were given vouchers instead of cash?

4. Reread James Gray's description of the 1930s on page 91. Write a first-person account of the summer of 1936 on the Prairies.

5. Choose a particular group such as Chinese-Canadians and write a paragraph describing conditions in that community during the Depression. Explain why conditions were so harsh. Include information you have learned from previous chapters.

6. What does the reaction of King George VI and Queen Elizabeth to the Squamish First Nation reveal about the social values of the era?

Responding to the Depression

Prime Minister Mackenzie King was unprepared to deal with a crisis on the scale of the Depression. He believed the situation was temporary and that, in time, the economy would recover. When desperate Canadians turned to the federal government for financial help, King told them this was the responsibility of municipal and provincial governments. The financial strain of the Depression, however, had bankrupted many municipalities. When the Conservative Opposition asked why some provincial governments were not being helped by the federal government, King said he would not give "a five-cent piece" to a Conservative provincial government.

King never lived down this impulsive remark. The Conservatives used his statement to build support during their 1930 election campaign. King lost to Richard Bedford Bennett and his Conservative **majority government**.

The Government's Response

Prime Minister Bennett was no more in favour of government relief than Mackenzie King had been. He once told a group of students that "one of the greatest assets a man can have on entering life's struggle is poverty." Nevertheless, Bennett's Conservative government introduced several measures to help Canadians through the Depression.

- Bennett's government introduced the Unemployment Relief Act, which gave the provinces $20 million for work-creation programs. In spite of this spending, the economy did not improve.

- Bennett tried to "use tariffs to blast a way" into world markets and out of the Depression. He raised tariffs by an average of more than 50 percent to protect Canadian industries, which provided protection for some businesses. In the long run, it did more harm than good, as other nations, in turn, set up trade barriers against Canada.

- The Prairie Farm Rehabilitation Act was introduced in 1935 to help farmers build irrigation systems and reservoirs. But by this time, drought and poverty had forced many families to leave their farms and move elsewhere.

- How did governments in Canada respond to the Great Depression?

- Why did the Great Depression cause conflict within Canadian society and elsewhere?

GO ONLINE • • • • • • • • • • • • • •
Find out more about Prime Minister Mackenzie King and the Depression.

? HISTORICAL INQUIRY

Interpret and Analyze

What did an economist like Mackenzie King and a wealthy lawyer and businessman like Richard Bennett think was the main cause and the best solution to the Depression in 1930?

FIGURE 4–11 As the situation in Canada grew worse, Prime Minister Bennett became a target for people's anger and frustration. A deserted farm was called a "Bennett barnyard"; a newspaper was a "Bennett blanket." Roasted wheat was "Bennett coffee." A "Bennett buggy" was an automobile pulled by horses when the owner could no longer afford the gas to run it.

KEY TERMS

On-to-Ottawa Trek a 1935 rail trip from Vancouver to Ottawa (stopped at Regina) by unemployed men to protest conditions at employment relief camps

Regina Riot a riot that occurred when police attempted to clear On-to-Ottawa trekkers from a stadium in Regina

New Deal a series of programs, such as social assistance for the aged and unemployed, introduced by U.S. president Roosevelt in the 1930s to deal with the Depression

? HISTORICAL INQUIRY

Communicate

Pretend you lived in a work camp in the 1930s. Write a short story about a typical day you had to endure. How would you feel?

FIGURE 4–12 Relief Camp Workers' Union newsletter

Historical Perspectives As the Depression continued, how was the worldview of the workers changing in the face of Canada's failure to deliver jobs and incomes for many families?

The growing number of jobless, homeless men drifting across the country frightened many middle-class Canadians. The "Red Scare" was still dominant in Canada, and Prime Minister Bennett feared these men would come under the influence of the Communist Party. In 1931, Bennett introduced a law outlawing communist agitation. Communist Party leader Tim Buck was convicted in defiance of this law, and spent two years in prison.

Work Camps Pay Twenty Cents a Day

In addition to relief payments and soup kitchens, Bennett created a national network of work camps for single men in an attempt to provide relief from the Depression. Work camps were usually located deep in the woods, so the men were completely isolated. Men worked on projects such as building roads, clearing land, and digging drainage ditches. They were paid $0.20 a day and given room and board. The food was terrible, and the bunks were often bug-infested. More than 170 000 men spent time in these camps.

The On-to-Ottawa Trek

In 1935, more than a thousand men left the relief camps in the interior of British Columbia in protest against camp conditions and to demand higher pay. They gathered in Vancouver, holding rallies and collecting money for food. Under the leadership of the Relief Camp Workers' Union, the men decided to take their complaints directly to the prime minister in a protest that became known as the **On-to-Ottawa Trek**. Crowding into and on top of freight cars, the trekkers rode through the Prairies. Many people supported them by donating food and supplies, while others joined the trek. By the time they reached Regina, Saskatchewan, there were more than 2000 trekkers and their protest had gained national attention.

Regina Riot

Bennett responded to the trekkers by calling in the RCMP to stop them in Regina. The protesters were confined in a local stadium, and only the leaders were allowed to continue on to Ottawa. The union leaders who met with Prime Minister Bennett had great hopes of being heard, but Bennett attacked the leaders as communist radicals and troublemakers.

Back in Regina, the RCMP were ordered to clear the trekkers from the stadium. The trekkers resisted, battling the RCMP and the local police for hours. The incident became known as the **Regina Riot**. One officer was killed, many were injured, and 130 men were arrested.

FIGURE 4–13 The On-to-Ottawa Trekkers
Gather Evidence How would protests of today differ from the On-to-Ottawa Trek? How might the government response be similar or different today? Explain.

When the federal government closed relief camps in 1936 and the provincial government reduced relief payments, many men were left destitute. In protest against the lack of government support, these men would conduct "sit-ins" at various buildings until the government responded to their complaints. In April, 1600 protesters occupied the Vancouver Art Gallery, the main post office, and the Georgia Hotel. Most of the protesters were convinced to end their sit-in without incident. At the post office, however, the men refused to leave; they were eventually evicted with tear gas.

Roosevelt's New Deal

When Franklin Roosevelt became the U.S. president in 1933, he introduced a "**New Deal**" that created public work programs for the unemployed and for farmers. His most drastic action was the introduction of the Social Security Act. This Act provided several social assistance programs, such as old age pension, unemployment insurance, and financial assistance for dependent mothers and children. Under the New Deal, the U.S. federal government spent billions of dollars to get the economy working again. The New Deal did not pull the United States out of the Depression. It did, however, help millions to survive, and it gave hope for the future in a time of national despair.

FIGURE 4–14 U.S. President Franklin Roosevelt priming the New Deal pump

Interpret and Analyze What is the message of this cartoon? Why has the cartoonist chosen the image of priming a pump to describe Roosevelt's New Deal?

KEY TERMS

laissez-faire an economic condition in which industry is free of government intervention

welfare state a state in which the government actively looks after the well-being of its citizens

Bennett's New Deal `Cause and Consequence`

Bennett was initially reluctant to spend government money on relief. But in his radio addresses prior to the 1935 election campaign, Bennett surprised listeners and his Cabinet colleagues by introducing his own version of Roosevelt's New Deal which included

- fairer, progressive taxation so that people who earned more money paid more tax
- insurance to protect workers against illness, injury, and unemployment
- legislation for workplace reforms that regulated work hours, minimum wages, and working conditions
- revised old-age pensions to help support workers over 65 years of age
- agricultural support programs to help farmers and the creation of the Canadian Wheat Board to regulate wheat prices

Many voters saw Bennett's change in policy as a desperate attempt to win votes and not as a true shift in his views. They questioned the value of social insurance programs for people who did not have a job and so could not make a claim. For most people it was too little and far too late.

FIGURE 4–15 To combat U.S. influence on Canadians, a public radio service was created, which became the Canadian Broadcasting Corporation (CBC) in 1936. The CBC ran Canadian-produced music and entertainment programs in French and English. French programming in Québec was very popular, but many English-speaking listeners still tuned in to popular U.S. shows.

CHECKPOINT

1. What actions did governments take to deal with the Depression? Explain.

2. What were the main complaints of relief camp workers?

3. Do you think the On-to-Ottawa Trek was a success or failure? Provide evidence to support your opinion.

4. Which three of Bennett's New Deal proposals do you think had the greatest impact on Canadians? Support your choices.

©P

counter points

How involved should the government be in the economy?

Before the Great Depression, governments generally did not interfere in the economy. Instead, they relied on a **laissez-faire** approach, letting the free enterprise system regulate itself. During the 1930s, the public pressured governments to create work programs and to provide money for those who could not help themselves. Some governments, most notably the U.S., followed the advice of British economist John Maynard Keynes who believed that governments needed to jump-start the economy. He supported spending money on programs that would put people back to work. Once they were working, people would spend money. The increased demand for goods would mean more jobs and more spending.

Opposition in the U.S. criticized Roosevelt's New Deal as a "...frightful waste and extravagance.... It has bred fear and hesitation in commerce and industry, thus discouraging new enterprises, preventing employment and prolonging the depression." In Canada, Prime Minister Bennett's campaign during the 1935 election promised his version of the New Deal. He said, "In my mind, reform means Government intervention. It means Government control and regulation. It means the end of laissez-faire." Mackenzie King, who won the election, believed that the economy would improve on its own in time. He warned that

> A house is not built from the top down. It is constructed from the ground up. The foundation must be well and truly laid, or the whole edifice will crumble. To seek to erect an ambitious program of social services upon a stationary or diminishing national income is like building a house upon the sands.
>
> –W. L. Mackenzie King, 1935

Many of the social programs created by the New Deal are part of today's "social safety net" in Canada and the U.S. These programs help to protect people and businesses during an economic crisis. Since the Depression, people have debated the role of the government in Canada's economy. Most Canadians believe that even if the country is not experiencing a depression, it

is the government's duty to provide basic services, such as education, health care, unemployment benefits, and other kinds of social assistance. This is referred to as a **welfare state**. Other people support a competitive state in which the government creates an atmosphere of competition for businesses by cutting spending on social programs and reducing taxes. Most Canadians believe in a mixed economy, where the government provides a certain level of social services, but is not overly intrusive in planning and running the economy (see Figure 4–16).

During the 2008 economic crisis, many governments referred to the lessons learned during the Depression to support intervention in the economy. With little opposition, the Canadian government provided $12 billion of economic stimulus. In the U.S., which was harder hit by this recession, the government supplied $787 billion to bail out failing industries and curb rising unemployment.

FIGURE 4–16 Levels of government involvement in the economy

Thinking It Through

1. Draw a flow chart to illustrate Keynes' theory of how government spending could lift a country out of a depression.

2. In a two-column organizer, summarize the arguments for and against government intervention in the economy during an economic slowdown and during a period of economic growth.

3. Why do you think there was little opposition to government intervention in the economy during the 2008 recession?

Politics of Protest

As Ottawa struggled to find ways to cope with the Depression, some Canadians looked to new political parties for solutions.

The Co-operative Commonwealth Federation (CCF)

The **Co-operative Commonwealth Federation** (**CCF**), founded in the Prairie provinces in 1932, was Canada's first socialist party and a forerunner of the New Democratic Party (NDP). The CCF believed that **capitalism** breeds inequality and greed and had caused the Depression. The CCF supported a socialist system in which the government controlled the economy so that all Canadians would benefit equally. Their ideas appealed to a wide variety of people who were dissatisfied with the government's response to the Depression. At the CCF's convention in Regina in 1933, J.S. Woodsworth was chosen as party leader. The party platform, known as the **Regina Manifesto**, opposed free-market economics and supported public ownership of key industries. It advocated social programs to help the elderly, the unemployed, the homeless, and the sick. Woodsworth also urged the government to spend money on public works to create employment. By 1939, the CCF formed the Opposition in British Columbia and Saskatchewan.

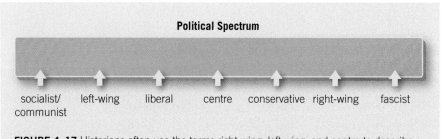

Political Spectrum

socialist/communist — left-wing — liberal — centre — conservative — right-wing — fascist

FIGURE 4–17 Historians often use the terms right-wing, left-wing, and centre to describe the position of a political party on the political spectrum. Right-wing parties value social tradition, economic freedom, and a strong military. Left-wing governments believe in social equality, the regulation of business, and a reduced military.

The Social Credit Party

The **Social Credit Party** was another political party from Western Canada that offered an alternative to Canadian voters. The party's leader, William "Bible Bill" Aberhart, was a charismatic preacher. Social credit was based on the belief that capitalism was a wasteful economic system. Under capitalism, banks hoarded money, preventing customers from buying goods that capitalism produced. Aberhart felt that the government should release money into the economy so that people could spend it. The theory of social credit appealed to many people from Alberta because the Depression had devastated their economy and they resented the power and control of the banks in Central Canada. Under Bible Bill's leadership, the Social Credit Party won 17 seats in the federal election of 1935 with nearly 50 percent of the popular vote in Alberta.

Aberhart promised each citizen a "basic dividend" of $25 a month to buy necessities. The federal government challenged the right of a province to issue its own currency, and social credit was disallowed by the Supreme Court. Despite this setback, the Social Credit Party remained in power in Alberta until 1971 under Aberhart's successors, Ernest Manning and Harry Strom.

WE PROPOSE TO TAKE OUR FIRST, DEFINITE STEP TOWARD THE ESTABLISHMENT OF SOCIAL CREDIT

FIGURE 4–18 William Aberhart came to power based on the popularity of his theory of social credit.

Evaluate and Draw Conclusions What is this cartoonist's opinion of the soundness of social credit?

©P

Union nationale

In Québec, Maurice Duplessis, a former Conservative, joined forces with some disillusioned Liberals to form the **Union nationale**, a party that supported **Québec nationalism**. The Union nationale relied heavily on the support of the Roman Catholic Church and rural voters. Duplessis blamed many of Québec's social and economic problems on the English minority in Québec, which controlled the province's economy. The Union nationale's political platform was based on improved working conditions, social insurance programs, publicly owned power companies, and a system of farm credits. During his first term, however, Duplessis' promises of reform evaporated, and he did little to improve economic and social conditions in Québec. Despite this, he remained premier until 1959 with the exception of one term from 1939 to 1944 (see Chapter 6).

FIGURE 4–19 Hon. Maurice Duplessis (third from the left) pictured here in August 1946

Provincial Responses

During the Depression, voters expressed their dissatisfaction with government inaction by voting out ruling provincial parties. As the CCF and Social Credit parties gained momentum in Western Canada, and the Union nationale gained power in Québec, voters in other provinces also made their voices heard by electing new governments.

In Ontario, the provincial Liberals came to power in 1934 for the first time in 29 years. The Liberal leader was a populist farmer, Mitchell Hepburn, who won wide support by championing the causes of "the little man." He railed against big business and was fond of flamboyant gestures, such as auctioning off the provincial government's fleet of limousines. Although Hepburn tried to improve Ontario's economy, he did little to help the unemployed and was against **unionization**.

Photographs convey information and provide insights into many areas of study in this textbook. Historical photographs are a useful primary source of information about past events. To make use of a photograph as a historical source, you must do more than look at the photograph; you need to interpret the information it provides. This is called decoding.

A photograph is an image created by a photographer. As such, it reflects that person's perspective. In the same way, any meaning you take from it will be influenced by your perspective (see Chapter 1, Building Your Inquiry Skills). It is important that you try to be open-minded when looking at photographs.

Paintings do not claim to represent reality. Photographs do, but they can be manipulated. Images can easily be altered with today's digital technology, so you must be aware of the intention of the photographer and how the photograph is being used when you try to decode its meaning.

Steps to Decoding Photographs

1. Examine the photograph carefully and describe what you see. Does the image have clues as to when it was taken and where? Who is in it? What is happening? Why was the image taken? Does the caption help to answer these questions?

Examine Figure 4–20. How many of the previous questions can you answer?

2. Analyze the image and ask questions. It may help to divide the image into sections to examine details. What are people in the image doing? Do their facial expressions and body language suggest anything? Are there signs, buildings, landmarks, or other clues visible? Analyze Figure 4–20 using these questions and any others you think are relevant.

3. Evaluate the photograph as a source of information. Do not simply accept the image as showing what happened. Is it reliable and credible? Is there bias in the presentation? (Review Building Your Inquiry Skills, Chapter 1.) What is your evaluation of Figure 4–20?

4. Draw conclusions based on the information you have collected and consider what information is missing. The photographer frames the image and the story by focusing only on a part of what he or she can see. Does outside information help you to better understand the contents of the picture? Read about the circumstances of the On-to-Ottawa Trek on page 104. Does this change your interpretation of the picture? Why or why not?

FIGURE 4–20 Police and On-to-Ottawa trekkers during the Regina Riot of July 1, 1935

©P

Interpret and Analyze

1. Apply the four-step decoding process to the images below and then answer the questions accompanying each image.

FIGURE 4–21 Relief camp in the 1930s. Compare and contrast the description of relief camps on page 104 with this photograph. Do you think the picture was staged? Which details do you consider most significant and why? Is it a fair representation of a bunkhouse in a 1930s relief camp? Why or why not?

FIGURE 4–22 Protesters at the G20 Summit held in Toronto in 2010. What point of view does this photograph represent? Why do you think so? What evidence is there in the image that the protesters were aware that the media were covering the event? Compare and contrast this image with Figure 4–20. Which image is a better source of information? Why?

- How did governments in Canada respond to the Great Depression?

KEY TERMS

Rowell-Sirois Report report of the Royal Commission on Dominion-Provincial Relations, a commission set up in 1937 to examine the Canadian economy and federal-provincial relations

equalization payments a federal transfer of funds from richer to poorer provinces

HISTORICAL INQUIRY

Formulate Questions

Suppose you were a voter in the 1935 election. What questions would you like to have asked the leaders of the five political parties who are running to win the most seats in the House of Commons and perhaps become prime minister?

A Change in Federal Government

By 1935, five years after Bennett was elected prime minister, voters were frustrated by his inability to deal with the crisis of the Depression. In the federal election, they returned Mackenzie King to power.

King did not support government intervention in the economy. He believed that in time, the economy would improve on its own. King also felt that spending money on social programs during a depression did not make economic sense, and that it was better to wait until the economy was strong before introducing these expensive programs.

King's views clashed with the findings of the National Employment Commission, which he had set up in 1936 to examine the state of unemployment in Canada. The commission recommended the federal government spend millions of dollars on job creation and training programs. King ended up spending only a fraction of what was recommended.

Federal-Provincial Tensions

In 1937, King created the Royal Commission on Dominion-Provincial Relations to examine the thorny issue of federal-provincial relations and to look into the responsibilities of the different levels of government. The unemployment crisis of the Depression had caused a great deal of tension between the federal and provincial governments. There was disagreement over which government had the right to collect tax money and which government should pay for social and unemployment assistance.

The Commission's findings, referred to as the **Rowell-Sirois Report,** recommended that the federal government give the poorer provinces grants, or **equalization payments**, to ensure that every province was able to offer its citizens the same level of services. The Commission also recommended that the federal government bear the responsibility for unemployment insurance and other social benefits such as pensions.

The wealthier provinces did not like the idea of equalization payments because they did not want their tax dollars going to other provinces. The provinces also felt that many of the Commission's recommendations would mean a loss of provincial power. By the time the Commission made its report, the economy had started to turn around. More people were finding jobs, and there was a mood of cautious optimism. Canada's involvement in the Second World War meant most of the Commission's recommendations were either pushed aside indefinitely or adopted later.

CHECKPOINT

1. **Historical Perspectives** List the political parties that were started during the Depression. Identify the supporters, leader, and policies of each party. Where on the political spectrum would each party sit?

2. What difficulties did provincial governments encounter in dealing with the problems of the Depression? Give examples from the province of Ontario.

3. What were Mackenzie King's views on government involvement in the economy?

4. What were the main recommendations of the Rowell-Sirois Report? Why did the wealthier provinces dislike these recommendations?

5. If you were a voter in the 1935 election, what questions would you like to have asked the leaders of the five political parties with candidates in the election?

Innovations
Medical Advances

During the 1930s, a number of Canadians pushed the boundaries of science and technology. As the government looked for ways to ease the economic suffering, Canadians tried to find ways to improve the lives of others, especially in the areas of health and medicine.

Pablum stands the test of time In 1930, doctors at Toronto's Hospital for Sick Children created Pablum, the first pre-cooked, vitamin-enriched cereal for infants. For 25 years, the hospital received a royalty for every package sold. In 2005, H.J. Heinz Company acquired the Pablum brand. How does the development of Pablum reflect the social conditions of the Depression?

A revolutionary brainwave Canadian doctor Wilder Penfield founded McGill University's Montréal Neurological Institute in 1934, which became an international centre for education and research on the brain. Penfield is most known for developing a surgical treatment for epilepsy known as the "Montréal Procedure." He used a local anesthetic so patients remained conscious during the operation, and then probed their brains to locate the site of the seizures. Doctors today still use maps of the sensory and motor sections of the brain that were drawn from these operations.

Saving lives on the front lines Norman Bethune was a Canadian doctor, inventor, and political activist. As a dedicated physician in Montréal during the Depression, Bethune provided free medical care to the poor and advocated for a social system of health care. He also volunteered for the Spanish Civil War (see Chapter 5). He was the first to set up a blood bank close to the front lines and organize a mobile blood-transfusion team.

During the turbulent years of the 1930s, Canada was led by two men who were studies in contrast. William Lyon Mackenzie King and Richard Bedford Bennett both had a profound effect on Canada. Yet history's judgement of each man has been vastly different.

King, one of the most dominant political leaders in Canadian history, was prime minister of Canada for almost 22 years, from 1921 to 1930, save for a few months in 1926, and from 1935 to 1948. One historian has called him the "...greatest and most interesting of prime ministers." Bennett led Canada for five years going from landslide victory in 1930 to disastrous defeat in 1935 after one term in office. Bennett's negative historical reputation comes from what was seen as his failure to find a solution to the Depression. He eventually left Canada and died in England as a member of the House of Lords, forgotten by Canadians and generally ignored by historians.

Bennett's One-man Show

In 1930, there were high hopes that the energy and competence Bennett displayed as leader of the Opposition would help the new prime minister find solutions to the economic crisis. However as the Depression worsened, so did his reputation. Bennett lacked the common touch and never wavered in his conviction that he was right. Even his supporters agreed that he liked to hear himself speak, paying little attention to the opinions of others. Members of his Cabinet accused him of running a one-man show, seldom informing them of important decisions. It was joked that when Bennett was mumbling to himself, he was holding a Cabinet meeting. This insensitivity toward the opinions of others and his unwillingness to compromise hindered Bennett's efforts to deal with the worsening Depression.

FIGURE 4–23 Bennett as a one-man government

Interpret and Analyze What is the cartoonist trying to say about Bennett? What techniques does the cartoonist use to convey his message?

Bennett was a millionaire bachelor who made his home in Ottawa in a suite occupying a whole floor of the luxurious Château Laurier Hotel. It was small wonder that poverty-stricken Canadians felt little affection for him. However, they did not see the private man who, according to Bennett, between 1927 and 1937 gave nearly $2.5 million to charities from his own income. Sometimes this was in response to the many letters he received from Canadians asking for his help (see the letters on page 101). Bennett secretly sent many of these people money. His generosity was uncovered in his private papers after his death.

King: The People Pleaser

King was a pragmatic and cautious politician who avoided making decisions if he could. He had a feel for the mood of the country and unlike Bennett, he was patient, willing to wait for events to unfold. He claimed that "it is what we prevent, rather than what we do that counts most in Government."

"My Government"

King was notorious for dull and ambiguous speeches that blurred the issues and seemed to promise everything to everyone. These speeches infuriated many listeners. In fact, King was a skilled negotiator who wanted desperately to keep Canada united—French and English, the different regions and social classes—and his vague manner was a deliberate technique to try to please everyone. His successes seemed to result from being the leader who divided Canadians the least.

After King's death, it was discovered that this apparently colourless man had, as he wrote in his diary, "a very double life." He had kept a detailed personal diary from his student days in the 1890s to his death in 1950. The nearly 30 000 pages in the diaries revealed that King was a believer in spiritualism, obsessed with clocks and mystical numbers. He held seances in which he communicated with the dead, especially with his mother, Wilfrid Laurier, and others.

1. Why was King a more successful politician than Bennett? Do you think his reputation as an effective leader is justified? Explain.

2. What were the strengths and weaknesses of each leader?

3. How was Bennett perceived by Canadians during the Depression? Do you think this image of him was justified? Explain your answer.

4. Is it necessary to know private details of the lives of our politicians to evaluate their role in Canadian history?

5. Should we judge politicians based on their accomplishments or personalities?

GO ONLINE

Read digitized copies of all of King's diary entries on the Library and Archives Canada website.

FIGURE 4–24 King as Wobbly Willy

Interpret and Analyze Mackenzie King was known for his reluctance to make decisions. Is the cartoonist effective in conveying this idea? Why or why not? Do you think a person from this era would have an easier or harder time interpreting the message? Explain your response.

HISTORICAL INQUIRY

Interpret and Analyze

Why did the protest parties with all their new ideas elect so few MPs in the 1935 federal election? Did King and the Liberals win the election, or did Bennett and the Conservatives lose the election? Whom would you have voted for in the 1935 election?

- What were the effects of the Great Depression on the global community?

The Depression and Global Politics

During the 1930s, many countries around the world were suffering from an economic slowdown. As in Canada, many people lost their jobs and were destitute, and governments looked for solutions to the economic crisis.

Germany After the War

Germany, in particular, suffered the consequences of the Depression. Since the end of the First World War, Germany had grown increasingly unhappy with the terms of the Treaty of Versailles. It bitterly resented the "war guilt" clause that required it to pay $32 billion in reparations to other countries. These payments put a great strain on the German economy, which had been ruined by war. To meet the payments, the government printed large amounts of money in the 1920s, which in turn lowered the value of the German currency. As German money became worth less and less, the price of basic goods continued to rise.

To control this inflation, Britain, France, and the United States agreed to give better terms for Germany's reparation payments. Germany made a modest recovery. However, when world stock markets collapsed in 1929, the weakened German economy was affected more than most countries. As you read at the beginning of this chapter, Germany's inability to make its reparation payments affected the economies of other countries and contributed to the causes of the global Depression.

GO ONLINE

Read more about the economic inflation in Germany following the First World War.

FIGURE 4–25 This photograph, taken in 1923, shows a German woman using several million marks to fuel her stove.

Evaluate and Draw Conclusions What can you conclude about the value of German currency from this photograph?

The Depression in Asia

The Empire of Japan, the only independent Asian nation with a colonial empire, developed a strong manufacturing industry after the First World War. Tariff barriers and the decline of international trade during the Depression greatly affected Japan's economy, which relied on raw materials from the United States and other countries. To deal with the slowdown, Japan adopted **Keynesian economics** and increased government spending to stimulate the economy. It also put into action an aggressive plan to expand its territory to gain resource-rich lands by invading China's northern province of Manchuria in 1931 (see Chapter 5).

KEY TERM

Keynesian economics an economic theory named for John Maynard Keynes (1883–1946) who advocated government intervention in the economy, especially during economic downturns

Russians Under Communism

After the Bolshevik Revolution in 1917, Russia experienced a series of political upheavals that led to a civil war. In 1922, Russia joined with several other communist countries to form the Union of Soviet Socialist Republics (U.S.S.R.) or Soviet Union. During the Depression, the Soviet Union's communist economic system insulated it from the economic slowdown experienced by other countries. It appeared to many as though the communist system worked, while the capitalist system had failed. This in turn increased people's interest in communism. But the people of the Soviet Union paid a price for their economic progress. Joseph Stalin's ruthless dictatorship robbed the Soviet people of their political and social freedom, and his economic and agricultural policies led to the deaths of millions of people (see Chapter 5).

Prelude to War

The economic crisis of the 1930s resulted in social and political instability around the world. As you will learn in Chapter 5, this instability was the perfect breeding ground for dictators who gained power by offering solutions and hope to desperate people. Ambitious plans to expand territories and resources led to a global military conflict, which had a profound impact on Canada's development and its reputation on the world stage.

CHECKPOINT

1. Explain why Germany was affected so deeply by the Depression.

2. How did other countries try to help Germany during the Depression?

3. What effect did the Depression have on Japan? How did Japan respond?

4. Why did communism gain attention during the Depression?

CHAPTER FOCUS QUESTION What were the causes and consequences of, and responses to, the Great Depression?

For most people, the Great Depression of the 1930s was a decade of hardship and despair. Formative historic events such as the Great Depression often lead to conflict. As you have seen in this chapter, the Depression highlighted weaknesses in the Canadian economy and its close ties to the United States. As the government struggled to provide relief to many suffering Canadians, regional political parties were created that offered new ideas and hope to Canadians. The Great Depression was a national crisis that, in many ways, divided the country: the rich and poor, the immigrants and non-immigrants, men and women, and Central and Western Canada.

1. Create an organizer such as the one below. Provide as many examples as possible for each category.

Causes	Consequences	Responses
Economic Cycle	New Political Parties	New Social Programs

Knowledge and Understanding

2. Continue the ongoing timeline assignment. Write the name and date of each event that occurred in this chapter on the timeline, and explain how the event contributed to Canadian independence.

3. What were the major weaknesses in the Canadian economy from 1919 to 1939? How did these weaknesses make the Depression in Canada particularly severe? How did Canada's economic problems compare to those of other countries? Why was there a reluctance on the part of many governments to take aggressive action to correct these problems?

4. a) In what ways did the federal and provincial governments respond to the needs of Canadians during the 1930s?

   b) What does this response say about the values that were held by society at the time? Use the personal memories in this chapter to support your answer.

   c) How successful were the government responses?

5. Suggest three actions that could have been taken to prevent the Depression. Why do you think these were not done?

6. Why were Aboriginal peoples, Asian men, single, unemployed, young men, and women in a particularly desperate situation in the 1930s?

Apply Your Thinking

7. Construct a cause-effect-consequence diagram for the Great Depression. Refer to Building Your Inquiry Skills on page 78. Use your diagram to list and explain three key lessons that today's governments should learn from the Great Depression.

Evidence

8. Why were the Prairie provinces the hardest-hit region of Canada during the Depression? Look for sources from within the chapter to support your answer. Be sure to consider the price of wheat during this time.

Evidence

9. Choose three images from the chapter that you think best illustrate the impact of the Great Depression on Canadians. Explain your reasons for choosing each of the photographs.

Communicate

10. With a partner or in a small group, imagine you are the founding members of a new political party in the 1930s. Your party is dedicated to solving the economic and social problems of the Depression. On a single page, write your party's name, a summary of the country's major problems, and a five- to ten-point declaration of your party's program. Include a catchy slogan or statement that sums up what your party stands for.

11. In a small group, discuss which political party each of the following would have supported during the Depression. Explain your choices.

a) owner of a small business

b) single unemployed person

c) farm wife

d) hourly paid worker

HISTORICAL INQUIRY

Evaluate and Draw Conclusions

12. The date is October 4, 1935. You are an adult living in Canada with a family to support. Choose a province in which to live. Then, write a letter using proper style and format to Prime Minister Bennett with a paragraph on each of the following topics:

- your ideas on the cause of the Great Depression
- the consequences of the Depression for you and your family
- how you plan to vote on election day, October 14, 1935, and why

End your letter with a concluding paragraph. Remember to sign it!

5

World on Fire: Canada and World War Two

? INVESTIGATE

Social, Economic, and Political Context

- What effect did the Second World War have on the role of women?

- What was the war's impact on the home front?

- What impact did conscription have on Canadian unity?

- What effect did the War Measures Act have on the legal rights of Canadians?

Communities, Conflict, and Cooperation

- Why were totalitarian leaders able to gain power in Europe and Asia?

- How did Canada get involved in the Second World War?

- What was Canada's military role in the Second World War?

Identity, Citizenship, and Heritage

- How did the war raise awareness of human rights issues?

- What factors contributed to Canada's emerging autonomy?

- How was Canadian identity strengthened by the war?

Five-year-old Warren Bernard reaches for his father's hand as he departs for war in 1940. Douglas Bernard was part of the Duke of Connaught's Own Rifles, British Columbia Regiment.

Historical Significance More people were killed during the Second World War than in any other war. Why would a five-year-old boy be so eager to run after his father? Why do many of the men and women in this picture appear to be smiling? Why would the Canadian government be eager to use this picture during World War II to sell war bonds?

TIMELINE

1939

Germany invades Poland

Britain and France declare war on Germany

Canada declares war on Germany

1940

Germany invades Denmark and Norway

Germany invades the Netherlands, Belgium, Luxembourg, and France

Evacuation of Dunkirk

National Resources Mobilization Act

France surrenders to Germany

The Battle of Britain

1940–1943

North African Campaign

1940–1944

Battle of the Atlantic

1941

Germany invades the Soviet Union

Japan bombs Pearl Harbor

U.S. declares war on Japan

Battle of Hong Kong

China officially declares war on Japan

CHAPTER FOCUS QUESTION

How did the Second World War impact Canada socially, politically, and economically?

On the Sunday of Labour Day weekend in 1939, Canadians gathered around their radios to hear King George VI address the rumours of war that had been heard across the country.

> *For the second time in the lives of most of us we are at war. Over and over again we have tried to find a peaceful way out of the differences between ourselves and those who are now our enemies. But it has been in vain. We have been forced into a conflict. For we are called, with our allies, to meet the challenge of a principle which, if it were to prevail, would be fatal to any civilised order in the world.*
>
> *–Historical Royal Speeches and Writings*

Once again, the world was at war. What would war mean to Canadians? How was this war different from the First World War? How was Canada different as a nation at the beginning of the Second World War? In this chapter, you will learn about the events of the Second World War and the contributions made by hundreds of thousands of Canadians during its course.

KEY TERMS

totalitarian state
Nazis
Holocaust
policy of appeasement
British Commonwealth Air Training Plan (BCATP)
total war
Allies
Axis
Dunkirk
Battle of Britain
Pearl Harbor
Battle of Hong Kong
Battle of the Atlantic
Bomber Command
Dieppe Raid
Italian Campaign
D-Day
Juno Beach
genocide
arsenal of democracy

1942
Internment of Japanese Canadians
Canadians vote in support of conscription
Allied raid on French port of Dieppe

1943
Allies begin bombing German cities
Sicily and mainland Italy invaded
Canadians win Battle of Ortona, Italy
Axis forces defeated in Stalingrad

1944
D-Day

1945
The Netherlands liberated
Germany surrenders
Bombing of Hiroshima and Nagasaki, Japan
Japan surrenders; war ends

- Why were totalitarian leaders able to gain power in Europe and Asia?

KEY TERMS

dictator a ruler with unrestricted power, without any democratic restrictions

totalitarian state a dictatorship in which the government uses intimidation, violence, and propaganda to rule all aspects of the social and political life of its citizens

five-year plans Stalin's plans for economic development in the Soviet Union over five years

fascist a form of authoritarian government that is totalitarian and nationalistic

Weimar Republic the democratic government in Germany after the First World War

Nazis members of the National Socialist German Workers' Party; the Nazis were extreme nationalists who took power in 1933 and controlled every aspect of German life through a police state

The Rise of Totalitarianism

As you learned in Chapter 4, the economic crisis of the 1930s led to social and political upheaval in countries around the world. During the Depression era, several charismatic leaders promised solutions to their citizens' woes, but soon emerged as powerful **dictators**.

The term *totalitarian* describes political philosophies that put the state above all else, including the rights of the individual. In a **totalitarian state**, the government has total control over all aspects of politics and society. It uses violence and intimidation to gain power, and then relies on its police force to maintain its control. Usually, the ruling party bans other political parties and does not tolerate any opposing ideologies. Propaganda and censorship reinforce the party message and control society. The government controls the economy and all the resources of the state, and uses these to further its goals. The state has one leader who has absolute power. In the 1930s, different forms of totalitarian states arose in Germany, Italy, Spain, the Soviet Union and, in a different way, Japan.

Stalin's Soviet Union

By 1917, the Communists had taken control of Russia. In 1924, Joseph Stalin became the leader of the Communist Party in what was now the Soviet Union. By 1928, he had gained total control of the Soviet Union and began to implement a series of **five-year plans** to industrialize the country and give the government complete control of the economy. The first step of Stalin's plan was to collectivize agriculture, which meant seizing all privately owned land. Next he created industrial projects, including building coal and steel mills, roads, and railways. Stalin focused on building industry and the military, practically ignoring the needs of the people. The government controlled all media and imposed strict censorship and travel restrictions on everyone. The secret police arrested anyone deemed to be a threat, and the government controlled the courts. During the Great Purge of the late 1930s, Stalin eliminated anyone he believed opposed the communist government or his power. Millions of people were convicted of crimes against the state and hundreds of thousands were executed. Many more Soviet people died of exhaustion or starvation in Gulags, labour camps that Stalin established in Siberia.

FIGURE 5–1 This statue of Joseph Stalin was unveiled in 1955 in Prague, Czech Republic. The monument was later destroyed by the Communist Party of Czechoslovakia in an effort to eliminate Stalin's influence and political system.

Gather Evidence What does Stalin's statue reveal about his personality and his views on leadership?

Mussolini's Italy

After the First World War, Italy suffered from chaotic economic and political conditions. Benito Mussolini took advantage of the situation. He established the **Fascist** Party, which emphasized nationalism and challenged Italy's democratic government. His new political movement found support in the government and with the middle class. Mussolini created the Blackshirts, gangs of fascists who intimidated their opponents by attacking communists and socialists in the streets. Their favourite tactic was forcing bottles of castor oil, a laxative, down a victim's throat. Promising to revitalize Italy and to restore Italian pride, the increasingly militaristic National Fascist Party won 35 seats in the election of 1921. Although the Fascists were anti-communist, Mussolini used the totalitarian model of the Soviet Union as a blueprint for his own plans to rule Italy. In 1922, Mussolini led the March on Rome: he gathered 26 000 Blackshirts outside the city and demanded that the government be turned over to him. Soon after taking power, Mussolini—who was called *Il Duce* ("the leader")—brought all communications, industry, agriculture, and labour under fascist control and turned Italy into a totalitarian state.

FIGURE 5–2 Fascist leader Mussolini (seen on left) and his Blackshirts march in Rome

Nazi Germany

Like Italy, Germany was politically and economically unstable at the end of the First World War. The kaiser had abdicated and a democratic government, the **Weimar Republic**, was set up. But the German people distrusted the government since it had signed the Treaty of Versailles, which had added to the country's economic struggles after the war. Many Germans wanted a leader who could solve the country's problems.

Hitler Comes to Power

In 1920, Adolf Hitler joined the National Socialist German Workers' Party, also known as the **Nazis**, and by 1921 he was the leader of the party. The Nazis gathered support throughout the 1920s by criticizing the Weimar Republic and the humiliating terms of the Treaty of Versailles. Hitler persuaded Germans that he could save the country from the Depression and make it a great nation again. In 1932, the Nazis became the largest party in the *Reichstag*, the German parliament, and in 1933 Hitler became chancellor of Germany.

Once in power, Hitler—called *Führer* ("the leader")—ruled his country through intimidation and fear. He banned all political parties other than the Nazis and used the Gestapo, a secret police, to enforce his rule. Hitler's government defied the terms of the Treaty of Versailles by stopping all reparation payments and rebuilding Germany's military. It also subsidized farmers and poured money into public projects. To the delight of the German people, unemployment went down and the economy improved.

HISTORICAL INQUIRY

Interpret and Analyze

Examine the pictures of the dictators and their supporters on pages 122–125. Why do these political leaders use uniforms as a key symbol in their public appearances? What does this suggest about what they think is the real basis of their political support and power? Why are military or police officers not allowed to run for political office in democracies? Why do retired military and police officers in democracies like Canada never campaign wearing uniforms? What do you think would be the public reaction if they did?

Kristallnacht a coordinated attack against Jewish people and their property carried out by Nazis in Germany on November 9, 1938

persecution to oppress or ill-treat because of race, religion, gender, sexual orientation, or beliefs

Holocaust the Nazi imprisonment and murder of 6 million Jewish people and 5 million other people during the Second World War

FIGURE 5–3 Under the Nazi regime, the Jewish Star of David was to be worn by all Jewish people for easy identification.

The "Master Race"

The Nazi Party believed that the German people were a "master race" of Aryans, a supposedly "pure" race of northern Europeans. Non-Aryans, including Jewish people, Roma ("Gypsies"), and Slavs, were considered inferior. People with mental or physical disabilities were despised because they destroyed the image of the master race. Communists and homosexuals were also targeted as undesirables. The Nazis banned non-Aryans and undesirables from teaching or attending schools and universities, holding government office, or writing books. As early as 1933, the Nazis set up concentration camps to isolate these people from German society.

Hitler's regime of hatred targeted Jewish people in particular. During his rule, he passed the Nuremberg Laws, which forced Jewish people to wear the Star of David at all times, banned marriages between Jews and Aryans, and made it illegal for Jewish people to be lawyers or doctors. The Nazi government also encouraged violence against Jewish people. On the night of November 9, 1938, Nazi mobs attacked Jewish homes, businesses, and synagogues across Germany. Many Jewish people were terrorized, beaten, and imprisoned for no reason. The attack was called *Kristallnacht* or "Crystal Night" because sidewalks in many parts of the country were covered with broken glass from windows. Their **persecution** escalated even more after that night. More laws were introduced which made it illegal for Jewish people to own businesses and restricted their travel. Eventually, Hitler and Heinrich Himmler, the head of Hitler's elite police unit, instituted the "Final Solution" and the **Holocaust**, which you will learn about later in this chapter.

FIGURE 5–4 The Nazis were brilliant propagandists, presenting selected information and using symbolism and pageantry to appeal to the emotions of the public.

Fascism in Spain

As in Germany and Italy, Spain struggled with economic and political strife after the First World War. During the Depression, Spain's democratic government was unable to prevent widespread poverty, and people became more and more dissatisfied. Led by General Francisco Franco, fascist rebels—called Nationalists—tried to overthrow the elected socialist government in 1936. This rebellion resulted in a brutal civil war that lasted three years. Although democratic governments around the world chose not to get involved in the conflict, socialist supporters from several countries went to Spain to join in the fight against Franco and fascism. More than 1200 Canadian volunteers, called the Mackenzie-Papineau Battalion (the Mac Paps), fought in the Spanish Civil War. They ignored the government when it prohibited Canadians from fighting in foreign wars. One of the volunteers was Dr. Norman Bethune, a Canadian surgeon and political activist (see Chapter 4).

FIGURE 5–5 Francisco Franco ruled Spain for 36 years.

Despite their efforts, Franco—with military support from Hitler and Mussolini—won the war and became the ruler of Spain in 1939. Once in control, Franco proved to be a brutal totalitarian dictator who ruled by intimidation and violence. Thousands of people were imprisoned in concentration camps or executed, and many others were used as forced labour to build railways and dig canals. Franco ruled Spain until he died in 1975.

Militarism in Japan

Japan also became a totalitarian state in the 1930s, but there were important differences between Japan and the fascist states in Europe. Many people had strong nationalist sentiments and notions of racial superiority. Japan had a government loyal to a single leader, the emperor. The country's parliament, called the Diet, had little power because government ministers answered only to the emperor. Much of the power rested with the military and the Zaibatsu, large family-run corporations, such as Mitsubishi. These groups took advantage of the political and economic problems of the Depression to gain control of the country. Influenced by European fascism, Japan took on many of its characteristics, including a Gestapo-like police force, the Kempeitai, which had the power to arrest, torture, or kill anyone thought to be an enemy of the state. Militarists took control of Japan in the 1930s and began strengthening the empire by conquering other countries and seizing their resources. During an attack on the Chinese city of Nanjing in 1937, Japanese soldiers killed 300 000 men, women, and children, and looted extensively.

FIGURE 5–6 Hirohito, the 124th emperor of Japan, reigned from 1926 until his death in 1989.

CHECKPOINT

1. In your own words, explain the term *totalitarian*.

2. **Cause and Consequence** Identify the forces at work that allowed Stalin, Mussolini, and Hitler to come to power and make their country a totalitarian regime. What conditions are common to all three situations?

3. How did the Nazis try to accomplish their goal of a "master race" in Europe?

4. Why did some Canadian volunteers become involved in the Spanish Civil War?

5. How were totalitarian leaders able to gain power in Europe and Asia?

KEY TERMS

policy of appeasement giving in to an aggressor's demands in the hopes that no more demands will be made

non-aggression pact an agreement between two countries not to attack each other

Causes of the Second World War

As you have read, different forms of totalitarianism took hold in Europe, the Soviet Union, and Japan during the 1930s. Like the colonialist leaders of pre–First World War empires, the totalitarian leaders of these states had nationalistic ambitions to expand their territory and resources. Germany and Italy felt that they had been cheated by treaties at the end of the First World War and wanted to right these wrongs. Japan wanted access to more resources to help support its industries. In other countries, leaders were conscious of the sacrifices their citizens had made during the last war and wanted to avoid another conflict at all costs. All these factors contributed to the Second World War.

Hitler's Imperialistic Ambitions

When Hitler came to power in 1933, he intended to make Germany a powerful nation again. Part of his plan involved uniting the "master race" of Germanic people and taking back territory that he believed belonged to Germany. In the years leading up to the Second World War, Hitler put his plan into action.

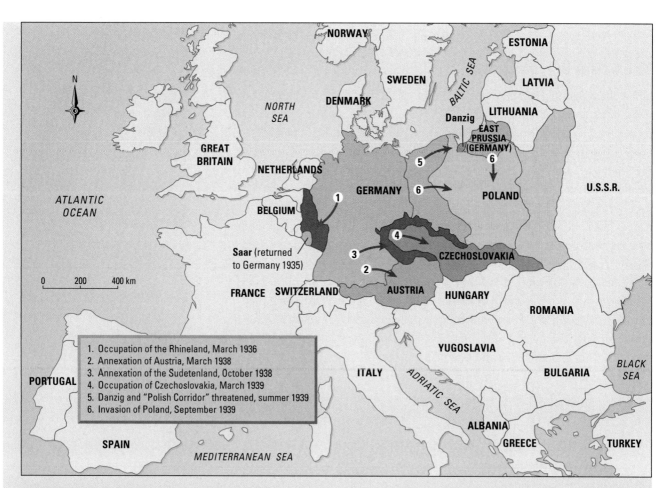

1. Occupation of the Rhineland, March 1936
2. Annexation of Austria, March 1938
3. Annexation of the Sudetenland, October 1938
4. Occupation of Czechoslovakia, March 1939
5. Danzig and "Polish Corridor" threatened, summer 1939
6. Invasion of Poland, September 1939

FIGURE 5–7 Hitler's aggression in Europe, 1936–1939

Evaluate and Draw Conclusions Which countries might have felt threatened by Germany's actions? Why? Italy, also ruled by a fascist government at the time, was Germany's ally. What difference might this alliance have made to the countries of Europe?

©P

Appeasing Hitler

In 1936, Hitler ordered his troops into the Rhineland, an area along Germany's western border that had been demilitarized and put under French protection by the Treaty of Versailles. Although this was a violation of the treaty, Britain and France chose not to act at the time. Two years later, Germany annexed, or took over, Austria. Again, this was another breach of the treaty, but Britain and France chose not to act. They were willing to make concessions to maintain peace. However, their weakness made Hitler bolder.

Next, Hitler set his sights on the Sudetenland, a territory populated by ethnic Germans given to Czechoslovakia at the Paris Peace Conference. When Hitler threatened to invade this territory, British and French leaders met with him in Munich to try to negotiate. In exchange for the Sudetenland, Hitler promised not to invade the rest of Czechoslovakia. British Prime Minister Neville Chamberlain announced to the world that the Munich Agreement and their **policy of appeasement** would secure "peace for our time." Only six months later, in March 1939, Hitler broke his promise and Germany invaded Czechoslovakia. Hitler's actions made it clear that the policy of appeasement had failed. Another war in Europe was looming.

The Nazi–Soviet Non-aggression Pact

After taking over Czechoslovakia, Hitler planned to unite East Prussia with the rest of Germany. This territory had been separated from Germany when the map of Europe was redrawn at the Paris Peace Conference, giving Poland a strip of land so it had access to the Baltic Sea and making Danzig an independent state under the protection of the League of Nations. Before Hitler could act, he had a problem to solve. If Germany invaded Poland, the Soviet Union would likely regard Germany's actions as a threat to its own security. In August 1939, Hitler stunned the world by signing a **non-aggression pact** with Joseph Stalin, leader of the Soviet Union, even though the Nazis hated communists and vice versa. Both countries pledged not to fight each other if one of them went to war, and they agreed to divide Poland between them. Germany was now free to make its move.

On September 1, 1939, German troops invaded Poland, and bitter fighting followed. This time, Britain and France responded immediately. They ordered Germany out of Poland by September 3, 1939. When Germany ignored this deadline, Britain and France declared war.

Failure of the League of Nations

While the policy of appeasement failed to prevent German aggression, the League of Nations was not effective in preventing nationalistic aggression in other parts of the world. The League was supposed to help maintain world peace, but it was too weak and did not have a military to enforce its decisions. The League's ineffectiveness in the following two military conflicts helped pave the road to war.

HISTORICAL INQUIRY

Gather and Organize

It is July 1, 1939. You are a representative of a country that participates in the Second World War. You are asked to set out your country's demands to avoid a war. You should take into account why the leaders of this country might consider war as a real policy option if their demands are not met. Work in pairs, with each pair representing a different country.

Japan Invades Manchuria

As part of its plans to expand its territory and influence, Japan invaded the Chinese province of Manchuria in 1931. The Chinese government appealed to the League of Nations to take action against Japan. The League condemned Japan's action and tried to negotiate. Japan merely withdrew from the League and continued with its policy of aggression. In 1937, it expanded its invasion of China and the two countries were at war.

Italy Invades Abyssinia

Like Hitler in Germany, Mussolini wanted to expand Italy's territory and power. Still bitter that Italy had not received more land in Europe after the First World War, Mussolini wanted to expand Italy's resources by adding to its African colonies. In the spring of 1935, Italy attacked Abyssinia (now Ethiopia). Abyssinia had never been colonized and was one of the few independent African nations. It fought hard against the Italian invasion and won support around the world. The League of Nations immediately voted to impose trade sanctions against Italy. But this action was not very effective because oil, a crucial import for Italy, was not included in the sanctions. At this point, the League still hoped for Italy's support if there was a new war with Germany.

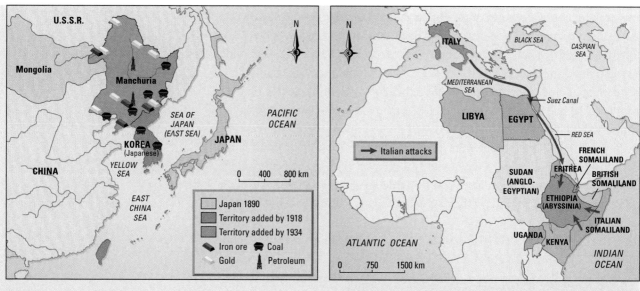

FIGURE 5–8 Japan's aggression by 1934

FIGURE 5–9 Route of Italians invading Ethiopia (Abyssinia), 1935

CHECKPOINT

1. **Cause and Consequence** In what ways did the treaties following World War I contribute to the causes of the Second World War? Compare the maps on pages 24, 55, and 126. How could Hitler attack the peace treaties in his speeches to the German people?

2. **Cause and Consequence** Why was France so determined to punish Germany severely after World War I? How is World War II an example of unintended consequences?

3. Why did the countries in the League of Nations fail to stop Japan's aggression in China and Italy's in Africa? What were the consequences?

4. When Stalin saw the League's failure to stop Germany's aggression, why would he have been tempted to make a non-aggression pact with Hitler and attack Poland?

©P

Canada's Response to the Threat of War

As events escalated in Europe, with Hitler's aggressive policies and the civil war in Spain, many Canadians asked why lives should be risked in another European war when Canada itself was not threatened.

Canada's Policy of Isolationism

Throughout the events of the 1930s, Canada practised **isolationism**, keeping out of affairs outside its borders. Prime Minister William Lyon Mackenzie King did not want Canada to become involved in another world conflict. For example, when Italy invaded Ethiopia in 1935, King stayed neutral, reiterating that Canada must look after its "own domestic situation" first. King had hoped that Britain's policy of appeasement toward Hitler would be successful. The First World War had deeply divided Canada on the issue of conscription, and Canadians had made many sacrifices in that overseas conflict. King knew that if he imposed conscription in this war, he and the Liberal Party would lose support in Québec. Besides, Canada was just starting to come out of the dark years of the Depression. The economy was slowly improving and King did not want the country plunged back into debt.

Canada's Response to Jewish Refugees

While King knew that the Nazis were tyrannizing people, he maintained Canada's isolationist policy. Like King, many Canadians believed that what was happening in Germany was a domestic issue that should not affect them. This attitude influenced Canada's immigration policies and attitudes toward Jewish **refugees** fleeing persecution in Europe.

KEY TERMS

isolationism the policy of remaining apart from the affairs of other countries

refugee a person displaced from his or her home and territory by war and other acts of aggression

[N]othing is to be gained by creating an internal problem in an effort to meet an international one.... We... must seek to keep this part of the Continent free from unrest.
–Diary of Mackenzie King, Tuesday, March 29, 1938

GO ONLINE
Read the detailed diary entry of King's visit with Hitler on the Library and Archives Canada website.

FIGURE 5–10 After meeting Hitler in Germany, Mackenzie King (centre) wrote the following in his diary on June 29, 1937: "[Hitler] smiled very pleasantly and indeed had a sort of appealing and affectionate look in his eyes. My sizing up of the man as I sat and talked with him was that he is really one who truly loves his fellow-men...."

deportation the act of sending someone back to his or her native land

Evaluate and Draw Conclusions

What reasons did countries offer for refusing to accept refugees in the 1930s? Consider Prime Minister King's statement on March 29, 1938 (see page 129). Have the reasons for rejecting refugees changed today? What counter-arguments have advocates for refugees offered in the past and today? To what degree do economic conditions or prejudice against refugees of different backgrounds influence people's attitudes both in the 1930s and today?

Anti-Semitism in Canada

Some Canadians supported the dictators who had seized power in Europe or approved of Hitler's policies and hatred of Jewish people. In Québec, some nationalists called for an independent Québec with a pure French-Canadian population. Anti-Semitism in Canada during the 1930s was not restricted to extremists. It was shared by many in mainstream society, and was reflected in newspapers and in general conversation.

Anti-Semitism and isolationism influenced Canada's immigration policies in the 1930s. After *Kristallnacht* in November 1938, Liberal Cabinet Minister Thomas Crerar recommended that 10 000 Jewish people be allowed to immigrate to Canada, but the Cabinet refused his suggestion.

Jewish refugees were seen as a burden on the state. As you read in Chapter 4, due to rising unemployment, Canada was reluctant to accept immigrants other than those from Britain or the United States who could support themselves. The government restricted immigration in the 1930s. As a result, the number of immigrants to Canada fell from 166 783 in 1928 to 14 382 in 1933. The number of **deportations** also increased to nearly 30 000 by 1936.

The SS St. Louis

Canada's immigration policy and refusal to accept Jewish refugees had tragic consequences in 1939. The S.S. *St. Louis* left Hamburg, Germany, in May with 907 Jewish passengers desperately trying to escape persecution. The *St. Louis* was denied entry in Cuba, South America, and the United States. Canada was the passengers' last hope. The Canadian government refused to let the *St. Louis* dock in any port because the passengers did not qualify for entry as immigrants. The ship was forced to return to Europe. Tragically, many of the people aboard later died in concentration camps during the Holocaust.

FIGURE 5–11 Passengers aboard the S.S. *St. Louis* looked to the Canadian government to accept them as refugees.
Interpret and Analyze At what stage of the journey was this photograph probably taken? Explain.

Canadians Speak Out

Many Canadians did not share the government's anti-Semitic views. Cairine Wilson, Canada's first female senator and chair of the Canadian National Committee on Refugees, spoke out against the banning of Jewish refugees from Canada. Prime Minister Mackenzie King was urged to offer the Jewish refugees sanctuary. In 1938, there were more than 150 000 Jewish people living in Canada. Rallies were held in many parts of the country in support of a more humane immigration policy. When the S.S. *St. Louis* was turned away and its passengers sent back to Nazi Germany, newspaper editorials also lashed out at the government:

● How did the war raise awareness of human rights issues?

> *This country still has the bars up and the refugee who gets into Canada has to pass some mighty stiff obstacles—deliberately placed there by the government.... Immigration bars... are undesirable.... We are deliberately keeping out of this country [people] and money who would greatly add to our productive revenues. We are cutting off our nose to spite our face.*
>
> —**Winnipeg Free Press,** *July 19, 1939, page 13*

FIGURE 5–12 On August 16, 1933, Toronto residents were enjoying a baseball game in Christie Pits, a downtown park, when members of an anti-Semitic club displayed a large swastika on a blanket. Several Jewish youths rushed to destroy the blanket and a riot ensued, injuring dozens.

Despite these objections, Canada still admitted only about 5000 Jewish refugees between 1933 and 1945, and anti-Semitic feelings sometimes erupted in Canadian communities (see Figure 5–12).

FASTFORWARD

Changing Attitudes

The Canadian Charter of Rights and Freedoms, enacted in 1982, guarantees that every individual has the right to live "without discrimination based on race, national or ethnic origin, colour, religion, sex, age or mental or physical disability." Due in large part to the Charter, discrimination of any form is unacceptable in Canada today.

CHECKPOINT

1. Why were many Canadians isolationist in the 1930s?

2. What reasons were given for Canada's admitting so few Jewish refugees fleeing persecution in Europe? Do you think that official reasons were the real reasons? Explain.

3. How do you think Prime Minister Mackenzie King could form such a misguided opinion of Adolf Hitler?

4. Why were the Jewish refugees so desperate to leave Germany? Provide specific information from this chapter.

5. Why do you think discrimination like this was considered acceptable by many people in the 1930s and is not acceptable today?

6. **Ethical Dimension** To what extent should Canadians be responsible for trying to stop human rights abuses in other countries?

KEY TERM

British Commonwealth Air Training Plan (BCATP) a program to train pilots and aircrew during the Second World War; it produced half of all Commonwealth aircrew and is the largest air training program in history

Canada Declares War

On September 1, 1939, Germany invaded Poland. Two days later, Britain and France declared war on Germany. In the First World War, when Britain declared war on Germany, Canada was automatically at war. But, in 1939, Canada was an autonomous country with no such obligation. Prime Minister Mackenzie King knew that once Britain became involved in such a major conflict, Canada would almost certainly support it, but the decision to join the war had to be a Canadian one, decided by Canada's Parliament.

Parliament Votes for War

On September 8, King called a special session of Parliament to decide whether Canada would join the war. He gave a strong speech in favour of declaring war. His Minister of Justice, Ernest Lapointe from Québec, also spoke in favour of the war. But Lapointe spoke bluntly about what conscription would do to Liberal supporters in Québec: "I am authorized by my colleagues in the Cabinet from Québec, to say that we will never agree to conscription and will never be members or supporters of a government that will try to enforce it." This statement helped win support for the war in Québec and convinced voters that Canada's involvement in the war was necessary. Conscious of how conscription had divided the country during the First World War, King assured Parliament, and Québec, that "So long as this government may be in power, no such measure [conscription] shall be enacted."

King's position on joining the war was supported by the opposition Conservative Party. Only J.S. Woodsworth, leader of the Co-operative Commonwealth Federation (CCF), argued against going to war. He believed that nothing could be settled by war and tried to convince the government that Canada should remain neutral. But Woodsworth did not find support for his pacifist position, and Parliament voted in favour of going to war. On September 10, 1939, Canada declared war on Germany.

FIGURE 5–13 Troops departing from Toronto's Union Station

Interpret and Analyze Carefully examine this photograph. How do you think most Canadians felt about going to war? Consider the feelings of those who were staying home as well as those who were going to fight.

Mobilizing Canada's Resources

● What was the war's impact on the home front?

Despite its willingness to join the war, Canada was not prepared for it. Its armed forces were small and unfit for combat. The Canadian army had only 4300 troops, a few light tanks, and no modern artillery. The air force and the navy were small with outdated equipment.

Unlike the First World War, there were no crowds cheering on the streets when Canada declared war in 1939. Many Canadians vividly remembered the horrors of the last world conflict. Still, Canada had no trouble finding volunteers. In September 1939, more than 58 000 people volunteered for service. The Canadian army initially rejected African-Canadian volunteers because of racist attitudes. As the war continued, however, African Canadians were encouraged to join the regular army and the officer corps.

As in the First World War, Aboriginal peoples volunteered at a higher percentage of their population than any other group in Canada. Among them was Thomas Prince, a Brokenhead Ojibway from Manitoba. Prince became a sergeant and served in Italy and France as part of an elite unit. One of Canada's most decorated soldiers, he received ten medals, including the Military Medal for bravery given to him by King George VI. During that incident—a 24-hour watch in which Prince's communication line was damaged by shelling—he "donned civilian clothing, grabbed a hoe and, in full view of German soldiers, acted like a farmer weeding his crops. He slowly inched his way along the line till he found where it was damaged, then, pretending to tie his shoelaces, quickly rejoined the wires..."

Many people still felt strong ties to Britain and volunteered from a sense of duty. Others were driven by a sense of new-found national pride. After years of economic hardship, some Canadians were attracted by the lure of a steady income. The first Canadian troops sailed from Halifax on December 10, 1939.

FIGURE 5–14 Sergeant Thomas George Prince (right) of the Brokenhead Ojibway Nation, Manitoba, stands with his brother, Private Morris Prince, at Buckingham Palace in London, England on February 12, 1945. Prince was decorated by King George VI with both the Military Medal and, on behalf of President Roosevelt, the Silver Star with ribbon.

The British Commonwealth Air Training Plan

GO ONLINE ● ● ● ● ● ● ● ● ● ● ● ●
Find out more about the contributions of Aboriginal peoples to World War II.

Mackenzie King hoped that Canada's contribution to the war effort would be mostly supplies and training, rather than troops, so that he could avoid the issue of conscription. In December 1939, Canada agreed to host and run the **British Commonwealth Air Training Plan (BCATP)**. Pilots and other flight personnel from all over the Commonwealth came to Canada to train with British instructors. Airfields were built on the Prairies and in other locations near small towns and villages. Old aircraft were refitted and returned to service for training purposes. The program was a major Canadian contribution to the war effort. The BCATP trained more than 130 000 pilots, navigators, flight engineers, and ground crew. The total cost was more than $2.2 billion, of which Canada paid more than 70 percent. Contrary to King's hopes, however, Canada's role in the war went far beyond its involvement in the BCATP.

FIGURE 5–15 A propaganda poster commissioned by the **Wartime Information Board**

Interpret and Analyze What three sectors of the workforce are represented here? How would this poster encourage the policy of total war?

Total War

The demands of **total war** meant that the federal government became more involved in planning and controlling the economy. In April 1940, the Department of Munitions and Supply was created and industrialist C.D. Howe was put in charge. Howe, whom you will learn more about in Chapter 6, was given extraordinary authority to do whatever it took to gear up the economy to meet wartime demands. He told industries what to produce and how to produce it. He convinced business leaders to manufacture goods they had never made before. Soon, Vancouver was building ships for the navy, Montréal was constructing new planes and bombers, such as the Lancaster, and Canada's car industries were producing military vehicles and tanks. Munitions factories opened in Ontario and Québec. If the private sector could not produce what Howe wanted, he created **Crown corporations** to do the job. Even farmers were told to produce more wheat, beef, dairy products, and other foods. Under Howe's leadership, the government ran telephone companies, refined fuel, stockpiled silk for parachutes, mined uranium, and controlled food production. Some called him the "Minister of Everything."

FIGURE 5–16 *Maintenance Jobs in the Hangar* by Paraskeva Clark (1898–1986)

Evaluate and Draw Conclusions Paraskeva Clark was a feminist whose painting conveyed a strong social message. How do this painting and the poster above it illustrate Canada's commitment to total war? What social message do they convey? How do you think more traditional artists and critics might have reacted to this type of painting in the 1940s?

CHECKPOINT

1. What assurance did Mackenzie King give Canadians during the debate on Canada's involvement in the war? Why did he do this?

2. What was the British Commonwealth Air Training Plan? Why was Canada chosen to host it? Why did King support the plan?

3. Compare Canadians' reaction to the announcement of the First World War with that of the Second World War. Why did many people still volunteer?

4. How did Canada's policy of total war change the economy? Why was the policy necessary?

©P

Axis Advances

With the declaration of war in September 1939, the **Allies** (Britain, France, and Commonwealth countries including Canada, Australia, and New Zealand) raced to get their forces organized. The alliance of Germany, Italy (1939), and Japan (1940) became known as the **Axis**. Allied troops were quickly stationed along France's border with Germany, where they waited for Germany's next move. But for seven months, from October 1939 to April 1940, nothing happened. This period became known as the "phony war," and many people started to believe there might not be a war.

These illusions were shattered when Germany renewed its *blitzkrieg* ("lightning war"), attacking Denmark and Norway in April 1940. The *blitzkrieg* was an extremely successful war tactic that used surprise, speed, and massive power to quickly overwhelm the enemy. War planes would often lead the attack, knocking out key enemy positions and supply lines. With lightning speed, German panzers (tanks) would crash through enemy lines, driving forward as far as they could. Soldiers would also parachute into enemy territory, destroying vital communication and transportation links. The attacks left the defending army confused and, eventually, surrounded.

Using these tactics, Germany quickly conquered Denmark and Norway. Germany then attacked the Netherlands, Luxembourg, and Belgium. Within weeks, all three countries were overrun. Hitler then set his sights on France.

Evacuation at Dunkirk

Within days of launching an attack on France through Belgium, German panzers reached the English Channel and surrounded Allied forces in the French port of **Dunkirk**. If the Allied troops surrendered, Britain would lose the bulk of its army. They had to escape before the Germans captured the town. In an act of desperation, the British navy rounded up every boat capable of navigating the English Channel. Hundreds of fishing boats, pleasure crafts, and ferries joined navy and merchant ships as they headed across the Channel for Dunkirk. The evacuation began on May 26. Two days later, the German **Luftwaffe** bombed the port of Dunkirk. The evacuation was finally completed on June 4, 1940.

It was a dramatic rescue. Nearly 340 000 Allied soldiers, thousands more than originally anticipated, were brought to safety in Britain. This could have been a disastrous loss for the Allies. Instead, the evacuation of Dunkirk was seen as a "miracle" and helped boost morale.

After the evacuation at Dunkirk, the German army continued to sweep through France. The French army proved to be no match for the German troops, and on June 22, 1940, France surrendered. Britain and the Commonwealth now stood alone against Germany.

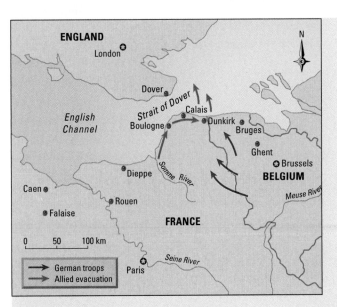

FIGURE 5–17 The Allied evacuation at Dunkirk

FIGURE 5–18 For almost two months, the German Luftwaffe bombed London day and night.

Evaluate and Draw Conclusions What is the likely target in this photograph? Where could people find protection from such attacks?

Battle of Britain

Once France fell, Hitler launched "Operation Sea Lion," his plan to invade Britain. For this scheme to succeed, the Royal Air Force (RAF) had to be defeated so that German forces could cross the English Channel and land in Britain. In July 1940, the Luftwaffe started a massive bombing campaign, aimed at destroying harbours and shipping facilities in southern England. In August, the Germans targeted airfields and aircraft factories. On August 24, German planes bombed several areas of London (some historians believe that this was accidental, while others claim it was a deliberate attack). In retaliation, the RAF bombed the German city of Berlin. This attack enraged Hitler. He ordered the Luftwaffe to bomb London and other British cities. These raids, which become known as "**the Blitz**," took place over many weeks, destroying buildings and terrifying and killing civilians.

Although the Germans had more aircraft than the British, they were unable to defeat the RAF. One reason was that the British had a very advanced radar system that warned them of German air raids. The British also used Spitfires and Hurricanes, two extremely effective fighter planes. In addition, the RAF was reinforced with pilots, planes, and supplies from Canada and other Commonwealth countries. In September 1940, as the RAF shot down more and more German bombers, Hitler finally gave up on his plans to invade Britain. During the **Battle of Britain**, more than 23 000 people, mostly civilians, were killed.

North African Campaign

Once Hitler was certain of victory in France, and days before the German Luftwaffe attack on Britain, Axis forces began what would become a three-year campaign in the deserts of North Africa. This campaign, known as the Desert War, was a struggle for the control of valuable resources and strategic positions.

As you read earlier, Italy wanted to increase its territories in Africa. Its first move had been to invade Abyssinia in 1935. Once Italy formally entered the war on the side of the Axis in June 1940, British cavalry and tank regiments immediately invaded Libya (an Italian colony). Italy, in turn, invaded Egypt with its sights on the Suez Canal, a major strategic point.

To have any hope of victory, the Axis had to dominate the Mediterranean by controlling its two access points: the Strait of Gibraltar and the Suez Canal (see map on page 137). Holding these waterways would give the Axis armies access to the oil-rich Middle East.

By December 1940, the British Commonwealth forces had all but destroyed the Italian army. German forces were dispatched to the area to support the Italians and to prevent an Allied victory in North Africa. Germany had hoped their Italian allies would quickly overrun Allied forces in the region. Instead, it now found its forces engaged on a second front.

Over the next three years, neither side won decisive victories. The tide turned in 1942 with a final Allied victory in North Africa in May 1943. The Allied forces could now focus on their next objective: the invasion of Sicily and the liberation of Italy, which you will read about later in this chapter.

Operation Barbarossa

After Germany's defeat in the Battle of Britain, Hitler launched "**Operation Barbarossa**" ("red beard") on June 22, 1941. This massive attack on the Soviet Union broke the non-aggression pact that Hitler had signed with Stalin in 1939. Hitler saw the Soviet Union as a source of raw materials, agricultural land, and labour for the German army, and conquering the Soviet Union was part of his long-term plans for a new German Empire.

The Soviets were unprepared for the attack, enabling the German army to strike deep into Russian territory. By autumn, they had reached the outskirts of Moscow and Leningrad (now St. Petersburg). But the Germans were ill-equipped for the long and bitterly cold Soviet winter and soon lost their advantage. In 1942, Germany launched another offensive in the Soviet Union, this time focused on the rich oil fields in the south. The German troops got as far as Stalingrad, but were stopped once again by the severe winter. The Germans could not turn back. Nor could they hope for reinforcements, since the Axis powers were also engaged in North Africa. After suffering more than 300 000 casualties, the German army began to retreat in 1942.

The Soviet army went on the offensive, retaking much of the territory it had lost. Hitler's aggression also assured that the Soviets joined the war on the Allies' side.

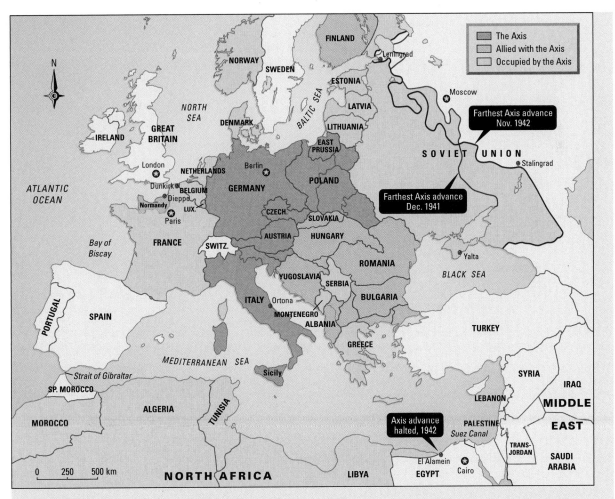

FIGURE 5-19 Extent of Axis control in Europe and North Africa, 1942

Gather and Organize Use this map and the text in this section to understand the scope of Axis control in Europe and North Africa.

Pearl Harbor the Japanese bombing of the U.S. naval base in Hawaii

Battle of Hong Kong Japan's attack on the British colony of Hong Kong in which there were heavy Canadian losses

Black Christmas December 25, 1941, the date Hong Kong fell to the Japanese

Pearl Harbor and Hong Kong

As you read earlier, Japan began a campaign to expand its territory in the 1930s. By 1941, it was prepared to invade American and European colonies in Southeast Asia to gain control of valuable resources such as oil, rubber, and tin. Japan knew such action would almost certainly involve the United States, which had thus far remained neutral in the war.

Japanese strategy depended on a quick and decisive strike against the United States. In a surprise attack on December 7, 1941, Japanese planes bombed the U.S. naval base in **Pearl Harbor**, on the island of Hawaii. More than 2400 people were killed and much of the American fleet was destroyed. Japan then bombed the U.S. territory of the Philippines. The surprise bombings stunned the Americans. On December 8, the U.S. joined the Allies and declared war on Japan. Japan's allies—Germany and Italy—then declared war on the United States. The whole world was now at war.

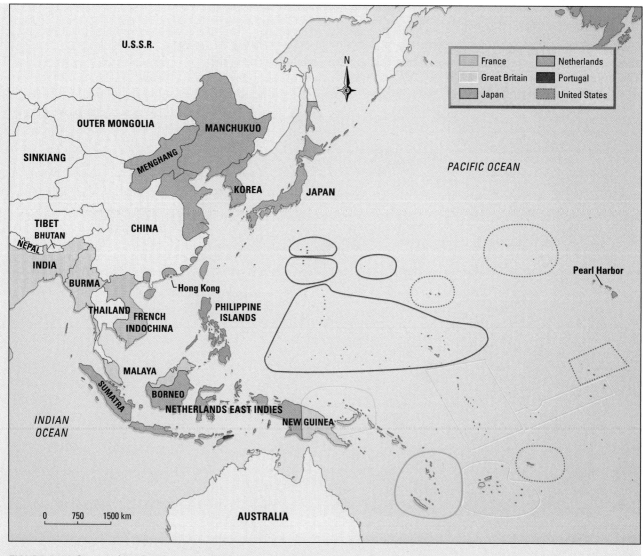

FIGURE 5–20 Control of the Pacific area in 1939

©P

Battle of Hong Kong

Only hours after bombing Pearl Harbor, Japan attacked Hong Kong, a British colony. Weeks earlier, Canada had sent two battalions, from Winnipeg and Québec, to reinforce the British and Commonwealth forces in Hong Kong. The Canadians were inexperienced and the 20 000 Allied soldiers were no match for the skilled Japanese soldiers. After 18 days of bitter fighting, Hong Kong fell to the Japanese on what would be known as "**Black Christmas**," December 25, 1941. Every Canadian was either killed or taken prisoner.

Nearly 1700 Canadian prisoners of war (POWs) faced brutal conditions and were later used as slave labour. More than 260 of these POWs died during three and a half years of imprisonment. Canadians at home were horrified to learn the fate of the soldiers and angry that troops had been sent to Hong Kong. The Japanese treatment of Allied troops may have encouraged the anti-Japanese sentiment that culminated in the internment of Japanese Canadians. You will read about this later in the chapter.

❓ HISTORICAL INQUIRY

Communicate

Posters that ask citizens to join the military are considered a form of propaganda (see page 122). Look at the poster on this page. How is this propaganda? Is it a powerful poster? Why or why not? What do you think of propaganda? Write a short opinion piece about the use of propaganda during wars.

• What was Canada's military role in the Second World War?

FIGURE 5–21 A recruitment poster issued after Canadian forces were defeated at Hong Kong

Interpret and Analyze What is this poster's message?

CHECKPOINT

1. Explain why German forces needed to invade Britain if they were to hold Western Europe. What efforts did they make to do this?

2. How did Canada contribute to the Allied victory in the Battle of Britain?

3. What strategic benefit was there to controlling the Mediterranean? Why would the Axis have needed to control this area?

4. Do you think it was an error on Germany's part to invade the U.S.S.R.? Explain.

5. Using the information about each of the major battles in this section, explain the strategic advantages of the Axis forces as well as how these eventually led to the major turning point that occurred in Stalingrad.

6. Why did the Japanese attack the U.S. navy at Pearl Harbor? How did this attack change the course of the war?

7. Why would Canada send troops to Hong Kong? Why were Canadians angry when they learned the fate of troops in Hong Kong?

Canada's Contribution to the War Effort

Canadians contributed to the war effort on all fronts. Over the course of the war, Canada expanded its navy and air force to help reinforce the Allies.

Battle of the Atlantic

When war broke out, the Royal Canadian Navy (RCN) had only 13 ships and 1819 sailors. Desperately short of equipment and personnel, Canada embarked on a massive building and training program so that by the end of the war, the RCN had grown to 400 vessels and more than 100 000 sailors. By 1941, the **Battle of the Atlantic** was in full swing and Canada's contribution was much needed. As in the First World War, Britain was almost completely dependent on food and military supplies from Canada and the United States. But the Allied supply ships bound for England were being attacked by "wolf packs" of German U-boats patrolling the Atlantic. Germany was trying to starve Britain by cutting off vital shipping routes.

The Allies Gain Momentum

For the first three years of the war, it seemed that the Allies would lose the Battle of the Atlantic. German submarines pounded convoys, sinking hundreds of ships. Some German submarines even sailed into the Gulf of St. Lawrence and up the St. Lawrence River to attack ships there. Gradually, the situation started to turn around. The British had cracked the German naval code, allowing the Allies to track German submarine movements more easily. As well, the Allies were building more ships than were being destroyed.

Canada's War at Sea

Canada also helped turn the tide. The RCN is credited with providing about half the escorts across the Atlantic. Better training of Canadian navy personnel and more sophisticated equipment contributed to the Allies' success. The Women's Royal Canadian Naval Service was created in 1942. Most "WRENs" were limited to shore-based jobs, and worked as wireless operators, coders, drivers, and operational plotters.

To protect supply ships from German torpedoes, the Allies sailed in convoys so warships could help to protect vessels carrying vital supplies. But even convoys did not stop the attacks. German U-boats destroyed hundreds of supply ships, sinking millions of tonnes of cargo. In response, Canada started building small warships, called **corvettes**, to escort convoys across the ocean. The corvette was quick and manoeuvred well, but it was not a very stable vessel. Nevertheless, the corvette was the best ship that could be built in such a short time. The corvettes were helped by long-range Liberator bombers, which could fly from bases in Britain and Canada to protect much of the convoy's route. By May 1943, the Allies believed they had won the Battle of the Atlantic.

FIGURE 5–22 This convoy, assembled in Bedford Basin, part of Halifax Harbour in Nova Scotia, was transporting war supplies to Europe.

Evaluate and Draw Conclusions Identify the smaller ships in the photograph. What might be the nature and function of these vessels?

War in the Air

Like the RCN, the Royal Canadian Air Force (RCAF) grew quickly once the war began. More than 215 000 people enlisted in the RCAF and, at one point, 35 Canadian squadrons were posted overseas. Canadian aircrews participated in bombing raids in North Africa, Italy, Northwest Europe, and Southeast Asia.

The Women's Division (WD) of the RCAF was created in 1941. Women trained as clerks, cooks, hospital assistants, drivers, telephone operators, welders, instrument mechanics, and engine mechanics. The RCAF refused to let licensed female pilots fly until later in the war. Women pilots ferried bombers to Britain, but they never took part in combat.

Bomber Command

The RCAF also participated in one of the most controversial missions of the war: night bombings over Germany. As part of Britain's **Bomber Command**, Canada's Bomber Group pounded German cities, including Dresden and Cologne, night after night. These cities were targeted for a number of reasons: to retaliate for the German air raids on English cities, to diminish German morale, and to destabilize German industrial centres. Tens of thousands of civilians were killed by these air raids. One of the worst attacks was on the city of Hamburg in July 1943. Relentless bombing by the Allies created a firestorm and the city was engulfed in flames. The city was practically destroyed and more than 40 000 civilians were killed.

The casualty rate for the RCAF aircrew was as high as seven out of ten. Nearly 10 000 Canadian Bomber Group members lost their lives during the war.

KEY TERMS

Battle of the Atlantic the struggle between the Allies and the Axis powers to control the Allies' shipping route across the Atlantic Ocean

corvettes small, fast warships built in Canada to help protect convoys in the Atlantic Ocean

Bomber Command the section of the RAF that directed the strategic bombing of Germany

FIGURE 5–23 Bombing raids on German cities, like Hamburg, shown here, killed thousands of civilians.

Interpret and Analyze Why were the conventional aerial bombings of England and Germany unsuccessful in stopping the war production of the English and German economies in World War II? What eventually brought the German economy to a halt?

CHECKPOINT

1. How did Canadian sea and air forces change over the course of the war?

2. How did Canada's navy help secure a successful outcome in the Battle of the Atlantic?

3. Explain why the corvette and the convoy system were so important to the Allied war effort.

4. What did Winston Churchill mean when he said everything in the war depended on the outcome of the Battle of the Atlantic?

5. Describe the contributions of women in the navy and air force.

6. Why do you think the casualty rate for the RCAF was so high?

7. Is the bombing of civilian targets ever justified? Explain your position.

Advances in War Technology

Technology played an important role in the Second World War and in many ways determined its outcome. Major technological advances were made in weaponry, communications, intelligence, and medicine.

Peril of the seas Both the Allies and the Axis powers used submarines, which were much more efficient than in the First World War. The Germans invented a snorkel that made it possible for U-boats to recharge batteries underwater, reducing the time on the surface, where it was vulnerable to attack.

A new type of terror weapon The German V-2 rocket had a range of 350 kilometres. V-2s were used with deadly effect against London in the closing days of the war. Wernher von Braun, the designer of the V-2, moved to the United States after the war. After becoming a U.S. citizen, he designed the *Gemini* and *Apollo* rockets that eventually led to the U.S. moon landing in 1969.

Finding the enemy Radar (radio detection and ranging) is an electronic system that uses radio waves to detect objects beyond the range of vision. It gives information about the distance, position, size, shape, direction, and speed of approaching aircraft. Radar was a deciding factor in the Battle of Britain.

The deadliest weapon The United States developed the atomic bomb, which permanently changed warfare. In this weapon, a sphere of concentrated radioactive material about the size of a baseball could easily destroy a city.

Technology in the air Airplanes played an important role in the First World War, but the development of multi-engine bombers was a major contribution to the defeat of Germany in 1945. These large aircraft were capable of carrying a substantial amount of ordnance that enabled saturation bombing. Many Lancaster bombers were manufactured in Ontario and ferried to Britain.

Secret codes The Germans developed a coding machine, known as "Enigma," which converted radio messages into code. This machine spurred the development of an early computer that could decode German signals.

Treating the wounded Great advances were made in medical technology as doctors tried to repair the hideous wounds of war. Penicillin, an antibiotic, was first isolated in 1929 by British scientist Alexander Fleming and was used to treat infections in humans in 1941. Recovery rates for wounded soldiers increased significantly due to penicillin. Below, a Canadian doctor treats a German soldier in 1944.

The Tide Turns

In 1942, the tide of the war finally began to turn. The Allied forces became stronger when the United States entered the conflict in December 1941. With the Americans' help, the Allies started to gain ground in North Africa. They were more and more successful against U-boats in the Atlantic and made important advances in the Pacific. On the Eastern Front, a determined Soviet Army had stopped the German advance at Stalingrad, thereby preventing Hitler from advancing across the Middle East toward Egypt.

We were sacrificial lambs… They were there waiting for us—they knew it was just a matter of time. In fact, one German at Dieppe actually asked us: "What took you so long?"

–Thomas Hunter

The Dieppe Raid

By the middle of 1942, the Soviet Union, now one of the Allied powers, had lost close to a million soldiers in its desperate fight against invading German troops. Stalin demanded that the Allies invade Europe from the west to weaken Germany by forcing it to fight the war on two fronts.

The Allies had hoped to postpone the full invasion of Europe, but they felt ready for a trial run. A smaller raid would allow them to test new techniques and equipment, and serve as a scouting mission for a future invasion. The 2nd Canadian Division was chosen to be the main attack force in a raid on the French port of Dieppe. The plan was to launch four pre-dawn attacks along the coast, followed by the main attack on Dieppe. Air force bombers and tanks brought in by ship would support the troops.

On the morning of August 19, 1942, one of the ships carrying Canadian soldiers to Dieppe met a small German convoy. The two sides engaged in a brief sea battle, and the noise alerted German troops on shore. To make matters worse, the ships were delayed and the troops landed in daylight. They were easily machine-gunned by waiting German soldiers. Allied tanks were ineffective because they could not get enough traction to move on the steep, pebbled beach. Communication between the ships and troops on land was poor. Believing the first wave of soldiers had reached the town, commanders sent reinforcements ashore. These troops, too, became trapped on the beaches. Unable to retreat or advance, they were easy targets for the German soldiers on the cliffs along the coastline.

GO ONLINE

Was the real intent of the Dieppe Raid to steal the German Enigma machine? Visit the BBC History website to find out more.

FIGURE 5–24 Dead Canadian soldiers and tanks on Dieppe beach, August 19, 1942

Interpret and Analyze Canadian troops were supported by tanks that arrived in transport ships, but most never advanced far from the shoreline. Find evidence in this photograph to suggest why tanks were useless in this attack.

TIMELINE	Major Canadian Battles, 1939–1945

September 1939–May 1943	May 26–June 4, 1940	August–October, 1940	December 7–25, 1941
Battle of the Atlantic	Battle of Dunkirk	Battle of Britain	Battle of Hong Kong

©P

Disaster or Learning Experience?

The **Dieppe Raid** was a terrible failure. Casualties were high. Of the nearly 5000 Canadian soldiers involved in the nine-hour battle, 907 were killed. Almost 600 were wounded and another 1946 were taken prisoner. Ross Munro, the Canadian war correspondent who accompanied the troops to Dieppe, described the raid and its devastating results:

> For eight hours, under intense Nazi fire from dawn into a sweltering afternoon, I watched Canadian troops fight the blazing, bloody battle of Dieppe. I saw them go through the biggest of the war's raiding operations in wild scenes that crowded helter skelter one upon another in crazy sequence. There was a furious attack by German E-boats while the Canadians moved in on Dieppe's beaches, landing by dawn's half-light. When the Canadian battalions stormed through the flashing inferno of Nazi defences, belching guns of huge tanks rolling into the fight, I spent the grimmest 20 minutes of my life with one unit when a rain of German machine-gun fire wounded half the men in our boat and only a miracle saved us from annihilation.
>
> *–Ross Munro,* **The Windsor Daily Star,** *1942*

Opinion is divided as to whether Dieppe was a valuable learning experience or a complete disaster. Some historians claim that the Allies were later able to launch a successful invasion based on what they had learned at Dieppe. Others maintain that the raid was poorly planned and taught the Germans more than it taught the Allies.

KEY TERM

Dieppe Raid the 1942 trial raid by Canadian troops against Germany's occupation of Dieppe; Canada suffered heavy losses

FIGURE 5–25 Ross Munro, Second World War correspondent for the *Canadian Press*

FASTFORWARD

HISTORICAL THINKING — **Ethical Dimension**

Reporting War

Today, news reports make it possible for us to see what is happening on a battlefield almost instantly. Many have argued, however, that what we see on the news is not always an accurate report of what is happening in a war zone. Several factors can influence what is reported on the news. For example, reporters "embedded" with combat units are often sympathetic to the young soldiers they live and work with. Back home, newspaper editors and television directors choose stories that will attract viewers so they can sell advertising. The government may also censor news reports to prevent security risks or to put their own slant on events. Some people argue that improved coverage of war is positive because it keeps us informed of what is happening in distant parts of the world. Others maintain that this coverage is negative because it hardens us to images of war so that we are no longer shocked by what we see.

1. Can a news broadcast ever completely avoid bias and show viewers the "truth"?

2. Should reporters tell us everything they see on the front lines?

August 19, 1942	July 1943–February 1945	June 6, 1944	September–November, 1944	February 8–March 10, 1945
Dieppe Raid	The Italian Campaign	D-Day	Battle of the Scheldt	Battle of the Rhineland

The Italian Campaign

After the failure at Dieppe, British Prime Minister Winston Churchill felt that the best way for the Allies to recapture Europe was through what he called the "soft underbelly" of Europe: an invasion of Sicily and Italy. The Allied victory in North Africa made it possible for forces to launch their attack from the south. The **Italian Campaign** ended up lasting almost two years and cost thousands of lives. The "underbelly" proved anything but soft.

Battle of Sicily

On July 10, 1943, Allied forces invaded Sicily. Once again, the Canadians proved themselves to be fierce opponents. They fought Italian and German soldiers through 240 kilometres of mountainous terrain, losing 562 soldiers in the battle. The Allies captured the island after 38 days.

This victory quickly led to Mussolini's downfall. He was overthrown and the new Italian government surrendered. The Germans, however, continued to defend their Italian territory.

Battle of Ortona

The Allies followed the Germans as they retreated to mainland Italy. Canadians were given the task of capturing the medieval town of Ortona on the Adriatic Sea. Before they could reach the heavily fortified Ortona, the Canadians had to capture several smaller villages, cross the river Moro, and fight across several kilometres of German-occupied territory. The regiment describes the battle:

FIGURE 5–26 Ortona after the Canadian advance

> *Throughout the night of December 8th–9th the RCR [Royal Canadian Regiment] maintained its position on the feature which came to be known… as "Slaughterhouse Hill." The fighting was most confused, the enemy appearing on several sides of the perimeter as well as within it… the incessant shellfire from both sides turned the night into pandemonium.*
>
> **–A Regiment at War, 1979**

Once they reached Ortona, advances were slow and battles were often fought house by house on the town's steep, rubble-filled streets. Canadians captured the town on December 28, 1943, but lost 1372 soldiers before the Germans withdrew. After capturing Ortona, Canadian troops advanced through Italy until they were sent to join the campaign in France. Nearly 6000 Canadians were killed in Italy.

CHECKPOINT

1. **Cause and Consequence** In 1942, Stalin wanted his allies to attack Germany in the west and force Hitler to fight on two fronts, thereby taking some pressure off the Soviet army. Why was Dieppe a failure in this context?

2. Was the invasion of Sicily and Italy a suitable substitute for an attack on Hitler's forces in northern Europe?

3. The Allies attacked Dieppe in 1942 and Sicily and Italy in 1943. What were the advantages for Allied troops in waiting until 1944 to launch the invasion of Normandy? What might have been the consequences for the Allies if Nazi Germany had defeated the Soviets at Stalingrad in 1943 and the USSR had withdrawn from the war?

Historical maps are useful documents that give specific information. They are a visual way of conveying facts as well as concepts. As with other historical documents, the information included in these types of maps is selective, so you must examine them carefully.

Steps to Reading a Map

1. Look at the title and legend of the map below. These should tell you the historical period of the map, its main purpose, and the other kinds of information that the map is meant to convey.

2. Examine the names (or symbols) closely. Look for patterns in the information. Why, for example, are some names bigger or bolder than others? Certain colours may be used to illustrate similarities in or differences between regions.

3. Now read the map by analyzing the information. Ask yourself: What is this map about? How is the information being communicated? What conclusions can be drawn from this map?

Interpret and Analyze

As you read about the events that occurred in Europe between 1942 and 1945, refer to Figure 5–27. Go through the three steps in reading a historical map, and answer the questions below.

1. What is the map about? What are the six pieces of information given in the legend?

2. The cartographer (map-maker) has shown a limited number of cities. How would you explain the choice of Dunkirk, Stalingrad, and Palermo?

3. What ideas does this map convey about

   a) the importance of the success of the North African campaign to the Allies?

   b) the role of the U.S.S.R. in defeating Germany?

   c) the importance of supremacy in naval forces for the Allies?

   d) the importance of an effective air force?

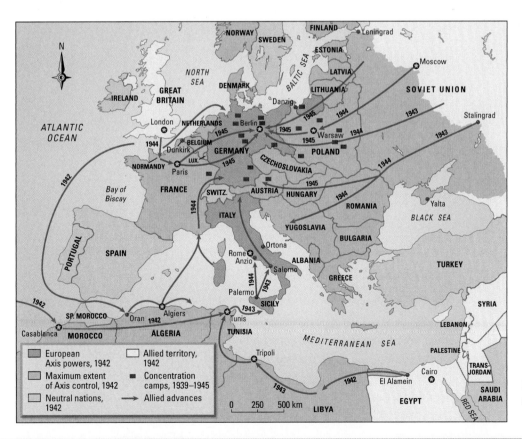

FIGURE 5–27 Allied advances on Germany, 1942–1945

- What was Canada's military role in the Second World War?

? HISTORICAL INQUIRY

Formulate Questions

Contact your local branch of the Royal Canadian Legion to see if there is a surviving veteran who could come to your class and talk about serving in one of the military campaigns of the Second World War. Prepare a list of questions that you would like to ask the veteran. Share these questions with the guest prior to the visit. Be aware that some veterans are unwilling to talk about their war experiences. Why might this be so? Instead of interviewing a surviving veteran, you might choose to research and find interview recordings and share them with the class.

Allied March to Victory

The Allies immediately followed their success in Italy with the biggest Allied invasion of the war. On **D-Day**, June 6, 1944, the Allies launched a full-scale invasion of Europe called "Operation Overlord." To avoid a disaster like Dieppe, the Allies planned and rehearsed the invasion down to the smallest detail.

The Allies launched their attack by landing their troops on five beaches along an 80-kilometre stretch of the Normandy coast in northern France. The beaches were code-named Sword, Juno, Gold, Omaha, and Utah. The soldiers on the beaches had massive air and naval support. The Allies were able to disrupt transportation and communication lines before the attack by dropping **paratroopers** behind enemy lines and bombing targets on the beaches. Their naval support also allowed the Allies to bring in more than a million troops, along with military vehicles and supplies, after the initial landing.

The D-Day invasions were also successful because the Allies had managed to keep the details of the attack a secret from the Germans. Although the Germans had anticipated an attack, they thought it would come from the north. The weather also helped the Allies. A storm delayed the initial attack and the Germans believed that the Allies would not attempt a landing in bad weather. As a result, the German defence was poorly coordinated.

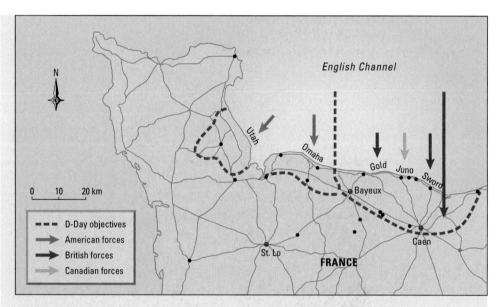

FIGURE 5–28 Allied invasion of Normandy on D-Day, June 6, 1944

Juno Beach

On the morning of June 6, 1944, 14 000 Canadian soldiers arrived at **Juno Beach** (see Figure 5–28) as part of the first wave of the attack. They had to make their way past the German defences, including concrete barriers, barbed wire, and land mines, to take the beach. By the end of the day, the Canadians had fought their way inland by about nine kilometres. Although they were successful, casualties from the day were high—359 Canadians died and 715 were wounded.

Battle of the Scheldt

It took the Allies weeks of constant fighting to expand their territory before they could begin an advance through France and Belgium toward Germany. The 11-month campaign was exhausting and there were several moving moments in which the Allies were welcomed as the liberators of Europe. In September 1944, for example, Canadians marched triumphantly through Dieppe where only two years earlier they had suffered a terrible defeat.

In October, Canadians were given the task of clearing enemy troops from the Scheldt River in Belgium. This river was important because it connected Antwerp to the North Sea. Although the Allies had already liberated Antwerp, German forces controlled the river and access to the sea. The Canadians achieved their goal after a month of bitter fighting, allowing the Allies to bring in supplies for their final advance into Germany.

Battle of the Rhineland

On February 8, 1945, the Allies—including approximately 175 000 Canadians—began their attack to drive the Germans back over the Rhine River and out of the Netherlands. The fighting was slow as soldiers struggled through mud and flooded fields against fierce German resistance. Nearly 23 000 Allied soldiers were killed, including more than 5300 Canadians. The Germans lost about 90 000 men, including 52 000 who were taken prisoner. On March 10, the German army withdrew to the east bank of the Rhine River, allowing the Canadians to continue north to liberate Holland.

Liberating the Netherlands

Once the Allied forces had reached the Rhine River and Germany, the Canadians were given a separate task: liberating the Netherlands. This was a difficult job. An earlier Allied attempt to free Holland had failed and German troops had practically destroyed the port cities of Amsterdam and Rotterdam and flooded much of the countryside. By the end of 1944, food and fuel supplies to the Dutch had been cut off and many were starving to death. The bitter winter of 1944–1945 made difficult conditions even worse.

KEY TERMS

D-Day June 6, 1944; the day Allied armies, including Canada, invaded France; the biggest Allied invasion of the Second World War

paratroopers soldiers trained to parachute from airplanes onto combat areas

Juno Beach the nine-kilometre stretch of beach in France where Canadian troops landed on D-Day

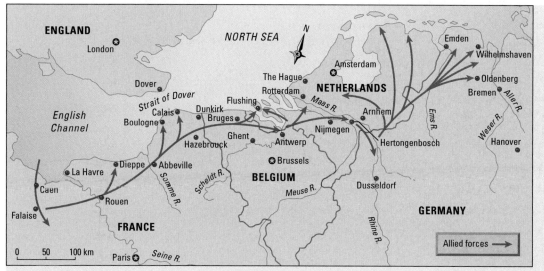

FIGURE 5–29 Allied liberation of France, Belgium, and the Netherlands, and invasion of Germany

Gather and Organize Use the text and the map to determine what route the Canadians used in their attack in the Netherlands.

FIGURE 5–30 Celebrating the liberation of Utrecht, in the Netherlands, by the Canadian Army, May 7, 1945

Interpret and Analyze Use the quotation and image to understand why Canadian troops were hailed as heroes in Holland.

Lasting Gratitude

After reaching the Rhine, it took another month of fighting to drive the Germans out of the Netherlands. On April 28, 1945, the Allies negotiated a truce with Germany, allowing them to bring much needed supplies to the Dutch people. Convoys of trucks carrying food and fuel eventually delivered thousands of tonnes of supplies to civilians.

As they liberated towns and cities throughout the Netherlands, Canadians were hailed as heroes in victory parades. Percy Loosemore, who travelled with Canadian soldiers, wrote:

> *When we entered Holland from Belgium, the Dutch people seemed overwhelmed with joy at their deliverance and the end of the war; for while the Belgians had been liberated for some time, the Dutch were celebrating both the end of the war in Europe and their own immediate liberation. Bunting hung everywhere; people cheered as we drove by… Once, when I stopped my car, children gathered around and proceeded to decorate our vehicle with flowers and coloured streamers. To witness the enthusiastic joy and happy faces of these people was a [great] pleasure to me… I was deeply moved.*
>
> –*Quoted in* **A Soldier's View, 2005**

GO ONLINE

To this day, the Dutch continue to show their appreciation to Canada for liberating the Netherlands. Use online resources to find out more.

Victory in Europe

While the Allies invaded Germany from the north and west, the Soviet Union attacked from the east. Facing certain defeat, Germany surrendered to the Allies on May 7, 1945. Hitler committed suicide in a bunker in Berlin before he could be captured. The war in Europe was over and the Allies declared May 8 as Victory in Europe (VE) Day.

FIGURE 5–31 At the Yalta Conference in February 1945, with an Allied victory only months away, Winston Churchill, Franklin D. Roosevelt, and Joseph Stalin (front row, from left to right) discussed the reorganization of post-war Europe, including occupation zones and new borders.

Japan Surrenders

After the Allied victory in Europe, the war in the Pacific intensified. By mid-1945, most of the Japanese air force and navy had been destroyed, but the army was still strong. In March 1945, the Americans, the main Allied force in the Pacific, had begun fire-bombing Japanese cities trying to force them to surrender. Although these bombing raids destroyed cities and killed thousands of people, the Japanese declared that they would "fight to the last person" and not surrender.

The Atomic Bomb

For some time, American and British scientists had been working on the **Manhattan Project**, a top-secret plan to develop an **atomic bomb**. In 1942, Canada was notified of the project and asked to contribute uranium, an important component of the bomb. The Canadian government agreed, and secretly bought the Eldorado mine at Great Bear Lake, Northwest Territories, to produce the uranium.

On August 6, 1945, an American bomber plane (named "Enola Gay" after the pilot's mother) dropped an atomic bomb over the Japanese city of Hiroshima. The destruction unleashed by the bomb had never been experienced before. Three days after the bombing of Hiroshima, a second atomic bomb was dropped on the city of Nagasaki. While precise casualty numbers are not available, it is estimated that the two bombings killed nearly 200 000 people—about 135 000 in Hiroshima and another 50 000 in Nagasaki. Long-term consequences, such as cancer, affected many more Japanese citizens.

The War Ends

The Japanese, realizing that they could not withstand the awesome power of the new U.S. weapon, surrendered on August 14, 1945. Finally, after six long years and the loss of millions of lives, the Second World War was over.

FIGURE 5–32 The nuclear detonation at Nagasaki on August 9, 1945, created a mushroom cloud that rose many kilometres into the air.

CHECKPOINT

1. What was D-Day? Why was it necessary? In what ways did the D-Day invasion differ from the raid on Dieppe? What role did Canadian troops play in both of these invasions?

2. In your own words, describe the situation in the Netherlands in the spring of 1945. Why were Canadian troops considered heroes in the Netherlands?

3. Compare and contrast how the war ended in Europe and Asia.

Are weapons of mass destruction ever justified?

On July 16, 1945, a group of American scientists tested the first atomic bomb—the most powerful weapon ever built until that time. The scientists who witnessed the test were awestruck by the power of what they had created.

Albert Einstein's theory of relativity was the basis of the atomic bomb, but he did not work on the Manhattan Project. However, he regretted even his indirect participation. Einstein met with fellow scientist Linus Pauling on November 11, 1954 and confessed:

> I made one great mistake in my life when I signed the letter to President Roosevelt recommending that atomic bombs be made; but there was some justification—the danger that the Germans would make them.
>
> –Quoted in Ronald Clark,
> **Einstein: The Life and Times, 2007**

Two atomic bombs, dropped on the Japanese cities of Hiroshima and Nagasaki, ended the war, but controversy regarding their use continues to this day. Was it necessary to use such a deadly weapon? Even before the atomic bomb was dropped, there were those who believed its use could never be justified. Admiral William Leahy, an advisor to U.S. President Harry Truman, opposed the bomb. In 1944, he advised Truman's predecessor, Franklin Roosevelt, not to use the bomb.

> Personally I recoiled at the idea and said to Roosevelt: "Mr. President, this would violate every Christian ethic I have ever heard of and all known laws of war. It would be an attack on the non-combatant population of the enemy...."
>
> It was my opinion that the use of this barbarous weapon at Hiroshima and Nagasaki was of no material assistance in our war.... The Japanese were already defeated and ready to surrender.... My own feeling was that in being the first to use it, we had adopted an ethical standard common to the barbarians of the Dark Ages. I was not taught to make war in that fashion, and wars cannot be won by destroying women and children....
>
> –I Was There, 1950

FIGURE 5–33 Hiroshima before the bombing

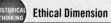

Colonel Paul Tibbets, commander of the air force squadron that dropped the bombs on Japan and pilot of the plane that dropped the bomb on Hiroshima, rejected such criticism because he felt it failed to take into consideration the "context of the times":

As for the missions flown against Japan on the 6th and 9th of August, 1945, I would remind you, we were at war. Our job was to win. Once the targets were named and presidential approval received, we were to deliver the weapons as expeditiously as possible, consistent with good tactics. The objective was to stop the fighting, thereby saving further loss of life on both sides. The urgency of the situation demanded that we use the weapons first—before the technology could be used against us.

–Quoted in news release by Airmen Memorial Museum, 1994

For almost 200 years, war strategists have been influenced by the writings of Carl von Clausewitz, a Prussian general and military theorist. In his book *On War*, he writes about his theory of absolute war:

To introduce into a philosophy of war a principle of moderation would be an absurdity. War is an act of violence pushed to its utmost bounds.

–Quoted in Gwynne Dyer, War, 1985

Weapons now exist that have the potential to destroy all life on Earth. Nations have stockpiled thousands of warheads hundreds of times more powerful than the first atomic bombs. Arsenals and laboratories store biological weapons designed to spread diseases. Governments maintain stores of deadly chemical weapons. Von Clausewitz could never have envisioned destruction on such a scale.

Thankfully, some nations have agreed to treaties that limit the testing of nuclear weapons and that reduce the arsenal of nuclear weapons. Still, both the United States and Russia have the capability to destroy the world several times over. Many other nations also have nuclear arms and large quantities of chemical and biological weapons.

Thinking It Through

1. What reasons did Admiral William Leahy give against using the atomic bomb?

2. What three arguments did Colonel Paul Tibbets give to support the use of the atomic bomb on Japan?

3. What do you think Albert Einstein meant by "...but there was some justification—the danger that the Germans would make them"?

4. Do you think there are any circumstances in which weapons of mass destruction can ever be justified? Explain your answer.

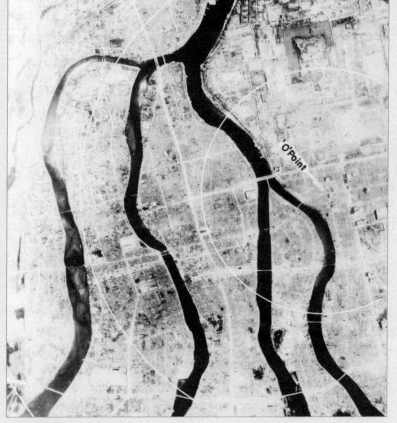

FIGURE 5–34 Hiroshima after the bombing

Crimes Against Humanity Ethical Dimension

Atrocities inflicted upon civilians and POWs during the Second World War brought the issue of human rights to the world's attention, and ultimately led to the Universal Declaration of Human Rights.

FIGURE 5–35 Survivors from the Buchenwald concentration camp. Elie Wiesel wrote about his experiences during the Holocaust in his book *Night*. Wiesel (inset and the farthest face on the right, second bunk from bottom) was later awarded the Nobel Peace Prize.

The Holocaust

The anti-Semitic and racist views of Hitler and the Nazi government were well-known in the 1930s. By 1941, the Nazi government adopted the "**Final Solution**"—a horrifying plan of **genocide**. Hitler ordered all Jewish people and "undesirables" to be shipped to concentration camps, such as Bergen-Belsen and Buchenwald in Germany, and Auschwitz and Treblinka in Poland. Upon arrival, guards stripped them of their clothes and valuables, shaved their heads, and separated families. The weak, the old, and the young were immediately killed in gas chambers. Healthy people worked as slave labourers. When overwork, starvation, and disease weakened them, they too were murdered. By 1945, the Germans had killed more than 6 million Jewish people and another 5 million Roma, Slavs, and other "undesirables." Though the Allies had known about German concentration camps, they did not realize the full extent of the horrors of the Holocaust until they pressed closer to Germany and saw the Nazi atrocities.

The Nuremberg Trials

In 1945, the Allies established an International Military **Tribunal** in Nuremberg, Germany, to prosecute prominent Nazi leaders and many others for atrocities committed during the war. Twelve defendants were sentenced to death and others were imprisoned. This is the first time in history that leaders of a country were charged for immoral acts during wartime. The Nuremberg Trials became a model for prosecuting war criminals in Rwanda and the former Yugoslavia.

A Canadian soldier at Bergen-Belsen wrote:

Tonight I am a different man. I have spent the last two days in Belsen concentration camp, the most horrible festering scab there has ever been on the face of humanity....

You have seen pictures in the paper but they cannot tell the story. You have to smell it and feel it and keep a stern look on your face while your heart tears itself into pieces and the tears of compassion drench your soul...

–*King Whyte,* **Letters Home, 1944–1946, 2007**

Atrocities in Asia

Liberators of Japanese POW camps also encountered terrible **war crimes** committed during the war. Mass killings, human experimentation, famine, torture, and forced labour were a few of the hardships suffered by POWs and civilians alike. Since many of Japan's wartime acts violated international law, the alleged crimes were subject to trial in international courts of justice, similar to the Nuremberg Trials. The Tokyo Trials heard these cases and passed sentence on military personnel found guilty of war crimes and **crimes against humanity**.

The War at Home

Canadians at home made enormous contributions to the war. Under the policy of total war, many Canadian factories were dedicated to producing supplies and war materials. In 1944, Canada produced 14 000 tanks and personnel carriers, more than 4000 aircraft, and 16 000 artillery pieces. Factories operated non-stop, and Canadians worked long hours to run them.

Changing Women's Roles

As in the First World War, women joined war industries in roles that were unusual for them at the time. They worked as welders, drillers, and punch-press or machine operators. "Rosie the Riveter" became a popular nickname for these working women. Women were in high demand as factory workers and many moved from rural areas to industrial centres. With government funding, some companies built dormitories close to their factories to house workers.

Canada's Wartime Economy

With so much increased production and employment, people suddenly had more money to spend. At the same time, there were fewer goods to buy as most of what was produced was shipped to Britain. Prime Minister Mackenzie King wanted to avoid soaring inflation and hoped to prevent the massive debt that had burdened Canada after the First World War so the government took the following steps:

- As Minister of Finance, James Ilsley enthusiastically encouraged Canadians to buy Victory Bonds. The government used the money to help finance the war, and people cashed in the bonds for profit after the war.

- Ilsley increased income taxes for added revenue.

- In 1941, the Wartime Prices and Trade Board, which had been set up in 1939, froze all wages and prices to try to prevent inflation.

- In 1942, King introduced food rationing, limiting the amounts of certain goods that Canadians were allowed per week. Each Canadian adult was limited to about 1 kilogram of meat, 220 grams of sugar, 250 grams of butter, and about 225 grams of coffee. Canadian rations were generous compared with those in England and the United States.

- What was the war's impact on the home front?

KEY TERMS

Final Solution the Nazis' plan to systematically kill all European Jews

genocide the systematic extermination of a religious or ethnic group

tribunal court of justice

war crimes the killing, torture, and hostage-taking of civilian populations, or the deliberate and extensive destruction of their property

crimes against humanity widespread attacks against civilians, including murder, enslavement, deportation, and torture

GO ONLINE

Use online resources for more information on how the Second World War transformed the lives of women.

FIGURE 5–36 Women were employed in non-traditional roles during the Second World War.

• What effect did the war have on the role of women?

Women and the War Machine

The Second World War changed Canadian society. Most young men joined the military and many went overseas. At the same time, industrial production greatly increased, meaning that more workers were needed. Although women in poorer families and on farms had always worked, the middle-class ideal was that women looked after the home and men went out to work. This pattern was so engrained that middle-class men resisted even the idea that their wives would go to work, believing that it would indicate, among other things, that the men could not provide for their families. During the Depression, governments wanted women to stay at home to keep more men employed. When the war changed everything, attitudes had to change too.

The National Selective Service Program

During the war, the National Selective Service program registered women for work in factories and established daycare centres in Ontario and Québec, where industry was concentrated. Women also joined the Canadian Women's Army Corps (CWAC), serving mostly as clerks, drivers, and nurses. By 1945, almost one-third of all Canadian women were employed in the war effort.

Ronnie, the Bren Gun Girl

Governments used propaganda and created stereotypes to mobilize the home front and to change the public's mind about women in the workforce. Working in the war effort had to seem glamorous, exciting, and patriotic. The Americans created Rosie the Riveter to idealize the working woman. Her posters show her with sleeves rolled up, ready to pitch in and help her country. Canada's stereotypical working woman was Ronnie, the Bren Gun Girl, who was, as opposed to Rosie, a real person working in a munitions factory.

Thinking It Through

1. In your own words, describe how the role of Canadian women changed from the Depression to the end of the Second World War.

2. Examine, describe, and compare the images of Rosie the Riveter and Ronnie, the Bren Gun Girl. What do they tell us about the societies they represent?

3. Describe social controls that might be used against a woman who chose to live independently rather than participate in the war effort.

FIGURE 5–37 Ronnie, the Bren Gun Girl—a real Canadian woman named Veronica Foster

FIGURE 5–38 Rosie the Riveter represented the idealized American woman contributing to the war effort.

©P

The Growing Demand for Social Change

In addition to regulating wages and controlling inflation, the Wartime Prices and Trade Board was also established to help reduce social unrest. It limited the power of trade unions by controlling wages so that striking would be less effective. The shortage of labour, however, often worked to the unions' advantage, and many ignored restrictions on the right to strike. Workers wanted higher wages but they also demanded the right to bargain. The board was unable to prevent steel workers in Nova Scotia and coal miners in Alberta and British Columbia from going on strike in 1943. In 1944, the federal government softened its policy, allowing workers the right to join a union and forcing employers to recognize their workers' unions.

The war also brought changes to the role of government. The wartime government had been involved in almost every aspect of Canadians' lives, and many Canadians wanted some of this involvement to continue. The Co-operative Commonwealth Federation party and its platform of social reform was becoming increasingly popular at both the national and provincial levels, a fact that was not lost on Prime Minister Mackenzie King. In 1943, the CCF made up the Opposition in Ontario. In 1944, it formed the government in Saskatchewan under T.C. "Tommy" Douglas. Mackenzie King had already brought in an unemployment insurance program in 1940. In 1945, he expanded Canada's social assistance by bringing in the Family Allowance program, which helped families cover the cost of child maintenance. Canada's policy of **"cradle to grave" social security** had begun.

The Conscription Crisis

Prime Minister Mackenzie King had promised there would be no conscription when Canada declared war in 1939. But the speed with which the Germans occupied Europe in 1940 stunned Canadians and made it clear that thousands of soldiers would be needed to fight against the Nazis. Canadians, including the opposition Conservative Party, demanded that their government do more for the war effort. In response to these demands, King's government quickly brought in the **National Resources Mobilization Act** (NRMA). This Act gave the government special emergency powers to take over the nation's resources. Most significantly, the NRMA allowed for conscription, although only for home defence.

FIGURE 5–39 The government reminded Canadians that everyone was involved in the war effort—and to be aware of possible spies in their midst.

Evaluate and Draw Conclusions How serious does the danger of spying and sabotage appear to be from this poster? What course of action does it suggest citizens take? What techniques does it use to create an impact on the viewer?

Canadians Vote on Conscription

As the war progressed, the Conservative opposition continued to pressure Mackenzie King to bring in conscription. But the prime minister knew that there would be strong resistance to conscription in Québec. As in the First World War, many Québécois did not feel connected to a war in Europe that did not directly affect Canada.

King decided to hold a plebiscite to get Canadians' views on conscription. He used the slogan "Not necessarily conscription, but conscription if necessary" to describe the government's position on the issue. On April 27, 1942, voters were asked whether they would release the government from its promise not to send conscripts overseas. In all provinces but Québec, the majority (over 80 percent) voted "yes." In Québec, over 70 percent voted "no." Once again, the issue of conscription divided the nation.

"Yes" to Conscription

Mackenzie King finally allowed conscription for overseas service by amending the National Resources Mobilization Act in August 1942. Many Québécois felt betrayed by King's actions. There were riots in Montréal to protest King's decision. The Québec legislature passed a motion condemning the federal government's actions.

King managed to avoid the issue of conscription for the next two years. But after heavy Canadian casualties during the campaigns in Italy and northwest Europe, there was a severe shortage of trained infantry. King could no longer avoid the issue and agreed to send conscripts overseas.

In 1944, King conscripted 15 000 men for active service under the NRMA. In the final months of the war, 12 908 NRMA conscripts were sent to Europe. Only 2463 of these Canadian conscripts ever reached the front.

FIGURE 5–40 Cartoon published in the *Montreal Gazette* in 1941

Interpret and Analyze What is the cartoonist's message?

Province	Yes (%)	No (%)
Ontario	84.0	16.0
Prince Edward Island	82.9	17.1
British Columbia	80.4	19.6
Québec	27.9	72.1

FIGURE 5–41 Plebiscite results for selected provinces, 1942

CHECKPOINT

1. What three initiatives did the Canadian government undertake to prevent inflation and pay for the war? How successful were these initiatives?

2. What social changes took place in Canada during the war? What demands were unions making?

3. **Cause and Consequence** What unintended consequences do you think resulted from women being a major part of the war effort?

4. Explain how Mackenzie King managed for five years to avoid sending conscripts overseas. Why did he eventually have to send conscripts overseas?

5. Why was Québec so opposed to conscription? What had changed between 1917 and 1944? How do you think people felt about conscripts? Why?

case study

• What effect did the War Measures Act have on the legal rights of Canadians?

Racism and Japanese Canadians

When war broke out, more than 22 000 Japanese Canadians were living in British Columbia. No evidence indicated that they supported Japan in the war, nor did the government consider these **enemy aliens** a security risk. But anti-Japanese sentiment grew in Canada after the bombing of Pearl Harbor and the invasion of Hong Kong in 1941. In early 1942, the Canadian government caved in to public pressure. For the second time in its history (see Chapter 2), the War Measures Act was invoked. All Japanese Canadians living near the British Columbia coast were "invited" to move to the Okanagan Valley. They would be settled in temporary "relocation centres." In the wake of anti-Japanese marches in Vancouver, about 750 people moved voluntarily. Soon, the government forced all Japanese Canadians, regardless of how long they had lived in Canada, to leave the coast.

Government officials separated families, sending members to different internment camps in the interior of British Columbia where they were held until the end of the war. David Suzuki, a famous Canadian environmentalist and broadcaster, was interned with his sisters and mother when he was six years old, while his father worked at a labour camp. Some families chose to go to Alberta or Manitoba. These locations were farther away, but at least families were allowed to stay together.

The situation worsened in January 1943. Federal government officials, called Custodians of Enemy Property, were given the power to confiscate and sell Japanese Canadians' property. People who had been relocated inland lost everything. Possessions were auctioned off and the owners received almost nothing.

In 1945, the federal government offered Japanese Canadians a choice: they could apply to be sent to Japan, which had been devastated by war, or they could agree to permanently settle east of the Rocky Mountains. Some people challenged Canada's right to deport innocent citizens, but the Supreme Court upheld the government's position. In all, 3964 Japanese Canadians were deported—2000 were Canadian citizens. Thousands of other Japanese Canadians were relocated to other parts of Canada.

In 1947, the government finally cancelled the policy. It was not until 1988 that the federal government apologized for its actions. As compensation, it agreed to pay the people still living who were affected by the policy $21 000 each. It also agreed to restore Canadian citizenship to any person who had been deported to Japan.

Thinking It Through

1. Why were Japanese Canadians relocated and detained during the Second World War?

2. How would posters like Remember Hong Kong (on page 139) contribute to anti-Japanese sentiment?

3. In your opinion, what would be just compensation for Japanese Canadians interned during the war?

4. Canadian veterans who were POWs in Asia were not compensated for being starved or used as slave labour in Japanese factories, even though their mistreatment violated the rules of war. (The Italians and Germans who were interned by the Canadian government were also not compensated.) People often cite the compensation given to Japanese Canadians as a reason why the Canadian government should negotiate with the Japanese for compensation for these veterans. Do you agree with this reasoning? Explain your thinking.

FIGURE 5–42 A Japanese Canadian family awaits relocation in 1942. Many families were separated, with men being interned separately.

Evaluate and Draw Conclusions Why do you think the men were interned separately?

- What was the war's impact on the home front?

KEY TERMS

arsenal of democracy a slogan coined by President Franklin D. Roosevelt in December 1940 promising to help the Allies fight the Germans by providing military supplies while staying out of the actual fighting

war brides foreign women who married Canadian troops serving overseas and then immigrated to Canada after the war

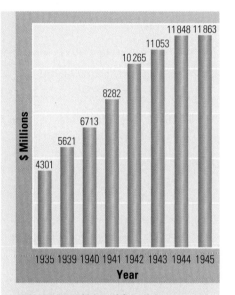

FIGURE 5–43 Value of Canada's gross national product (GNP), 1935–1945. GNP is a measure of the value of all goods and services produced by a nation.

Gather Evidence Why did Canada's GNP increase significantly during the war?

What the War Meant to Canada

The Second World War had many long-lasting economic, social, and political consequences for Canada. As you will read in the next chapter, these consequences ushered in tremendous changes in post-war Canadian society.

Economic Growth

Arsenals supply armies with weapons. In 1940, before the United States entered the war, President Roosevelt called the United States the "**arsenal of democracy**." Roosevelt promised to arm and support the Allies, while staying out of the actual fighting. Canada, as part of the Empire, supplied both soldiers and an arsenal, providing Britain with the weapons and resources it needed to resist Germany from 1939 onwards.

Under its policy of total war, Canada provided major military and economic support to the Allies. The value of goods it produced rose from $5.6 billion in 1939 to $11.8 billion in 1945. During the war, Canada gave the Allies billions of dollars in financial aid.

Virtually every sector of the Canadian economy boomed. There was a rapid increase in the production of aluminum, which was used in the manufacture of aircraft. Wood and paper production rose, as did mining and smelting. There was also a great increase in the demand for petroleum to fuel tanks, trucks, and airplanes. A wave of exploration led to discoveries of new oil fields in Alberta. Many jobs were created in production, transportation, processing, and providing services for the new industries.

The wartime boom brought another important change to the Canadian economy. Agriculture, once the most important sector of Canada's economy, was overtaken by manufacturing. Canadian cities and the industrial areas around them became much more important contributors to the economy after the war. During the period from 1939 to 1949, Canada had transformed itself from a rural economy to a modern industrial nation.

Societal Changes

The Second World War changed Canadian society in several ways. Women were employed in great numbers during the war. Their contribution helped to raise their profile in society and promote their rights as workers. There was a significant wave of immigration as about 48 000 **war brides**—along with approximately 21 000 children—arrived from Europe to join their soldier-husbands after the war. The government encouraged war brides to come to Canada by paying for their trip. Once they arrived, many faced a difficult adjustment as they became members of a new culture and society.

In addition to war brides, thousands of people displaced by the war came to Canada to start a new life. After the war, Canada eventually loosened some of its immigration restrictions to allow more people to come to Canada to meet the growing demand for labour. But, for the most part, Canadian immigration policy remained unchanged. It allowed mainly immigrants from preferred countries in Europe to enter Canada.

Building an Identity

Canada's enormous contribution to the war, in both human and economic terms, gave it a new role on the world stage. Just two decades earlier, Canada had been a colony in the British Empire. By the end of the Second World War, Canada had emerged as a major player in a global conflict, with one of the world's largest navies and fourth-largest Allied air force. Once again, Canadian troops proved themselves on the battlefields, and were recognized for their contribution to the Allied victory. In addition, the efforts of Aboriginal, Asian, and African Canadian soldiers—along with those from other minority groups—during the war helped further civil rights for all Canadians. Although many Canadians were killed, wounded, and captured, the Second World War became a defining event in the development of Canada's identity.

> *But it was a good war for Canada too, because it made us a great nation. I mean... it showed us what we could do. We just weren't a bunch of wheat farmers and Nova Scotia fishermen and lumbermen in B.C. We were a nation. A big and tough and strong nation.*
>
> *—Quoted in Barry Broadfoot, Six War Years, 1974*

- How was Canadian identity strengthened by the war?
- What factors contributed to Canada's emerging autonomy?

Country	Casualties
Canada	42 000
Britain	326 000
France	340 000
Germany	325 000
Soviet Union	8 668 000
Japan	1 506 000
United States	295 000

FIGURE 5–44 Allied and Axis military casualties

Interpret and Analyze Casualty numbers for the Second World War vary widely depending upon their source. Give some possible explanations.

FIGURE 5–45 In May 1946, more than 100 African Canadian veterans attended a welcome home banquet in their honour.

? HISTORICAL INQUIRY

Formulate Questions

Assume the role of a news reporter in Canada during the Second World War. Prepare a list of questions that you would ask a soldier returning home. Prepare to answer a similar set of questions from a classmate.

CHECKPOINT

1. **a)** How did the war end the Depression?

    b) What were the major changes in Canada's economy during this period?

2. In what ways did the war change the social make-up of Canada? In what ways was it unchanged?

3. In your opinion, which branch of the armed forces had the greatest impact on the outcome of the war? Provide evidence from the chapter.

4. Do you agree that "it was a good war"? Explain.

5. **Historical Significance** What were the three most significant ways that the Second World War changed Canada?

CHAPTER FOCUS QUESTION — How did the Second World War impact Canada socially, politically, and economically?

Unlike in the First World War, Canada entered the Second World War as a recognized and independent nation. Even so, ties to Britain were still very strong. After Britain declared war on Germany in September of 1939, Canada almost immediately followed suit. The war put the development of Canadian industry into overdrive. On the home front, women took over many of the jobs formerly done only by men and everyone had to adjust to rationing and the rigours of a war economy. Canadians fought in Hong Kong, Dieppe, Italy, Normandy, and

Holland. The Canadian navy grew enormously during the war, protecting the sea lanes over which the products of Canadian forests, farms, and factories travelled to Britain and Russia to help the war effort. Canadian pilots and crews fought in the Battle of Britain and flew thousands of missions over Europe. The need for more personnel brought back conscription, which again threatened to split the nation. Canada's participation was critical to the war effort and won the nation increased status in the post-war world.

1. Complete the following organizer to show the impact of the Second World War on Canada.

Event	Description	Significance of the Event	Long-lasting Consequences

Knowledge and Understanding

2. Continue the annotated timeline showing steps to Canadian autonomy that you started in Chapter 2. Review the events that are covered in this chapter. Write the name and date of each event on the timeline and explain how the event contributed to Canadian independence.

3. Outline the causes of the Second World War.

4. Describe how the war changed women's roles and how you think this may have changed Canadian society.

5. Explain the significance of each of the following to Canada:

   a) Battle of Hong Kong
   b) Dieppe Raid
   c) Battle of Britain
   d) Battle of Ortona
   e) Battle of the Scheldt
   f) Battle of the Atlantic
   g) D-Day
   h) Liberating the Netherlands

6. The Nazis killed millions of Jewish people in the Holocaust during the Second World War, but their anti-Semitism became official government policy in the 1930s. What position do you think the Canadian government should have taken toward Germany before the war? Might the war have been prevented if other countries had protested? Explain.

7. Find examples in the textbook of divisions within Canada that were exacerbated by the war.

Apply Your Thinking

Historical Significance

8. Use the organizer you created in Question 1. Which three events had the greatest impact on Canada? Provide evidence to support your opinion.

Cause and Consequence

9. Could war have been avoided if Britain, France, and their allies had stood up to Hitler's demands earlier than they did? Why do you think politicians were so ready to appease Germany in 1938? Prepare reasoned arguments for both sides of these questions.

10. During the Second World War, Canada and its allies practised "total war." Explain how this contributed to the Allied victory. How successful would Canada have been if it had participated in the war on a limited basis, such as with the war in Afghanistan?

Communicate

11. Discuss with a partner how the following countries and groups might have viewed Canada at the end of the Second World War. Be prepared to discuss your ideas with the class.

    a) Britain

    b) the Netherlands

    c) United States

    d) Japanese Canadians

    e) Canadian women

HISTORICAL INQUIRY

Evaluate and Draw Conclusions

12. It's December 1945. Organize a conference of surviving representatives of countries that participated in the July 1939 conference (see Historical Inquiry box, page 127). Ask each country's representative to respond to the following:

    • How did World War II change your country and your people?

    • Could the war have been avoided in 1939? How?

    • Will your country join the new United Nations?

    What lessons should countries learn from the failure of the League of Nations to prevent and limit wars?

13. Read the quotations on the bombing of Hiroshima on pages 152–153, keeping in mind that quotations must always be understood in context.

    a) What moral question is raised here?

b) Briefly summarize the arguments presented and rank them by how strong you think they are.

c) Do you think photos of the bombing victims have influenced the use of nuclear weapons? Explain.

d) In your opinion, where does the responsibility for the bombings of Hiroshima and Nagasaki chiefly lie? Explain.

e) Faced with the same factual information as Truman, would you have decided to use the atomic bomb?

Having found the bomb we have used it. We have used it against those who attacked us without warning at Pearl Harbor, against those who have starved and beaten and executed American prisoners of war, against those who have abandoned all pretense of obeying international laws of warfare. We have used it in order to shorten the agony of war, in order to save the lives of thousands and thousands of young Americans.

– U.S. President Harry S. Truman, 1945

FIGURE 5–46 A woman and child who survived the atomic bomb dropped on Nagasaki, Japan, on August 9, 1945. Their faces are burned from the heat of the explosion.

Thinking It Through

Use this study guide to continue synthesizing your learning about Canada's history. Referring back to the focus questions for chapters in this unit will help you review your understanding.

STEP 1 Unpacking Knowledge

List and summarize the important events, persons, and concepts or ideas you learned in Chapters 4 and 5. Pick five events, persons, and concepts from each chapter.

Chapter 4	Chapter 5
Decade of Despair: Canada in the Great Depression	**World on Fire: Canada and World War Two**
Events:	
Persons:	
Concepts:	

STEP 2 Organizing Your Understanding

Historical Significance

Now cull your information by using the categories shown below. For example, make sure the events are not just events, but are "historically significant." Then rank the importance of each event, person, and idea from most important to least important within each section and chapter.

	Chapter 4	Chapter 5
Category of Information	**Decade of Despair: Canada in the Great Depression**	**World on Fire: Canada and World War Two**
Historically significant events		
Influential people		
Ideas and concepts that are of critical importance for the period		

©P

STEP 3   Making Connections

Each chapter in Unit 2 focuses on a world-changing event—the Great Depression in Chapter 4 and World War II in Chapter 5. Create two diagrams or paragraphs, the first describing how the two events are linked and the second showing how and why each event involved Canada.

STEP 4   Applying Your Skills

Historical Perspectives

Evidence

Examine these images of Germans taken during the Depression. The men and women shown were among millions of unemployed in prewar Germany. The car on the next page is homemade; the model Zeppelin was built and displayed by unemployed people scouting for donations.

Is it possible to generalize about life in Germany during the period from these images? How might you use this evidence to make a case for the Depression being a cause of World War II? How was the situation in Germany similar to that in Canada and other countries during this period? How was it different?

▲ **SOURCE 1:** Unemployed young people in Berlin play cards during the Great Depression

◀ **SOURCE 2:** Two unemployed men in Germany drive a homemade car.

▲ **SOURCE 3:** An unemployed German displays a miniature Zeppelin, a German-made airship that had been used extensively, and to great effect, during World War I.

©P

Evidence

Ethical Dimension

The costs of the Canadian war effort had to be borne by the Canadian people through taxation and other methods. The government also raised money by selling Victory Bonds, also called war savings certificates, that paid interest when they matured. The campaign to sell bonds was expensive but millions were sold to the Canadian public.

Answer the following questions about this poster, which features a special Christmas offer to Canadians buying war savings stamps and cerificates.

◀ **SOURCE 4:** Free greeting cards were offered to those buying war savings stamps and certificates.

- What is the explicit (obvious) message of this poster? What is its implicit (implied) message?
- Identify two reasons why this poster was released during the Christmas season.
- Who do you think "Miss Canada" represents? Why might this kind of image be featured on this offer? Do you think such an ad would appear today? Why or why not?

UNIT

3

Canada, 1945–1982

Nuclear tensions and a Cold War during the post-war years saw Canada's role in the world evolve. Attitudes, economy, and national identity were reshaped as Canada struggled to find its place as a neighbour to one of the world's military and economic superpowers—the United States. Canadian society and identity were influenced by renewed questions regarding immigration, multiculturalism, Aboriginal rights, and the role of Québec. In addition, the rise of youth culture changed how Canadian society understood itself and its values.

During the 1950s, Canada experienced a boom in both its economy and population. Cities expanded into suburbs due to post-war immigration and a baby boom. Teenagers embraced new rock'n'roll music.

The Cold War became a reality for Canadians in 1945 when a Soviet spy ring was uncovered in the country. Canada struggled to remain independent of its superpower neighbour, the U.S., during the Cold War years.

During the 1960s and 1970s, the huge youth population engendered a culture of activism and protest that challenged social norms and government policies. A separatist crisis also divided the country.

In 1969, the Liberal government of Pierre Trudeau released the White Paper to address the issues facing Aboriginal people. Harold Cardinal, an Aboriginal Cree leader, rejected it, saying it was nothing more than "a program of assimilation." In the end, the White Paper was shelved. The event became a catalyst for Aboriginal rights advocacy in Canada.

SOUTH AMERICA

ATLANTIC OCEAN

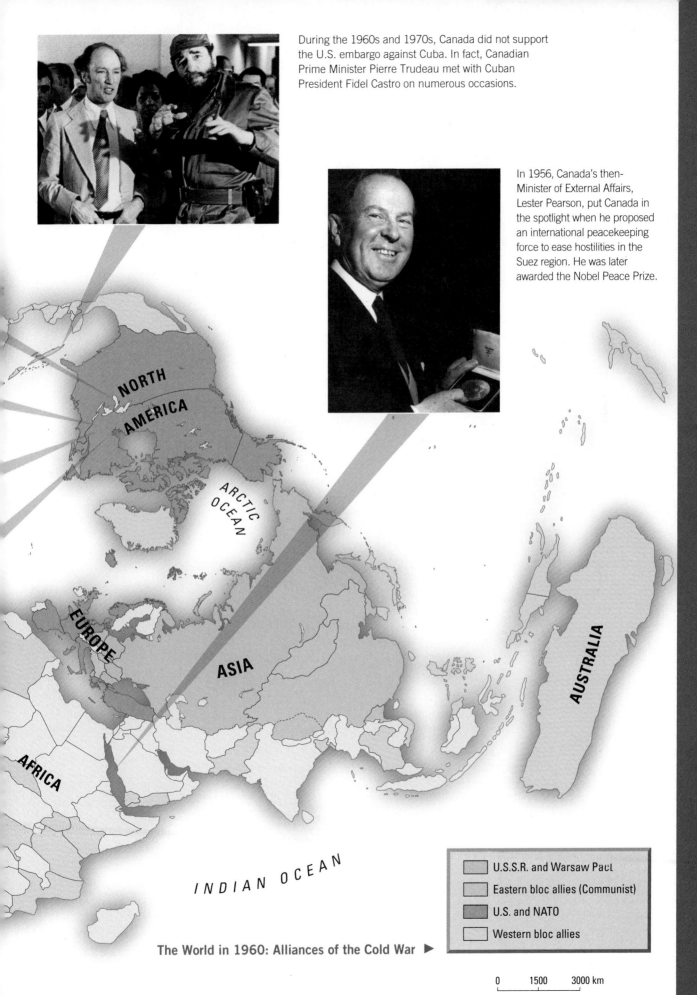

During the 1960s and 1970s, Canada did not support the U.S. embargo against Cuba. In fact, Canadian Prime Minister Pierre Trudeau met with Cuban President Fidel Castro on numerous occasions.

In 1956, Canada's then-Minister of External Affairs, Lester Pearson, put Canada in the spotlight when he proposed an international peacekeeping force to ease hostilities in the Suez region. He was later awarded the Nobel Peace Prize.

NORTH AMERICA

ARCTIC OCEAN

EUROPE

ASIA

AUSTRALIA

AFRICA

INDIAN OCEAN

The World in 1960: Alliances of the Cold War ▶

U.S.S.R. and Warsaw Pact

Eastern bloc allies (Communist)

U.S. and NATO

Western bloc allies

0   1500   3000 km

6

Refining an Identity: Canada in the Post-War Years

? INVESTIGATE

Social, Economic, and Political Context

- How did people improve their working conditions after the Second World War?
- How was the role of women redefined after the Second World War ended?
- What were the characteristics of the post-war economic boom?
- How does industrial development affect the environment?
- What was the impact of American investment on the Canadian economy?

Communities, Conflict, and Cooperation

- In what ways did Canadian society change after the Second World War?
- What was Canada's involvement in the Cold War?
- Describe Canada's involvement in the UN.
- What was Canada's response to conflicts during the late 1940s and the 1950s?

Identity, Citizenship, and Heritage

- What challenges did Aboriginal people face in the 1940s and 1950s?
- How was Quebec nationalism expressed in the 1940s and 1950s?
- What measures has Canada taken to promote a distinct Canadian identity?

Elvis Presley appears at Toronto's Maple Leaf Gardens in 1957.

Evaluate and Draw Conclusions Why would selling out Maple Leaf Gardens be a significant accomplishment in the 1950s? What does this tell you about the influence of American popular culture in Canada? What, if anything, do you think the rock 'n roll revolution of the 1950s had in common with the Roaring Twenties?

TIMELINE

1945
Second World War ends
United Nations created

1947
Immigration of displaced persons from Europe begins
Oil discovered at Leduc, Alberta

1948
Louis St. Laurent becomes prime minister

1949
Newfoundland becomes Canada's 10th province
NATO formed
Communists take over China

1950
Korean War begins

CHAPTER FOCUS QUESTION

How did Canadian political decisions reflect a concern about the growing influence of the United States over Canada?

Evidence
Historical Significance
Ethical Dimension
HISTORICAL THINKING
Continuity and Change
Historical Perspectives
Cause and Consequence

On April 2, 1957, Elvis Presley arrived in Toronto to perform two shows at Maple Leaf Gardens. Although *Toronto Star* reporter Hugh Thomson didn't care much for him—he compared Presley's appeal to that of a "bulldozer in mating season"—he admitted the 22-year-old singer knew how to work an audience.

Following the show, more critics expressed their disapproval. The manager of a major opera company who was visiting Toronto called Presley "vulgar" and "tasteless." He said it was a desperate state of affairs when young people were being brought up on comic books and Elvis. Canadian religious leaders claimed that teens who listened to rock 'n' roll would eventually be forced to admit their music was a "mockery and a sham."

Why might Thomson and many other adults have been so hostile to 1950s teenagers' love affair with rock 'n' roll? How did popular culture in the 1950s reflect a society turning away from the tough times of the war years?

As you will see in this chapter, the 1950s brought new lifestyles, new products, and new values to Canadian society. At the same time, the Canadian economy boomed and consumerism grew in importance—factors that favoured the growth of youth culture. People were also on the move. Cities grew larger and hundreds of new suburbs were developed. Economic growth attracted many new immigrants to Canadian cities. With few environmental protections, industry often polluted the environment without consideration for the long-term consequences of development.

Internationally, Canada sought a middle path, maintaining strong relations with Britain and the Commonwealth and good, but independent, relations with the United States. Carving out an independent foreign policy for Canada was a challenge during the period known as the Cold War, but Canadian governments successfully maintained our independence.

KEY TERMS

Massey Commission
Canada Council for the Arts
Canadian Radio-television and Telecommunications Commission (CRTC)
Cold War
communist
capitalist
superpowers
middle power
North Atlantic Treaty Organization (NATO)
Warsaw Pact
North American Aerospace Defence Command (NORAD)
Distant Early Warning (DEW) Line
United Nations (UN)

? HISTORICAL INQUIRY

Formulate Questions

There are five main headings in this chapter. Individually or in pairs, scan the chapter, make a list of these five headings, and change each of them into a question. Which historical thinking concept do you think will be addressed in each section?

1951	1952	1953	1955	1956	1957
Massey Commission report	First CBC Television broadcast	Canadian government begins to resettle Inuit families in the Arctic	Warsaw Pact formed	Lester Pearson helps to defuse the Suez crisis	John Diefenbaker becomes prime minister

The Changing Face of Canada

The end of the Second World War marked the beginning of a population boom in Canada. Those who had postponed marriage because of the war began to start families. Generally, families were larger than they are today—three or four children was the average. In all, 6.7 million children were born in Canada between 1946 and 1961, making up almost one third of the population. The increase in the birth rate that took place in Canada as well as Australia and the United States became known as the **baby boom**. For a time Canada's birth rate was the highest in the industrial world, peaking in 1959. The baby boom among the First Nations population also peaked in the late 1950s. In addition, post-war immigration brought thousands of new Canadians into the country—people eager to take part in the prosperity of the post-war years.

Post-War Immigration

From 1905, when Clifford Sifton's "open-door policy" ended, up until the 1960s, Canada had a somewhat restrictive **immigration policy**. Immigrants of British and European origin, especially northern Europeans, were preferred because it was thought that they would adapt the most easily to the Canadian way of life. Immigrants of other origins did arrive, but the government limited their numbers. After the Second World War, nearly 1 million veterans returned to Canada. Not all of them came home alone: many Canadian bachelors serving overseas married there.

War brides formed just part of the wave of immigrants that arrived in Canada after the Second World War. Millions of refugees were stuck in camps across Europe at the end of the war. They included concentration camp survivors and others uprooted by the war. Canada accepted 165 000 such **displaced persons**, settling them in communities across the country.

FIGURE 6–1 Most war brides were British, although some came from France and the Netherlands.

Gather Evidence What challenges do you think these women might have faced in their new homeland?

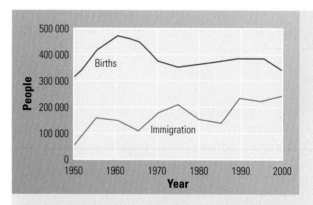
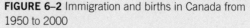

FIGURE 6–2 Immigration and births in Canada from 1950 to 2000

Interpret and Analyze What trends in birth and immigration rates can you see on this graph? To what extent do they match up? What might account for this?

Other immigrants were attracted by new possibilities in Canada and wanted to escape war-torn Europe. Unable to practise their former trades or professions in Canada, some of these newcomers had a hard time. Nevertheless, refugee children absorbed English quickly at school, and their parents found that a job, any job, opened up new opportunities. More than 2 million immigrants arrived between 1945 and 1960.

Unlike immigrants before the First World War, who had settled largely on farms in Western Canada, post–Second World War immigrants usually settled in the cities of Central Canada where their cultures and hard work enriched Canada in many ways. Older areas of larger cities, vacated as veterans and their families moved to the suburbs, became home to vibrant new communities.

In 1956 when a violent revolution broke out in Hungary, federal and provincial governments relaxed entry requirements in order to allow Hungarians wanting to escape communism to immigrate to Canada. More than 37 000 Hungarians came to Canada. Many Czechs and Slovaks came to Canada from Czechoslovakia in 1968–1969 under similar circumstances. (You will read about communism in eastern Europe later in this chapter.)

HISTORICAL INQUIRY

Communicate

How much did Canada's population grow between 1945 and 1960? How important was the baby boom and immigration to this growth? Research the statistics and create a bar graph to illustrate the growth of each group. Share and compare your graph with a classmate.

The Rise of the Suburbs

After the war, developers began building thousands of new homes for Canada's growing population. Many were in the outlying areas of cities, the suburbs, where land was less expensive. Cheap land encouraged low-density building: big houses on large lots with lawns, patios, even swimming pools. In time, suburban subdivisions became "bedroom communities" with their own schools, parks, and churches. Commuters travelled to work in the cities and returned home to the suburbs at the end of the day.

Increased economic development supported suburban life. Both business and manufacturing were booming and fewer than six percent of Canadians were unemployed throughout the 1950s. It was also a time of tremendous technological innovation, as you will see later in the chapter.

The Age of the Automobile

In the 1950s, Canadians fell in love with cars and bought 3.5 million of them. Automobile culture changed Canada's neighbourhoods. For people living in the suburbs, a car was a great convenience. Although suburban houses were often plain and functional, cars grew steadily fancier with lots of chrome, fins, and fancy tail lights.

The automobile represented all the elements of the post-war era: fascination with technology, progress, and personal freedom. Few thought of the downside costs. Enormous V8 engines needed lots of fuel, which increased society's dependence on oil. Atmospheric pollution, in the form of smog, also became a problem.

FIGURE 6–3 Throughout the 1950s, cars were made longer, lower, and wider than previous models. Every fall, manufacturers unveiled new models with eye-catching improvements.

Historical Significance What does this design suggest about the importance of the automobile at this time?

Women in the Fifties

Suburban life was centred on the traditional middle-class family, with a stay-at-home mother at its heart. The father's role was to be the breadwinner, supporting the family on his earnings. Popular women's magazines denounced working mothers as the cause of delinquent children. This was a far cry from the propaganda during the war that had urged women to work outside the home.

Fashions of the day emphasized femininity: long, full skirts; narrow waists; and high heels. New gadgets such as electric floor polishers, pop-up toasters, and electric food mixers promised to make housework seem less like drudgery. Women were encouraged to beautify themselves and their homes by consuming new products.

Many women came to resent suburban life. They felt isolated and trapped in a role that did not allow them to develop their potential. By the mid-1960s, many women were looking for a different way of life.

FIGURE 6–4 Not all women in the 1950s lived the suburban dream. Many urban women, particularly immigrants, worked in low-paying factory jobs or as domestic help.

Gather and Organize Compare the situation of women in the 1950s with that of women you know today.

The Birth of Teen Culture

Because the "boomer" generation is the largest age group in Canada, it influenced Canadian culture and the economy for decades to come. Boy Scouts, Girl Guides, and other youth organizations flourished, as did minor sports. Governments built thousands of new schools, arenas, and playgrounds to accommodate the needs of "boomers." Manufacturers developed and made new products for the baby-boomer market.

Baby boomers spent more time in school than earlier generations. Before the war, the average Canadian child received only eight years of schooling and only one in ten students finished high school. For the boomer generation there were no wars or economic hardships to force students out of school and into the adult world. The result was the invention of the "teenager." Rock 'n' roll, a musical style developed in the mid-1950s, soon became the favourite of many teenagers. The roots of rock 'n' roll were in African-American music—gospel, blues, and rhythm and blues (R & B). Legendary performers B. B. King, Bo Diddly, and Chuck Berry (sometimes called the originator of rock 'n' roll) were musical influences on Elvis and countless others.

In Canada, Paul Anka of Ottawa, Ontario created a series of smash hits including his first, "Diana," as well as "Lonely Boy" and "Put Your Head on My Shoulder." Anka's sound was more pop than rock, but his records sold millions of copies. Folk music also gained popularity, mostly because of American folk stars Pete Seeger and Woodie Guthrie. In Canada, the Travellers folk group formed during the summer of 1953, eventually signing a record deal with Columbia Records of Canada. Folk music would later go on to be an important part of the '60s protest movements (see pages 206–207).

FIGURE 6–5 Canadian singer and composer Paul Anka, shown here in his twenties, went on to have a long career in music and acting. Anka also collaborated with Michael Jackson on the 2009 hit "This Is It."

FIGURE 6–6 With lots of leisure time and money to spend from part-time jobs, teenagers in the 1950s developed a new sense of independence and group identity.

Gather Evidence What hair and clothing styles that you identify with the 1950s do you see in this photograph?

Television and the Consumer Society

In the early 1950s, a television set cost about 20 percent of an average annual income. Neighbours and relatives would gather to watch at the homes of those lucky enough to own a set. But television quickly became something of a necessity, especially for families with children. The first shows were in black and white; colour TV did not come to Canada until 1966. And what were Canadians watching? American programs topped the list. The kids tuned in to *Howdy Doody, Roy Rogers, Lassie,* and *The Mickey Mouse Club.* Families came together to watch game shows, comedies, Westerns, and variety shows like *The Ed Sullivan Show,* a Sunday night institution that featured everything from comedy, classical music, and circus acts to teen pop stars.

The scrimping and saving of the 1930s and the rationing of the war years were now left far behind. The advertisers that sponsored television shows were sending the powerful and appealing message that consumption was the road to happiness. They were selling the good life: bigger cars, more household appliances, new "improved" products. TV also encouraged youngsters to become consumers, introducing them to sweetened cereals, Barbie dolls, and Davy Crockett hats. Advertising was one of the biggest areas of economic growth during the decade—with companies doubling their spending to $11.9 billion by 1960 in the United States.

GO ONLINE

Find pictures and descriptions of consumerist technologies, such as the television, using the Canada Science and Technology Museum's website.

FIGURE 6–7 Television shaped the values of the time. American shows promoted the ideal of a traditional, wholesome, family-centred lifestyle.

Historical Perspectives To learn about the values and attitudes of the fictional characters in this photo, what questions would you ask?

CHECKPOINT

1. How did the automobile culture change neighbourhoods? What businesses developed because of the automobile culture?

2. Describe the roles of women and men in the 1950s. Discuss reasons why you think many accepted these roles.

3. What effect did television have on many people's buying habits in the post-war period?

4. **Continuity and Change** How would being a teenager in the 1950s be similar to and different from being a teenager today?

The age of the consumer really began in the 1950s. The economy was prospering and Canadians were able to buy the new gadgets and inventions that were introduced into the marketplace during this period.

Advertisements were an important part of this process. They created powerful messages to make people want to buy things that would make their lives better, easier, and more glamorous.

Some people would argue that advertisements are, in fact, a form of propaganda. Both advertisements and propaganda try to influence people's emotions in order to make them think and act in certain ways. During the First and Second World Wars the Canadian government used propaganda posters to create support for the war across the country and to encourage people to purchase war bonds. After the war, advertisers continued to use similar techniques to create a need for the products and lifestyle they were selling.

Here are some questions to consider when you are looking at advertisements and propaganda.

1. What product or viewpoint is being sold?

2. What mood is created and why?

3. Does the written material provide information or is it there to generate an emotional response?

4. If people are shown, what are they like?

5. What social attitudes are reflected?

Interpret and Analyze Evidence

1. How do the poster and the advertisement appeal to the viewer's emotions?

2. Evaluate how effectively these two images deliver their messages. Explain.

3. Compare the way women are portrayed in the advertisement and the propaganda poster. Does the portrayal of women differ today? Explain how.

FIGURE 6–8 What message does this propaganda poster convey?

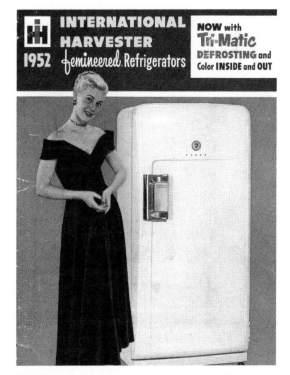

FIGURE 6–9 This advertisement is not only selling a brand of refrigerators, but it is also selling a lifestyle. Why might women find this ad appealing?

Massey Commission a body set up by the federal government to study the state of Canadian culture

Canada Council for the Arts the group that funds Canadian artists and supports the arts in Canada

Canadian Radio-television and Telecommunications Commission (CRTC) the agency that regulates the amount of foreign material broadcast over the airwaves in Canada and imposes rules requiring Canadian content

Protecting Canadian Culture: The Massey Commission

Television was a powerful cultural influence. Many Canadians saw world events unfolding through an American lens as they watched popular newscasts from the United States. Children of the 1950s grew up identifying more with American culture and values than any generation before them. In 1949, the Liberal government of Louis St. Laurent established the **Massey Commission** to investigate the state of Canadian culture. When the Commission reported in 1951, it suggested that Canadian culture needed to be protected from U.S. influences. Measures taken as a result of its recommendations included the following:

- Canadian television would be used to promote national communication and for cultural education in drama and music. The CBC, which already had a national radio network, was put in charge of the development of television. It opened its first two stations in Toronto and Montréal in 1952. Two years later, four more cities were added. By 1960, 90 percent of Canadian homes had a television and access to the CBC.

- The National Film Board (NFB) would be strengthened.

- The government would become involved in funding universities and the arts. Consequently the **Canada Council for the Arts** was created, which awarded grants to writers, artists, and theatres.

What If...

Imagine that measures had never been put in place to protect Canadian culture. To what extent do you think that Canadians' choices in the books they read, the music they listen to, and the movies and television shows they watch would be different today? Give examples from your own experience to support your answer.

Another important step in the protection of Canadian culture was the creation of the **Canadian Radio-television and Telecommunications Commission (CRTC)** in 1968. This agency would regulate the amount of foreign material broadcast over the airwaves and impose rules requiring Canadian content.

Each of these measures encouraged the growth of arts and culture in Canada and had profound consequences for Canadian identity in the post-war years.

FIGURE 6–10 The National Ballet of Canada was established in 1957. This photograph shows Canadian ballet stars David Adams and Lois Smith in a 1950s National Ballet of Canada production of *Swan Lake*.

TIMELINE	Protecting Canadian Culture					
1936	**1939**	**1951**	**1952**	**1957**		**1968**
CBC Radio begins broadcasting	National Film Board established	Massey Commission report	CBC Television begins broadcasting	Canada Council for the Arts established		CRTC formed

Aboriginal Communities in Transition

The post-war years were times of transition for Aboriginal communities. Those who had served in the military during the war—3000 status Indians and thousands more non-status Aboriginal people and Métis out of a total population of 166 000—still faced institutionalized racism and other barriers when they returned home. Aboriginal soldiers were denied the same benefits as other veterans.

Education Issues

Education was always a concern for Aboriginal people. For many decades, Aboriginal children were forced to leave home to attend residential schools. Here they were isolated from their home communities and families and forced to abandon their culture and language. The purpose of the schools was the assimilation of Aboriginal children into mainstream Canadian culture.

Although compulsory attendance in residential schools ended in 1948, many remained in operation during the 1940s and 1950s. In fact, as a result of the baby boom, the 1950s were peak years in the residential school system—with 76 schools in operation. The last residential school did not close until 1996. Residential schools were underfunded and relied on the forced labour of their students. Students in many facilities received a poor education.

In response to the demands of Aboriginal parents, the federal government began to fund off-reserve education. By 1960, thousands of Aboriginal youth were attending provincial schools with certified teachers and modern equipment. However, teachers were often not trained to meet the needs of Aboriginal students. This, and the fact that many students had to commute long distances by bus or board far from home, worked against their academic success.

Changes to the Indian Act

In 1951, a number of changes were made to the Indian Act that governed the lives of First Nations peoples. Women gained the right to vote in band elections, and potlatches and wearing traditional regalia were no longer illegal. However, the Indian Act maintained the federal government's power to define Indian status and band membership and continued to control the political and economic lives of Aboriginal people.

> • What challenges did Aboriginal people face in the 1950s?

> *Broadly speaking, the residential school system attempted to eradicate the culture of generations of Aboriginal people, a practice identified in the United Nations Declaration on the Rights of Indigenous Peoples as cultural genocide.*
> *—Beverly Jacobs and Andrea J. Williams, in From Truth to Reconciliation: Transforming the Legacy of Residential Schools, 2008*

GO ONLINE • • • • • • • • • • •

First-hand accounts of the residential school experience can be found in *They Came for the Children*, published by the Truth and Reconciliation Commission.

FIGURE 6–11 A class of First Nations students at a residential school

Interpret and Analyze How does this photograph illustrate the role of residential schools in assimilating Aboriginal children into mainstream Canadian culture?

CHECKPOINT

1. Make a web diagram showing social changes in Canada after WWII. Include and show their relationships for the following: war brides, immigration, the baby boom, suburbs, youth culture, and Aboriginal communities.

2. What is the role of the CRTC? Do any media threaten Canadian identity today? Explain.

3. The Canadian government's ability to define Aboriginal status has been called "paternalistic." Do you agree or disagree with this statement? Explain your response.

The High Arctic Relocation

FIGURE 6–12 The Inuit community of Qausuittuq (Resolute) in 1956. It was formerly in the Northwest Territories and is now part of Nunavut.

FIGURE 6–13 The new territory of Nunavut was created in 1999.

> *My mind went into shock when I heard the fear in my father's voice. I remember he said, "I don't know how we are going to survive here." We were put in an area where there was nothing but rock. It was such a desolate land. There was no place to seek warm shelter, or fetch water or hunt.*
>
> *–Lizzie Amagoalik, relocated to Resolute Bay in 1955*

GO ONLINE

Visit the Nunavut Tunngavik website to read more first-hand accounts of the High Arctic relocation experience.

Governments have sometimes relocated indigenous peoples with little consideration of their needs and rights. The resettlement in 1953–1955 of Inuit families to the High Arctic almost 2000 kilometres away from their former homes was such a case.

In the summer of 1953, the Canadian government relocated several Inuit families from Inukjuak (formerly known as Port Harrison) in northern Québec and Pond Inlet in Nunavut (formerly the Northwest Territories) to Grise Fjord and Resolute Bay. A second group of families was moved from Inukjuak two years later.

The families volunteered for the move because hunting in their area was poor, but they were not told about conditions in the Arctic or about how difficult it would be to return to Québec if they wished to do so. Families were dropped off without firewood or housing at the onset of the Arctic's four-month winter darkness. Survivors today still talk about their struggles: hunger, defending themselves from polar bears, and living in igloos until they could get wood to build houses.

In the 1980s, a suit was initiated against the federal government arguing that the relocation was done to assert Canadian sovereignty in the Far North rather than to benefit the Inuit. The Arctic had become strategically important for defence during the Cold War. (You will read about the Cold War later in this chapter.)

In 1989, the federal government created a program to help those relocated (and their descendants) who wished to return south. In 1996, the government gave cash compensation to the survivors, and in 2010, an official apology was offered for the "mistakes and broken promises of this dark chapter of our history."

Thinking It Through

1. Look up the term "paternalism." Was government action in the High Arctic relocation program paternalistic? Explain.

2. Would a relocation program such as this one be possible today? Explain.

©P

New Times, New Leadership

Canada's leadership changed little during the early post-war years. Mackenzie King, who had guided the country through the war, retired and his successor, Louis St. Laurent, pursued very similar policies. The Liberals were finally put out of office when the Progressive Conservatives formed a minority government headed by John Diefenbaker in 1957. Diefenbaker called a snap election in 1958 and won the largest majority government in Canadian history.

- What measures has Canada taken to promote a distinct Canadian identity?

The Changing Face of Federal Politics

When Mackenzie King retired in 1948 at the age of 73, he had been in power longer than any Canadian prime minister before him. He was succeeded by Louis St. Laurent as a new age of politics was born. King had governed in the days before television. Today's television commentators would probably have focused on his personal life or pompous speeches, but during his years in power such things were not considered important. By the early 1950s, however, the media was playing a much larger role in Canadian life.

St. Laurent entered politics late in life and during the 1949 election campaign, the Liberal Party election organizers worried about how they could sell this rather shy, reserved, elderly man to the Canadian public. Then, during a campaign stop at a railway station, a reporter noticed St. Laurent, who was a father of five and grandfather of twelve, chatting with a group of children. Newspapers soon began referring to St. Laurent as "Uncle Louis." The media thus created the image of St. Laurent as a kindly relative. The Liberal advertising agency made sure the nickname stuck. From that time on, the media has played an influential part in Canadian politics.

Louis St. Laurent and Canadian Autonomy

Louis St. Laurent was born in Compton, Québec, to an English-speaking mother and a French-speaking father. He was nearing retirement after a successful law career when he was approached by Mackenzie King to become Minister of Justice in his government. St. Laurent was elected to the Commons in 1942 and provided key support to King during the conscription crisis of the Second World War. When King retired, St. Laurent seemed to be the right man to take over as prime minister.

St. Laurent led a progressive government that expanded federal social welfare programs, such as old-age pensions and family allowances. He also brought in hospital insurance, another important step on Canada's road to universal health care. His other major domestic contributions were in the areas of protecting Canadian culture (see page 178) and gaining Canada more autonomy from Britain. Measures St. Laurent took as prime minister to increase Canadian autonomy included

- appointing the first Canadian-born Governor General, Vincent Massey

FIGURE 6–14 St. Laurent on the campaign trail

Interpret and Analyze What impression does this photograph give of St. Laurent? What elements in the photograph suggest that it was carefully posed? How does this photo reinforce his campaign nickname, "Uncle Louis"?

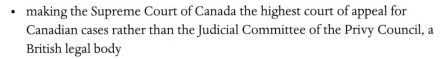

- making the Supreme Court of Canada the highest court of appeal for Canadian cases rather than the Judicial Committee of the Privy Council, a British legal body

- negotiating with Britain to give the Canadian Parliament the power to amend portions of its own constitution without appealing to the British Parliament. This resulted in the British North America (No. 2) Act, 1949

St. Laurent also played a leading role in Canadian post-war peace and defence initiatives, as you will see later in the chapter.

John Diefenbaker

Louis St. Laurent fought and won election campaigns in 1949 and 1953. When the next election rolled around in 1957, the 75-year-old St. Laurent was looking tired and depressed. By comparison, the new Progressive Conservative leader, John Diefenbaker, seemed energetic. Used to public speaking as a defence attorney in Saskatchewan, "Dief" proved to be a great campaigner and a witty orator. Television carried his image across the nation, and he led his party to a narrow election victory. Diefenbaker was the first Westerner to become prime minister. St. Laurent resigned and the defeated Liberals chose a new leader, the diplomat Lester "Mike" Pearson.

Of German extraction, Diefenbaker was the first Canadian prime minister whose father was of neither English nor French background. He saw himself as a Prairie **populist**, one who spoke for and listened to ordinary people. Ordinary people, in turn, responded to him. A colleague recalled the 1958 campaign: "I saw people kneel and kiss his coat. Not one, but many. People were in tears. People were delirious."

Newfoundland Joins the Confederation

Prime Minister St. Laurent was part of the negotiations that resulted in Newfoundland joining Canada. The process of expanding Canada from sea to sea had been set in motion by Prime Minister King at the end of the Second World War. Until 1932, Newfoundland had been an independent, self-governing dominion within the British Empire. During the Depression, however, the island had suffered so badly that its government had gone bankrupt. Democracy was temporarily suspended and Britain set up a special commission to govern Newfoundland.

In 1948, the islanders were given the opportunity to vote on their political future in a **referendum**. They were offered three options: to continue to be governed by special commission, to be a self-governing dominion within the British Empire, or to join Canada. J.R. "Joey" Smallwood, a skillful Newfoundland politician, argued that union with Canada would bring modernization to the province. Yet, many Newfoundlanders believed the benefits could not make up for the higher taxes and loss of identity that Confederation would bring. Some preferred economic union with the United States.

FIGURE 6–15 Governor General Vincent Massey shakes hands with the newly re-elected Prime Minister John Diefenbaker on May 12, 1958.

In a referendum in June 1948, only 41 percent of Newfoundlanders favoured Confederation. A larger number, 44.6 percent, voted in favour of returning to the self-governing dominion status, while 14 percent preferred government by commission. As no option won a clear majority, another vote was scheduled for late July. This time, the commission option was dropped, and the Confederation option won 52 percent of the vote.

The Terms of Union were negotiated with the federal government under Prime Minister St. Laurent, and on March 31, 1949, Newfoundland became part of Canada. That same year, Joey Smallwood was elected premier of the new province, a job he held for more than two decades.

Resettlement in Newfoundland

Newfoundlanders had joined Canada in the hope that Confederation would bring better health care, education, and employment opportunities. It was difficult, however, to provide these services in Newfoundland's outports—isolated fishing settlements connected to the outside world only by occasional ferry service. In 1954, the provincial government introduced a "centralization" program that offered compensation to people who wanted to move to larger centres. Families were paid an average of $301, which is about $2430 in today's dollars. By 1959, about 2400 people from 29 communities had been resettled. Unfortunately, prosperity did not follow relocation. In fact, Newfoundland's unemployment rate climbed. The social impact of losing homes, traditions, and a unique way of life in the outports could not be measured. Some Newfoundlanders still feel grief and resentment over the resettlement.

KEY TERMS

populist someone who appeals to the concerns of ordinary citizens

referendum the process of referring a political question to the people for a direct vote

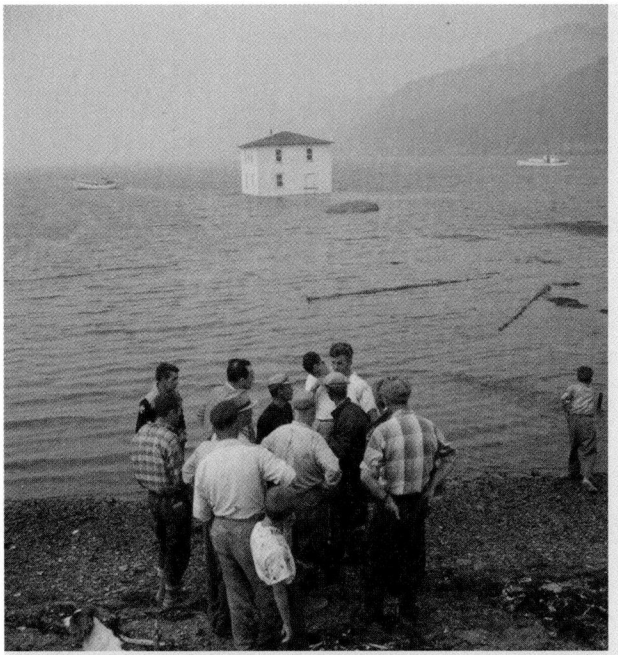

FIGURE 6–16 Resettlement continued in Newfoundland throughout the 1960s and into the 1970s. This house was towed from Silver Fox Island, Bonavista Bay, to its new location in Dover, Newfoundland.

Interpret and Analyze How does the resettlement in Newfoundland show the tensions that sometimes exist between progress on the one hand, and cultural and lifestyle traditions on the other?

Duplessis and the Roots of Québec Nationalism

- How was Québec nationalism expressed in the 1940s and 1950s?

From 1936 to 1939, and again from 1944 to 1959, Québec was controlled by Premier Maurice Duplessis and his party, the Union Nationale. Duplessis was a strong Québec nationalist who promoted the idea of Québec as a distinctive society, a "nation" rather than just another Canadian province. To emphasize his province's difference from English-speaking Canada, Duplessis introduced a new flag for Québec bearing the French symbol, the fleur-de-lys. He fiercely opposed the growing powers of the federal government in the post-war years.

Under Duplessis, the Roman Catholic Church was the main defender of Québec culture. Priests urged people in Québec to turn their backs on the materialism of English-speaking North America. The Church praised the old Québec traditions of farm, faith, and family. It ran Québec's hospitals and schools. Religion played a role in every part of the curriculum, and the schools taught children to accept authority. The elite few who attended high school and university received a fine education, but the emphasis was on traditional

FIGURE 6–17 Conditions at the American plants were often poor. Workers at the American-owned Johns-Manville asbestos plant in Québec walked off the job in February 1949 to protest unsafe working conditions and poor pay. Duplessis was determined to break the strikes and encouraged police to shoot at workers. In the end, workers achieved a 10-cent raise but discontent about foreign-owned companies in Québec could not be stopped.

subjects such as classical languages and philosophy. As a result, Québec produced many priests, lawyers, and politicians, but few scientists, engineers, or business people.

While Duplessis tried to keep out the influence of foreign culture, he encouraged foreign investment in Québec. The province guaranteed cheap labour, since union activity was either discouraged or banned. It also promised low taxes. Québec would benefit from the new investment, but so would Duplessis. In return for favourable business conditions, companies were expected to contribute generously to the Union Nationale.

Bribery and corruption became the trademarks of the Duplessis regime. One of the worst cases was that of the "Duplessis Orphans." Thousands of children housed in orphanages financed by the province were falsely certified as mentally ill and moved into insane asylums, which were funded by the federal government. For many Québécois, the Duplessis era is *La Grande Noirceur*, the Great Darkness.

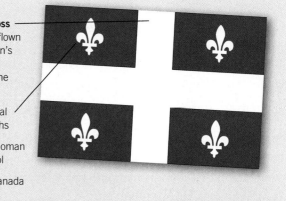

blue flag with white cross (left) the flag of France flown by Samuel de Champlain's ship as it sailed up the St. Lawrence River for the first time in 1603

fleur-de-lys used on royal seals of French monarchs

sacred heart of Jesus Roman Catholic religious symbol

maple leaf symbol of Canada

FIGURE 6–18 The present-day provincial flag of Québec (right) was adopted in 1948. Compare it to the previous Carillon Sacré-Coeur flag.

Interpret and Analyze What might account for the differences in the symbols on the two flags?

CHECKPOINT

1. **a)** Why was Confederation so hotly debated in Newfoundland in 1949?

   b) Only 52 percent of Newfoundlanders voted to join Canada. Do you think this was enough of a margin to warrant such a huge political change? Should it have been necessary for a greater percentage to support the change? Give reasons for your view.

2. **a)** Explain how the media was important in creating the image of politicians in this period.

   b) How is the current prime minister presented in the media? Use pictures from different sources to compare the images created. Include editorial cartoons.

3. Create a web diagram summarizing Québec society and politics under Maurice Duplessis.

Post-War Prosperity

• What were the characteristics of the post-war economic boom?

The Second World War had transformed Canadian industry and society. As the war ended, the government needed to find ways to ease the transition from a wartime to a peacetime economy. But planning for peace was complicated—a million people who had worked in war-production industries and close to half a million in the armed services were about to lose their jobs.

Veterans returning to Canada were eager to come home but anxious about the future. Would they find jobs? Many had enlisted in the armed forces right out of high school or had been unemployed during the Depression. However, new laws ensured that they got their old jobs back if they wanted them and that the years they had been at war were counted as years of service on the job. Government policy encouraged women to leave factories to make room for men, which freed up many jobs. Veterans who wished to attend university or trade school received free tuition and living allowances. Veterans and war widows got preference for government jobs. The Veterans' Land Act gave veterans mortgages at lower rates. These government interventions saved Canada from economic recession.

Spreading the Wealth

As a wartime measure, the provinces had transferred their economic powers to the federal government. Prime Minister Mackenzie King wanted this to become permanent, but provinces were not willing to give up a power conferred on them at Confederation. In the end, the provinces gave in and transferred taxation powers to the federal government. In return, they received government grants for social services such as health care and education. Through equalization or transfer payments, the federal government would then transfer money to the poorer provinces.

Meanwhile, C.D. Howe, Minister of Reconstruction, Trade, and Commerce, gave economic incentives such as generous tax breaks to private industry. Soon, factories were producing washing machines, automobiles, and other items that were in demand, and Canada's economy was booming.

FIGURE 6–19 A 1943 National Film Board poster promoting the "Canada Carries On" series. These films documented Canada's war involvement and sought to inform viewers that the war would bring prosperity to Canada.

Cause and Consequence

C.D. Howe was one of Canada's most influential politicians in the post-war period. When the Depression forced him to close his engineering business in 1935, he entered politics as a Liberal MP. Howe rose quickly in government. During the war, he ran the country's economy, and after it he manoeuvred the provinces into giving the federal government more control.

In two decades as a Cabinet minister, Howe was responsible at one time or another for railways, canals, airlines, munitions, war supplies, transition to peacetime, pipelines, trade, and commerce. He was, people said, the "Minister of Everything."

Howe admired the efficiency of the American economy and was impatient with debates over economic issues in Canada's House of Commons. Howe's short temper and determination to force his plans through eventually made him unpopular.

FIGURE 6–20 Howe (second from left) with Winston Churchill and W.L. Mackenzie King, 1944

KEY TERMS

boom town a town that enjoys sudden prosperity or develops quickly

boom-and-bust cycle a term used to describe a healthy (booming) economy and/or one that is failing (bust)

Rich Resources and New Industries

Traditional industries such as mining and forestry remained at the heart of the Canadian economy. Massive development of mines, forests, smelters, and the like encouraged the economic boom of the post-war period. One of the most important developments was the discovery of oil at Leduc, Alberta, in 1947. It was Canada's entry into the international oil market.

Wherever new mines and wells developed, resource companies carved **boom towns** in the wilderness, sometimes airlifting in heavy equipment, construction material, and other supplies. Employees lived in tents, trailers, and temporary shanties often far from the nearest town or city. Although they were very well paid, many workers—mostly single men—were starved for distractions. Gambling and alcoholism were chronic problems.

While resource industries developed in frontier areas, manufacturing in southern Ontario grew tremendously. By the 1950s, more than half of the nation's factories and plants and 99 percent of its automobile industry were located in Ontario, close to transportation routes and markets.

In later decades, when resource industries in other parts of the country were in the "bust" part of the **boom-and-bust cycle**, Ontario did well. Those in other provinces deeply resented Ontario's seemingly privileged position and its apparent immunity from economic downturns.

FIGURE 6–21 Sudbury, Ontario, became a centre for nickel mining.

Innovations
1950s Technology

Even a famous science fiction writer could not have guessed how much technology would transform life in the decades after the Second World War. H.G. Wells, author of books such as *The Time Machine* (1895) and *The Shape of Things to Come* (1933), predicted that by 1950 soldiers would wage war from bicycles and drop bombs from balloons. In reality, the atomic bomb had demonstrated the awesome power of science. It was soon replaced by the even more powerful hydrogen bomb. While military technology was developing rapidly, everyday life, too, was being changed by new inventions.

Ballpoint pen After the war, manufacturers competed to produce the first reliable ballpoint pens.

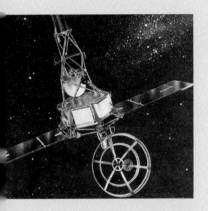

Satellite The Russians launched the first artificial satellite, Sputnik, in 1957, with the Americans following in 1958. The space race had begun. Today, artificial satellites are used in weather forecasting, television transmission, and supplying navigation data for aircraft and ships. They are also used for military purposes such as surveillance and tracking missile launches.

Television transformed the way Canadians entertained and educated themselves. TV exposure could make or break political careers and start social movements.

Heart pacemaker Technology transformed medicine. In 1957, the first wearable heart pacemaker and artificial heart valves extended the lives of people who, just years before, would not have survived.

Transistor radio In 1948, Bell Telephone announced the invention of the transistor, an electronic device for amplifying and switching that is durable, small, and inexpensive. In 1955, Sony Corporation sold the first transistor radios, and over the next decades the radios grew smaller and more portable. Radio, which was predicted to die out in the age of TV, was revived, as teens could now take their music with them wherever they went.

Vinyl was invented by the chemist who also discovered bubble gum. This new synthetic product allowed for the invention of many new products in the years after the Second World War. Fire-resistant, waterproof, flexible, and cheap, it was used to make a host of items including long-playing records, convertible automobile roofs, and garden hoses.

- How does industrial development affect the environment?

KEY TERM

megaprojects large-scale construction projects that require a huge capital investment; the construction of the St. Lawrence Seaway is an example

FIGURE 6–22 Trans-Canada Highway in Northern Ontario

- What was the impact of American investment on the Canadian economy?

Giant Projects for a Giant Land

As towns across Canada grew, governments improved infrastructure—roads, sewer systems, power plants, schools, and hospitals—using taxes from business and workers in the booming economy. The money paid out to construction companies created more jobs and stimulated the economy as workers spent their wages. The federal government under Louis St. Laurent undertook **megaprojects** that changed the Canadian landscape.

Few people realized at the time that many projects and industrial processes had hidden costs. The greatest of these was pollution. Solid industrial wastes were simply buried, creating toxic landfills on which housing, schools, and playgrounds were sometimes constructed. Pulp and paper and petrochemical plants dumped wastes directly into streams, contaminating lakes and rivers. Industry simply wanted high productivity and low costs.

Trans-Canada Highway	• construction began in 1950 to upgrade and pave roads along the Trans-Canada Route
	• 7821-kilometre road from St. John's, Newfoundland, to Victoria, British Columbia; would be the longest national highway in the world
Trans-Canada Pipeline	• natural gas pipeline completed in 1958 to carry gas east from Alberta all the way to Québec
St. Lawrence Seaway	• system of locks that would allow large ships from the Atlantic to travel all the way to Lake Superior
	• built cooperatively by Canada and United States between 1954 and 1959
	• grain for export could be loaded directly onto ships; business increased in inland ports; hydro plants developed at dam sites

American Investment: A Continuing Issue

In 1945 President Franklin Roosevelt and Prime Minister Mackenzie King discussed economic cooperation between their two countries. King described it to Parliament this way: "It involves nothing less than a common plan [for] the economic defence of the western hemisphere." But Canadians wondered if Canada was becoming the "49th state."

The United States, like Canada, had a booming economy in the post-war years. When it began to run short of raw materials, it looked to Canada as a vast storehouse of minerals and other natural resources. Canadians, for their part, recognized that they needed investment to extract resources such as oil, uranium, and iron ore. By 1957, Americans controlled 70 percent of oil and gas investment, 52 percent of mining and smelting, and 43 percent of Canadian manufacturing. In addition, U.S. companies had opened numerous branch plants in Canada.

There were advantages and disadvantages to U.S. investment. Branch plants provided many Canadians with good jobs in manufacturing, and Canadian industries benefited from U.S. technology. However, profits from the branch plants went back to the parent corporations in the United States. To many critics, it looked as though Canada was losing control of its economy.

©P

The debate continued for decades, until the North American Free Trade Agreement (NAFTA) brought about a new economic relationship in 1994. (You will read about NAFTA in Chapter 8.)

The Labour Movement in Canada

The wealth of Canada was not entirely in the hands of others. Canadian tycoons built up commercial empires that commanded vast resources and employed many people. In Central Canada, E.P. Taylor and the Bronfman family controlled the production of many consumer goods and the stores that sold them. In New Brunswick, K.C. Irving became one of the world's richest men with businesses ranging from gas stations to timber and newspapers.

At the same time, members of trade unions fought for a greater share of the country's prosperity. In 1946 and 1947, strikes were frequent as workers fought for the right to form unions and pressed for wages that would support a family. As a result, wages rose, for example, from $0.67 per hour in 1945 to $0.95 per hour in 1948. Workers won a major victory in establishing the 5-day, 40-hour workweek and increasing fringe benefits such as paid vacations. These hard-won benefits eventually became standard for many workers across the country. Non-industrial unions grew rapidly, including organizations for teachers, nurses, civil servants, postal workers, and police.

FIGURE 6–23 Newfoundland lumbermen on strike, March 1959

- How did people improve their working conditions after the Second World War?

The Limits of Prosperity

Some groups did not share the prosperity of the times. The working poor in cities—including many immigrants—washed dishes, cleaned offices, sweated in meat-packing plants, or toiled at sewing machines under miserable conditions. Women who could not afford to be stay-at-home wives and mothers were at a particular disadvantage. Society disapproved of working mothers, and employers discriminated against female workers by paying them lower wages than those paid to men.

CHECKPOINT

1. Why did the problem of post-war unemployment not arise?

2. What are transfer payments? Why were they instituted?

3. Explain the importance of one of the megaprojects of the 1950s.

4. Which groups were marginalized in the 1950s and 1960s? Why do you think this was so?

5. Why was American investment necessary and controversial?

6. Why were unions important?

7. Why were women workers at a disadvantage in the 1950s?

- What was Canada's involvement in the Cold War?

FIGURE 6–24 The government gave Soviet embassy clerk Igor Gouzenko and his family new identities, after which they settled in Ontario. Gouzenko wrote a book about his experiences and occasionally appeared in public, as in this television interview. He always wore a hood, afraid that the Soviet spy agency, the KGB, would kill him.

Historical Significance

The Cold War and Post-War Diplomacy

In 1945, a Russian citizen, Igor Gouzenko, was working as a clerk at the Soviet embassy in Ottawa. In September of that year, Gouzenko went to the *Ottawa Journal* with documents proving that a Soviet spy ring was operating within the Canadian government. When no one at the newspaper believed him, Gouzenko took his pregnant wife and child in tow and brought the documents to the offices of the RCMP, the Department of Justice, and the prime minister. Still no one believed him—until Soviet agents broke into his apartment. Finally Gouzenko and his family got protection from Canadian authorities.

Canadian officials informed the British and American governments of the spy ring. In February, 1946, the RCMP made several arrests. The spy ring was likely trying to discover information about the atomic bomb, but it appeared that the Soviets had learned very little. The Gouzenko affair brought Canadians into the new reality of the post-war world—the period of intense hostility and suspicion known as the **Cold War**.

Origins of the Cold War

During the Second World War, the United States and the Soviet Union had been allies even though they had little in common except their opposition to the Axis powers. Once the war was over, tensions between the two countries surfaced. At the heart of the conflict were differences in their political and economic systems. The Soviet Union was **communist**, which meant that the

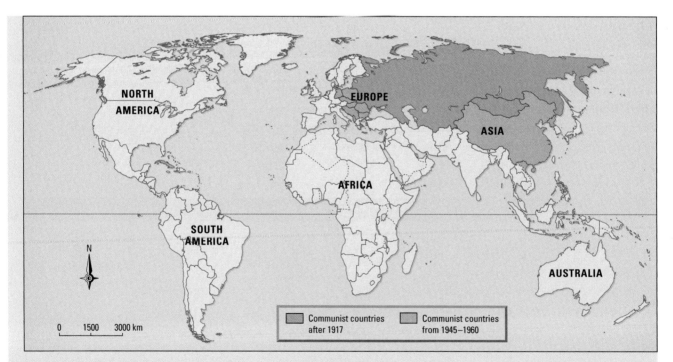

NORTH AMERICA

EUROPE

ASIA

AFRICA

SOUTH AMERICA

AUSTRALIA

N

0   1500   3000 km

Communist countries after 1917   Communist countries from 1945–1960

FIGURE 6–25 After the October 1917 revolution in Russia, two countries were recognized as communist. The post-war world, after 1945, saw the addition of 12 new communist countries, most of which were in Eastern Europe.

Interpret and Analyze How does this map contribute to your understanding of American concerns about the spread of communism?

government controlled all industry and commerce. Under communism, political opposition was not tolerated. The United States and most Western countries were **capitalist**. Their economies were based on private enterprise, with individuals investing in business for profit. Citizens had basic freedoms such as freedom of the press and freedom of speech.

Western countries were suspicious of communism. As in the decades following the First World War, they feared that communists planned to overthrow Western societies in a world revolution. The Soviet Union, for its part, was suspicious that the Western countries might try to invade Soviet territory through Europe. The Soviets took over the countries of Eastern Europe in the years following the Second World War and established communist governments in them. The West, particularly the United States, saw this expansion as proof of Soviet designs on the world.

As a result, the war years were not followed by peace and cooperation, as so many had hoped. Instead hostility increased between the Soviets and the Americans. But this was not traditional warfare; it was a Cold War in which there was no direct confrontation between the **superpowers** but a series of conflicts that broke out around the world. At the same time, both sides built up huge stockpiles of sophisticated arms, including the atomic bomb and other nuclear weapons and also spied on one another. The rivals became superpowers, each capable of inflicting massive destruction.

Canada aligned itself closely with U.S. interests while trying to remain true to the goals and values of Canadians—not an easy task. Through the early part of the 20th century, Canada had achieved independence from Britain; in the latter half, Canada struggled to keep U.S. influences from weakening its national identity.

The Cold War at Home

When the Igor Gouzenko story hit the media, the Canadian public was shocked to learn that a communist spy ring had been operating in Canada. During the early decades of the Cold War, many Canadians worried that an open war between the Soviet Union and the United States would result in a rain of nuclear bombs and missiles on Canada. The federal government in Ottawa developed civil defence plans, and cities prepared to protect their populations. Some cities had nuclear shelters in deep basements or subway tunnels. If an attack were to occur, sirens would sound a warning and people would try to find shelter. Schools ran drills to teach students to "duck and cover" or to lie in ditches. The fear of a nuclear Third World War was very real. Ironically, however, the existence of nuclear weapons—and the threat of mass destruction—probably prevented an all-out war between the superpowers.

FIGURE 6–26 Students doing a duck-and-cover drill
Interpret and Analyze Why were students taught this manoeuvre? How effective do you think it would have been?

counter points

Was the "Red Menace" real?

The "Red Menace" referred to the threat from the communist Soviet Union and its allies. Communists became known as "Reds" because the flags of the Communist International and the Soviet Union were red. The Gouzenko Affair had shown that it was possible for communists to infiltrate democratic governments and institutions in North America.

In the United States, Senator Joseph McCarthy and the House Un-American Activities Committee (HUAC) instituted a "witch hunt" for communists. McCarthy terrified people with secret lists of supposed communists who had, according to him, infiltrated all parts of American society.

The Committee interrogated thousands of suspected communists. For instance, many prominent figures in the entertainment industry, including movie stars, were forced to testify before the Committee because they had once belonged to socialist organizations or had simply attended meetings of such groups.

Many Canadians also feared the spread of communism, as is evident in the following quotation:

> *No longer could western governments fail to acknowledge that Soviet Russia was conducting a gigantic conspiracy for the overthrow of governments throughout the free world.*
>
> –*Clifford Harvison, RCMP Commissioner, 1950s*

The "Red Menace" sometimes became an issue in local elections, as the quotation below and poster on page 193 demonstrate.

> *Toronto's Communists took a lacing in the civic elections with Ald. Charles Sims and Trustee Mrs. Edna Ryerson of Ward 5 remaining as the only stooges of Stalin on either city council or board of education.... On the Board of Education three Communist aspirants fell by the wayside. In Ward Four, where Mrs. Hazel Wigdor, a Commie, retired, Comrade Samuel Walsh took a shellacking....*
>
> –*Globe and Mail, January 2, 1948*

Unlike U.S. President Dwight Eisenhower, Prime Minister Louis St. Laurent refused to outlaw communism. He reminded Canadians that such tactics were the trademarks of dictatorships, not democracies. Two of Canada's future prime ministers, Lester Pearson and John Diefenbaker, both supported St. Laurent's moderate approach.

> *Let us by all means remove the traitors from positions of trust, but in doing so, I hope we may never succumb to the black madness of the witch hunt.*
>
> –**Lester Pearson, quoted in The Red Scare**

> *I frankly state that in 1948 my own party came out in favour of outlawing communism. I was the only one to oppose it. I received a very unusual lack of welcome. The Conservative Party was going to sweep Canada with that policy. I said, "You cannot do it. You cannot deny an individual the right to think as he will."*
>
> –*John Diefenbaker, House of Commons, 1970*

FIGURE 6–27 Although Joseph McCarthy had many supporters in the United States, he was feared and hated by many people.

©P

• What measures has Canada taken to promote a distinct Canadian identity?

Nevertheless, injustices did take place in Canada.

• Union leaders who fought for better conditions for workers came under suspicion.

• Defence industries secretly sent lists of their employees to Ottawa for screening and dismissed workers suspected of communist sympathies.

• The RCMP Special Branch put artists, peace activists, union leaders, and intellectuals under surveillance.

• Québec Premier Maurice Duplessis used the so-called "Padlock Law" to shut down organizations and newspapers that criticized his government, and to arrest those who sought better rights for workers.

FIGURE 6–28 A Toronto municipal campaign poster, 1947

Thinking It Through

1. In the United States, and to some extent in Canada, governments and government agencies used un-democratic tactics and violated the civil liberties of those suspected of communist sympathies. Why do you think the rule of law was broken so often at this time?

2. Maurice Duplessis' government used the so-called Padlock Law to close down newspapers that Duplessis thought were communist or leftist and the publications of other groups he did not like. What fundamental Canadian right does this violate? How would this law stand up against the Canadian Charter of Rights and Freedoms?

3. Why did a current and two future prime ministers defend Communist Party members' rights to freedom of conscience, thought, belief, opinion, and association?

4. Find out to what extent anti-terrorist policies after 2001 followed the same pattern as the communist witch hunts of the 1950s.

5. Is banning certain political, social, or economic groups ever justified? Explain.

6. What makes evidence credible? Why is it so important that credible evidence of guilt be established in a democratic society?

? HISTORICAL INQUIRY

Gather and Organize

Who was Fred Rose, Member of Parliament from Cartier in Montréal? What does his career suggest about the origins of the Cold War in Canada? Why was he arrested and convicted?

● What was Canada's involvement in the Cold War?

KEY TERMS

middle power a nation that is not a super-power but has international influence

North Atlantic Treaty Organization (NATO) the mutual defence organization set up to protect several Western European countries, Canada, and the U.S. from possible aggression from the U.S.S.R. after the Second World War

United Nations (UN) an organization established in 1945 to bring peace and security to the world

Warsaw Pact a post–Second World War military alliance established in 1955 involving the Soviet Union and the Soviet-bloc countries of Albania, Bulgaria, Czechoslovakia, East Germany, Hungary, Poland, and Romania

North American Aerospace Defence Command (NORAD) a defence agreement signed in 1958 between Canada and the United States (known as the North American Air Defence Agreement until 1981)

Distant Early Warning (DEW) Line radar stations in northern Canada set up between 1958 and 1960 to detect Soviet activity over the North Pole

HISTORICAL INQUIRY

Interpret and Analyze

Compare the maps on pages 169 and 195. Consider why many Canadians were prepared to help the United States build and staff radar stations across Canada's territory. How did the launch of the USSR's sputnik satellite influence people's attitudes?

NATO and the Warsaw Pact

Prime Minister St. Laurent saw Canada as a "power of the middle rank" and his government expanded Canada's international role accordingly. He believed that although Canada had a close relationship with both the United States and Britain, it could nevertheless act independently of these two nations. As a **middle power**, Canada was in the position of effectively representing the interests of smaller nations. St. Laurent was an enthusiastic supporter of Canada's participation in the **North Atlantic Treaty Organization (NATO)** and the **United Nations (UN)**.

In 1949, Canada joined with the United States, Britain, and other Western European nations to form NATO, a military alliance. An attack on one NATO member was to be treated as an attack on all. NATO members agreed that if conventional weapons were not sufficient, they would use tactical weapons, that is, short-range nuclear weapons such as artillery shells or bombs. As a last resort, they would be prepared to wage total nuclear war.

Since the United States was by far the most powerful member of the alliance, much of NATO's activity served American policy first and foremost. Canada's close ties with the United States made maintaining an independent foreign policy very difficult. When NATO admitted West Germany as a member, the Soviet Union initiated the **Warsaw Pact**, a military alliance with Eastern European communist countries, to counter it.

Much of the northern hemisphere was now effectively divided into two hostile camps. Armies constantly practised for war and added to their arsenals of weapons. Everywhere, spies and counterspies probed for weaknesses in their enemy's security—searching for secrets, carrying out assassinations, and promoting revolutions and counter-revolutions.

Canada's Commitment to NATO

Canada made a serious commitment when it joined NATO. It agreed to keep a full army brigade and several air squadrons in Europe, mostly in West Germany. It built and supplied military bases overseas. Canadian ships and aircraft tracked the movements of Soviet submarines. Canadian forces participated regularly in military exercises with Canada's allies. Perhaps most significantly, by joining NATO, Canada had to adapt its defence policy to those of its allies.

NORAD and North American Defence

In 1958, Prime Minister Diefenbaker signed an agreement with the United States committing Canada to the **North American Aerospace Defence Command (NORAD)**. (NORAD was originally called North American Air Defence Command; it was renamed in 1981.) This meant that Canada and the U.S. had become part of a joint coordinated continental air defence against the threat of attack from the Soviet Union.

Canadian and American fighter forces, missile bases, and air-defence radar were controlled from a command station deep within Cheyenne Mountain, Colorado. NORAD had a force of 1000 bombers at its disposal at any one time, some of which were always in the air armed with nuclear weapons. A Canadian command post, under joint control, was established deep inside tunnels at North Bay, Ontario.

©P

When the Cold War began, it looked like Europe would be the battle-ground between West and East. However, when long-range bombers were developed that could carry warheads to distant targets, North America also became vulnerable. To protect against direct Soviet attack from the air, the United States built three lines of radar stations across Canada between 1950 and 1957—the Pinetree Line, the Mid-Canada Line, and the **Distant Early Warning (DEW) Line** (see map below). These stations were designed to detect a surprise Soviet attack over the North Pole, giving the United States time to launch a counterattack.

The DEW Line, and other radar stations, compromised Canadian sovereignty. For the first time, the U.S. stationed military personnel in Canada, alarming many Canadians. To visit the DEW Line, Canadian members of Parliament and journalists had to fly to New York and gain security clearance from U.S. authorities.

FIGURE 6–29 The NORAD emblem. What might the elements of this emblem represent?

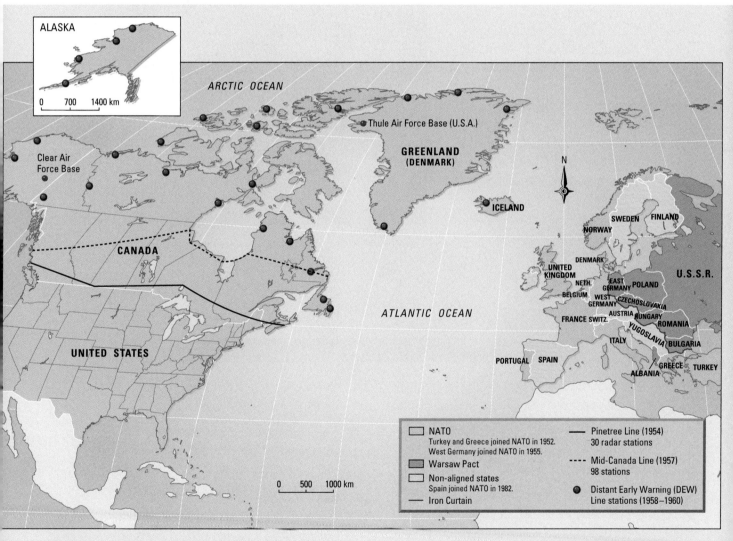

FIGURE 6–30 Countries of NATO and the Warsaw Pact. The dividing line between the Western European and communist countries was known as the "Iron Curtain," and movements of people and information from one side to the other was tightly restricted.

Interpret and Analyze Why would countries in Western Europe feel threatened by the countries of the Warsaw Pact and vice versa?

intercontinental ballistic missiles missiles equipped with nuclear warheads that have a range of 5500 kilometres

Most Canadians, however, showed little interest in this loss of independence, which the government had "sold" as the price of added security against an attack from the Soviet Union. Soon, the superpowers had developed **intercontinental ballistic missiles** armed with nuclear warheads. Missiles launched from the U.S.S.R. could reach North American cities within 30 minutes, rendering radar stations in Canada less effective.

FAST FORWARD

Terrorist Threats

The Cold War of the 1950s prompted the government to create military alliances and build weapons to protect Canadians from communist spies and attack. Fifty years later, when terrorists attacked the Twin Towers of the World Trade Center and other targets in the United States on September 11, 2001, governments around the world again took strong measures to protect their citizens. In both cases, the threat was real. Some people say that in times of terrorist threats, citizens should be willing to sacrifice their rights and freedoms in the interest of security. Others claim that security measures that erode citizens' rights to privacy, for example, may not even be necessary. In your opinion, which measures are necessary?

FIGURE 6–31 People around the world were horrified by evidence of torture of terrorist suspects by U.S. military personnel. This 2004 photograph was taken at Abu Ghraib prison in Iraq.

CHECKPOINT

1. What was the Cold War? Why did the Soviet Union want to have a buffer of countries between it and Western Europe?

2. **a)** Why was communism considered a threat to democracy?

   b) What groups of Canadians came under suspicion of being communists? What actions were taken against some of these people?

3. Identify a) NATO, b) NORAD, c) the DEW Line.

4. Why was Canada willing to enter an air defence agreement with the United States?

5. What commitments did Canada make as a member of NATO? How did membership in NATO affect Canada's foreign policy?

6. **Historical Significance** Read the feature on the following page. How might Canada's identity have been different if the Avro Arrow project had not been cancelled? What different role might Canada have played in international affairs?

Innovations
The Avro Arrow: Supersonic Jets

By the end of the Second World War, advances in technology had completely changed aviation. Jet fighters developed by Britain and Germany made propeller-driven warplanes obsolete. Canada, which had many aeronautical engineers in the early 1950s, was a leader in the field. Even though the Avro project was cancelled in 1959, the memory of the Arrow remains.

Delta-winged interceptor By 1958, the A.V. Roe (Avro) Company had developed the Arrow (CF 105), capable of flying at twice the speed of sound (Mach 2). The Arrow was to have exceptionally powerful and state-of-the-art engines and be faster than almost any other interceptor of the day.

Turbojet engine The Arrow, which was to be powered by two huge Iroquois jet engines, had a very specific purpose: to shoot down Russian nuclear-armed bombers.

The Concorde supersonic jetliner which first flew in 1969, used delta-wing design, similar to that of the Arrow. The Avro project was cancelled in 1959 by the Diefenbaker government. The existing planes were scrapped, and most of Avro's designers and engineers moved to the United States. Many Canadians feel that they lost an opportunity to establish a world-class space and aeronautics industry in Canada.

? HISTORICAL INQUIRY

Evaluate and Draw Conclusions

Why did Prime Minister Diefenbaker cancel the Avro Arrow in 1959 if it was on the leading edge of fighter-jet design?

GO ONLINE

Read more about John Humphrey and the creation of the Universal Declaration of Human Rights at Historica Canada.

Planning for Peace

Despite growing tensions at the end of the Second World War, world leaders began making plans for an international agency that would work to prevent future conflict and alleviate human misery.

Canada and the United Nations

In October 1945, delegates from 51 countries signed a charter that established the United Nations (UN). It was based on the idea of collective security, as the League of Nations had been before it. Canada played an important part in drafting its Charter. Membership in the United Nations is open to all recognized nations. Two bodies govern the United Nations: the General Assembly and the Security Council.

The use of the veto in the Security Council has often prevented the United Nations from taking decisive action. By 1955, as the Cold War escalated, the veto was used 78 times, 75 of which were by the Soviet Union. However, when permanent members agree on a course of action, the United Nations has the potential to implement it.

The founders of the UN also pledged to abolish disease and famine and to protect human rights. Canadian John Humphrey was the leading author of the Universal Declaration of Human Rights. Various agencies such as the **World Health Organization** (**WHO**) and the **United Nations Children's Fund** (**UNICEF**) are designed to accomplish these goals. In addition, the UN established the International Monetary Fund (IMF) to stabilize the world economy by helping countries that face great debt and the collapse of their currencies. The United Nations has benefited millions of people worldwide, especially through its social and economic agencies and peacekeeping operations. As with all international organizations, however, countries pursue their own agenda within it.

Canada has been a strong supporter of the United Nations since its creation and has aided refugees from war or natural disasters and worked on development projects—such as building schools, dams, and roads—in various countries. Canadian peacekeepers have been involved in almost every UN operation since the start of these missions in 1956.

FIGURE 6–32 The UN Security Council is responsible for keeping peace. It issues calls for ceasefires and creates peacekeeping forces. Canada has had a seat on the Council in every decade since the United Nations was formed, until 2000. In 2010, Canada lost its bid for a seat.

The General Assembly
Seats
• each member nation has a seat
What it does
• provides a forum in which members can debate issues
• has three powers it can use against aggressor nations
– condemn the actions through speeches and resolutions
– use economic sanctions
– deploy armed forces
How decisions are made
• each member nation has the right to vote

The Security Council
Seats
• 5 permanent members, the "Big Five"—Britain, France, the United States, Russia, and China (represented by the government in Taiwan until 1971)
• 10 non-permanent members, each holding a two-year term
What it does
• maintain peace and security
• deploy peacekeeping missions
How decisions are made
• decisions need the consent of 9 members
• each of the "Big Five" has the power of veto—the right to reject actions with which they disagree

The Korean Conflict

Though the threat of nuclear annihilation kept the major powers from open war, both sides supported their own interests in the developing world. The Second World War had left the Asian country of Korea divided. The Soviet Union and communist China supported North Korea, a communist state. The United States supported South Korea which had a fragile democracy. In 1950, war broke out when North Korea invaded South Korea.

> • What was Canada's response to conflicts during the late 1940s and the 1950s?

The United Nations called on its members to assist South Korea. (The Soviet Union was boycotting the UN at the time because it refused to give communist China a seat. Therefore it could not exercise its right to veto.) Prime Minister Louis St. Laurent sent thousands of Canadian troops and three naval destroyers to Korea. The UN force, led by American General Douglas MacArthur, tried to drive the invaders back over the border into North Korea. Meanwhile, Lester Pearson, Canada's Minister of External Affairs, urged all sides to agree to a ceasefire. At one point, the United States considered using the atomic bomb, but luckily, it did not. In addition, General MacArthur made plans to invade China. Had either of these things happened, a third World War would likely have resulted.

Although a ceasefire was reached in 1953, the war had increased tensions between the West and the communist nations. Global attention returned to this part of the world in the 1960s when American involvement in Vietnam escalated. (You will read about the Vietnam War in Chapter 7.)

Sandwiched between the Second World War and the Vietnam War, the Korean conflict is often called "Canada's forgotten war." Canada sent more than 25 000 soldiers to fight in Korea. More than 1500 were seriously wounded and another 516 died. The Korean War has technically not ended: the Republic of Korea (South) and the Democratic Peoples' Republic of Korea (North) have yet to sign a peace treaty.

FIGURE 6–33 Lester Pearson with the Nobel Peace Prize that he won in 1957 for helping to defuse the Suez crisis

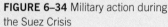

GO ONLINE

Learn more about the Suez Crisis and Lester Pearson on the Nobel Prize website.

The Suez Crisis and Pearson's Nobel Peace Prize

A crisis over the Suez Canal in Egypt gave Canada another chance to take a leading role at the United Nations. The Suez Canal links the Mediterranean and Red Seas and provides the shortest sea route from Europe to the Indian Ocean. It was opened in 1869 and was privately owned by British and French investors.

In 1956, Egypt's president, Gamal Abdel Nasser, took over the canal and threatened to ban ships travelling to and from Israel. In response, Israel, Britain, and France planned "Operation Musketeer" to regain control of the canal. Ignoring a UN Security Council resolution to cease hostilities, they landed troops in the canal zone. The Soviet Union immediately offered Egypt financial and military aid.

The United States was angry with its allies, Britain, France, and Israel, for not consulting the U.S. government before attacking Egypt. Nevertheless, the United States threatened retaliation against any Soviet involvement. Canadian public opinion on the crisis was divided. The Conservative Party and many other Canadians felt it was their duty to support Britain. Liberal Prime Minister Louis St. Laurent, however, denounced the British and French military intervention.

Once again, Lester Pearson went to the United Nations to try to work out a solution. He proposed that a multinational peacekeeping force be created and installed in the war zone to maintain ceasefires and oversee the withdrawal of troops. The United Nations agreed, and the United Nations Emergency Force (UNEF) was formed and sent to the Suez area to bring hostilities to a peaceful end. The force, under the command of a Canadian general, was chosen from countries not directly involved in the conflict. The UNEF remained stationed on the Israel-Egypt border until 1967.

In the following years, Canada gained a reputation as an impartial and peace-loving country, willing to pay the costs of sending peacekeepers to troubled areas of the world. In 1998, the United Nations celebrated 50 years of peacekeeping around the world. During that time there were 49 peacekeeping operations; 36 of which were created by the Security Council between 1988 and 1998.

FIGURE 6–34 Military action during the Suez Crisis

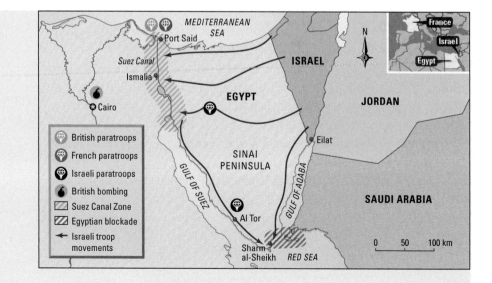

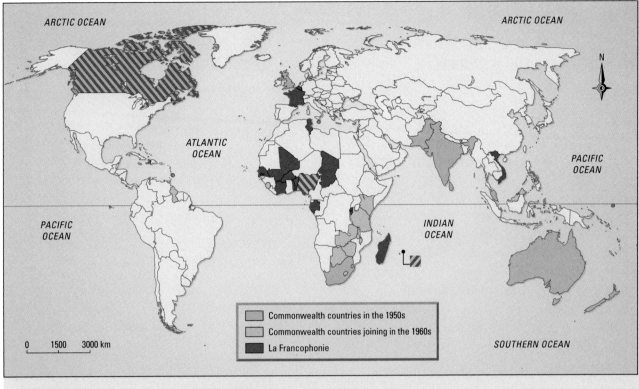

Commonwealth countries in the 1950s
Commonwealth countries joining in the 1960s
La Francophonie

FIGURE 6–35 La Francophonie and the Commonwealth

The Commonwealth and la Francophonie

Canada was in a good position to build international understanding through its membership in two other organizations, the Commonwealth and la Francophonie. The Commonwealth is made up of countries that once belonged to the British Empire. La Francophonie is an organization of French-speaking states, many of which are former colonies of France. Both organizations have many members that are less industrialized, and both offer a forum for discussing the economic problems of poverty-stricken countries.

In 1950, Commonwealth countries, including Canada, established the Colombo Plan to provide money and aid to less-developed countries in the organization. Canada contributed in a number of ways, for example, by inviting overseas students to study in Canada and by sending Canadian experts overseas to give technical assistance. Most Canadian aid under the Colombo Plan went to India and Pakistan.

CHECKPOINT

1. **a)** What is the purpose of the UN General Assembly?

   b) Why were the five permanent members of the Security Council given veto powers? How did this power create a stalemate in the United Nations?

2. What caused the Korean War? How did Canada participate?

3. What important roles did Canada play in the Suez crisis?

4. How would the experiences of the 1930s have influenced the United States and its many allies in the UN to come to the aid of South Korea in 1950? Consult Figure 5–7 on page 126 and Figure 5–8 on page 128.

CHAPTER FOCUS QUESTION — How did Canadian political decisions reflect a concern about the growing influence of the United States over Canada?

As you learned in this chapter, the years following the Second World War brought many social, economic, political, and technological changes to Canada. These changes altered the lives of many Canadians and helped to usher in a new era of prosperity and growth. There were also many fundamental shifts in Canada's international focus in the early post-war years, shifts that had a profound effect on the way Canadians viewed themselves and also on the way Canada was seen by the rest of the world. The transformation in national identity that had begun after the First World War, and was strengthened by the Second World War, grew and developed in the second half of the century.

1. Create an organizer such as the one below; provide specific examples of at least three or four decisions made by the Canadian government to limit the influence of the U.S. on Canada. Explain why the decision was made and evaluate its effectiveness at limiting American influence on Canada.

2. Rank the decisions in order from most to least effective. Provide reasons for your rankings.

3. If you had been advising the Canadian government, what other decisions would you have made to limit American influence on Canada? Explain why you would have made these decisions.

Decision made by the Canadian government	Reason for the decision	Explain the effectiveness of the decision
1.		
2.		
3.		

Knowledge and Understanding

4. Continue the ongoing timeline assignment. Write the name and date of each event in this chapter on the timeline and explain how the event contributed to Canadian independence.

5. You learned in earlier chapters that Canada began to gain autonomy from the beginning of the 20th century. To what extent did Canada become more independent in the post-war era? In what ways did Canada become less independent during this same period?

6. Compare the resettlement of Newfoundland (page 183) with the High Arctic Relocation of 1953 (page 180). In each case, what was the motive of the government? What was the lasting impact of each program?

7. Explain how the economy of Canada was transformed during the post-war era.

a) How might this transformation have affected the way Canadians viewed themselves?

b) What effect did it have on how other countries viewed Canada?

8. During the late 1940s and early 1950s, a "Red Scare" was alive and well in Canada and the United States. What effect do you think this threat had on Canada's military decisions? Support your opinion with specific examples from the textbook.

Apply Your Thinking

Historical Significance

9. Using the information from the Chapter Focus organizer above, list the two political decisions that you believe had the longest-lasting effect on limiting the influence of the U.S. on Canada. Write a paragraph explaining why these decisions were so effective at limiting American influence over Canada.

10. What does it mean to be a middle power? Select three examples from the textbook that you think demonstrate Canada's role as a middle power during the Cold War. Support your choices with at least two reasons.

11. How significant was Canada's role in Cold War events? Provide supporting evidence for your opinion.

Communicate

12. Complete a PMI chart on the three megaprojects (Trans-Canada Highway, Trans-Canada Pipeline, and St. Lawrence Seaway). How does each of these projects continue to influence the Canadian economy?

HISTORICAL INQUIRY

Evaluate and Draw Conclusions

Imagine Canada had refused to participate in NATO and/or NORAD. Use the map below, as well as the map showing NATO and Warsaw Pact countries on page 195, to guide your thinking and to formulate answers to the following questions:

13. How might Canada–U.S. relations have been affected if Canada had decided to remain neutral during the Cold War?

14. What do you think the U.S. reaction might have been to such a decision?

15. Did Canada really have a choice on whether or not to join these military alliances?

16. Do your answers to these questions change the views you expressed in Questions 5 and 8?

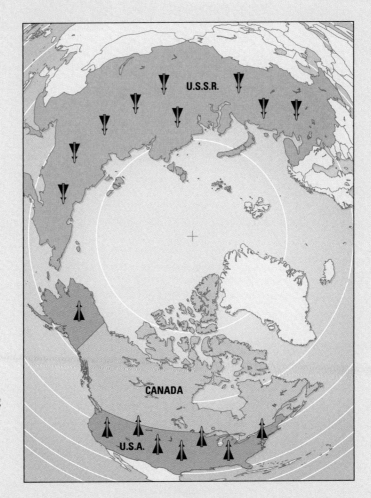

FIGURE 6–36 The United States and the Soviet Union both stockpiled weapons in the years following the Second World War.

Gather Evidence Where is Canada on this polar projection? In what way does this projection clarify Canada's decision to join NORAD?

7

Social Upheaval:
Canada from 1960 to 1982

? INVESTIGATE

Social, Economic, and Political Context

- How did Canada respond to changing social values after 1959?
- How did changes to social policies affect women and minority groups in Canada?
- How did Canadian social programs evolve?
- How did Canadian voters signal a change in political and social values?
- How did the Canadian government respond to economic challenges?

Communities, Conflict, and Cooperation

- How did Aboriginal people respond to challenges in the 1960s and 1970s?
- What effect did the War Measures Act have on the legal rights of Canadians?
- What was Canada's involvement in the Cold War?
- What was Canada's response to world conflicts?

Identity, Citizenship, and Heritage

- What was the impact of Québec nationalism on Canadian identity?
- What measures did Canada take to promote a distinct Canadian identity in the 1960s and 1970s?
- How was regionalism expressed in the 1960s and 1970s?

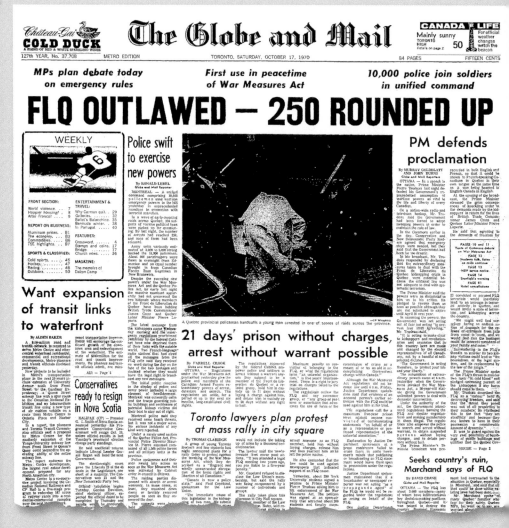

The front page of the *Globe and Mail*, October 17, 1970

Cause and Consequence After seven years of violent attacks on public institutions, the Front de libération du Québec kidnapped two political leaders, and Prime Minister Trudeau invoked the War Measures Act. What would be the consequences of this decision—for violent and for peaceful separatists?

TIMELINE

1960
Québec's Quiet Revolution begins

1961
Vietnam War begins

Berlin Wall built

1962
Medicare established in Saskatchewan

Cuban Missile Crisis

1963
Federal election over the issue of nuclear warheads on Canadian soil

Lester Pearson elected prime minister

1964
Beatles perform in Montréal, Toronto, and Vancouver

1965
Maple Leaf flag adopted

1966
Canada Pension Plan introduced

Medical Care Act passed

CHAPTER FOCUS QUESTION

How did Canada's political, social, and economic policies reflect a new independence from the 1960s to 1982?

On the night of March 7, 1963, three Canadian army buildings in Montréal were bombed with Molotov cocktails (homemade firebombs). The mysterious letters "FLQ" were painted on the walls. The next day, a document from an organization claiming responsibility for the bombings was delivered to the news media:

> The Front de libération du Québec is a revolutionary movement of volunteers ready to die for the political and economic independence of Québec. The suicide-commandos of the FLQ have as their principal mission the complete destruction, by systematic sabotage of:
>
> all colonial [federal] symbols and institutions, in particular the RCMP and the armed forces;....
> all commercial establishments and enterprises which practise discrimination against Quebeckers, which do not use French as the first language, which advertises in the colonial language [English];
> all plants and factories which discriminate against French-speaking workers.
>
> ...INDEPENDENCE OR DEATH
>
> **–Revolution by the People for the People**

How did this crisis emerge? What had happened between English and French Canadians to make the relationship so strained? How could the crisis be resolved?

The 1960s and 1970s were tumultuous times in Canada and around the world. A culture of activism and protest developed that challenged both social norms and government policies. The continuation of the Cold War brought with it the Vietnam War and the Cuban Missile Crisis. The Canadian government tried to carve out a path of international relations independent of the United States while also dealing with an economic recession at home.

HISTORICAL INQUIRY

Formulate Questions

There are four main headings in this chapter. Individually or in pairs, scan the chapter, make a list of these four headings, and then change each of them into a question. Which historical thinking concept(s) do you think will be addressed in each section?

1967	1968	1969	1970	1971	1972	1973	1976	1980
Canada's centennial, Expo 67	Pierre Trudeau elected prime minister; CRTC established	Woodstock	October Crisis; Trans-Canada Highway completed	National Action Committee on the Status of Women established; Trudeau government restricts foreign ownership of Canadian business	Canada defeats Russian hockey team	Oil crisis in Canada; Pierre Trudeau first Canadian prime minister to pay an official visit to the People's Republic of China	Montréal Olympics	Referendum on Québec sovereignty

- How did Canada respond to changing social values after 1959?

KEY TERMS

counterculture a subculture, especially of young people, with values or lifestyles that are in opposition to those of the dominant, established culture

draft resisters citizens who refuse to join the army to fight in a war during conscription

Toward Social Change

By the early 1960s, Canadians were beginning to accept the teen culture that had evolved after the Second World War. They had very little choice—by 1965, as a result of the baby boom, more than half the population of North America was under the age of 25. The sheer number of young people in North America and Western Europe created a powerful culture of protest— a "youthquake." The young people were joined by other groups calling for change to society, among them members of the women's movement, the environmental movement, and Aboriginal nations.

The "Youthquake"

The transition began with the so-called "British invasion" of pop culture led by four young men from Liverpool—the Beatles. Boys' hair became longer, girls' skirts shorter. This was the start of the hippie phenomenon. Large numbers of young people embraced rock music, new clothing styles, sexual promiscuity, and experimentation with drugs as a protest against mainstream society. With slogans such as "Make love, not war" and "Turn on, tune in, drop out," they strove to be different from earlier generations. Canadian youth participated in these international cultural trends, becoming part of the **counterculture**.

Some young people had aims that went beyond culture. They held strong political beliefs and rejected the consumerism of post-war society in the hope that the world would change for the better. Some became involved in women's, environmental, and Aboriginal rights movements. Others demonstrated to support greater student participation in university affairs. Many joined in protests against the war in Vietnam, demonstrating outside the American embassy in Ottawa and in front of Parliament hoping to persuade Canadian leaders to take a stronger stand against the war. Canadian youth had a particular incentive to protest the war in Vietnam because many had the opportunity to get to know American **draft resisters** personally. Between 1965 and 1975, an estimated 40 000 American men came to Canada to avoid serving in Vietnam.

FIGURE 7–1 Hippies rejected traditional societal values. Their clothes, hair, beliefs, music, and opposition to the Vietnam War were an expression of deep dissatisfaction with their parents' values, particularly materialism and respect for authority. The 1960s term "generation gap" summed up the differences between youth and their parents.

Evaluate and Draw Conclusions Why do you think some members of the older generation might have disapproved of scenes such as this?

Popular music of the day reflected these concerns. Protest songs condemned racism, war, and the devastation of the environment. Protest singers such as Bob Dylan and Saskatchewan native Joni Mitchell attracted a wide following. Rock groups such as the Beatles, the Rolling Stones, and the Canadian band The Guess Who ("American Woman," "Share the Land") captured the mood with songs of protest and free love. Aboriginal singer Buffy Sainte-Marie and African-American artists like Marvin Gaye also used their music to highlight the social conditions of their peoples.

Canadian artists got a boost from the Canadian Radio-television and Telecommunications Commission (CRTC) in 1971. That year, new Canadian content rules stated that 25 percent of radio air time had to be devoted to Canadian music. Before then, it had been difficult to get stations to play home-grown music unless the artist was well known.

The youthquake showed Canadian governments that young people were becoming more politically aware. Soon, politicians began making an effort to appeal to them by increasing spending on employment and activities for youth. In 1972, the voting age for federal elections was lowered from 21 to 18. Most provinces lowered the voting age around the same time.

FIGURE 7–2 "Universal Soldier," a song by Canadian singer-songwriter Buffy Sainte-Marie, expressed the anti-war sentiments of many people, young and old.

Protest and Mockery

Political protests marked the 1960s. Even Woodstock, a huge music festival held in 1969, turned into a kind of protest against the establishment. A new political party, the Rhino Party, which grew out of the protest movement of the 1960s, fielded candidates who made far-fetched promises such as moving the nation's capital from Ottawa to Moose Jaw, Saskatchewan, or making Swedish Canada's official language. The Rhinos made a joke out of politics, but their criticisms were very serious. They used publicity to question and mock the system itself, rather than any one political party or politician.

? HISTORICAL INQUIRY

Gather and Organize

Canadian songwriter and singer, Gordon Lightfoot, wrote "Black Day in July" in 1967. What protest was he witnessing?

FAST FORWARD

HISTORICAL THINKING — Historical Perspectives

Political Protest

Political protests still take place in the tradition of the 1960s and 1970s. The 1990s and 2000s saw an increase in the number of organized protests against economic globalization and human rights abuses. During the G20 Summit held in Toronto in 2010, world leaders met to discuss the global financial system and world trade. Protests occurred before and during the meeting, led by a coalition of groups fighting poverty, globalization, and consumerism. Although some Canadians approved of the protest, the ensuing violence was disturbing to many. More than a thousand people were arrested, many of whom later voiced concerns over police brutality.

FIGURE 7–3 Protesters took to the streets of Toronto during the G20 Summit of 2010.

Evaluate and Draw Conclusions If you were responsible for ordering the police to break up a demonstration, what criteria would you use to help you determine that such an order was necessary?

KEY TERMS

feminist a person who supports the idea that women are equal to men and deserve equal rights and opportunities

pressure group a group of people who get together around a particular issue to try to influence government policy

❓ HISTORICAL INQUIRY

Interpret and Analyze

Women have played a very important role in Canada's history. How were women's roles in World War One, World War Two, and the 1960s important turning points for women and for Canada? Consult sources in your community, in the library, and on the Internet.

FIGURE 7–4 Women burn bras in a protest at Toronto City Hall on International Women's Day, March 8, 1979.

The Women's Movement

Women had been expected to fill men's shoes in industry and manufacturing during the Second World War. However, when veterans returned and women were no longer needed in these jobs, post-war society expected them to return to their traditional role as housekeepers. Many felt isolated in the suburbs and trapped by roles that did not allow them to develop their potential. Many working women continued to hold low-paying jobs such as waitressing, hairdressing, secretarial work, and retail sales. Employers could legally discriminate against them in both wages and benefits. University-educated women were expected to work as either teachers or nurses—other professions were difficult for women to enter.

In 1963, Betty Friedan's book *The Feminine Mystique* became a best-seller. It argued that women were trapped in gender roles that were reinforced by images in the media. Friedan urged women to liberate themselves from these traditional roles and fulfill themselves as human beings by acquiring an education and pursuing careers. Friedan's ideas transformed the lives of many women during this period. Just as they had done during the suffrage movement of the early years of the century, **feminists** joined together to fight for women's rights.

In 1967, responding to pressure from women's groups, Prime Minister Lester Pearson's government set up the Royal Commission on the Status of Women. The Commission thoroughly examined how Canadian women were treated and the problems they faced. It made recommendations that included the following:

- Women should have the right to work outside the home.
- Society in general, as well as parents, should take some responsibility for children; therefore, daycare services should be provided.
- Women should be entitled to paid maternity leave from their jobs.
- The federal government should do all it can to help overcome discrimination against women in society.

Several women's groups joined forces to form the National Action Committee on the Status of Women (NAC) in 1971. This **pressure group** lobbied both federal and provincial governments to act quickly on the Commission's recommendations. One of NAC's key victories was the inclusion of a clause guaranteeing the equality of women in Canada's Charter of Rights and Freedoms, which came into force in 1982 (see Chapter 8).

Canadian feminists demanded that women be promoted to positions of responsibility in government, business, education, and the civil service. They argued against stereotyping women and the kinds of work they do. They also pressed for changes to the education system, under which girls were not encouraged to excel in math and sciences—subjects more likely to lead to well-paying jobs. Soon, more Canadian women were becoming engineers, doctors, politicians, and company presidents—pursuing careers in which they had previously been under-represented. "Sexism," "male chauvinism," and "sexual harassment" became common terms to describe behaviour and attitudes that were no longer acceptable.

©P

The Environmental Movement

Canada's prosperity was won at a great cost. Many environmental challenges facing the world today had their roots in this period. It was not until 1962 that North Americans began to be aware of the extent of environmental damage. In that year, an American scientist, Rachel Carson, published a widely read book titled *Silent Spring*. In it, she warned that pollution of air, water, and soil was threatening life on Earth. She criticized the chemical industry for producing toxic pesticides such as DDT, a contact poison, and claiming that they were safe. For years, farmers had been pumping weedkiller and chemical fertilizers into the soil and, indirectly, into the groundwater. Homeowners casually used the insecticide DDT around their houses and yards. Nevertheless, "pollution" did not become a common word until the late 1960s.

At first, business and governments resisted any attempts to limit pollution, but public concern over the environment rose steadily. Environmental groups were established to lobby governments to control pollution and as awareness grew, legislation changed. Greenpeace was created in 1970 by a small group of activists in British Columbia to draw attention to environmental concerns.

FIGURE 7–5 Initially, little was done to address the issues raised in Rachel Carson's groundbreaking book, *Silent Spring*.

up close and personal ○ Greenpeace: Warriors for the Environment

In the fall of 1971, 11 people with a shared vision of a green and peaceful world set sail from Vancouver on an old fishing boat. They were headed toward Amchitka Island, Alaska, to "bear witness" to underground nuclear testing by the United States. Not only were they concerned about the immediate consequences for the region's ecology, including the possibility of earthquakes and tsunamis along Pacific coastlines, but they also had a strong anti-nuclear message to spread.

Although their mission was unsuccessful, and the U.S. detonated its bomb, it was that country's final nuclear test in the area. Some believe that this voyage and the global environmental awareness that resulted was the beginning of the end of the Cold War. Today, Greenpeace is an international organization with more than 40 offices and 2.8 million members around the world. Through direct action, Greenpeace seeks to

- protect biodiversity in all its forms
- prevent pollution and abuse of Earth's oceans, land, air, and fresh water
- end all nuclear threats
- promote peace, global disarmament, and non-violence

FIGURE 7–6 Crew of the boat *Phyllis Cormack*, also known as *Greenpeace*; inaugural protest mission

Prime Minister
John George Diefenbaker

- born 1895, Neustadt, Ontario
- lawyer
- first elected to Commons in 1940
- prime minister 1957–1963

Domestic Record

- served as a lieutenant during the First World War
- championed the Canadian Bill of Rights to guarantee certain rights for all Canadians
- appointed James Gladstone, a Blackfoot from the Northwest Territories, Canada's first Aboriginal senator, in 1958
- cancelled the Avro Arrow project in 1959
- extended franchise to all Aboriginal peoples in 1960

International Record

- opposed apartheid and played a role in South Africa withdrawing from the Commonwealth
- signed North American Air Defence Agreement (NORAD) with the U.S. in 1957
- allowed two squadrons of American Bomarc anti-aircraft missiles deployed in Canada (1958)

Challenging Social Values

Although there had been groups fighting for **civil liberties** in Canada during the 1930s and 1940s, it was not until the 1960s that there was a dramatic increase in activism for social change. Organizations formed during this time include the Canadian Civil Liberties Association and the National Indian Brotherhood. Canadian chapters of Human Rights Watch and Amnesty International also started at this time.

Diefenbaker and the Canadian Bill of Rights

John Diefenbaker's government set the stage for reform when it introduced the **Canadian Bill of Rights** in 1960 to protect a person's fundamental human rights. These rights included

- freedom of life, liberty, security of person, and the enjoyment of property
- the right to equality before the law and its protection
- freedom of religion
- freedom of speech
- freedom of assembly and association

Although Diefenbaker did not feel he had enough provincial support to make the Bill of Rights part of the Constitution, the fact that it had been passed by Parliament gave it considerable influence. Most of the rights protected by the Bill were included in the Charter of Rights and Freedoms in 1982. (You will read more about the Charter in Chapter 8.)

Legal Reforms

In 1969, the Liberal government, under Prime Minister Pierre Trudeau, passed Bill C-150, which made major changes in social legislation. These included

- recognizing the right of women to have access to contraception;
- recognizing the right to abortion (with certain limitations); and
- legalizing homosexuality between consenting adults.

Legalizing these activities, formerly considered criminal and immoral, signalled a huge shift in Canadian social values.

Trudeau was criticized for his progressive social policies, but refused to back down, saying that "There's no place for the state in the bedrooms of the nation." Trudeau also changed Canada's divorce law in 1968, making divorce more freely available to reflect what was happening in society.

In 1970, feeling that the abortion law did not go far enough, women protesters chained themselves inside Parliament, forcing it to close. Dr. Henry Morgentaler also challenged abortion laws. Juries refused to convict Morgentaler despite the fact that he had performed thousands of abortions. The law had become unenforceable.

In 1976, Bill C-84 passed in the House of Commons by a narrow margin (131–124), ending the death penalty. Although Bill C-84 did not have widespread public support, Trudeau and his Cabinet were determined that Canada should join other progressive nations and abolish capital punishment.

FIGURE 7–7 In 2008, Dr. Henry Morgentaler was named a member of the Order of Canada. Morgentaler was a crusader for women's right to abortion. He opened an abortion clinic in 1969 and was arrested many times.

Women's Rights

Women's rights activists protested against Canadian laws that supported traditional roles for women. The reforms in divorce and abortion legislation were welcomed by many people. These were important steps toward women's equality. Many unions joined the fight for women's rights. For example, the Canadian Union of Postal Workers was the first to win the right to paid maternity leave for its members.

Gay Rights

Before Bill C-150 was passed, gay men and lesbians could be arrested and sent to prison, denied employment, and otherwise persecuted. In the 1960s, gay rights activists began to organize to draw attention to these injustices. This took tremendous courage, as the attitudes of many Canadians, churches, and members of governments at all levels were strongly anti-gay. Gay people began to publicly show pride in their sexual orientation and resist persecution.

During the 1970s, the push for gay rights continued. In 1971, Everett George Klippert—the last man in Canada to be arrested, prosecuted, and imprisoned for being gay—won his freedom. If not for Bill C-150, Klippert, labelled a dangerous sexual offender just because of his sexual orientation, might have been held indefinitely. By the end of the decade, Québec had become the first province to include sexual orientation in its Human Rights Act, and the Canadian Immigration Act no longer listed homosexuality as a reason to keep someone out of the country.

Although the Canadian Human Rights Commission recommended that sexual orientation no longer be grounds for discrimination in 1979, it would not be until the 1990s that this injustice was resolved. Nonetheless, the strides made by gay men and lesbians from the late 1960s until the early 1980s helped to ensure many future successes and also called attention to discrimination against people who are transgender.

KEY TERMS

civil liberties basic individual rights protected by law, such as freedom of speech

Canadian Bill of Rights a federal document that set out the rights and freedoms of Canadians; it was enacted in 1960 under the leadership of Prime Minister John Diefenbaker

FIGURE 7–8 Toronto's Pride Week celebrated its 25th anniversary in 2005. It continues to be a celebration of diversity, drawing up to 1 million visitors to the city.

CHECKPOINT

1. a) Name three protest movements that emerged in Canada during the 1960s.

b) What kind of impact do you think each of these groups has since had on Canadian society?

2. Many young people of the 1960s and 1970s believed they could change the world. List some of their aims. Do you think they succeeded? Explain.

3. Which group benefited most from Bill C-150? Support your answer.

- What measures did Canada take to promote a distinct Canadian identity in the 1960s and 1970s?

KEY TERM

multiculturalism a policy of encouraging the expression of the cultures of many ethnic groups that make up a country's population

...support and encourage the various cultures and ethnic groups that give structure and vitality to our society. They will be encouraged to share their cultural expressions and values with other Canadians and so contribute to a richer life for us all.

—House of Commons

? HISTORICAL INQUIRY

Interpret and Analyze

How was Canada's multicultural heritage recognized in the Charter of Rights and Freedoms?

Immigration and Multiculturalism

By the 1960s, many Canadians had a somewhat more open attitude toward people of other cultures and countries. This was reflected in new immigration regulations as illustrated by the timeline below. In 1962, Citizenship and Immigration Minister Ellen Fairclough—the first woman to serve as a federal Cabinet minister—introduced regulations in the House of Commons that eliminated racial bias from Canada's immigration policy. The new rules focused on immigrants' education level, skill, and job prospects, and banned discrimination based on race, ethnicity, or religion. This reform led to the points system, introduced by the Liberal government of Lester Pearson in 1967. Under this system, immigrants earned points in several categories such as education, job prospects, age, and bilingualism, up to a certain maximum. This system survives today.

In 1971, an official policy of **multiculturalism** was introduced by Prime Minister Trudeau. The policy encouraged the country's various ethnic groups to express their cultures. Multicultural activities were organized across the country. For example, heritage language classes were provided to help children learn the language of their parents. Festivals were held for cultural communities to share their music, dances, foods, games, arts, crafts, and stories. Programs were designed to make all residents feel at home in Canada, regardless of their origins. These programs were also intended to prevent racism by promoting respect for all cultures.

TIMELINE

Canadian Immigration Milestones

1900	Chinese Immigration Act increases $50 head tax to $100; in 1903 it is raised to $500.	
1908	Continuous Passage Act requires immigrants to travel directly to Canada, thus restricting immigration from India.	
1919	New Immigration Act excludes people from Canada for reasons of race, culture, and political beliefs.	
1923	Law is passed prohibiting almost all immigration from China; this law was revoked in 1947.	
1931	Admission to Canada is restricted to American citizens, British subjects, and agriculturalists with economic means.	
1939	The *St. Louis*, a ship carrying 930 Jewish refugees from Germany, is turned away from Canadian ports. It returns to Europe where three quarters of the passengers are killed by the Nazis.	
1947	Between 1947 and 1952, more than 186 000 displaced persons come to Canada from wartorn Europe.	
1962	New regulations eliminate most of the racial discrimination in Canada's immigration policy.	
1967	Immigration to Canada becomes "colour blind." The points system is introduced, which assigns potential immigrants points in categories such as education, age, fluency in French or English, and job opportunities in Canada.	
1976	Immigration regulations change to allow immigration of family members with relatives already in Canada.	
1978	Refugees make up 25 percent of all immigrants to Canada until 1981.	
1981	Canada's census reveals that 16 percent of Canadians are immigrants.	

FIGURE 7–9 In 1972, many South Vietnamese people fleeing war sought refugee status in Canada.

The Other Canada

While many Canadians benefited from the booming economic times of the 1950s and 1960s, others were **marginalized**. Governments expropriated properties for the building of freeways and other projects. Citizens sometimes organized themselves to preserve their communities, though this was not always the case—especially when the people affected were poor and not used to speaking out on public issues. In the 1960s, two thirds of Toronto's Chinatown was bulldozed for the construction of a new city hall. In Nova Scotia, officials ordered the destruction of the African-Canadian community of Africville and the forced removal of its residents. The people of these communities were angered at the way they had been **disenfranchised** by government.

KEY TERMS

marginalized to be pushed aside and made less important in terms of social standing and power

disenfranchised to be deprived of basic legal rights

GO ONLINE
Visit the Africville Museum and learn more about this community that endured for 150 years.

FIGURE 7–10 By the 1960s, racism and neglect had made Africville one of the worst slums in Canada, but its destruction brought an end to a vibrant community. In 2010, the mayor of Halifax apologized to the descendants of the Africville community.

Evaluate and Draw Conclusions What connections can you make between the relocation of people in Africville and the relocations in Newfoundland and the High Arctic that you read about in Chapter 6? What conclusions can you draw from these events?

Aboriginal Nations: Decades of Action

Canada's First Nations had fared badly economically in the boom years following the Second World War. In addition, many had also suffered from environmental damage caused by resource industries. For example, mercury poisoning from a pulp and paper mill contaminated the fish caught and eaten at the Whitedog and Grassy Narrows reserves in Ontario. (See page 309.) The development of mines, highways, pipelines, and boom towns disrupted the hunting grounds and way of life of other First Nations.

- How did Aboriginal people respond to challenges in the 1960s and 1970s?

GO ONLINE
Visit the Elections Canada website to read more about Aboriginal people winning the right to vote in 1960.

Organizing for Change

When Aboriginal people living on reserves won the right to vote in 1960, it did little to improve their living conditions. They continued to suffer from serious problems, including poverty, poor health, and inadequate housing and education. Those who left to try their luck in the large cities often faced hostility and discrimination. By the late 1960s, Aboriginal peoples were organizing to pressure Ottawa and the provincial governments to bring about change.

White Paper of 1969 the government report proposing dramatic changes to the lives of Aboriginal peoples, including the elimination of the Indian Act

Red Paper Aboriginal response to the federal government's White Paper of 1969; the Red Paper caused the government to change its policies

lobby to try to influence the opinions and votes of public officials for or against a cause

The Government believes that its policies must lead to the full, free and nondiscriminatory participation of the Indian people in Canadian society. Such a goal requires a break with the past. It requires that the Indian people's role of dependence be replaced by a role of equal status, opportunity and responsibility, a role they can share with all other Canadians.

–Foreword of the White Paper

The Liberal government of Pierre Trudeau issued the **White Paper of 1969** to address the issues facing Aboriginal people. The White Paper, prepared by Indian Affairs Minister Jean Chrétien, proposed dramatic changes to the lives of Aboriginal people. Among its recommendations, the White Paper proposed that

- the Indian Act be repealed
- Aboriginal people be given control and ownership of their lands
- the provincial governments take over the same responsibility for Aboriginal people that they have for other citizens
- substantial funds be made available for economic development for Aboriginal people
- the Department of Indian Affairs be closed down

The White Paper would end special status for Aboriginal peoples and place them on an equal footing with other Canadians. Its intent was to encourage Aboriginal people to leave the reserves, seek jobs in the cities, and become part of mainstream Canadian society. Assimilation would supposedly bring an end to their problems.

Aboriginal people were furious. They saw the White Paper as an attack on their right to maintain their unique identity. Harold Cardinal, an Alberta Cree leader, explained their response:

Ironically, the White Paper concludes by... calling upon Indian organizations... to assist [in the process it recommends].... It is difficult to envision any responsible Indian organization willing to participate in a proposal that promises to take the rights of all Indians away and attempts to... legislate Indians out of existence. It is a strange government and a strange mentality that would have the gall to ask the Indian to help implement its plan to perpetrate cultural genocide on the Indians of Canada. It is like asking the doomed man on the gallows if he would mind pulling the lever that trips the trap.

–The Unjust Society, 1969

The National Indian Brotherhood led the attack. Instead of assimilation into "White" (non-Aboriginal) society, they demanded self-government for Aboriginal peoples and control over their own affairs. When they presented their paper, *Citizens Plus,* which became known as the **"Red Paper,"** Trudeau and Chrétien abandoned the White Paper.

FIGURE 7–11 Harold Cardinal speaks to Prime Minister Trudeau and other Cabinet members at an Ottawa meeting in 1970. A delegation of about 200 First Nations peoples representing most provinces attended the meeting.

GO ONLINE •
Read the first page of the White Paper (Statement of the Government of Canada on Indian Policy) and the preamble to Citizens Plus (the Red Paper). What areas of difference can you find? How do the perspectives differ?

Educational Reform

As the residential school system began to wind down by the 1970s, many First Nations took over the education of their children. "Band schools" emerged across the country where Aboriginal children could study their own languages and learn about their own values, cultures, and traditions. The lack of secondary schools near the reserves, however, meant that most Aboriginal children were forced to leave home if they wanted to continue in school. As part of a government-run "boarding home program," some high-school students were sent to live with families and attend school in cities such as Toronto, Thunder Bay, and Sudbury. But loneliness drove many to return to their reserves before graduating.

Environmental Action

Aboriginal peoples began taking action in another area: the environment. Industries were expanding, some of them in and around reserves. Many Aboriginal groups were concerned that hydroelectric and natural gas projects would jeopardize their hunting, fishing, and trapping activities.

Probably the most significant Aboriginal victory during the 1970s was won by the Inuit, Métis, and Indian Brotherhood (later Dene) of the Yukon and Northwest Territories as they **lobbied** to halt the construction of oil and natural gas pipelines that were to run through their lands in the Mackenzie Valley. They demanded a study to determine its impact on their lands and on the environment.

The federal government agreed to investigate the issue. The Berger Commission conducted hearings all over the North, listening carefully to Aboriginal concerns. In 1977, the commission recommended that construction of the Mackenzie Valley Pipeline be suspended for 10 years pending an in-depth environmental study and negotiations with the Aboriginal peoples about financial compensation, self-government, and other issues.

In fact, construction was suspended for much longer. However, once land claims associated with the pipeline were settled, and once the Aboriginal communities of the Northwest Territories had negotiated for partial ownership of the project, supporters of the pipeline hoped construction would begin. On March 11, 2011, the Mackenzie Valley pipeline project was approved by the federal Cabinet. Environmental concerns over the project persist.

FASTFORWARD

Responsible Business

Today, many Aboriginal peoples are willing to collaborate with business, as long as environmental standards are upheld. Proceeds from large projects can benefit Aboriginal communities, and many leaders welcome the financial independence. Agnes Spence, a Cree band councillor in Nelson House, Manitoba, sums it up this way: "First Nations are trying to do something for themselves."

Today, the Aboriginal Pipeline Group is partnering with oil companies on the Mackenzie pipeline; four Cree communities in Manitoba are working with Manitoba Hydro on multiple dam projects; and dozens of gold, copper, nickel, and diamond mines (like the one below)—the result of partnerships between Aboriginal peoples and the mining industry—are operational from coast to coast.

CHECKPOINT

1. Explain the importance of the following in the development of Aboriginal identity:

   a) the 1969 White Paper and the Red Paper

   b) the Mackenzie Valley Pipeline and the Berger Commission

2. Give examples of the federal government's attempts to assimilate Aboriginal people into Canadian society.

3. List three changes that occurred for minority groups in Canada during the 1960s and 1970s.

4. **Historical Perspectives** Write a short paragraph supporting or opposing the following statement: The policy of multiculturalism promoted a shift away from assimilation and toward acceptance of diversity in Canada.

Politics and Government

As the first of the baby boomer generation reached maturity, politicians faced new priorities and demands from Canadians. John Diefenbaker and Lester "Mike" Pearson dominated Canadian politics in the early 1960s. But by 1967, Canada's centennial year, both Diefenbaker and Pearson seemed out of touch with the times. Diefenbaker was defeated in a leadership convention in September 1967, and Pearson announced his intention to retire in December of the same year. Many Canadians wanted a leader who could appeal to a new generation of voters. The answer was the charismatic Pierre Trudeau who came to power on the strength of "Trudeaumania" and the youth vote.

Diefenbaker Versus Pearson

Diefenbaker and Pearson had different styles and visions of Canada. They were bitter rivals, fighting four national elections in 10 years. Diefenbaker was passionately committed to what he called "unhyphenated Canadianism"—a belief in the equality of all Canadians, whatever their heritage. A staunch nationalist, he also believed in preserving Canada's British connections and standing up to the Americans. Diefenbaker championed human rights, introducing the Canadian Bill of Rights. In addition, he was the first prime minister to include a woman in his Cabinet and to appoint an Aboriginal senator. In 1960, his government gave Canada's status Indians living on reserves the right to vote in federal elections. While Diefenbaker's beliefs made him popular among many Canadians, they were also the source of his problems. In particular, French Canadians, who saw their culture as distinct, did not appreciate Diefenbaker's version of "unhyphenated Canadianism."

By contrast, Pearson and his Liberals appealed to younger, urban voters, especially in Central Canada. Pearson's vision of Canada was based on two founding peoples: French and English. He believed that Canadians should sever their British connections and that Canada needed an identity that would be meaningful to all Canadians. Pearson won the election of 1963; Diefenbaker never again led the country. Pearson was responsible for modernizing Canada. His government introduced a trial abolition of capital punishment and easier divorce laws. Above all, he is remembered for introducing Canada's flag in 1965.

The Flag Debate

For some Canadians, the Red Ensign was too British to be the symbol of modern Canada. Still, many opposed a new flag both for reasons of tradition and because they felt that Pearson was giving in to pressure from Québec. An emotional debate split the country. In general, English Canadians wanted to keep the Red Ensign; French Canada wanted a new flag. Finally, after hundreds of suggestions from across Canada, the red-and-white maple leaf design was chosen. On February 15, 1965, Canada's new flag was raised on Parliament Hill for the first time. Ironically, English Canadians have come to regard the flag with pride and affection, while people from Québec, disillusioned by the bitter debate, continue to fly primarily the fleur-de-lys.

GO ONLINE • • • • • • • • • • • • • • •
Ever wonder how the first official Canadian flag went missing? Find articles on this and other flag facts in CBC's archives.

FIGURE 7–12 Diefenbaker and the Conservatives wanted to keep the Red Ensign (top) with its traditional links to Britain, while the Liberals wanted a new design, favouring the three maple leaf flag (centre). A multi-party committee selected the maple leaf flag we use today, recognized around the world as the symbol of Canada.

Historical Significance What do you think might have motivated Pearson to initiate the change of flags in the 1960s?

©P

Social Welfare

Pearson's government continued to build on the social welfare programs started by Mackenzie King. During the war, King was looking for a way to keep the support of voters who remembered the hardships of the Depression and were attracted by the Co-operative Commonwealth Federation (CCF), the political party that stood for social benefits. As a result, he introduced unemployment insurance in 1940 and family allowance, or the "baby bonus," in 1944. In 1966, Pearson's government began the Canada Pension Plan, which improved on existing pension schemes. It also introduced the Canada Assistance Plan to help the provinces finance social assistance programs for people in need. In the same year, Pearson introduced Canada's system of universal health care, the **Medical Care Act.**

- How did Canadian social programs evolve?

KEY TERM

Medical Care Act an Act passed by Parliament in 1966 that provided free access to physician services for Canadians

---

up close and personal | **Tommy Douglas: What Makes Him the Greatest Canadian?** | **HISTORICAL THINKING** Historical Significance

Before 1966, most Canadians who fell seriously ill could spend their life savings on medical care. Many had to depend on charity, or face debt or bankruptcy to pay medical bills. Despite bitter opposition from doctors, Saskatchewan Premier T.C. "Tommy" Douglas introduced a complete medicare program that allowed all people in the province to seek medical treatment without paying out of their own pockets. When the bill was finally passed in Saskatchewan in 1962, it illustrated to the rest of Canada that a medicare system was possible.

In the same year, Tommy Douglas left provincial politics to become leader of the New Democratic Party (NDP), which grew out of the CCF. Fearing that the NDP might capture votes with a campaign for national medicare, the Liberals added health care to their party platform. As a result, the national Medical Care Act was passed in 1966. This Act meant that federal and provincial governments would now share the cost of medical care by doctors and hospitals for all Canadians, with funding coming from taxes.

Today, Canadians identify medicare as the social program they value most.

FIGURE 7–13 Tommy Douglas with supporters after winning the New Democratic Party leadership in August 1961

Evaluate and Draw Conclusions In 2004, Tommy Douglas was voted the Greatest Canadian of all time in a nationwide CBC contest. Why might Canadians have such high regard for him?

CHECKPOINT

1. Explain several social changes introduced by John Diefenbaker, Lester Pearson, and Tommy Douglas.

2. **a)** Why did Prime Minister Pearson believe a new flag was necessary?

b) How important do you think a flag is in asserting identity? Should it be a criminal act to show disrespect to a flag? Discuss your views with the class.

KEY TERMS

Quiet Revolution a period of rapid change and reform that modernized Québec society during the years 1960 to 1966 under the Liberal provincial government of Jean Lesage

FLQ (*Front de libération du Québec*) a revolutionary movement founded to work for an independent, socialist Québec

Parti Québécois (PQ) a Québec provincial party that advocates separation from Canada

Trudeau: A New-Style Politician

Pierre Elliott Trudeau was a French Canadian who was also a strong federalist. He appealed to many young Canadians. Previous leaders had seemed formal and serious; Trudeau was relaxed and witty. He drove a flashy sports car and was a "hip" dresser. A bachelor until 1971, he dated celebrities, went to New York nightclubs, hung out with the rich and famous, and eventually became an international celebrity himself. He delighted in joking with reporters. Crowds of admirers swarmed him at his public appearances. Young people responded to him as though he were a rock star, and "Trudeaumania" gripped the nation. He succeeded Lester Pearson as prime minister in 1968, just as radical separatists were becoming increasingly violent.

Trudeau also had a clear vision of what he thought Canada should be: a "just society" for all Canadians. He believed that government had a duty to protect the rights and freedoms of people and to foster their economic and social well-being. He also supported individual freedom and thought that governments should not interfere with personal liberties.

FIGURE 7–14 Pierre Trudeau stands before a crowd during a visit to Newfoundland in 1971. Trudeau had charisma and used the media very well. Media coverage is a "two-edged sword." The media can bring down a politician as easily as it can raise him or her up.

Interpret and Analyze What qualities do you think help politicians to "sell" themselves to a mass audience? Do any contemporary politicians have the mass appeal that Pierre Trudeau had?

- What was the impact of Québec nationalism on Canadian identity?

Québec Nationalism

In 1960, after Duplessis' death in 1959, Jean Lesage and the Liberals came to power with an election slogan that announced it was "Time for a Change." Once in power, Lesage's first step was to stamp out corruption. Government jobs and contracts were now to be awarded according to merit. Wages and pensions were raised, and restrictions on trade unionism were removed.

The government also began to modernize the province's economy, politics, education, and culture. This wave of change became known as the **Quiet Revolution,** and it transformed the face of Québec. It took control of social services and the education system. Students were now required to take more science and technology courses to prepare for the new Québec. Above all, Québécois were encouraged to think of themselves as citizens of the 20th century. As new attitudes began to take hold, the influence of the Roman Catholic Church declined.

In the 1962 election, the Liberals went one step further. They campaigned, and won, with the motto *Maîtres chez nous*—"Masters in our own house"—with the aim of strengthening Québec's control of its own economy. Among other things, the government bought several hydro companies and turned them into a provincially owned power monopoly, Hydro-Québec.

The Birth of Separatism

Québec nationalism and the separatist movement grew in the 1960s and 1970s. Québécois resented what they perceived as injustices at the hands of English-speaking Canadians. Why was Ottawa, the national capital, so overwhelmingly English speaking? Why did federal politicians from Québec seldom hold key Cabinet posts? Why did Francophones not have the right to their own schools and hospitals in the rest of Canada, even though Anglophones enjoyed those rights in Québec? Why was Québec's Francophone majority expected to speak English in stores and at work?

For some, the only solution lay in a Québec controlled entirely by Québécois—a new country independent of Canada. Some extremists joined terrorist groups such as the **FLQ** *(Front de libération du Québec)* in the name of *le Québec libre*—"a free Québec." The FLQ blew up mailboxes and attacked symbols of English-Canadian power in Québec. Many Québécois supported the aims of the terrorists, if not their methods.

In 1967, Québec Cabinet minister René Lévesque left the Liberal Party and, a year later, formed the **Parti Québécois (PQ).** Lévesque believed that Québec and Canada would do better to "divorce" peacefully than to continue a "marriage" of two cultures that seemed imposed and unworkable.

HISTORICAL INQUIRY

Gather and Organize

Research and make a list of the new political parties that elected members to the House of Commons since 1914.

HISTORICAL INQUIRY

Evaluate and Draw Conclusions

A number of new protest political parties have emerged in Canadian federal elections over the past 100 years. What five questions would you ask about a new political party? What criteria would you use to determine if the new party was successful? What were the consequences for other political parties and for Canada?

GO ONLINE

Find more information about René Lévesque and the Parti Québécois.

FIGURE 7–15 A Canadian army engineer lies injured after an FLQ bomb, which he had removed from a mailbox, exploded in his hands. On May 17, 1963, a total of 13 bombs were placed in mailboxes in the Montréal suburb of Westmount.

Evaluate and Draw Conclusions How might Canadians across the country have responded to images such as these?

Prime Minister
Lester Bowles Pearson

- born 1897, Newtonbrook, Ontario
- professor, author, diplomat
- first elected to Commons in 1948
- prime minister 1963–1968

Domestic Record

- served in the Canadian Army Medical Corps and Royal Flying Corps during the First World War
- introduced maple leaf flag in 1964
- established the Canada Pension Plan
- introduced universal medicare
- established the Canada Student Loans Plan

International Record

- Canadian ambassador to the U.S. in 1945 and attended the first conference of the UN
- saw Canada join NATO in 1949
- president of the UN General Assembly (1952–1953)
- won the 1957 Nobel Peace Prize for his part in creating the UN peacekeeping force
- criticized U.S. involvement in Vietnam

A Bilingual Nation

Lester Pearson, who had become prime minister during Québec's Quiet Revolution, was convinced that Canada would face a grave crisis unless French Canadians felt more at home in Canada. In 1963, he appointed the **Royal Commission on Bilingualism and Biculturalism** (the "Bi and Bi Commission") to investigate solutions. The Commission's report called for Canada to become bilingual, with English and French as its two official languages. Perhaps more importantly, it recommended that Canada adopt a bilingual strategy that would promote both languages across the nation, including the protection of French and English linguistic minorities. For example, parents would be able to have their children attend schools in the language of their choice in regions where there was sufficient demand.

When Pierre Trudeau succeeded Pearson in 1968, he was determined to do more to persuade people from Québec that their future lay with Canada. In 1969, his government passed the **Official Languages Act**, making Canada officially bilingual. All federal government agencies were now required to provide services in both languages, and more Francophones were appointed to senior government positions. Trudeau also called on French and English Canadians, especially young people, to increase their understanding of each other's cultures—and provided money to help make this happen.

These tactics were met with mixed reviews. Some loved them, some hated them. Some Canadians embraced the idea of bilingualism with enthusiasm. For example, many parents enrolled their children in French immersion classes. Others, especially Western Canadians, felt that the federal government was forcing French on them. They believed that Ottawa was focusing too much attention on Québec, while the West and its concerns were largely ignored. Francophones in Québec were also unimpressed. They wanted "special status" for Québec in Confederation. Trudeau, however, insisted that Québec was a province just like any other.

FIGURE 7–16 This 1976 cartoon shows then B.C. Minister of Human Resources, Bill Vander Zalm, Prime Minister Trudeau, and Québec Premier René Lévesque. Many people in British Columbia, farthest from Québec geographically, opposed the Official Languages Act.

Interpret and Analyze What is happening in the cartoon? What is the cartoonist saying about Western Canada's reaction to bilingualism? About regionalism in Canada? About Pierre Trudeau's views?

©P

The October Crisis

Trudeau disliked the very idea of separatism and took a forceful stand against Québec nationalists. In October 1970, members of the FLQ kidnapped British diplomat James Cross. In exchange for Cross's safe release, they demanded the release of FLQ members serving prison sentences and a public reading of the FLQ manifesto. Québec Premier Robert Bourassa agreed to most of the demands but refused to release any FLQ prisoners. In response, the FLQ kidnapped Québec Labour Minister Pierre Laporte.

Alarmed by the deteriorating situation in Québec, Trudeau took drastic action. At the urging of Bourassa and Montréal Mayor Jean Drapeau, he imposed the War Measures Act. Until then, the Act had only been used in wartime. The Act suspended Canadians' civil rights—anyone could be arrested and detained without being charged with an offence. Membership in the FLQ became a crime. When asked how far he would go to defeat the FLQ, Trudeau replied, "Just watch me."

On October 16, 1970, federal troops patrolled the streets of Ottawa and Montréal, and armouries across the country were locked down. Hundreds of pro-separatist Québécois were arrested and held without charge. Imposition of the War Measures Act was fiercely criticized, but Trudeau was undeterred. After all the rights legislation that had been passed by the Liberals under Trudeau, many people were shocked by this hardline approach.

One day later, police found the body of Pierre Laporte in the trunk of a car. His murder increased pressure on the government to crack down on the FLQ and find the remaining hostage, James Cross. Montréal police located Cross after he was held in captivity for 60 days. His kidnappers negotiated safe passage to Cuba in exchange for Cross's release. The October Crisis was over. Of the 450 people detained under the Act, most were released and only a small number were ever charged.

- What effect did the War Measures Act have on the legal rights of Canadians?

FIGURE 7–17 Soldiers patrol the streets of Montréal during the October Crisis.

Historical Perspectives Do you think it was wise to put on a show of force during the Crisis? Explain.

FIGURE 7–18 On October 16, 1970, several thousand Montréal students protested the imposition of the War Measures Act and showed support for the FLQ.

What If . . .

Imagine there was a terrorist threat in your community and the government imposed the War Measures Act. What civil rights would you be prepared to give up? What rights do you think are too important to give up, even in an emergency?

Robert Bourassa and Bill 22

Premier Robert Bourassa had taken office just months before the October Crisis in 1970. Although most people in Québec did not support radical separatist movements, it was clear Trudeau's Official Languages Act had not gone far enough to satisfy the Francophone majority in the province. In 1974, Bourassa responded with **Bill 22**, the first provincial legislation passed in

Bill 101 also called the "Charter of the French Language," Bill 101 strengthened the position of the French language in Québec

sovereignty-association a proposal by Québec nationalists that Québec have political independence yet retain close economic ties or association with Canada

Québec aimed at protecting the status of the French language. Bill 22 made French the official language of Québec in several areas. It was to be the language of civic administration and services, and the main language of instruction.

Bill 22 forced hundreds of thousands of business and professional people in Québec who were not proficient in French to move out of the province. Toronto eventually surpassed Montréal as the business capital of Canada. Many Anglophones were angered by what they saw as the loss of their language rights. Many Francophones, however, did not think that Bourassa had gone far enough. In the next election, Bourassa and the Liberals lost to the Parti Québécois.

The PQ in Power

In 1976, the Parti Québécois won the provincial election. It was a stunning victory for René Lévesque and his party, which had won only seven seats in the 1970 election.

Shortly after taking office, the PQ government passed **Bill 101**, sometimes referred to as the "Charter of the French Language." Its purpose was to reinforce Bill 22. Under Bill 101,

- all children were to be taught in French (with some exceptions)
- French was the official language of the courts and government, and the workplace
- all outdoor signs had to be in French

The Québécois welcomed the new language law. Many felt that their culture and language were endangered. The birth rate in Québec had fallen, and most new immigrants were educating their children in English. To non-Francophones, however, Bill 101 was a symbol of oppression. Many people in the rest of Canada felt that the PQ's policies were extreme. They looked to the federal government to stand up to the separatists.

In 1980, Lévesque's government called a referendum on Québec. He asked Québécois to give him a mandate to negotiate a new agreement with Canada based on what he called **sovereignty-association**. Québec would become politically independent, yet maintain a close economic association with Canada. (You will read more about the referendum in Chapter 8.) Forty percent of Québécois voted "yes," but it was not enough to give Lévesque the go-ahead. However, in the years ahead, support for sovereignty-association would increase.

FIGURE 7–19 Québec Premier René Lévesque at a PQ rally after his party's victory in the 1976 provincial election

CHECKPOINT

1. What did Pearson and Trudeau do to address rising Québec nationalism?

2. Do you think the Official Languages Act was an effective way to address dissatisfaction in Québec?

3. **a)** What motivated the FLQ? What tactics did they use?

   b) Had you lived in Québec in the 1960s, how do you think you would have reacted to the FLQ? Write a letter to the editor explaining your view.

4. Make a timeline of events during the October Crisis. Identify events that you think were most significant. Give reasons for your choices.

5. In Québec elections, the Parti Québécois won 23.5 percent of votes in 1970, more than 30 percent in 1973, and 41 percent in 1976. What do you think accounted for these results in each case?

©P

The use of the War Measures Act by Prime Minister Trudeau remains controversial. Was he justified in invoking such powerful legislation?

The following documents give different points of view. Read each document and identify the circumstances under which the statement was made, and what position was taken.

Source 1

The kidnapping in broad daylight of a Québec Cabinet minister [Laporte] in front of his own... residence had a dramatic effect on [the government's] view of the crisis we were facing. We began to believe that perhaps the FLQ was not just a bunch of pamphlet-waving, bomb-planting zealots after all; perhaps they were in fact members of a powerful network capable of endangering public safety, and of bringing other fringe groups—of which there were a large number at the time—into the picture, which would lead to untold violence. If all these groups coalesced [came together], the crisis could go on for a very long time, with tragic consequences for the entire country.

–Pierre Trudeau, Memoirs, 1993

Source 2

...[T]he list of people arrested, without warrant, on the strength of suspicions, prejudice, or pure idiocy, exceeded the incredible number of four hundred.... Deprived of all their rights, beginning with habeas corpus, a great many of them were to remain in custody for days and weeks. As much as, if not more than in 1917, when there was at least the excuse... of a real world war, the whole of Québec found itself behind bars as Trudeau and company now attempted to justify their act before Parliament, the existence of which they seemed just to have remembered.

–René Lévesque, Memoirs, 1986

Source 3

...[T]here were no fine distinctions drawn between separatism and terrorism in the general round-up in October 1970.... After the crisis had passed, rather than issuing an apology for such overzealous police work, the prime minister boasted that separatism was "dead." Other... Liberals agreed: the FLQ crisis had been an opportunity to "smash separatism" and the government had taken it.

–The Structure of Canadian History, 1984

Source 4

As for the objection that Trudeau was acting to squash separatism and... the Parti Québécois, we have the statements of both the prime minister and one of his supporters... during the crisis. On October 17, [Bryce] Mackasey stressed to the House of Commons that the Parti Québécois was "a legitimate political party. It wants to bring an end to this country through democratic means, but that is the privilege of that party." Trudeau... made the same point in November to an interviewer.

–Canada Since 1945: Power, Politics, and Provincialism, 1989

Interpret and Analyze Evidence

1. Are these documents primary sources or secondary sources? Explain in each case.

2. Summarize each document's main argument.

3. Which documents support Lévesque's claims? Trudeau's claims?

4. Which documents do you consider to be the most credible sources? Justify your choices.

5. Write one or two paragraphs giving your view on whether the use of the War Measures Act was justified. Support your view with details from the text and the documents above.

● How did the Canadian government respond to economic challenges?

KEY TERMS

embargo the prohibition by a government or organization that prevents certain goods from being shipped in or out of a country

regional disparity differences in income, wages, and jobs in one area compared with another

Western alienation the feeling on the part of Western Canada that federal policies favour Central Canada; it has led to the rise of several regional parties

GO ONLINE • • • • • • • • • • • • • •
Check out more about inflation at the Canadian Encyclopedia.

Economic Challenges

When the Trudeau era began, Canadians could look back on nearly two decades of economic growth. People old enough to remember the dark days of the Depression were amazed by the prosperity they were enjoying. Many Canadians believed that the post-war boom would continue indefinitely. High unemployment and poverty were surely problems of the past, never to be seen again. But within just a few years, this optimism was badly shaken.

The Problem of Inflation

A variety of factors caused the economic crisis, but one of the most important was an oil **embargo** imposed in 1973 by the Organization of the Petroleum Exporting Countries (OPEC). In that year, war broke out in the Middle East between Israel and its Arab neighbours. Many Western countries, including Canada, supported Israel. In retaliation, OPEC, which included Saudi Arabia, Kuwait, and other Arab oil-producing countries, refused to sell oil to these countries. Almost overnight, oil and gas prices jumped about 400 percent.

The huge increase in oil prices started a round of inflation that would last most of the 1970s. The prices of all manufactured products went up sharply, and Canadians found that the purchasing power of their dollar fell steadily. Suddenly, they were heading for tough economic times.

As prices rose, Canadian workers began to demand higher wages; but as their wages increased, so did prices, and inflation spiralled. At the same time, businesses were failing. Their energy and labour costs had soared while the demand for their products was down. Unemployment rates rose from the average of 3 to 5 percent during the 1950s and 1960s to a high of 12 percent by 1983.

For the average Canadian family, the 1970s were unsettling times. Inflation stretched household budgets and increased the need for women to enter the workforce. Dual-income families became common. By 1978, the average family's buying power had fallen for the first time since the end of the Second World War.

FIGURE 7–20 Canada's high rate of inflation in the 1970s was tied to massive oil price increases generated by the oil crisis of 1973.

Cause and Consequence What would it mean if prices went up more than 14 percent a year, but your income remained the same?

Regionalism

To make matters worse, two economic problems that had plagued Canada in the past resurfaced. Both were the result of regionalism. The first of these problems was **regional disparity**, or the economic gap between the poorer and more prosperous regions of Canada. As in the Depression of the 1930s, industries based on natural resources were hit the hardest in the recession of the 1970s. The fishing industry in Atlantic Canada and the forestry, mining, and fishing industries in British Columbia suffered massive layoffs. Ontario and Québec were less affected, and the other provinces resented them. The Trudeau government increased transfer payments to the provinces to be used for social services. It also spent millions of dollars on regional projects to help economic development in certain areas, especially the Atlantic provinces.

The second problem of **Western alienation** had long existed. Many Westerners believed that Ottawa's policies favoured Central Canada at the expense of the West. In the 1970s, Westerners were shocked when, in response to the oil crisis, the federal government froze the price of domestic oil and gas and imposed a tax on petroleum exported from Western Canada. The money raised by the tax would subsidize the cost of imported oil in the East. These actions infuriated Albertans. Along with their premier, Peter Lougheed, they felt that Alberta had the right to charge world prices for its oil:

> *The Fathers of Confederation decided that the natural resources within provincial boundaries would be owned by the citizens through their provincial governments.... We view the federal export tax on Alberta oil as contrary to both the spirit and the intent of Confederation.*
> *–Federal–Provincial Conference on Energy, 1974*

To deal with a renewed oil crisis and rising gas prices, the Liberals also brought in the National Energy Program (NEP). The NEP aimed to reduce oil consumption, protect Canadians from rising oil prices, and make Canada oil self-sufficient.

- How was regionalism expressed in the 1960s and 1970s?

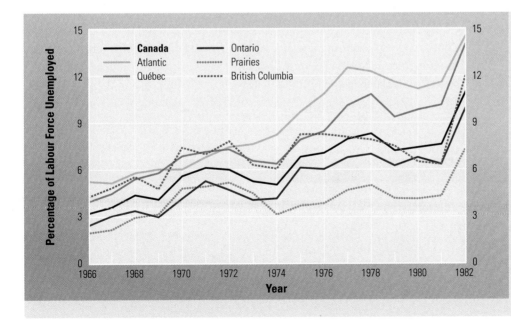

FIGURE 7–21 Regional unemployment rates, 1966–1982

Interpret and Analyze
Which regions had the highest unemployment rate? Which had the lowest? How did the rate in British Columbia vary in relation to other provinces? What might account for the difference?

The program provided funding to Canadian petroleum companies to drill for oil in promising sites in the Arctic and off the coast of Newfoundland. It also encouraged consumers to switch from oil to gas and electric sources of power. Alberta, once again, reacted angrily. By 1984, oil prices had fallen and the NEP had been dismantled.

The Future of Energy

Today's energy crisis is caused by a vastly increased world demand for hydrocarbons. To meet demand, and to diminish the climate-changing consequences of burning petroleum and coal, new technologies are now in widespread use. Many governments actively promote energy conservation; some even use tax incentives. In January 2010, the government of Ontario signed a $7 billion deal with Korean technology company Samsung to develop green energy technology and to construct solar and wind power facilities in that province. This technology is expected to create jobs and bring financial benefits.

FIGURE 7–22 Solar collectors like this one may soon be a common sight in some areas of Canada.

- What measures did Canada take to promote a distinct Canadian identity in the 1960s and 1970s?

HISTORICAL INQUIRY

Communicate

Why and how did Premier Brad Wall of Saskatchewan persuade Prime Minister Stephen Harper to stop a foreign takeover of Potash Corporation in his province in 2010? Write a short essay to support your research.

Expanding Horizons

During the 1970s, Canadians were again asking themselves whether the United States had too much influence over the Canadian economy. Prime Minister Trudeau was particularly interested in finding new trading partners so that Canada would no longer depend so heavily on the U.S. as the major customer for its exports. Trudeau tried to interest the European Economic Community in expanding trade with Canada. Those countries, however, were more eager to strengthen trade links among themselves. And the newly industrialized countries of Southeast Asia, the so-called "Asian tigers," showed little interest in a special agreement with Canada.

Reluctantly, the Trudeau administration accepted the reality of Canada's continuing economic dependence on the United States. The government tried to strengthen its control over the economy and culture through programs and agencies such as the NEP, the CRTC (see Chapter 6), and the Foreign Investment Review Agency (FIRA), which reviews all major proposed foreign investments to determine whether they serve Canada's national interest.

CHECKPOINT

1. What economic problems arose in the 1970s? How did Trudeau propose to deal with them? What was the outcome?

2. What would be the consequences of high inflation for
   a) people on fixed incomes and pensions?
   b) workers who were not in unions?
   c) a family seeking a loan to buy a house?

3. How did the problems of this period influence the growth of regionalism and Western alienation?

©P

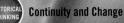
Innovations
A New Age of Technology and Medicine

The Second World War spurred a wave of new technology that continued into the 1960s and 1970s. Computers and other communications technologies were revolutionizing the way Canadians worked, played, and communicated. With satellite broadcasting, Canadians had access to hundreds of television stations. New discoveries in science and medicine, such as the artificial heart and the Pill, revolutionized Canadians' thinking about their own health and, in some cases, their social roles.

"Giant step for mankind" Space travel became a fact in the 1960s. U.S. astronauts from the *Apollo 11* spacecraft landed on the moon in the lunar module "Eagle." The first person to set foot on the moon's surface was Neil Armstrong on July 21, 1969.

The pill The first oral contraceptive was approved for use in the United States in 1960. Although Canada didn't formally approve "the pill" as birth control until 1969, it had been available for medical reasons. Between 1960 and 1965, prescriptions for the pill increased by 7400 percent. Physicians began to recognize the seriousness of preventing unwanted pregnancy but were still more comfortable writing prescriptions for married women.

Information to go The first computer microchip, invented in 1971, revolutionized computer technology. Computers had been in use since the end of the Second World War, but they were very big and slow at processing information. The microchip made computers smaller, more portable, and cheaper. The first flexible disk drive was invented in 1976.

Transplanting futures The 1960s and 1970s saw dramatic advances in medicine. The first successful heart transplant took place in 1967.

Information at your fingertips The Internet was formed in 1969 when the U.S. Defense Department and four U.S. universities linked their computers to create the Advanced Research Projects Agency Network (ARPAnet). Its aim was to decentralize the Defense Department's computer system and make it less vulnerable to attack by the Soviet Union.

• What was Canada's involvement in the Cold War?

FIGURE 7–23 For many people, the 1961 construction of the Berlin Wall to separate the German city into two zones—one communist and one capitalist—was a frightening symbol of Soviet power and aggression. It appeared that the Cold War was still going strong.

A More Independent International Policy

As the Cold War intensified during the early 1960s, tensions developed between Canada and the United States. Even at the personal level, the leaders of the two countries did not get along: Prime Minister John Diefenbaker and U.S. President John Kennedy strongly disliked each other; President Johnson treated Lester Pearson with contempt; Trudeau had nothing but scorn for President Richard Nixon. These differences were particularly obvious during the most serious crisis of the Cold War: the Cuban Missile Crisis, which took the world to the brink of nuclear war. Later, the Vietnam War further strained Canada's relations with the United States.

The Nuclear Issue in Canada

The Cuban Missile Crisis caused a debate about Canada's defence policy and the government's stand on nuclear weapons. Should Canada accept nuclear weapons on its territory, as the United States wished? When the Avro Arrow was scrapped (see Chapter 6), Canada accepted U.S. **Bomarc missiles** that were capable of carrying nuclear warheads. The years that passed before the missiles were actually installed, however, allowed time for second thoughts.

In 1963, the ruling Conservative Party was divided on the issue. The Minister of External Affairs felt Canada should be a non-nuclear nation. He argued that it was hypocritical to urge the United Nations to work for disarmament while accepting nuclear weapons. The Defence Minister, in contrast, insisted that nuclear weapons were vital in protecting Canada against communist aggression. Meanwhile, the anti-nuclear movement was growing among Canadian citizens. Many were starting to realize that nuclear war would amount to global suicide.

During the election campaign of 1963, the Liberals, under the leadership of Lester Pearson, proposed that Canadian forces accept nuclear weapons under certain conditions. Prime Minister Diefenbaker and the Conservatives, however, appealed to Canadian nationalism, including Canada's right to decide for itself on international matters. Many business leaders and influential newspapers supported the Liberals, fearing that Diefenbaker's anti-Americanism would injure trade with and investment from the United States. The nuclear issue split the country. Diefenbaker was narrowly defeated in the election of 1963, and the Liberals formed a minority government. This federal election was the first to be fought over Canada–U.S. relations since 1911.

FIGURE 7–24 Prime Minister Trudeau and American President Richard Nixon are smiling in this staged photograph. In reality, Nixon and Trudeau disliked one another. Nixon particularly resented Trudeau's support of Cuba, which ran counter to American policy.

case study

The Cuban Missile Crisis: Canada–U.S. Relations Deteriorate

In 1959, Cuban rebels led by Fidel Castro overthrew Cuba's pro-U.S. dictator, Fulgencio Batista. The United States reacted angrily, imposing trade and economic sanctions on Cuba. In 1961, a group of Cuban exiles, supported by the U.S., landed in Cuba with the aim of overthrowing the Castro government. The "Bay of Pigs" invasion was a failure, which encouraged Cuba to turn to the Soviet Union for support.

In October 1962, U.S. surveillance showed that the U.S.S.R. was installing offensive nuclear missile bases in Cuba. Missiles launched from these sites were a direct threat to U.S. security. President Kennedy announced a naval and air blockade of Cuba. U.S. forces and NORAD were readied for war. Armed B-52 bombers were constantly in the air. The world seemed to be poised on the brink of war.

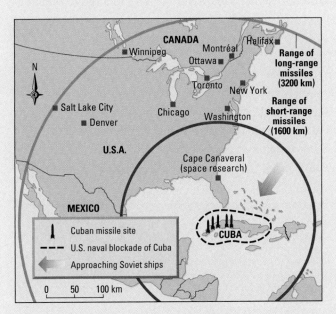

FIGURE 7–25 Projected range of Cuban missiles

At first, Soviet Premier Nikita Khrushchev refused to remove the missiles. He put the armed forces of the U.S.S.R. on full alert and Soviet ships steamed toward U.S. ships blockading Cuba. At the last minute, Khrushchev agreed to dismantle the missile bases in exchange for a promise that the U.S. would not invade Cuba.

After the Missile Crisis ended, relations between the U.S. and Cuba continued to be difficult. The U.S.

FIGURE 7–26 On October 22, 1962, U.S. President John F. Kennedy gave a dramatic radio and television address explaining his position on the Cuban Missile Crisis to the American public.

tightened its economic embargo and restricted its citizens from doing business with or visiting Cuba. (Not until 2015 did Cuba and the United States begin to talk about ending the embargo and lifting travel restrictions.)

During the crisis, the United States expected Canada, its partner in NORAD, to provide unconditional support of its policies. Prime Minister Diefenbaker, however, preferred that the United Nations send a fact-finding mission to Cuba to verify the U.S. surveillance.

Diefenbaker was reluctant to have Canada drawn into a major conflict that seemed largely rooted in U.S. policy and interests. At first, the Canadian government refused to place Canada's NORAD forces on alert. Nor did it allow U.S. planes with atomic weapons to land at Canadian bases. The Americans were furious.

Diefenbaker believed he was defending Canada's independence, but a poll later showed that 80 percent of Canadians thought he was wrong. Canadian troops were eventually put on alert but the damage to Canada–U.S. relations had already been done.

Thinking It Through

1. The Monroe Doctrine is a U.S. policy from 1823, which gives the U.S. the right to intervene if foreign governments interfere in countries in the Americas. Was President Kennedy justified in using the Monroe Doctrine to support his actions during the Cuban Missile Crisis? Explain.

2. In your opinion, should Canada have supported the United States during the Cuban Missile Crisis? Give reasons for your answer.

3. "At the time of the Cuban Missile Crisis, the U.S. had missiles of its own in Europe that were capable of striking Soviet targets." To what extent does this statement affect your thinking about the crisis?

©P

The Vietnam War

The war in Vietnam profoundly affected politics and society in the United States and Canada. Vietnam was divided, almost in half. North Vietnam had a communist government. The government in South Vietnam, more a dictatorship than a democracy, was supported by the United States. The Americans felt that if the south fell to communism, then it would not be long before other Asian states fell, a sort of domino effect. At first, the United States sent military advisors and economic help to the South Vietnamese, but by the 1960s it was sending troops as well. By 1966, there were 317 000 U.S. soldiers in Vietnam, and the number kept growing. At the same time, the U.S.S.R. and communist China supplied weapons and aid to North Vietnam.

The war in Vietnam was the first war recorded by television cameras. Nightly newscasts brought the events of the war into the living rooms of millions of Americans. In 1968, the public was horrified to learn of a massacre of Vietnamese civilians by U.S. troops in the village of My Lai. That same year, North Vietnamese forces simultaneously attacked cities throughout South Vietnam during the Tet Offensive. They even briefly seized the U.S. embassy in the capital city of Saigon (today's Ho Chi Minh City). Americans, who had been assured that they were winning the war, were stunned.

As Americans watched Vietnamese villages being bombed, and their own young men returning home disabled or in body bags, many began questioning the war. As more and more Americans disagreed with their government's actions, massive anti-war protests swept across the country.

Canada's Reaction to the War

Canadians were divided in their response to the war in Vietnam. Many people still saw communism as a real threat to Western security. However, as the war raged on, more and more Canadians turned against American policy. Until 1968, most opponents of the war were students, but opposition soon came from a much wider group of Canadians.

FIGURE 7–27 Images of American soldiers in Vietnam encouraged anti-war sentiments.

Interpret and Analyze How might seeing images such as this one in newspapers and on television influence young people to oppose the war? Why do you think today's wars do not generate so much interest from young people?

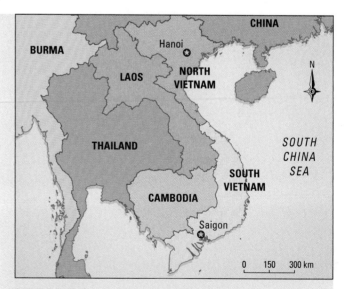

FIGURE 7–28 Southeast Asia during the Vietnam War

©P

During the Vietnam War, the U.S. drafted young men to serve in the armed forces. Beginning in 1965, thousands of American draft resisters and deserters who were opposed to the war came to Canada. Anti-draft groups were established in many cities to help them get settled and support their protests against the war. The U.S. government was unhappy about Canada accepting resisters.

The Canadian government tried its best to stay neutral during the Vietnam War, but its close relationship with the U.S. made this complicated. Canada did not send troops to fight in the war, although thousands of Canadians did join the U.S. forces voluntarily. Some Canadian companies benefited from the war by selling goods such as berets, boots, airplane engines, and weapons to the U.S. Defense Department. In 1965, when Prime Minister Pearson spoke out against a U.S. bombing campaign in North Vietnam, he was severely reprimanded by President Lyndon Johnson.

FIGURE 7–29 This demonstration was one of hundreds of anti-war protests in Canada.

Interpret and Analyze Do you think Canada was right to offer American draft resisters and deserters a safe haven?

The Vietnam War Ends

In 1969, President Richard Nixon took office in the United States, with a pledge to pull American troops out of Southeast Asia. By 1972, the Americans began to withdraw. The last American combat forces left South Vietnam in 1973. Less than two years later, a massive North Vietnamese military offensive crushed the South Vietnamese army. Vietnam, ravaged by decades of war and destruction, was unified under communist rule. Those who did not support the new regime were stripped of their property and forced into "re-education" camps, where they were pressured to support their new leaders.

Many anti-communist Vietnamese fled. They took to the seas in boats hoping to find freedom. These "boat people" made their way to refugee camps in Malaysia and Hong Kong where they applied for refugee status. Thousands of Vietnamese were accepted into Canada and became citizens.

CHECKPOINT

1. **Historical Significance** Of the innovations shown on page 227, which one do you think had the greatest impact on society? Explain your answer.

2. Identify the following and explain the role each played in the Cuban Missile Crisis: a) Nikita Khrushchev, b) Fidel Castro, c) John F. Kennedy, d) John Diefenbaker.

3. What questions about nuclear weapons did the Cuban Missile Crisis raise in Canadians' minds? Why did these questions divide Canadians?

4. What consequences did the Cuban Missile Crisis and the Vietnam War have for Canada–U.S. relations?

5. How did U.S. policy deal with Cuba after the Cuban Revolution? How did Canada's policy differ?

6. How would you explain the war in Vietnam to someone who knew nothing about it? Answer the following questions: What? Where? When? Why?

7. **Evaluate and Draw Conclusions** Why did Canada accept so many Vietnamese boat people in the 1970s?

Should Canada's foreign policy be independent of the United States?

As you learned in Chapter 6, Canada has a long history of international involvement and the Canadian military has been in many places in the world. Mostly, our troops have been part of United Nations peacekeeping missions, in Cyprus and Suez, for example. Peacekeeping allowed us to actively participate in international conflict while still maintaining a non-combative role—and a largely independent foreign policy. We were not directly involved in either the Cuban Missile Crisis or the war in Vietnam, even though both were very important to our superpower ally, the United States. However, in 1990, we joined the U.S.-led coalition against Iraq and sent ships and planes into that

conflict. Although our commitment was relatively small, it represented a shift in Canada's foreign policy. More recently, as part of NATO, Canada took on a more active combat role, particularly since the 9/11 attacks and the beginning of America's "War on Terror."

Between 2001 and 2011, Canadian troops fought in Afghanistan as part of the NATO force there. This was a significant departure from peacekeeping. Defeating the Taliban in Afghanistan was an important NATO goal, but it was also fundamental to the geopolitical goals of the United States. Was Afghanistan important to Canada? Should we have been involved? Are we helping the U.S. achieve its goals rather than our own?

FIGURE 7–30 Two images of Canadian forces: above, combatants in Afghanistan, and left, under a UN peacekeeping mandate in Haiti

Interpret and Analyze Compare these images. What differences do you see in the soldiers? How might these differences be interpreted by citizens of the countries in which they are stationed?

● What measures did Canada take to promote a distinct Canadian identity?

In today's world, with the threat of international terrorism, is it really possible for a middle power closely allied to a superpower, as Canada is, to have an independent foreign policy?

Consider these opinions for and against Canadian participation in Afghanistan. The first is from an article in *The Tyee* newspaper, published in October, 2006. Byers argues that following the American lead has meant that Canada's peace-keeping reputation has been sacrificed. The second is from an interview in *Maclean's* magazine with commentator Andrew Coyne. Coyne thinks Canada's mission in Afghanistan is necessary. He also makes the point, in this excerpt, that helping the U.S. has other benefits.

Against:

Wrapped up in the distinction between the peacekeeping opportunities in Lebanon and Darfur and the counter-insurgency mission in Afghanistan is the additional issue of reputation costs, most notably the cost to Canada's international reputation for independence and objectivity, and thus our ability to lead and persuade on a wide range of issues. Where would we gain the most in terms of our international reputation: continuing with a failing counter-insurgency mission in Afghanistan, or leading a humanitarian intervention to stop the genocide in Darfur?

For:

There's a crasser, more self-interested reason for why we should stay. Just now we're having a devil of a time convincing the Americans we're as serious about fighting terrorism as they are. The issue has all sorts of obvious implications for our trade relations. Sticking it out in Afghanistan would be a fine way to prove our credentials. Whereas clearing out before the job's done risks giving aid and comfort, not just to the enemy, but the French and Italians.

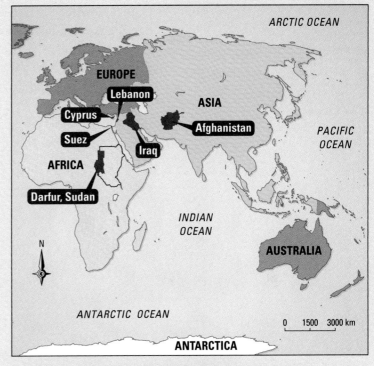

FIGURE 7–31 Canadian peacekeeping missions

Thinking It Through

1. In your opinion, does Canada have an international role that is different from, and independent of, that of the U.S.? How would you define that role?

2. Summarize Coyne's argument in a sentence and support it with two examples of Canadian military action from the 20th century. Do the same for Byers' argument.

3. Research Canada's participation in the Gulf War. Compare this with Canada's participation in the Afghan operation in terms of length of commitment, military resources provided, cost of the war, and casualties.

4. Research by the Department of National Defence on the mission in Afghanistan found that as the mission went on, Canadian support for it decreased. By 2011, the year combat ended, only 60 percent of Canadians supported the mission. Write a brief description of Canadian foreign policy goals as you see them and include an explanation of why or why not the Afghan mission fits the goals.

- What was Canada's involvement in the Cold War?

KEY TERMS

trade and aid the process of stimulating the economies of developing countries with aid so that they can access global markets and trade with developed nations

tied aid aid given to a foreign country with conditions attached

Trudeau's Foreign Policy

The Vietnam War and the Cuban Missile Crisis highlighted the differences between American and Canadian foreign policy. As prime minister, Pierre Trudeau reflected the changing attitudes of the time. One of his goals was to chart a course in foreign policy that was less dependent on U.S. approval.

This intention was clearly signalled in 1970, when Canada officially recognized the communist government of the People's Republic of China. Even though Trudeau defied U.S. policy, his decision made sense to most Canadians. Mainland China was a great power, a major purchaser of Canadian wheat and other goods, and potentially a significant trading partner.

At the same time, Trudeau did not wish to anger the U.S. Neither did he think Canada could act on foreign or economic affairs without considering the U.S. to some extent. He explained his views in a now famous speech:

Let me say that it should not be surprising if these policies in many instances either reflect or take into account the proximity of the United States. Living next to you is in some ways like sleeping with an elephant. No matter how friendly or even-tempered is the beast... one is affected by every twitch and grunt.

–Speech to the National Press Club, Washington, 1969

FIGURE 7–32 In 1976, Trudeau became the first leader of a NATO country to pay a state visit to Fidel Castro's communist Cuba. At the end of a speech, he surprised and delighted the audience by proclaiming "Viva Cuba" and "Viva Castro."

Evaluate and Draw Conclusions Why would his words be controversial in Canada and the United States?

Defence Revisited

Trudeau's approach to national defence was a sharp departure from that of previous governments. Lester Pearson had referred to Canada and the United States as "defence partners." Trudeau believed that Canada needed to re-evaluate this policy. He took steps to scale back Canada's participation in the nuclear arms race with the Soviet Union in the hope that this would ease Cold War tensions. These steps included the following:

- From 1970 to 1972, Canada's NATO forces gave up their nuclear missiles in Europe.
- The Bomarc missile sites that Pearson had accepted in 1963 were dismantled. A new jet fighter, the CF-18 Hornet, was armed with conventional rather than nuclear warheads.
- The national defence budget was cut by 20 percent and Canada's NATO contingent in Europe was reduced to half its former strength.

Military officers, diplomats, and officials from the U.S. embassy in Ottawa were outraged, but the government pursued its new course.

At the same time, Canada continued to participate in NATO and NORAD, alongside the United States. American vessels and submarines armed with nuclear missiles were permitted to dock in Canadian ports. American branch plants in Canada accepted contracts from the U.S. Defence Department to develop nuclear technology or other war materials, sometimes over strong protests from Canadian pacifists.

Canada's International Profile

Throughout Trudeau's period in office, the Cold War continued to dominate international affairs. The world remained divided between the West (the U.S. and its allies) and the East (communist China, the Soviet Union, and countries friendly to it). Trudeau wanted Canada to be a middle power, strong enough and respected enough to chart an independent foreign policy.

Outside the two rival power blocs, most of the world's people lived in countries not officially allied with either superpower. African and Asian nations emerging from colonial rule after the Second World War tried to remain detached from Cold War rivalries—at least for a time. But other divisions were emerging. Most new nations were located in the southern hemisphere. They were also, for the most part, far less industrialized than countries in the northern hemisphere. So, while the Cold War split the world politically between East and West, a huge economic gap separated the rich North from the poor South.

The Trudeau government aimed to bridge both gaps in order to promote world peace and understanding among nations. As a middle power, Canada could build links between East and West and North and South. Trudeau's efforts to reduce nuclear weapons and to establish trade and sporting links with communist states were part of this plan. Trudeau called for more aid for the poor countries of the world. He believed that the prosperous nations of the North should be helping the poverty-stricken countries of the South to develop their economies and improve the living conditions for their people. This policy of "**trade and aid**" became the cornerstone of Trudeau's foreign policy in bridging the North–South gap.

In 1968, a new government body known as the Canadian International Development Agency (CIDA) was formed. CIDA's responsibility was to boost foreign aid to less industrialized countries. Countries receiving aid would have to agree to use it to buy products manufactured in Canada. In this way, Canada would benefit as well. This was known as **tied aid**, and it made up more than half the total development aid Canada extended to less industrialized nations. During Trudeau's administration, the total amount of aid Canada extended to developing countries increased from $278 million in 1969 to more than $2 billion in 1984.

FIGURE 7–33 Paul Henderson celebrates after scoring the winning goal for Canada in the Canada–U.S.S.R. hockey series in 1972. This popular event was one of many steps taken by Canada to lower Cold War tensions. Why do you think winning the series meant so much to Canadians?

`Historical Significance`

What If...

Imagine Canada had taken a stronger military stance during the 1960s and 1970s. How might Canada's image as a middle power have been affected? Would the Canada–U.S. relationship have been different?

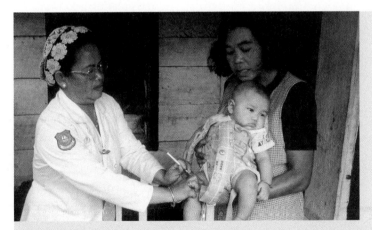

FIGURE 7–34 Canadian-sponsored immunization program in the Philippines

Cause and Consequence How would Canadian programs, such as immunization, improve living conditions in less industrialized countries? How would improved living conditions promote peace?

Prime Minister
Pierre Elliott Trudeau

- born 1919, Montréal, Québec
- lawyer, law professor, author
- first elected to Commons in 1965
- prime minister 1968–1979, 1980–1984

Domestic Record

- changed the Criminal Code to decriminalize homosexuality, make it easier to divorce, and legalize abortions

- passed the Official Languages Act in 1969 to officially make Canada bilingual

- invoked the War Measures Act during the October Crisis in 1970

- campaigned against Québec separatism during the 1980 referendum

- passed the Constitution Act in 1982, which entrenched the Canadian Charter of Rights and Freedoms in the Canadian Constitution

- appointed Jeanne Sauvé Canada's first woman Governor General in 1984

International Record

- won the Albert Einstein Peace Prize in 1984 for negotiating the reduction of nuclear weapons and easing Cold War tensions

- first leader of a NATO country to visit Cuba

- recognized Communist China before the United States did

The Cold War Renewed

While Trudeau was trying to bridge the economic gap among countries during the early 1970s, tension between the United States and the Soviet Union eased, and the two countries agreed to reduce the number of their nuclear weapons. In 1972, at the Strategic Arms Limitation Talks (SALT I), the U.S. and the Soviet Union signed the **Anti-Ballistic Missile Treaty** (ABMT) and an interim agreement on strategic offensive arms. This marked a breakthrough in relations between the two superpowers.

In 1979, however, the Soviet Union invaded Afghanistan. It also sent medium-range missiles to Eastern Europe. In response, NATO announced that it, too, was deploying more advanced missiles in Europe. In protest against the Soviet occupation of Afghanistan, many Western nations, including Canada, boycotted the 1980 Olympic Games held in Moscow.

Sovereignty in the Arctic

Canada and the United States were soon drawn into a confrontation over territory. Canada claimed sovereignty, or possession, of the islands of the Arctic and the waterways between them, including the Northwest Passage. (See The High Arctic Relocation, page 180.) In 1968, oil was discovered at Prudhoe Bay in Alaska, and American oil companies were interested in establishing a regular tanker route through the Northwest Passage to the east coast of the United States—in other words, through an area Canada believed was its own. The following year, an American oil tanker, the *Manhattan*, travelled along this route without Canadian approval. The Canadian government became alarmed that the U.S. was treating the Northwest Passage as an international waterway, rather than as part of Canada's Arctic possessions.

Canada was also concerned about the fragile Arctic ecosystem. Greater tanker traffic through the Northwest Passage increased the likelihood of an oil spill that could spell environmental disaster. The government announced it was extending Canada's territorial limit from 3 to 12 miles (about 5 to 19 kilometres) offshore. In addition, it passed the Arctic Waters Pollution Prevention Act, creating a 100-mile (160-kilometre) pollution-free zone around the islands of the Canadian Arctic. Within this zone, strict environmental regulations would be enforced, and oil tanker traffic would be controlled. Despite protests from Washington, the oil companies involved in the Alaska development agreed to respect Canada's rules.

Canada won support for its moves in the Arctic region from a number of nations with Arctic territories. At the United Nations, a conference on a "Law of the Sea" was suggested, endorsing the idea that the nations of the world should act together to protect the oceans as "the common heritage of mankind." Canada renewed talks about a 12-mile territorial sea and a further 200-mile economic zone for every country whose land mass faced an ocean. Canada also suggested that oil or mining companies active in environmentally sensitive areas should pay a special tax and channel some of their revenues into local economic development. To date, these suggestions have been adopted by more than 160 nations as part of the Law of the Sea Convention.

The Politics of Global Warming

In recent years, global warming has severely weakened Arctic ice and made the region easier to navigate. Canada now faces a serious threat against what some see as its sovereign territory. Many countries lay claim to the region—and the seabed—of the Arctic Circle. At stake is the Arctic's many important resources: oil, natural gas, diamonds, gold, and silver.

The Northwest Passage is enormously beneficial to Canada as well. Prime Minister Stephen Harper announced that Canada will build a deep-water port in the High Arctic. Will this be enough to protect Canada's sovereignty in the Arctic? Though Inuit governments and organizations are generally positive, the Inuit have mixed feelings about these developments, which will significantly change their lives. Paul Kaludjak of the Arctic Athabaskan Council (AAC) expressed the council's view:

> The Canadian government does not have a strategy to assert our sovereignty. Instead, individual departments have reacted to events. We need a long-term plan that knits together federal and territorial agencies and Inuit organizations. We all have roles to play. Asserting Arctic sovereignty is a national, not a federal, project.
>
> *–Arctic Athabaskan Council Newsletter, November 2006*

In 2013, Canada announced that it would file a claim to the Arctic that would include the North Pole.

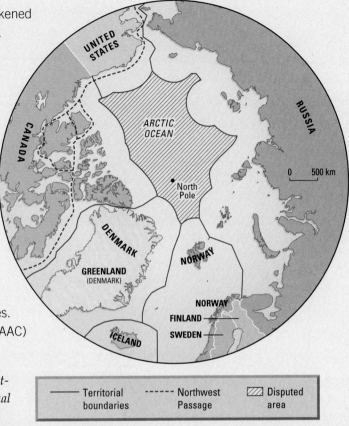

FIGURE 7–35 How might the extension of territorial limits affect Canadian sovereignty in the Arctic? Do you think Canada should defend its claims to the region?

Evaluate and Draw Conclusions What military assets and capabilities do you think Canada would need to back its claims?

CHECKPOINT

1. What do you think Trudeau meant when he said that living next to the United States is like sleeping next to an elephant?

2. List the ways in which Trudeau distanced Canada's foreign policy from that of the U.S. in the 1970s. What were the reasons for this shift?

3. How did Trudeau try to bridge the gap between rich and poor countries?

4. Where did Cold War tensions increase from 1979 to 1984? What was Canada's response?

5. What steps did Canada take in the 1960s and 1970s to uphold its rights in the Arctic? How did the Arctic relocation of 1953 help lay the groundwork for Canadian sovereignty in the Arctic? Do you think these efforts—and Canada's most recent efforts—will ultimately be effective?

CHAPTER FOCUS QUESTION How did Canada's political, social, and economic policies reflect a new independence in the 1960s and 1970s?

By 1967, Canada had a population of 20 million people, half of whom were under 25 years of age. The needs, views, and priorities of youth affected everything from politics to social priorities. In politics, Pierre Trudeau and his policies seemed to reflect the times. The country experienced a separatist crisis to which Trudeau responded forcefully. Canadians also thought a lot about their ties to the United States, particularly after Americans became involved in the unpopular Vietnam War. And, perhaps for the first time, the environment became an important national and international issue.

1. Make a three-column chart like the one shown below for the key people, events, and ideas of the 1960s and 1970s, and early 1980s. Use the information in the chapter to fill in the chart, including a brief explanation of each item and a sketch to help you visualize the concept.

Key People	Key Events	Key Ideas

Knowledge and Understanding

2. Continue the ongoing timeline assignment you began in Chapter 2. Review the events that are covered in the chapter. Write the name and date of each event on the timeline and explain how the event contributed to Canadian independence.

Cause and Consequence

3. In 1982, the National Indian Brotherhood, the lobby that led the fight against the Liberal White Paper, became the Assembly of First Nations. How might the debate over the White Paper have catalyzed the formation of this national advocacy group?

4. How successful was the Canadian government in dealing with the economic challenges of the 1960s and 1970s? Provide evidence from the textbook.

5. What was the October Crisis? Why was this event a challenge to Canadian unity? How did Trudeau respond? What were some unintended consequences?

6. What is inflation? What caused the inflation of the 1970s? Why would inflation affect Canadian unity? (Hint: Think about regionalism.) How did the National Energy Program add to the problem?

7. Write a summary explaining the Vietnam War to modern newspaper readers who know little about it. Answer the following questions: a) Who? b) What? c) When? d) Where? e) Why?

8. "The Vietnam War helped define Canada as a nation since it encouraged Canadian leaders to distance their country from U.S. foreign policy." Explain this statement in your own words.

9. How successful was Canada at keeping its independence from the U.S. during the 1960s and 1970s? Create a two-column chart like the one below. Provide examples of independence and rate their success.

Evidence of Canadian Independence from the U.S.	Success Rate (high/moderate/low)

Apply Your Thinking

10. Using the chart from Question 1, select at least five events that you think were the most significant to Canada's independence during the 1960s and 1970s. Provide evidence to support your opinion.

Historical Significance

11. Assess the impact of Québec nationalism both on Québec and on the rest of Canada.

12. List and then rank Trudeau's largest national and international challenges. Provide evidence from the textbook to support your choices.

13. Using websites suggested by your teacher, research world and United States indigenous peoples' rights activism in the 1960s and 1970s. How would you describe the influence of this activism on Aboriginal rights movements in Canada? Give reasons for your answer.

Communicate

Ethical Dimension

14. Trudeau was right to impose the War Measures Act in 1970. Present a reasoned argument for or against this statement.

Evaluate and Draw Conclusions

15. The period from 1960 to 1982 was a time of varied and widespread social activism. Look at the photos in the collage below and respond to the following:
    - How might these images influence other groups or individuals?
    - Analyze the photos and explain why each group was protesting.
    - Is there a common theme or goal for the groups?
    - Describe some of the methods used by the groups to achieve their goals.
    - Evaluate which methods were the most successful in drawing attention to the groups' causes and explain why this was the case.
    - Which of these methods are still used today?
    - From your knowledge, how successful were the groups in achieving their goals?
    - Individually, with a partner, or in a small group, research one of the causes below and share your findings with the class. What was the historical significance of this issue and group?

Thinking It Through

Use this study guide to continue synthesizing your learning about Canada's development as a country. As you work through the following steps, refer back to the focus questions for Chapters 6 and 7, shown here.

STEP 1 Unpacking Knowledge

Create a T-chart by writing a chapter focus question on each side. Look through the unit and list all the items you could use as evidence to answer these questions.

The more specific the evidence is to a question, the closer to the question you will write it down. For example, if an item could be used to answer both questions, you will write it in the middle of the chart. If it is an item specifically about Canada/U.S. relations, it will be located in that column, closer to the top.

How did Canadian political decisions reflect a concern about the growing influence of the United States over Canada?	How did Canada's political, social, and economic policies reflect a new independence from the 1960s to 1982?

STEP 2 Organizing Your Understanding

Examine your T-chart from Step 1 and identify trends and themes in the evidence you have listed. What answer is emerging for each chapter focus question?

Using your T-chart, create a ranking ladder for each question. Select the strongest pieces of evidence for each chapter focus question and write your choices in descending order of importance.

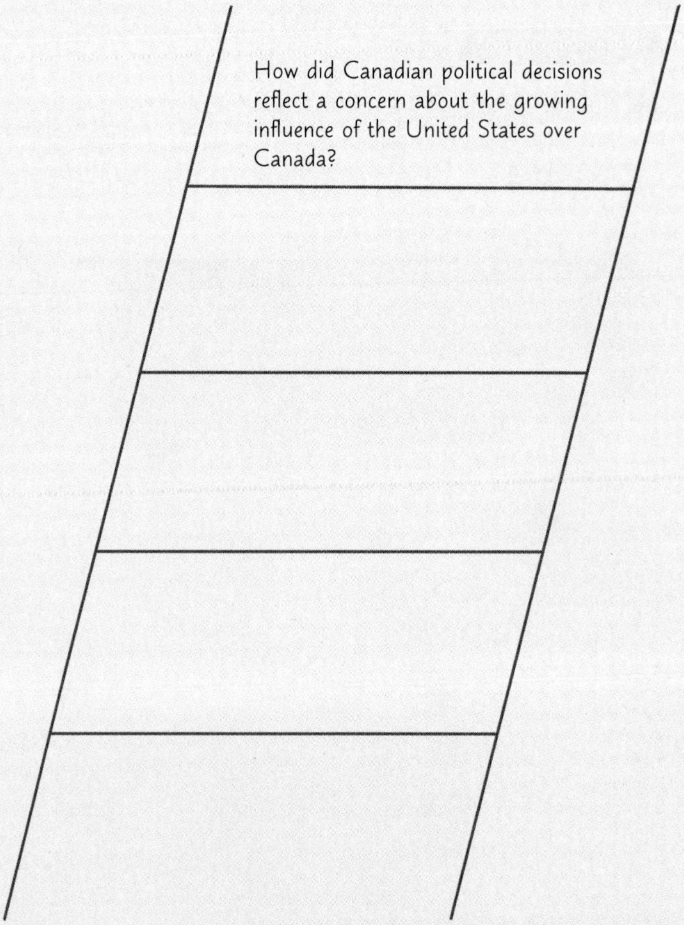

How did Canadian political decisions reflect a concern about the growing influence of the United States over Canada?

©P

STEP 3 Making Connections

Interview someone who grew up in Canada during the Cold War/post-war era (1945–1982). Write three interview questions that address any gaps in your understanding of historical change that took place during the period. Identify historical patterns that you feel stayed much the same and write three interview questions to confirm your hypothesis. Make sure you consider the three relevant overall expectations for the course as you prepare your questions:

- ☐ Social, Economic, and Political Context
- ☐ Communities, Conflict, and Cooperation
- ☐ Identity, Citizenship, and Heritage

Be prepared to share interview responses with the class.

STEP 4 Applying Your Skills

Examine the following quotations and images and discuss the perspectives reflected in each source. Remember to identify who made the statement or who is in the image and what part they played in the event. What position does each represent? What might be the goals of each speaker, photographer, or figure? Who might agree with each position at the time? Who might disagree?

GROUP A

▼ **SOURCE 1:** Text from Bell Telephone ad for a kitchen extension phone:

First, it's a great help in running the house—near shopping lists and at your fingertips for calls to the plumber or other repairmen.

Next, it saves you trouble. Biscuits won't burn, or a pot boil over, because a telephone call took you out of the kitchen. And you can still keep a watchful eye on playing children.

It saves you lots of steps, too. Your husband, like you, will find it one of the most useful phones in your house.

▼ **SOURCE 2:** Remarks by the Hon. Judy LaMarsh, Canada's Secretary of State, 1965 to 1968

Women understand that men must often be kept from soiling themselves with the little dirty details of life in order to accomplish the big shiny jobs unimpeded.

Why you **need** a kitchen extension phone

Thinking It Through

▼ **SOURCE 3:** Prime Minister Trudeau's "Just watch me" impromptu interview with Tim Ralfe of the CBC and Peter Reilly of CJON-TV, October 13, 1970

Ralfe: *I still go back to the choice that you have to make in the kind of society that you live in.*

Trudeau: *Yes, well there are a lot of bleeding hearts around who just don't like to see people with helmets and guns. All I can say is, go on and bleed, but it is more important to keep law and order in the society than to be worried about weak-kneed people who don't like the looks of...*

Ralfe: *At any cost? How far would you go with that? How far would you extend that?*

Trudeau: *Well, just watch me.*

Ralfe: *At reducing civil liberties? To that extent?*

Trudeau: *To what extent?*

Ralfe: *Well, if you extend this and you say, ok, you're going to do anything to protect them, does this include wire-tapping, reducing other civil liberties in some way?*

Trudeau: *Yes, I think the society must take every means at its disposal to defend itself against the emergence of a parallel power which defies the elected power in this country and I think that goes to any distance. So long as there is a power in here which is challenging the elected representative of the people I think that power must be stopped and I think it's only, I repeat, weak-kneed bleeding hearts who are afraid to take these measures.*

▼ **SOURCE 4:** Reaction of the FLQ to the invocation of the War Measures Act, October 17, 1970; communiqué released on December 8, 1970

The present authorities have declared war on the Québec patriots. After having pretended to negotiate for several days they have finally revealed their true face as hypocrites and terrorists.

The colonial army has come to give assistance to the "bouncers" of Drapeau the "dog." Their objective: to terrorize the population by massive and illegal arrests and searches, by large and noisy deployments, and by making shattering statements on the urgent situation in Québec, etc.

▲ **SOURCE 5:** Soldiers guard a side entrance to Montréal City Hall, October 15, 1970.

©P

▼ **SOURCE 6:** Background on Canada and NATO provided by the Canadian Defence & Foreign Affairs Institute:

The [NATO] agreement was signed in Washington on April 2, 1949. Its original membership included twelve countries—the United States, Canada, United Kingdom, France, Denmark, Iceland, Italy, Norway, Portugal, Belgium, Netherlands, and Luxembourg. In signing the agreement Canadian External Affairs Minister Lester Pearson said that Canadians "feel deeply and instinctively" that the treaty is "a pledge for peace and progress."

▼ **SOURCE 7:** Speech by Gunnar Jahn, Chairman of the Nobel Committee, on awarding the Peace Prize to Lester Pearson in 1957:

Mr. Pearson has frequently been mentioned as one of the most enthusiastic supporters of NATO. In this organization for defense of the countries whose life pattern is based on democracy and personal freedom, he finds a guarantee for the maintenance of peace and human rights in the world. ...

Lester Pearson would be the last to believe that military force can secure peace in the long run. This is what he said in 1955:

"No person, no nation, no group of nations can view with comfort ... the prospects of a world where peace rests primarily on the deterrent effect of collective military strength ...."

STEP 5 Thinking Critically

Evidence

Ethical Dimension

Now that you have reviewed the Unit 3 content, practised skills, explored sources, and gathered evidence, it is time to synthesize your learning. Read the following comments from Canada25, a non-partisan organization dedicated to bringing the ideas of young Canadians into public policy debate, and then complete the activity below.

As a relatively young country with a tradition of offering assistance to our allies to attain mutual goals, Canada needs to define its values and objectives, both at home and abroad. Although everyone agreed that our traditional role as peacekeeper and "helpful fixer" was a vital one that we should continue to fill, our international reputation in these areas has clearly suffered over the years, evidenced by our failure to facilitate consensus on important contemporary global issues. Perhaps it is a question of confidence and boldness where Canada has been weak in the past, but what underlies these qualities must be real. Are we hoping to restore the reputation of the Pearson/Trudeau years or create a completely new one... or is the answer somewhere in between? How important is our international reputation—is it really soft power? Is it enough that other nations "like us"?

–David Eaves, Canada25

What do you think Canada's values and objectives should be at home and abroad? How do you think Canada should act on the world stage? On what principles or actions should we base our reputation? Prepare a position statement that clearly states your argument and defends it. Refer to the procedure for defending a position as outlined in Chapter 8.

By the end of the millennium, Canada was continuing to define its identity at home and abroad. A second Québec referendum would show that nearly 50 percent of Québécois wanted sovereignty—a vote that rocked the nation. A few years later, the United States would experience the devastating attack known as 9/11. Once again, Canada chose to support its closest ally while following its own foreign policy. Throughout the new century, Canada adapted to a new digital universe and to the new business models ushered in by technology. Old conflicts found new voices, such as the peaceful protest movement Idle No More, which presented new challenges to the traditional concept of governance in the 21st century.

Innovative communication technologies such as Facebook and Twitter changed the interaction between individuals, corporations, and government. Social movements embraced these technologies and gained a greater voice and reach. Cyberbullying is a new term that has entered the language.

The creation of Nunavut in 1999 signalled the success the Aboriginal peoples had achieved by the end of the century in negotiating new land agreements with the Canadian government. The concept of assimilation, long controversial, was no longer sustainable in any form.

The unexpected tragedy of the World Trade Center changed global perspectives on the concept of terrorism and fuelled a sense of fear. Canadians died in New York. Canada made a commitment to fight in Afghanistan but refused to join the U.S. invasion of Iraq.

In the last decade the average temperature of the globe increased. The Arctic ice cap is melting and various regions of Canada have seen dramatic climate events. There are those who say it is not happening, but others insist that climate change poses the most serious threat to global stability yet.

On April 17, 1982, Queen Elizabeth II and Prime Minister Trudeau signed the new Constitution Act into law in Ottawa. Canada was finally an independent nation, and Trudeau's dream of a Charter of Rights and Freedoms enshrined in the country's constitution had become a reality.

EUROPE

ASIA

PACIFIC OCEAN

AFRICA

INDIAN OCEAN

AUSTRALIA

0   1000   2000 km

In the 1990s, Canada participated along with other countries in several United Nations missions overseas. Some of these missions were actual peacekeeping missions, while others involved the use of military force. Canadians debated this shift in Canada's traditional role. Was this the right direction for Canada?

8

A New Direction: Redefining Our Values at Home and Abroad

Social, Economic, and Political Context

- In what ways did Canadian society change after 1982?
- How did changes to social policies affect women and minorities in Canada?
- How did changes to the Constitution affect Canadian society?
- How did the Canadian government respond to economic challenges after 1982?
- How does globalization affect living standards?

Communities, Conflict, and Cooperation

- How did Aboriginal groups respond to challenges in the late 20th century?
- What was Canada's involvement in the Cold War and its end?
- What was Canada's response to modern world conflicts?
- How did Canada participate in UN initiatives?
- What contributed to Canada's world presence?

Identity, Citizenship, and Heritage

- How did Canada's multiculturalism policy affect minority groups?
- What was the impact of Québec nationalism on Canadian unity?
- What measures did Canada take to promote a distinct Canadian identity?

Canadian soldier Patrick Cloutier (left) and University of Saskatchewan student Brad Laroque at the Kahnesatake reserve in Oka, Québec, September 1, 1990

Historical Significance In addition to Oka, where have other standoffs occurred between Aboriginal peoples and Canadian governments? What has been at the root of these disagreements? Why have the Canadian armed forces been called in during some of these protests? Do you think this photo helps or hinders dialogue between Aboriginal peoples and the Canadian government?

TIMELINE

1982	1985	1987	1990	1991	1990s
Constitution patriation	Peak of the debt crisis	Meech Lake Accord signed	Meech Lake Accord dies Oka Crisis in Québec	The Royal Commission on Aboriginal Peoples started	Asian countries become major sources of immigration

CHAPTER FOCUS QUESTION

How did Canada and Canadian identity change as a consequence of social, economic, and cultural trends at the end of the millennium and beyond?

In the summer of 1990, events in the Québec town of Oka made headlines across the nation. The town council decided to expand a golf course into long-disputed land that the Mohawk Nation at the nearby Kanesatake reserve considered sacred.

The Mohawks decided to stop construction of the golf course by blockading the land. In response, the mayor of Oka called in Québec's provincial police. On July 11, the police advanced on the Mohawk lines, gunfire broke out, and an officer was killed. It was not clear which side had fired the fatal shot.

From that point, events snowballed. The police blockaded Kanesatake. Mohawks from the nearby Kahnawake reserve barricaded the road to a bridge that ran through their reserve, blocking motorist access to part of Montréal. There were nightly violent confrontations involving the population of nearby Québec communities, the police, and the Mohawks. Across Canada, other Aboriginal groups demonstrated their support by blockading highways and railway tracks that ran through their reserves.

As the tense standoff continued, Québec Premier Robert Bourassa called in the Canadian Forces. Troops with heavy weapons moved into the area. Negotiations to end the crisis were tense. Toward the end of September, members of other bands persuaded the Mohawks of Kanesatake to end the standoff. Eventually, the disputed land was purchased by the federal government and given to Kanesatake.

KEY TERMS

Multiculturalism Act
distinct society
notwithstanding clause
Meech Lake Accord
Bloc Québécois
self-government
Free Trade Agreement (FTA)
North American Free Trade Agreement (NAFTA)
Rwandan genocide

? HISTORICAL INQUIRY

Formulate Questions

There are seven main headings in this chapter. Individually or in pairs, scan the chapter, make a list of these seven headings, and then change each of them into a question. Which historical thinking concept(s) do you think will be addressed in each section?

1992	1993	1994	1995	1999	2001
Charlottetown Accord rejected	Collapse of the Conservative Party	Widespread access to Internet	Second Québec referendum	Nunavut created	Canadian Forces at war in Afghanistan
The Algonquins and the governments of Ontario and Canada begin negotiating a land claim agreement					

Popular Culture and the Spirit of the Age

As the millennium approached, popular culture—which mirrored a growing group of young people, from teens to those in their early thirties—reflected some of the cynicism and confusion that seemed to characterize the era. The revolutionary optimism of the 1960s seemed almost naïve from the perspective of the 1980s, 1990s, and 2000s. Environmental disasters, economic shocks such as the stock market crash of 1987 and perennial high unemployment among young workers made for an uncertain future.

FIGURE 8–1 Canadian rap artist k-os. Rap and hip-hop culture, which emerged in the 1980s, incorporates music, language, and dance as well as fashion.

Youth culture tended to fragment into subgroups—each identifying with a style of music, a way of dressing, and an attitude toward life. The list of musical styles that came and went included new wave, punk, glam rock, heavy metal, grunge, alternative, pop, house, rap, hip hop, and gangsta. Fashionable looks ranged from mullets to big hair to neon-dyed buzz cuts, from dancewear to ripped jeans to belly shirts. Body piercing and tattoos became popular with everyone from punks to preppies.

These decades saw a huge rise in consumerism and materialism. Brand names and designer labels became extremely powerful marketing tools. Yet at the same time, people became more aware of the social and environmental consequences of their consumption. Some refused to buy products such as running shoes because they were produced in sweatshops, often by children, in developing countries. Naomi Klein's book *No Logo: Taking Aim at the Brand Bullies*, which criticized branding and globalization, became a best-seller.

The Boomers and After

Most baby boomers were between the ages of 20 and 40 in the 1980s. They were still the largest demographic group in history, and eventually became the holders of power and wealth. As their parents retired, boomers moved into influential positions in government and business. The huge growth in the economy since the 1990s is due, in large part, to the fact that these were the peak earning and spending years of the boomers. Their comparative wealth changed the way people expected to live their lives. Travel had become less expensive and the price of consumer goods relative to wages dropped.

FIGURE 8–2 *The Simpsons*, which began its phenomenally successful run in 1989, has an anti-establishment message. It mocked the lifestyle of the boomers.

Financially secure boomers became known as "yuppies," which stood for young urban (or upwardly mobile) professionals. Yuppies were not afraid to spend their money. They took expensive holidays, bought the latest electronics, fancy cars, and expensive houses. The opening decade of the 21st century saw a huge explosion in goods and services aimed at aging boomers, including retirement communities, health and anti-aging products, and cosmetic surgery.

Aging Boomers

The disproportionately large size of the baby boomer generation, the increased longevity of the population, and declining birth rates all add up to problems for Canada in the future. As the boomers retire in large numbers, there will not be enough workers entering the workforce to replace them. Some experts predict that by 2020, Canada will face a labour shortage of 1 million workers. The skills and talents of the boomers will be sorely missed. In addition, pension costs, health services, and old-age benefits required by aging boomers will put huge pressure on the Canadian economy. The rising costs of these social programs will force young Canadians to pay higher taxes than previous generations.

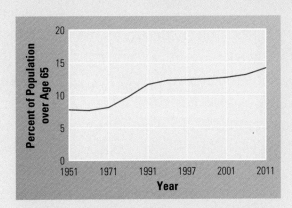

FIGURE 8–3 This graph shows the number of Canadians over age 65 as a percentage of the total population.

Interpret and Analyze What trend do you notice on this graph? What factors do you think might account for this trend?

1. What are some of the negative consequences of an aging population?

2. How might the large number of aging boomers impact your life?

Generations X and Y

The generation immediately following the baby boomers was much smaller than its predecessor. Called Generation X, or the Gen Xers, they were the first of the so-called "latchkey kids," children of single working parents or those who lived in households in which both parents worked. Canadian author Douglas Coupland, who wrote a novel called *Generation X*, described them as "underemployed, overeducated, intensely private and unpredictable." Gen Xers were not, generally, as interested in politics and social change as the boomers. They came of age during times of economic difficulty when all the good jobs seemed to be taken. As a result, they tended to be more cynical and less optimistic about the future. The widespread introduction of computers and the Internet had a huge effect on the lifestyles of the Gen Xers. Popular television shows, such as *Seinfeld* and *Friends*, made fun of the supposed self-centredness of Gen Xers.

Generation Y, made up of people born between the mid-1970s and the end of the 1990s, was even more heavily influenced than the Gen Xers by new technologies such as computers, video games, and cellphones. The buying power of Generation Y forced manufacturers to keep up with its demands for better and faster computing and networking products, and these have fundamentally changed the way society operates.

GO ONLINE

Read "Get Ready for Generation Z," about people born after 1995. What characteristics about your demographic ring true? Which ones seem inaccurate or stereotypical? Explain and share your responses with others.

HISTORICAL INQUIRY

Interpret and Analyze

How have new technologies (see pages 250–251) changed the lives of Canadians? What are the advantages and disadvantages of the technological revolutions? Who is included, and who is left behind?

Innovations
Toward the Future

By the end of the 20th century, most Canadian homes had relatively powerful computers and Internet access. Cell phones, first invented in the 1980s, were widely available by 2000. In the 1990s, some Canadians began to "telecommute": to work from their home or car, keeping in touch with the office via computer. In many industries, computers displaced humans. A new knowledge-based economy emerged, one in which knowledge, skills, and the ability to adapt to new situations became more important than ever before.

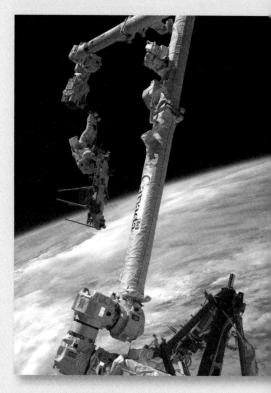

At home, at work Laptop computers became popular with the public in the late 1980s. As they improved over the years, they gave people more freedom by allowing them to take their work with them wherever they went.

Canada reaches out The first *Canadarm* was designed and built by Spar Aerospace in 1981. The remote arm that is attached to NASA's space shuttles allows crews to launch and recapture satellites. Without this technology, much of the world's satellite communication would be impossible.

THE MOBILE PHONE TIMELINE

1983
The first commercial wireless call is placed on the Motorola DynaTAC mobile phone. After the successful test call, a second call is placed to the grandson of Alexander Graham Bell.

1996
Motorola launches the first ever clamshell, or "flip" mobile phone.

1999
Nokia introduces the idea of "small and light" to the mobile phone market.

2002
The Samsung SGH becomes the first phone with active-matrix liquid-crystal display, resulting in low weight and good image quality.

©P

The car with wings

John DeLorean had a futuristic vision of a car and produced the "DeLorean" between 1981-83. Fashioned with brushed stainless steel and featuring "gull-wing" doors, the car became instantly popular based on its appearance. Unfortunately, North American consumers found it heavy and overpriced. But the DeLorean made a comeback with the 1985 release of *Back to the Future* as the time machine taking Canadian actor Michael J. Fox (Marty McFly) and American actor Christopher Lloyd ("Doc" Brown) on a wild adventure.

Picture perfect

You may take graphics editing for granted but there was a time when it was very difficult to alter an image—and something to leave to the pros. With Adobe's release of the first photoshopping software in 1990, "Photoshop" became synonymous with the tools we still use today to create, alter, enhance, or morph pictures at school, in business, or just for fun.

2003

A Canadian company, BlackBerry, produces a phone with a large screen and full keyboard.

2007

Apple releases the first iPhone—a "smart phone" with a touch-screen interface.

Hello Dolly Scientists announced the first cloning of a mammal, a sheep named Dolly, in 1996. This technological breakthrough raised ethical questions about human cloning.

KEY TERMS

Multiculturalism Act or Bill C-93, was adopted in 1988 to provide a legal framework for multiculturalism in Canada

Canadian Charter of Rights and Freedoms the bill identifying human rights that are guaranteed to everyone in Canada; enacted in 1982 and embedded in the Constitution of Canada

❓ HISTORICAL INQUIRY

Gather and Organize

Which section of the Canadian Charter of Rights and Freedoms mandated the "preservation and enhancement of the multicultural heritage of Canadians"? (To get started, see pages 259–260.)

The Growth of Multiculturalism

During the 1980s, Canada became more multicultural than ever before. Government policies encouraged immigrants with money and business skills to create jobs by investing in existing companies or starting new ones. Figures 8–4 and 8–5 show how the countries of origin of immigrants changed over the years.

Unlike immigrants who had arrived earlier in the century in search of good farmland, later immigrants were drawn to Canada's cities. For instance, in 2001, 43.1 percent of immigrants to Canada settled in Toronto; 18 percent settled in Vancouver; and 12 percent settled in Montréal.

As new cultures took root in Canada, some issues were raised. For example, traditional Canadian holidays, such as Easter and Christmas, are rooted in the Christian faith and culture. These holidays presented a challenge for schools with large multicultural populations. One solution was to highlight the festivals of groups represented in sufficient numbers in the school. For example, Chinese New Year, the Muslim holy month of Ramadan, and Sikh holy days such as Baisakhi were celebrated in some schools. These festivals offered students a better understanding of the beliefs and customs of Canada's multicultural society.

Multiculturalism Act

The Canadian **Multiculturalism Act** (Bill C-93) was enacted by Parliament in 1988, to provide a legal framework for existing multiculturalism policies across Canada. In the spirit of the Bill of Rights and the **Canadian Charter of Rights and Freedoms** (read more about the Charter in Figure 8–18 on page 260), the Multiculturalism Act aimed to reinforce racial and cultural equality with legal authority. The Act ensured that all federal institutions took into account the multicultural reality of Canada.

The federal government further recognized the growth of Canada's multicultural communities by establishing the Department of Multiculturalism and Citizenship. Supporters say the government's multiculturalism policy helped strengthen national unity by drawing all Canadians closer together in mutual respect.

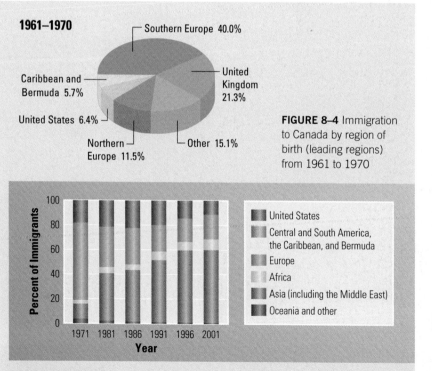

1961–1970
- Southern Europe 40.0%
- United Kingdom 21.3%
- Other 15.1%
- Northern Europe 11.5%
- United States 6.4%
- Caribbean and Bermuda 5.7%

FIGURE 8–4 Immigration to Canada by region of birth (leading regions) from 1961 to 1970

Percent of Immigrants / Year (1971, 1981, 1986, 1991, 1996, 2001)

Legend:
- United States
- Central and South America, the Caribbean, and Bermuda
- Europe
- Africa
- Asia (including the Middle East)
- Oceania and other

FIGURE 8–5 Immigration to Canada by region of birth from 1971 to 2001

Evaluate and Draw Conclusions Based on these graphs, find evidence to support the following conclusion: The sources of Canadian immigration changed almost completely between 1961 and 2001.

❓ HISTORICAL INQUIRY

Interpret and Analyze

How was Canada's multicultural heritage recognized in the Charter of Rights and Freedoms?

Toward a More Just World

The rights movements of earlier decades (see Chapter 7) continued to gain strength during the 1980s and 1990s. Equality rights for women were enshrined in the Constitution in 1982. Tests for job suitability, such as height and strength requirements that favour men, were challenged in the mid-1990s. In 1985, Bill C-31 gave Aboriginal women the right to Aboriginal status even if they married non-Aboriginals. Under Bill C-31, Aboriginal people who had lost their status through enfranchisement also gained it back. This bill brought the Indian Act in line with gender equality under the Canadian Charter of Rights and Freedoms.

• How did changes to social policies affect women and minorities in Canada?

A Spirit of Generosity

A renewed sense of responsibility to help those in need became part of the world view of many Canadians in the 1980s. In 1984, CBC reporter Brian Stewart brought the world's attention to the famine in Ethiopia. Canadian recording stars such as Neil Young, Bryan Adams, Joni Mitchell, and Robert Charlebois got together to form the supergroup Northern Lights and recorded the song "Tears Are Not Enough" to raise money for famine relief. Proceeds from the recording eventually raised more than $3 million. American musicians also created a similar supergroup. USA for Africa recorded "We Are the World" in 1985. Bob Geldof founded Band-Aid in 1984—comprised of Irish and British musicians—and recorded "Do They Know It's Christmas?" This recording, along with the Live-Aid concerts that followed, each raised money for international aid efforts. Similar concerts continued into the next century.

FIGURE 8–6 Joni Mitchell (with music) and Neil Young (right) record "Tears Are Not Enough" with The Northern Lights.

FIGURE 8–7 Canadian organizations have also stepped forward to help people around the world. Montréal's Cirque du Soleil, founded in the 1980s, has a global citizenship mandate. The company works with individuals and groups around the world to help those at risk. Since 1989, Cirque du Soleil has donated one percent of the company's gross revenue to social and cultural programs. Cirque du Monde, a program that targets at-risk youth ages eight to 25, teaches circus skills, team-building, and creativity. The program is now available to 50 communities worldwide.

Gay Rights in the 1980s and 1990s

Although not every public figure discloses his or her sexual identity, in the 1980s, remaining closeted was the norm. So when federal MP Svend Robinson revealed in 1988 that he was gay, there was a swift national reaction. While some Canadians called for his resignation, many young people wrote to him saying that for the first time, they felt free to be themselves without compromise.

After Robinson's announcement, more gay and lesbian politicians came out, including Bloc Québécois MPs Réal Ménard and Raymond Gravel, New Democrat MPs Libby David and Bill Siksay (both of British Columbia), Progressive Conservative MP Scott Brison, and Liberal MP Mario Silva. Gay rights activism also accelerated during this period. Although some bills that prohibited discrimination based on sexual orientation failed to pass, discrimination was outlawed by the mid-1990s.

In 1990, Robinson turned his attention to the rights of LGBT servicemen and women in Canada's military. He persuaded Canadian Forces Captain Michelle Douglas to sue the Department of National Defence for dismissing her as "not advantageously employable due to homosexuality." In 1992—before Douglas even had a chance to present her case at trial—the Canadian military announced that it would no longer discriminate on the basis of sexual orientation. The decision came more than two decades before the U.S. military would announce a similar policy, and distinguished Canada as a country that respects the complex diversity of its populace.

FIGURE 8–8 Since the 1990s, Canadian society has become more aware of the challenges facing LGBT youth. Canadian entertainer Rick Mercer tells young people, "so if you're being bullied at school because you're different, please tell someone about it."

GO ONLINE
Watch Rick Mercer's complete rant on teen suicide. Have things changed since 2011? If so, are things better or worse?

… Sexual orientation … is a deeply personal characteristic that is either unchangeable or changeable only at unacceptable personal costs.
—*Supreme Court Justice Gérard La Forest, 1995*

Equality Rights and the Charter

After the Charter became law, its impact on LGBT rights was felt almost immediately. At issue was Section 15, which guarantees equality before and under the law. While "sexual orientation" was not included as a prohibited ground for discrimination, by the end of the 20th century, many people believed this was the Charter's intent.

In 1995, the Supreme Court handed down a decision that stated Section 15 must be interpreted to include sexual orientation. In *Eagan v. Canada*, Justice Gérard La Forest noted that being gay is similar to having a certain racial, national, or ethnic origin. This idea confirmed the equality rights of LGBT Canadians and helped them secure one last right: the right to marry.

In the years that followed, gay marriage would be made legal in nine provinces, including Ontario. Then in 2005, the passage of the *Civil Marriage Act* legalized gay marriage throughout Canada and marked an important step toward the achievement of a free and just society. The Act gave same-sex couples full access to all the rights and benefits previously enjoyed only by heterosexual married couples, such as access to a spouse's medical benefits.

In 1978, 21-year-old Terry Fox, who had lost a leg to cancer, decided to run across Canada. The goal of his run, which he called the Marathon of Hope, was to raise money for cancer research. Fox started his run by dipping his leg into the Atlantic Ocean in St. John's, Newfoundland, on April 12, 1980. He intended to run all the way to the Pacific Ocean on the west coast of Vancouver Island.

Fox set himself a gruelling pace—42 kilometres per day. By the time he reached Southern Ontario, crowds of people were lining his route cheering him on.

When Fox was approaching Thunder Bay, he was forced to stop his run due to pains in his chest. He went to the hospital where doctors discovered that the cancer had spread to his lungs. He died in 1981, and was mourned across the country.

Canadians honour Terry Fox with annual Terry Fox Runs and have donated hundreds of millions of dollars to the cause he championed. He is considered one of Canada's heroes.

1. Terry Fox hoped to raise $21 million for cancer research. So far, his organization has raised more than $650 million worldwide. Why do you think his goal has been surpassed on such a grand scale?

FIGURE 8–9 Terry Fox was named a Companion of the Order of Canada in 1980.

CHECKPOINT

1. How did Canadian immigration policies and patterns develop between 1960 and 2000? Present your answer in the form of a timeline or chart.

2. Explain how the Canadian model of a "cultural mosaic" differs from the American model of a "melting pot."

3. Québec has long pressed for a greater share of immigrants to Canada and a greater say on who can enter. Why do you think this is so?

4. **Cause and Consequence** What impact has computer technology had on Canadian society?

5. Create a timeline of key events in the acceptance of LGBT Canadians using information from Chapters 7 and 8. Indicate why you think each event was important.

6. Which technological innovation has had the most impact on your life? The least? Might this change in the future? Explain.

7. Why do you think Canada introduced an official policy of multiculturalism? Do you think the policy had its intended effect? Support your views with examples.

The 1980s and 1990s were an exciting period for music in Canada. Energized by Canadian content regulations that forced radio stations to play more Canadian music (see page 207), artists seized the opportunity to create a distinctively Canadian brand. Even when the sound was inspired by mainstream genres of the day—rock, disco, funk, and rap—bands seemed to form in every corner of the country, often creating music that would stand the test of time. Here is a look at some of the players who were part of the period.

MuchMusic If you were a Canadian teen in the early '80s, your exposure to music came mostly via radio stations, as well as the American MTV—provided you could receive its broadcasts in your area. Then in 1984, Canada launched MuchMusic, the first specialty channel in the country devoted to music videos. The music video changed how music was marketed in the '80s and '90s. Suddenly, it was important to be a great entertainer or dancer as well as a good musician. Artists who knew how to exploit the new genre, such as Michael Jackson and Madonna—or Canadian bands Platinum Blonde and The Northern Pikes—often achieved success.

FIGURE 8–10 After MuchMusic launched in 1984, it created a number of musical variety shows that showcased Canadian talent, including the popular *Electric Circus* and *City Limits*, which featured alternative rock videos.

FIGURE 8–11 Toronto's Platinum Blonde embraced the popularity of music videos and scored several major hits on both sides of the border between 1983 and 1986.

The Rheostatics are a Genie-award winning band from Etobicoke, Ontario, that formed in the 1980s and disbanded in 2007. Some of their albums—notably *Whale Music* and *Melville*—have been voted, by both critics and audiences, the best Canadian music ever recorded. Although the band started out in the 1980s with an American soul sound (its horn section was dubbed The Trans-Canada Soul Patrol), the group soon gravitated to Canadian themes, writing songs devoted to hockey ("The Ballad of Wendel Clark, Parts I and II"), poverty in Ontario ("Bad Time to Be Poor"), and later, at the invitation of the National Gallery of Canada, the Group of Seven painters.

FIGURE 8–12 The Rheostatics play their farewell concert at Toronto's Massey Hall in March 2007.

Great Big Sea is a band from Newfoundland and Labrador that became well known in the early '90s. The band got their break at Memorial University in Newfoundland when they composed two original songs for the winter carnival talent show and won first prize. Their sound combines rock with the traditional musical genres of Ireland, Scotland, and Cornwall. Initially, the band played mostly local gigs in and around St. John's, but by 1996, they had won their first Entertainer of the Year Award at the East Coast Music Awards. They continued to take the prize every year until 2001, when they voluntarily withdrew their name so that other bands could complete. Great Big Sea has also been nominated for several Juno Awards.

FIGURE 8–13 Great Big Sea often refers to Canadian history in their material. "Recruiting Sergeant," from their 1997 self-titled album, tells the story of the Royal Newfoundland Regiment, which served during the First World War.

The Dishrags were a pioneering all-female punk band from Victoria, British Columbia. (Punk was a rock music genre that developed in in the late 1970s in North America and Britain.) They started their group in high school when their youngest member was only 15 years old, and performed in the late '70s and early '80s. When the British band The Clash made their first trip to Canada, they invited The Dishrags to open for them, increasing the group's exposure. Despite their age, lack of experience, and gender (audiences often mocked them for being girls), The Dishrags persevered and became popular on both the Canadian and U.S. west coasts.

FIGURE 8–14 The Dishrags in the 1980s. Few punk bands were composed entirely of women, and The Dishrags had to fight for acceptance.

Arcade Fire is a Montréal-based indie rock band that became popular in the 2000s and has achieved critical acclaim for their unique sound, beginning with a self-titled extended-play recording in 2003 and the album *Funeral* in 2004. The group surprised many in the music industry when their 2011 album *The Suburbs*

FIGURE 8–15 Arcade Fire typically uses many instruments in a single performance, including rock staples guitar and drums, along with violin, viola, xylophone, glockenspiel, French horn, accordion, harp, and mandolin.

won Best Album at the Juno and Polaris Awards in Canada, Best International Album at the Brit Awards, and Best Album of the Year at the Grammy awards, beating other major-label artists.

Singer and songwriter **k.d. lang** was born in Edmonton, Alberta. An internationally acclaimed pop and country music singer, lang has won eight Junos and four Grammy awards; she is also a member of the Canadian Music Hall of Fame. Her first big hit was the 1992 album Ingénue, featuring the songs "Constant Craving" and "Miss Chatelaine." That same year, she came out as a lesbian. In 2004 lang recorded *Hymns of the 49th Parallel*, featuring covers of Canadian musicians such as Neil Young and Joni Mitchell. In 2010 she performed Leonard Cohen's "Hallelujah" for the opening ceremonies of the Vancouver Olympics.

FIGURE 8–16 k.d. lang is also a well-known animal rights activist and a supporter of LGBT rights.

1. If you were to write a music feature such as the one you just read, what artist you would be sure to include? What other aspects of Canadian identity would you choose to represent? When you make your choice, consider the artist's significance, either as someone who had an impact on Canadian music or who reflected a trend in Canadian culture.

2. Choose a Canadian artist and research them in depth. How is their identity reflected in their music? You might consider their Canadian identity or something more specific, such as their sense of belonging to particular community.

patriate to take control of a document from a former colonial government

distinct society a phrase that refers to the recognition of the unique nature of Québec within Canada; it often has the sense that Québec should have special powers and privileges to protect its language and culture

• What was the impact of Québec nationalism on Canadian unity?

Constitution and Discord

In the 1970s, the October Crisis and the election of the Parti Québécois (PQ) made it clear that the threat of Québec separatism was very real. Concerns about separatism contributed to Prime Minister Trudeau's determination to **patriate** Canada's Constitution. He hoped that a "made in Canada" Constitution would make Québécois feel more comfortable about their position. Québec discontent and the Constitution continued to define Canadian affairs well into the 1990s. Twice during this time, PQ governments tried and failed to win referenda that would have separated Québec from the rest of Canada.

Trudeau vs. Lévesque

In Chapter 7, you learned that Québec Premier René Lévesque called a referendum on sovereignty-association in 1980. Lévesque had envisioned an arrangement between Québec and Canada whereby Québec would become politically independent, or *"maîtres chez nous,"* yet maintain a close economic association with Canada. This partnership would include

• free trade between Canada and Québec

• a common currency for the two nations

• common tariffs against imported goods

Although Québécois ultimately voted "no" to sovereignty-association, Trudeau was aware of the growing threat to unity that the concept posed. He promised to negotiate a new Constitution, which proved popular among Québécois who wanted a Constitution that recognized Québec as an equal partner in Confederation and as a **distinct society** within Canada.

FIGURE 8–17 This cartoon showing Prime Minister Trudeau and Premier Lévesque offers one view of sovereignty-association.

Interpret and Analyze
According to the cartoonist, how did sovereignty-association differ from separation? What was this cartoonist's view of Lévesque? How do you know?

NOW REMEMBER, I'VE CHANGED THE OPERATION FROM COMPLETE SEPARATION TO SOVEREIGNTY ASSOCIATION... THAT MEANS WE'LL BE COMPLETELY SEPARATE ... EXCEPT FOR WHERE I'M ATTACHED TO YOUR WALLET...

The Canadianese Twins

Patriating the Constitution

The British North America (BNA) Act had been Canada's Constitution since 1867. The Act set out the powers of the federal and provincial governments and guaranteed the language and education rights of Québec's Francophone majority. Since the BNA Act fell under British jurisdiction, no changes could be made without the British Parliament's approval.

Amending the Constitution

Prime Minister Trudeau wanted to patriate the Constitution so that the Canadian government would have sole authority to make changes to it. Trudeau hoped, above all, to include in the Constitution a clear statement of the basic rights to which all Canadians were entitled.

As a first step, Trudeau needed to come up with a formula for amending, or making changes to, the Constitution. Questions such as the following needed to be considered: How many provinces need to be in agreement to make a change to the Constitution? Should Québec, as the Francophone partner in Confederation, be given veto power? Getting both the federal and provincial governments to agree to an amending formula was difficult.

While Québec pushed for more power, the Western provinces saw patriating the Constitution as a way to have more say in affairs that affected them. Most of the provincial premiers outside of Québec felt that the Charter would make the courts more powerful than provincial legislatures. In Québec, Lévesque feared that the Charter could be used to override his language laws or any other legislation that might be passed to protect Québec's distinct society.

A series of meetings failed to resolve the concerns that divided the provinces and the federal government. In a final attempt to reach an agreement, the prime minister and the premiers met in Ottawa on November 4, 1981. Over late-night meetings in the kitchen of the National Conference Centre, federal Justice Minister Jean Chrétien and the justice ministers from Saskatchewan and Ontario hammered out what came to be called the "Kitchen Accord." The provincial premiers were awakened in their rooms at the Château Laurier Hotel and asked to approve the deal.

Including a Notwithstanding Clause

The premiers agreed to accept the Charter if an escape clause were added. This was the **notwithstanding clause**, which allowed the federal government or any of the provinces to opt out of some of the clauses in the Charter. An agreement on the amending formula was also reached. Changes to the Constitution could be made only with the agreement of "seven out of ten provinces representing 50 percent of Canada's population." This meant, in effect, that Québec could be excluded as long as Ontario was included.

René Lévesque argued against the deal but Trudeau accepted the compromise. He maintained that the federal government had so many members from Québec that it could speak for that province. Lévesque and the people of Québec felt that the federal government and the other provincial premiers had ganged up to deny Québec recognition of its distinct status. The Québec provincial government refused to sign the proposed Constitution.

> • How did changes to the Constitution affect Canadian society?

KEY TERM

notwithstanding clause a clause in the Canadian Constitution (Section 33[1]) that enables Parliament or the legislature of a province to allow an Act to stand even though it contravenes the Charter of Rights and Freedoms

GO ONLINE
Use the CBC's digital archives and other sources to learn more about the Constitutional debate.

? HISTORICAL INQUIRY

Gather and Organize

Who were the other two members of the Kitchen Cabinet that drafted the Kitchen Accord along with Jean Chretien?

The Canadian Charter of Rights and Freedoms

Few laws have had as profound an effect on the life of Canadians as the Canadian Charter of Rights and Freedoms. The Charter protects your fundamental freedoms and guarantees your democratic mobility, equality, legal, and language rights. The Charter gives you the right to challenge in court any law you believe violates your Charter rights. The courts do not always agree with the challenges made, but Canadians generally believe that the Charter offers them a chance to stand up for their rights, even against powerful government interests.

Limiting the Charter

The Charter sets limits on some rights to make sure that one person's rights do not take precedence over someone else's. The Charter also allows the federal and provincial governments to have the final say in which laws are passed.

So, what does the Charter mean to you, a student in high school? The following chart summarizes and explains the key points.

Section	Rights	What does this mean to me?
1	Guarantee of rights and freedoms	• I can live as a free citizen in a democratic nation, with certain legal limitations.
2	Fundamental freedoms of conscience and religion; thought, belief, opinion, expression, and the press; peaceful assembly; association	• I can follow any religion I choose. • I can believe what I want. • I can express my opinions openly without fear. • I can associate with whomever I choose. • I can meet with others peacefully.
3–5	Democratic rights	• Once I am 18, I can vote in elections at least once every five years. • Once I am 18, I can run as a candidate in elections.
6	Mobility rights	• I can enter, remain in, or leave Canada. • I can live, work, or study wherever I wish in Canada.
7–14	Legal rights	• I have a right to life, liberty, and security of person. • I have the right not to be arbitrarily arrested and detained. • I have the right to a fair trial if I am accused of a crime. • I have the right to humane treatment.
15	Equality rights	• I can live, study, and work regardless of my race, religion, national or ethnic origin, colour, sex, age, and mental or physical ability. • I have the right to be treated as "equal before and under the law."
16–22	Official languages of Canada	• I can communicate with and receive federal government services in English or French. • I can use French or English in any federal court.
23	Minority language educational rights	• I can have my children educated in either French or English where sufficient numbers of students exist.
24	Enforcement	• I can take the matter to court should any of the above rights and freedoms be denied.
25–31	General	• Aboriginal peoples of Canada retain any rights previously established. • Charter to be interpreted consistent with the preservation and enhancement of multiculturalism. • Rights under the Charter are guaranteed equally to both sexes.

FIGURE 8–18 Some of the human rights protected by the Canadian Charter of Rights and Freedoms

©P

Trudeau went ahead without Québec's agreement and asked the British Parliament to pass the **Canada Act**, which included the Canadian Charter of Rights and Freedoms, a new amending formula, and the notwithstanding clause. The British Parliament passed the Canada Act, and Queen Elizabeth II came to Canada. On April 17, 1982, the queen and Prime Minister Trudeau signed the new Constitution Act into law in Ottawa. As the rest of Canada celebrated, flags in Québec flew at half-mast and Premier Lévesque led an angry demonstration through the streets of Québec City. The last step toward making Canada a completely independent nation had been taken, but the process had revealed cracks in national unity that would continue to trouble Canadians in the years that followed.

KEY TERM

Canada Act an Act of the Parliament of the United Kingdom passed in 1982 at the request of the Canadian government to patriate Canada's constitution

Trudeau Steps Down

Trudeau's dream of a Canadian Constitution and a Charter of Rights and Freedoms had become a reality. He felt he had played his part and was growing tired of politics. On February 28, 1984, he left his official residence at 24 Sussex Drive in Ottawa for a walk through the snowy streets of the capital. It was then that he decided to retire from politics. The Trudeau era had come to an end.

John Turner, who had served in the Cabinet under both Pearson and Trudeau, won the leadership of the Liberals. He called an election soon after, and the Liberals suffered a disastrous defeat by Brian Mulroney's Progressive Conservatives, winning only 40 seats in the House of Commons. By the time the next election was called, Mulroney had introduced a Free Trade Agreement with the United States. Turner and Mulroney found themselves in the midst of a rancorous election debate over Canada's future—whether to join the emerging global economy or protect Canada, culturally and economically. It was a battle that Mulroney won decisively (you will read about it later in this chapter). Turner resigned his position and was replaced by Jean Chrétien.

FIGURE 8–19 Queen Elizabeth II signs Canada's Constitution Act, April 17, 1982.

Historical Significance Why would the Canadian government want to have the queen sign the Act in Canada?

CHECKPOINT

1. Would you describe Lévesque's plan for sovereignty-association as a plan for separation from Canada? Why or why not?

2. Do you think Lévesque was betrayed by the Kitchen Accord? Why or why not?

3. Do you think section 1 of the Charter is necessary? Why or why not?

4. Why was the notwithstanding clause included in the Charter? This clause has rarely been used. Why do you think that is the case?

When you defend a position on an issue, you present arguments that you hope will persuade others. To do this, you need to use facts and anecdotes that support your position. Remember that a well-structured argument is very different from simply expressing opinions or ideas on a subject.

Know what you are talking about. Understanding the basis for your argument is the key to defending it. Do research to gather facts and evidence to support your position. Learn the meaning of any terms you are using.

Clarify your position. You should begin by clearly stating your point of view. This statement is the thesis of your argument and needs to be as specific as possible.

Anticipate objections. Learn what objections might be raised by those who disagree with you. Be ready to counter objections with well-reasoned and well-supported points.

Practising the Skill

Québec separation has been a major issue in Canada for many decades. Read the three positions on separatism: the first by a Grade 11 student from Kitchener, Ontario; the second from a Québec sovereigntist group's Web posting; and the third from a grand chief and chairman of Québec's Grand Council of the Crees.

1. *It is my belief that as citizens in this country, we must be conscious of this movement [separatism] and take action to convince Québec to stay. We have so far spent billions of dollars on protecting the French language and the Québec way of life.*

   We have even let the rights of Anglophone citizens (English-speaking people in Québec) be violated for the sake of the French culture in acts such as Bill 101.

   There is evidence to show that if Québec ever did separate, its language and culture would be even more at risk than it is now. Canada is one of the main reasons that the French language is as strong as it is today. We have passed many laws to protect it....

   —*Claire Lehan, "Separatism is an issue for all of Canada, not just Québec," 2006*

2. *....some people regard the measures taken to protect French as excessive and systematically fight against it with the aid of the Canadian government. It is our view that all citizens, regardless of their origins or the communities they belong to, are entitled to freedom of expression; and indeed Québec's Bill of Rights is among the most progressive on that score. This individual freedom of expression can, in our view, coexist harmoniously with the legitimate promotion of the French language which, in the North-American context, requires appropriate legislation.*

   —*Québec Sovereignty: A Legitimate Goal, posted on the Internet by Intellectuals for the Sovereignty of Québec (IPSO)*

3. *The fundamental and constitutional rights of Aboriginal peoples in Québec are clearly a major obstacle for the secessionists. They claim that they have a historic right to determine their future on the basis of a distinct language, history, and culture. On what ground can they possibly deny, as they do, that we too have this right? The separatists claim that they have the right to choose to end their ties with Canada. On what basis can they possibly claim, as they do, that the Crees and the Inuit do not have the right to choose instead to maintain and renew our relationship with Canada?*

   —*Grand Chief Matthew Coon Come, speech at the Canada Seminar, Harvard Center for International Affairs and Kennedy School of Government, October 28, 1996*

Evaluate and Draw Conclusions

1. **Evidence** Which opinions in each argument could be strengthened by citing specific, credible evidence?

2. Explain why knowing your subject and knowing the meaning of terms are important to defending a position on an issue.

3. With a partner, scan blogs, newspaper or magazine articles, or TV news shows for issue statements that you think state a position that needs to be defended or is being defended. Assess the strengths and weaknesses of each statement.

Mulroney, Québec, and the Constitution

Conservative leader Brian Mulroney became Canada's prime minister in September 1984. He was unlike Trudeau in many ways. Prime Minister Mulroney worked to forge closer links with the United States and developed a close personal relationship with President Ronald Reagan, with whom he shared a conservative philosophy. He was also more aligned with U.S. ideas about the economy than Trudeau.

Reopening the Constitution Debate

By 1984, most Canadians outside Québec felt that the issues of the Constitution and Canadian unity had been settled. Yet, when John Turner called an election later that year, Brian Mulroney, the leader of the Progressive Conservatives, returned to the issue of the Constitution. To build support from separatists in Québec during the election campaign, Mulroney promised to repair the damage of 1982 by obtaining Québec's consent to the Constitution "with honour and enthusiasm."

Once elected, Mulroney looked for an opportunity to make good on his promise. The time seemed right when René Lévesque retired and the pro-federalist Liberal Party, led by Robert Bourassa, took office in Québec. Mulroney's first priority was to negotiate an agreement to have Québec sign the Constitution. But by then, other provinces had their own demands. For example, Newfoundland and Alberta wanted more control of their resources—Newfoundland of its fisheries, and Alberta of its oil industries. As well, both Alberta and Newfoundland demanded reforms to the Senate that would give them a stronger voice in Ottawa.

Western alienation, which had grown during the oil crisis of the 1970s, had come to a head once again over a government contract to repair air force jets. Ottawa awarded the multibillion-dollar contract to the Bombardier company of Montréal, even though Bristol Aerospace of Winnipeg had made a better proposal. Westerners were convinced that the contract went to Bombardier just to "buy" Conservative votes in Québec.

The Meech Lake Accord

Prime Minister Mulroney called the premiers to a conference to discuss the Constitution at Meech Lake, Québec, in 1987. He proposed a package of amendments that included an offer to recognize Québec as a distinct society. The **Meech Lake Accord** also included giving more power to the other provinces. All provinces, for example, would have the power to veto constitutional change. In a radio discussion, Premier Bourassa announced Québec's support for the accord:

> History will say... that [the] Meech Lake Accord was a unique chance for Canada. If it is accepted Canada will be and could be a great country. If it is rejected, it is hard to predict what will be the future.
>
> –*Robert Bourassa*

- What was the impact of Québec nationalism on Canadian unity?

KEY TERM

Meech Lake Accord a package of constitutional amendments that would define Québec as a distinct society within Canada

GO ONLINE ••••••••••••••

Read more about reopening the Constitution debate and the Meech Lake and Charlottetown Accords.

Prime Minister
Martin Brian Mulroney

- born 1939, Baie-Comeau, Québec
- lawyer, author
- first elected to Commons in 1983
- prime minister 1984–1993

Domestic Record

- passed the Multiculturalism Act in 1985 to recognize and promote multiculturalism as an essential part of Canadian heritage and identity
- launched the Meech Lake Accord (1987), which proposed giving the provinces more say in federal matters and declaring Québec a distinct society within Canada
- apologized in 1988 to Japanese Canadians for their internment during the Second World War
- introduced the Goods and Services Tax (GST) in 1991
- tried to pass the Charlottetown Accord (1992), which proposed that provinces have more power, that the Senate be reformed, and advocated Aboriginal self-government

International Record

- negotiated the Free Trade Agreement with the U.S. in 1987
- expanded free trade to include Mexico in the North American Free Trade Agreement (NAFTA) in 1992
- opposed apartheid in South Africa

FIGURE 8–20 Elijah Harper, a Cree member of the Manitoba legislature, opposed the Meech Lake Accord because it did not recognize Canada's Aboriginal nations as a distinct society.

- How did Aboriginal groups respond to challenges in the late 20th century?

However, the accord had many critics. Former Prime Minister Pierre Trudeau argued that the designation of Québec as a distinct society would create "two solitudes" in Canada. It would, he said, simply isolate the Francophones of Québec and make them less, rather than more, a part of Confederation. Many Québécois, on the other hand, saw this clause as a way of protecting French culture and language. Other critics also focused on the "distinct society" clause. They worried that it might be used in Québec to override the Charter and deprive specific groups of their rights. Aboriginal peoples pointed out that they too had a distinct society that needed to be recognized and protected. Others argued that Canadians had not been given enough opportunity to have their say on the issue.

Two provinces, Manitoba and Newfoundland, withheld their support from the Meech Lake Accord, and it died in June 1990. The failure of the accord was seen as a rejection of Québec itself, even a "humiliation." Support in Québec for separation had soared to 64 percent. Lucien Bouchard, a powerful Québec member of Mulroney's Cabinet, resigned in protest and formed a new national party, the **Bloc Québécois**. The Bloc would run in federal elections but it remained committed to Québec separation.

The Charlottetown Accord

Prime Minister Mulroney was not willing to let the Constitution debate end. He appointed a "Citizens' Forum," a committee that travelled across the nation to hear the views of Canadians on the Constitution. Eventually, Mulroney and provincial premiers proposed a package of constitutional amendments called the Charlottetown Accord. It answered Québec's concerns in ways similar to the Meech Lake Accord, but it also advocated the principle of Aboriginal self-government. In addition, the Charlottetown Accord proposed reforming the Senate. In response to pressure from the Western provinces, the Senate would become an elected body with equal representation from all parts of the country.

The Charlottetown Accord was put to a national referendum in October 1992. Although Mulroney warned that rejection of the accord would endanger the very future of the nation, 54.3 percent of Canadian voters rejected it. The greatest opposition came from British Columbia, where 68.3 percent voted "no." B.C. voters felt that the accord gave Québec too much power and they objected to the guarantee that Québec would always have 25 percent of the seats in the House of Commons, regardless of the size of its population. Many voters in Québec, on the other hand, believed that the Charlottetown Accord did not give them enough power because most of the Senate seats would go to the West. They also objected to Aboriginal self-government because it would affect a large portion of northern Québec.

©P

The 1995 Québec Referendum

Perhaps angered by events in the Constitution debates, Québécois again elected the separatist Parti Québécois in 1994. In 1995, Premier Jacques Parizeau called a provincial referendum on full sovereignty. The "yes" forces reminded Québécois of their "humiliation" in the rejection of the Meech Lake Accord. On October 30, 1995, the nation held its breath as the referendum votes were counted. The results: 49.4 percent of the people of Québec had voted "yes" to sovereignty. The close vote shocked Canadians.

The threat of separatism lessened somewhat in the following years. Lucien Bouchard, who became Québec's premier in 1996, talked periodically of a new referendum, and the federal government under Prime Minister Jean Chrétien prepared guidelines for any future vote, stressing that the costs of sovereignty would be high for Québécois. Chrétien sent the legal question of Quebec's right to separate to the Supreme Court of Canada. The Court ruled that Québec could not leave Canada unilaterally. However, Canada had to negotiate a separation if a substantial majority of Québecers voted "yes." In response to this ruling, Chrétien and Minister of Intergovernmental Affairs Stéphane Dion introduced the **Clarity Act**. The Clarity Act stated that any future referendum questions had to be clear and that Ottawa would determine what a substantial majority would be, rather than a 50 percent plus one majority.

As the century closed, support for separatism appeared to decline. Liberal gains in Québec in the 2000 federal election and the resignation of Premier Bouchard seemed to support Chrétien's tough stand on separation.

KEY TERM

Clarity Act (Bill C-20) legislation passed by the Chrétien government requiring separatist referendums to pass with a "clear majority" rather than 50 percent plus 1, before Quebec could negotiate separation

FIGURE 8–21 In 1995, people came to Québec from across Canada to tell Quebecers that they wanted them to stay in Canada.

Evaluate and Draw Conclusions How does this photograph demonstrate support for the "no" side? How does a symbol such as the Canadian flag play a part in national events such as the referendum campaign?

CHECKPOINT

1. Why was it difficult to patriate the Constitution?

2. Why do you think that it was so difficult for the provinces and the federal government to agree about the Constitution?

3. Why did Brian Mulroney reopen the Constitution debate? Why did the Meech Lake Accord fail? Why did the Charlottetown Accord fail?

4. How did the Québec referendum of 1995 differ from that of 1980?

5. Why did the results of the 1995 Québec referendum shock Canadians? What action did the federal government take?

6. **Cause and Consequence** How might the rest of Canada have changed if the 1995 referendum had passed?

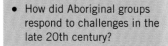
- How did Aboriginal groups respond to challenges in the late 20th century?

GO ONLINE • • • • • • • • • • • • • • • • •
Find out more about residential schools.

The Fight for Aboriginal Rights

The crisis in Oka, Québec, which you read about at the beginning of the chapter, ended after about two and a half months of tense and sometimes violent confrontation. Oka served as a wake-up call to the government and people of Canada. Canada's Aboriginal peoples had demonstrated again that they were prepared to fight for their rights.

The Legacy of Residential Schools

Even though the residential school system had been dismantled by the final decade of the 20th century, its consequences continued to haunt Aboriginal people who had lived through it. In 1990, a new aspect of the residential school legacy was brought to light. The Grand Chief of the Assembly of Manitoba Chiefs, Phil Fontaine, spoke out about the physical and sexual abuse he suffered at a residential school. Others soon came forward with horrifying stories of abuse.

These accounts led to the creation of the Royal Commission on Aboriginal Peoples. Eventually, hundreds would share painful stories of their residential school experiences and the trauma of being forcibly removed from their family, culture, and language. Soon, the very churches that had once encouraged the assimilation and religious conversion of Aboriginal children were working with the government to figure out a way to compensate the victims.

Eighteen years after Fontaine first spoke out, Prime Minister Stephen Harper would read an official apology to Aboriginal people in the House of Commons. You will read more about this event in Chapter 9.

FIGURE 8–22 In an interview with the CBC in October 1990, First Nations leader Phil Fontaine publicly revealed for the first time the horrors of the Canadian residential school system.

©P

1850s–1860s	Assimilation of Aboriginal people through education becomes official policy.
1892	Federal government and churches officially partner in operation of residential schools.
1920	Indian Affairs Minister Duncan Campbell Scott makes residential school attendance mandatory.
1958	Indian Affairs inspectors recommend abolition of residential schools.
1970s	Residential schools begin to be transferred to Indian bands.
1986	United Church apologizes for its role in residential schools. Eventually Anglican, Presbyterian, and some Catholic churches also offer apologies.
1996	Last government-run residential school closes.

KEY TERMS

self-government the right of a colony or cultural group to define the structure, laws, and policies that will govern its affairs

specific claims First Nations' claims to land based on the belief that the government did not fulfill its obligations under a treaty or other agreement related to money, land, or other assets

comprehensive claims the assertion of the right of Aboriginal nations to large tracts of land because their ancestors were the original inhabitants

HISTORICAL INQUIRY

Evaluate and Draw Conclusions

First Nations leaders regularly say that we are all treaty people; that all Canadians are treaty people. What do you think they mean?

The Path to Self-Government

In 1982, the Assembly of First Nations was formed to represent Aboriginal peoples in their dealings with the federal government. During the constitutional negotiations, the Assembly pressured political leaders for legal recognition of Aboriginal rights. As a result, Aboriginal rights were entrenched in the Charter of Rights and Freedoms. In 1985, Parliament also passed Bill C-31, which gave Aboriginal band councils the power to decide who had the right to live on Aboriginal reserves. Previous decisions of this sort had been made by the federal government's Department of Indian Affairs.

The increase in band council powers raised the question, "What other powers should be transferred from the federal government to the band councils?" The stage was set for discussions about **self-government**. Aboriginal peoples argued that self-government would give them the right to manage resources and gain control of their education, culture, and justice systems. This would then give them the tools needed to tackle social and health concerns in their communities.

But how would self-government work in practice? Should reserves be run as municipal or town governments by the band members? Or would Aboriginal lands and reserves across Canada eventually join together to form something like a province? Furthermore, by what means could Aboriginal nations lay claim to lands that they considered to be theirs?

Aboriginal land claims have been of two types. **Specific claims** have arisen in areas where treaties between Aboriginal peoples and the federal government have been signed, but their terms have not been kept. For example, the agreed-upon size of a reserve may have decreased as land was taken away to build highways or other projects. **Comprehensive claims** have questioned the ownership of land in large parts of Canada that were never surrendered by treaty.

FIGURE 8–23 The eagle and the bear in the logo of the Assembly of First Nations are symbols of strength.

GO ONLINE •••••••••••••••••••

More details on Aboriginal self-government can be found on the Government of Canada website.

FIGURE 8–24 Victoria Island, in Ottawa, has been a centre of trade and cultural exchange for Algonquin people for centuries. It is considered a special place because it is located where three rivers meet. The island currently features an Aboriginal centre, a guided tour, performances of traditional dance, a cafe, and a crafts workshop.

The Algonquin Land Claim

For more than 200 years, the Algonquins of Ontario have been asserting their rights to their traditional territory along the Ottawa River and its tributaries. A number of treaties covering the area were signed during that time, but none was signed with the Algonquins. However, a reserve was established at Golden Lake in 1873.

Since 1992, the Algonquins and the governments of Ontario and Canada have been trying to negotiate a treaty, or land claim agreement. The claim covers 36 000 square kilometres of eastern Ontario and includes Algonquin Park and cities and towns such as Ottawa, Pembroke, Arnprior, and Smiths Falls. About 10 000 people of Algonquin ancestry are covered by the claim.

Negotiations were complicated because only a small part of the Algonquin population had previously been registered by the federal government. The bulk of the Algonquin population was considered non-status, which meant they had no formal recognition. Who had a right to be considered Algonquin and how they would be represented in the negotiations proved to be contentious. Today the Algonquins of Ontario are represented by the Pikwàkanagàn First Nation and nine other First Nation communities. An added complication to negotiation is the fact that the area includes 1.2 million other people whose rights needed to be considered.

An agreement-in-principle was reached in 2012, but had not been ratified as of 2015. The 2012 agreement-in-principle says:

- 475 square kilometres of Crown land in 200 separate parcels will be transferred to Algonquin ownership

- no private land will be expropriated and no new reserves will be created

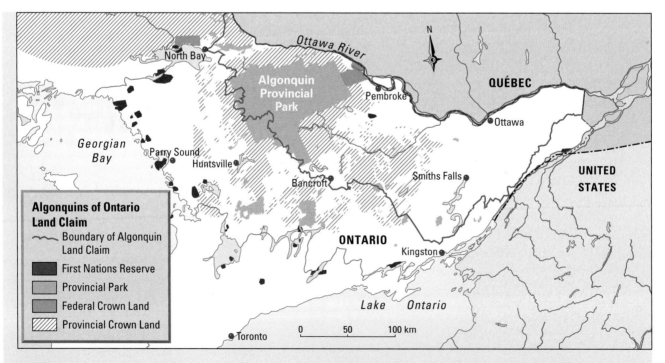

Algonquins of Ontario Land Claim
- ∿ Boundary of Algonquin Land Claim
- ▪ First Nations Reserve
- ▪ Provincial Park
- ▪ Federal Crown Land
- ▨ Provincial Crown Land

FIGURE 8–25 The Algonquin land claim covers more than 36 000 square kilometres in eastern Ontario. The boundaries of the claim are based on the watershed in the area. Note that the land claim includes Ottawa. The Algonquins call the Ottawa River the *Kiji Sibi*, which means "Great River."

©P

- Algonquin Park will remain accessible to everyone

- Algonquins will have the right to hunt, fish, and gather plants for domestic purposes on Crown land throughout the year

- $300 million will be transferred to the Algonquins

TIMELINE

A History of the Algonquin Land Claim

1763	The Royal Proclamation confirms Aboriginal ownership of their traditional territories.
1772	Algonquins object that traders are infringing on their territory.
1819–1822	Britain signs a treaty, known as the Rideau Purchase, with the Mississauga people. It covers much of the traditional Algonquin territory but the Algonquins are not a party to the treaty.
1820s–30s	The Algonquins formally complain many times that the Rideau Purchase ignores their rights.
1840s	An attempt to establish an Algonquin reserve at Bob's Lake north of Kingston fails.
1873	Golden Lake Reserve is created, later called the Algonquins of Pikwàkanagàn First Nation. This is the only Algonquin reserve established in Ontario.
1923	The Williams Treaty, signed with the Mississaugas, covers Algonquin Park and other areas within traditional Algonquin territory, but ignores the Algonquins.
1983	The Algonquins of Pikwàkanagàn make a formal land claim under rules enacted by the federal government in the 1970s. They claim the southern side of the Ottawa River basin.
1990	Pikwàkanagàn and a number of non-status Algonquin communities in the region meet to explore how the interests of those communities will be represented in the negotiations.
1991	Ontario enters into negotiation of the Algonquin claim.
1992	The federal government joins the formal negotiations with the Algonquins of Pikwàkanagàn and several non-status Algonquin communities.
2012	An agreement-in-principle is reached and a voters' list is compiled.

We and our ancestors have … from the remotest antiquity, held, used, occupied, possessed, and enjoyed as hunting grounds the tract of land lying on either side of the River Ottawa and Little Rivers as far as Lake Nipissing…. We … do not presume to venture to entertain the belief that the lands already … converted and erected into Townships for Settlement by the Government … will be restored to us but we do believe that a fair and reasonable compensation for the lands … will be allowed ….

—Petition by the Algonquins to the Lieutenant Governor of Upper Canada, 1835

Nunavut

Self-government and land claims continue to be important issues in many other parts of Canada. The creation of the territory of Nunavut in 1999 resulted from the largest treaty ever negotiated in Canada. It gave the Inuit of this northern area political control over 2 million square kilometres of the eastern Arctic. Aboriginal land claims and self-government will continue to be a powerful force for change in shaping the nation into the 21st century.

FIGURE 8–26 Celebrating the creation of Nunavut in Iqaluit, the territory's capital, in April 1999

Aboriginal artists and entertainers are an important part of Canadian culture. Aboriginal writers, visual artists, and actors are recognized and have won acclaim around the world.

Tomson Highway (born 1951) is a Cree from Manitoba. After studying music and literature in Ontario and in England, he joined a performing arts company. He is a playwright whose works include *Dry Lips Oughta Move to Kapuskasing* and *The Rez Sisters*. He became Artistic Director of Native Earth Performing Arts in Toronto, one of only a few Aboriginal theatre groups in North America.

Daphne Odjig was born in 1919 on Manitoulin Island, Ontario. Her grandfather was a stone carver who told her about the history and legends of her people. Odjig later moved to British Columbia, where her paintings were inspired by the landscape of the B.C. interior and the West Coast islands. She published her memoirs, *A Paintbrush in My Hand*, in 1992, and in 1998 received the Achievement Award in Arts and Culture from the National Aboriginal Achievement Foundation.

Joseph Boyden (born 1966) is a highly acclaimed Canadian novelist and short story writer of Irish, Scottish, and Ojibwa descent. His first novel, *Three Day Road*, is about two young Cree, Xavier and Elijah, who sign up for the military during the First World War. It is inspired by Ojibwe Francis Pegahmagabow, the legendary First World War sniper. Boyden's second novel, *Through Black Spruce*, follows the story of Will, son of one of the characters in *Three Day Road*, and his niece, Annie, who has returned to the bush from the city where she has been searching for her missing sister. Joseph Boyden won the prestigious Scotiabank Giller Prize for *Through Black Spruce* in 2008.

I ask Elijah where I can find rounds for the Fritz rifle. Elijah'd promised me more a while ago, and only a handful is left now. I think he is holding out. Elijah covets this gun, but I am responsible for taking down the Hun sniper who loved the dead. The night of the day I killed my first human was the first time I felt like an ancestor, an awawatuk *raider and warrior. I prayed to* Gitchi Manitou *for many hours on that day and the following day, thanking him that it was I who still breathed and not my enemy. Since that time I am able to shoot at other men and understand what I do is for survival, as long as I pray to* Gitchi Manitou. *He understands. My enemy might not understand this when I send him on the three-day road, but maybe he will on the day that I finally meet him again.*

***Excerpt from* Three Day Road**

FIGURE 8–27 *It Gets Hot on the Rocks by Noon* by Natalie Bertin of Newmarket, Ontario

©P

Adam Beach (born 1972) is a Saulteaux First Nations actor who has appeared in films such as *Smoke Signals, Flags of Our Fathers*, and *Windtalkers*. He also appeared in the CBC series *Arctic Air*. Born on the Lake Manitoba/Dog Creek First Nation Reserve, Beach got the acting bug in high school, when he attended drama class and began performing in local theatre. In 2008, he was nominated for a Golden Globe Award for best actor for his work in the television film *Bury My Heart at Wounded Knee*.

John Kim Bell (born 1952) was born on the Kahnawake Mohawk reserve in Québec. He studied violin and piano as a youth. In 1980, he was appointed apprentice conductor of the Toronto Symphony Orchestra. He went on to devote his time to promoting opportunities for Aboriginal artists and, in 1993, he established the National Aboriginal Achievement Award.

Bill Reid (1920–1998) discovered in his teens that his mother was Haida. He became interested in traditional Haida carving techniques and began to create wooden masks and totem poles using traditional techniques. Reid's work inspired other Aboriginal artists to return to traditional art forms.

FIGURE 8–28 Adam Beach is a Saulteaux First Nations actor.

Susan Aglukark (born 1967) was raised in Arviat, Northwest Territories, now part of Nunavut. She has developed a distinctive musical style, fusing traditional Inuit chants with modern pop melodies.

1. What themes and concerns are evident in the works of the Aboriginal artists featured here?

2. Explain the importance of these artists to young Aboriginals in Canada.

FIGURE 8–29 One of Bill Reid's most famous works, *The Spirit of Haida Gwaii, the Jade Canoe*, sits in the international terminal at the Vancouver International Airport.

The Royal Commission on Aboriginal Peoples

In 1991, one year after the Oka Crisis, the federal government launched an extensive study of the issues that affected Aboriginal peoples. The Royal Commission on Aboriginal Peoples travelled across the country for five years, gathering information and talking to Aboriginal and non-Aboriginal Canadians. It released a five-volume report of its findings in 1996. The report concluded that sweeping changes were needed to help mend the relationship between Aboriginal peoples and the government. The report also presented strategies to close the economic gap between Aboriginal and non-Aboriginal peoples and improve social conditions.

Ten years later, the Assembly of First Nations published a "report card" describing the progress that had been made on the recommendations of the Royal Commission. The report card stated the following statistics:

- One in 4 First Nations children lives in poverty compared to 1 in 6 Canadian children.

- Life expectancy for First Nations men is 7.4 years less, and 5.2 years less for First Nations women, compared to Canadian men and women, respectively.

- Unemployment is over 50 percent, and rises to over 60 percent for those without high school completion.

The report card also noted that Canada was one of two countries that voted against the UN Declaration on the Rights of Aboriginal People. The report card concluded that "Canada has failed in terms of its action to date."

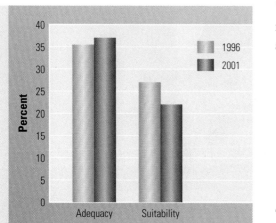

FIGURE 8–30 Percentage of on-reserve Aboriginal homes meeting Canada's standards for adequate housing and suitable living conditions

---

CHECKPOINT

1. What was the government's response to demands that it acknowledge its part in the ill treatment of Aboriginal children in residential schools? Do you think this response was adequate? Give reasons.

2. Explain the importance of
   a) the Assembly of First Nations
   b) specific land claims
   c) comprehensive land claims
   d) the Algonquin land claim in Ontario

3. **Evidence** How does the Algonquin petition from 1835 mirror the agreement-in-principle reached in 2012?

4. **a)** Why do you think the creation of Nunavut is significant?

   b) What challenges do you think are posed for Nunavut by having 29 000 people politically control 2 million square kilometres of land? How do you think e-mail and other modern technologies can help?

5. Summarize the contributions of Aboriginal artists to Canadian society.

6. What were the conclusions of the Royal Commission on Aboriginal Peoples? Does this surprise you? Explain.

7. Make a list of at least five events that contributed to Aboriginal Canadians affirming their identity and position in society. Explain why you chose each item.

©P

New Economic Ideas

By 1981, the oil crisis, inflation, and high interest rates had all taken a toll on Canada's economy. As the world slipped into an economic recession, many Canadians faced serious financial difficulty. The recession meant more unemployment and poor job prospects for young people. Canadians looked back wistfully on the confident 1950s and 1960s.

During the boom years, Canada had been a nation of savers. Now it was becoming a nation of spenders. But there was an important difference. In the past, Canadians had bought most of their goods with cash. Now they were experiencing the credit-card revolution, and consumerism was to become a way of life for the next decades. At the same time, governments cut public services and transfer payments to the provinces to deal with the national debt. Such measures dramatically changed Canadians' expectations.

An Uncertain Future

When Trudeau decided to retire in 1984, the government faced huge economic problems. Years of high unemployment and interest rates had resulted in a faltering economy. The National Energy Program (NEP), which was intended to shelter Canadians from soaring world oil prices, had failed.

High unemployment meant that government revenues fell as fewer people paid income tax and more required government assistance. The government had to borrow money to pay for social services, and the **national debt** grew tremendously. Both provincial and federal governments often ran a **deficit** as government expenditures (the amount of money spent) were greater than revenues (the amount of money taken in, mostly through taxes). Although reluctant to do so, the Trudeau government had begun to cut social programs and offer tax breaks to corporations to help stimulate the economy.

Mulroney and the Debt Crisis

Prime Minister Brian Mulroney's approach to Canada's economic problems was inspired by conservative governments in the United States and Britain, which were cutting back on the role of government in the economy. U.S. President Ronald Reagan thought the solution to economic problems lay in the hands of corporations and wealthy citizens. He believed that if they were given large tax breaks, they would reinvest in the economy and create new jobs for everyone else. This became known as the "trickle-down effect." In Britain, Conservative Prime Minister Margaret Thatcher took a similar line. She lowered taxes and drastically cut spending on social benefits.

Mulroney planned to use this approach to cut the debt. He would save money by trimming social programs, and the savings would help to pay off the debt. He would also stimulate the economy by cutting taxes. At the same time, the Mulroney government tightened economic links with the United States. Over the years, some Canadians continued to express concern that U.S. companies controlled too much of the Canadian economy. Some measures had been put in place to limit U.S. investment, such as the Foreign Investment Review Agency (FIRA), which was formed by the Trudeau government in

- How did the Canadian government respond to economic challenges after 1982?

KEY TERMS

national debt the amount of money owed by a federal government; most of Canada's national debt money is owed to Canadians who hold Government of Canada savings bonds, treasury bills, and so on

deficit the amount of money a government owes when it takes in less money than it spends

What If...

Imagine the federal government had not cut transfer payments to the provinces. Would supporting Canada's social safety net be worth running a deficit?

FIGURE 8–31 Brian Mulroney built close ties with the U.S. and shared the economic and political ideals of President Ronald Reagan. When the two leaders met in 1995, an event known as the "Shamrock Summit" because both men had Irish heritage, it was seen by the Americans as a turning point in Canada-U.S. relations. The Mulroney government reversed many of the programs previously enacted by Trudeau's Liberals.

1973 to block any foreign investment that seemed not to be in Canada's interest. Now Mulroney announced that Canada was "open for business." He dismantled FIRA and replaced it with Investment Canada, a body that would encourage suitable foreign investment. Mulroney also came to believe that free trade with the United States would help businesses to thrive, raise the employment rate, and increase government revenues.

Mulroney's plan to cut the debt did not work as planned. Canada was hit by a recession in 1990. Businesses failed and workers lost their jobs. Once again, the debt increased and the government was forced to increase, rather than cut, taxes. Failure to tackle the debt contributed to the defeat of the Conservative Party in 1993, when only two Tories won seats in Parliament.

Down the Road to Free Trade

In 1987, Mulroney started negotiations that led Canada into the **Free Trade Agreement (FTA)** with the United States. The agreement removed tariffs on goods crossing the border, and opened Canada to U.S. investment as well as opening the United States to Canadian investment.

Free trade proved to be a very controversial issue for Canadians. Supporters of free trade made arguments that included the following:

- By eliminating tariffs, Canada would attract more U.S. investment. This would help Canadian industry grow and benefit the whole economy.

- Free trade would give Canada access to the larger U.S. market, which would increase our productivity and growth. With more demand, Canadian products could be sold at lower prices to compete with imports.

- A free trade agreement would attract U.S. firms to Canada to take advantage of our natural resources, skilled workers, and well-planned transportation system.

People who were against the Canada–U.S. Free Trade Agreement put forward arguments that included the following:

- Once protective tariffs were removed, U.S. branch plants that had moved to Canada to avoid paying tariffs would simply return to the U.S. As a result, hundreds of thousands of jobs would be lost.

- Canadian businesses could not compete against giant U.S. companies that would flood the Canadian market with cheap goods and services.

- Free trade threatened Canada's independence. Economic union would also lead to pressure for political union.

FIGURE 8–32 Free trade was a popular topic for cartoonists.

Interpret and Analyze What opinion about free trade does the cartoonist express? How do the relative sizes of the hands help to put across this message?

©P

After much heated debate, the FTA was established in 1989. It included the following points:

- Tariffs between Canada and the U.S. would be eliminated. Complete free trade would be achieved by 1999.

- Cultural industries were exempt from the agreement, allowing Canada to retain protection for publishing, television and films, and the arts.

- The agreement included mechanisms to ensure fair competition between the two countries and fewer conditions on investment.

KEY TERM

North American Free Trade Agreement (NAFTA) the agreement signed in 1992 and implemented in 1994 between the United States, Mexico, and Canada to create a free trade zone among the countries

North American Free Trade Agreement (NAFTA)

In 1992, the Mulroney government expanded the free trade zone by signing the **North American Free Trade Agreement** (**NAFTA**), which included free trade with Mexico. This agreement also proved to be controversial. The major fear of NAFTA's opponents was that companies operating in Canada would move to Mexico to take advantage of the low wages and less strict anti-pollution laws. Those who supported NAFTA argued that while a few companies might move to Mexico, most would remain in Canada because Canadian workers are better educated and skilled. Canada had other attractions, such as transportation and communication systems, social services, and social stability. Although the Conservatives were defeated in 1993, their policies linked Canada's political and economic fortunes much more closely to those of the United States.

The Collapse of the Conservatives Under Kim Campbell

By the time the 1993 election came around, Prime Minster Mulroney was quite unpopular. Many supporters left to join the Reform Party in the west and the Bloc Québécois in Québec. An economic recession and the introduction of the Goods and Services Tax (GST) also upset many voters. Mulroney decided to step down. In June, 1993, Kim Campbell, a Cabinet minister from Vancouver, B.C., was elected leader of the Conservative party and became Canada's first female prime minister. Although Campbell appeared popular at first, Canadians were tired of the Conservative Party. In the 1993 election, Canadians elected only two Conservative MPs and Campbell lost her own seat. The Conservatives remained unpopular for the next two elections.

CHECKPOINT

1. How did Mulroney's ideas about government differ from those of the Liberals? What other politicians inspired Conservative policies?

2. **Evidence** Describe the FTA and NAFTA. Why are these agreements controversial? Find evidence to show that NAFTA has benefited or damaged the Canadian economy.

- How did the Canadian government respond to economic challenges after 1982?

Prime Minister

Joseph Jacques Jean Chrétien

- born 1934, Shawinigan, Québec
- lawyer
- first elected to Commons in 1963
- prime minister 1993–2003

Domestic Record

- first prime minister to win three consecutive terms since Mackenzie King
- supported federalism during the referendum on Québec sovereignty in 1995
- appointed Beverley McLachlin as the first female Chief Justice of the Supreme Court of Canada in 2000
- passed the Youth Criminal Justice Act, which came into effect in 2003, creating a separate criminal justice system for youths between the ages of 12 and 18

International Record

- led a series of "Team Canada" missions to improve international relations and trade
- supported Canadian involvement in NATO's campaign in Yugoslavia (1999)
- refused to send Canadian troops to support the U.S. invasion of Iraq in 2003
- ratified the Kyoto Protocol, committing Canada to a reduction of greenhouse gas emissions (2002)

Chrétien Comes to Power

Economic issues were brought to the forefront in the 1993 federal election campaign. Liberal leader Jean Chrétien quickly gained popularity by opposing the unpopular Goods and Services Tax. He also pledged to renegotiate NAFTA and to scrap the Conservatives' $5.8 billion order for new military helicopters. Chrétien further promised to fire the very unpopular governor of the Bank of Canada, John Crow. On October 25, 1993, the Liberals won 177 seats, enough for a strong majority government.

When Jean Chrétien and the Liberals came to power in 1993, they inherited a staggering national debt of close to $459 billion. Their solution was to inject $6 billion into the economy through public works such as road repairs and new bridges. These projects would create jobs, and workers would then spend their earnings and boost the economy.

The Liberals Tackle the Debt

Chrétien's Liberals had little opportunity to judge the effectiveness of their policy. At the end of 1994, interest rates shot up. Provincial and federal governments used 43 percent of revenues to pay interest on the debt. Minister of Finance Paul Martin announced that Canada could no longer afford "big government" nor could it fund social services as it had in the past. He eliminated more than 40 000 jobs in the federal civil service and drastically reduced money transfers to provinces for post-secondary education, health care, and welfare. The provinces were thus forced to cut programs as well. To try to enhance the effects of the cuts, Martin put extra money into the Canada Pension Plan and Employment Insurance—programs essential to Canada's "social safety net."

The government was reducing the deficit, but Canadians paid a high price. For example, universities and colleges had to raise their tuition fees. Through the 1980s and 1990s, health care costs rose rapidly. New drugs and technologies were expensive and an aging population meant more demand on the system. At the same time as the federal government was cutting transfer payments to the provinces, less money was available for health care. Hospital wards were closed, the length of hospital stays was reduced, staff were cut and registered nurses were replaced by aides with less training. Some patients went to the United States for treatment because the services they needed were not available in Canada.

FIGURE 8–33 Prime Minister Jean Chrétien supported Finance Minister Paul Martin's deficit-cutting measures, many of which went against Liberal policies set up while Chrétien was in Trudeau's Cabinet.

Continuity and Change How might cutting social programs change Canadian expectations and values?

There were other problems. Growing numbers of Canadian children were living in poverty. More Canadians were homeless, and many had to rely on food banks. Food banks reported that 40 percent of their users were children, although only 26 percent of Canada's population was children. In the new millennium, social services were more hard pressed than ever to meet the needs of Canadians.

A New Era of Globalization

One of Chrétien's priorities was to expand Canada's trading opportunities. He sent "Team Canada" trade missions to Asia and Latin America to secure deals for Canadian investment and exports. The Canadian government also signed free trade agreements with Chile and Israel, and joined APEC (Asia–Pacific Economic Cooperation) to promote cooperation, freer trade, and economic growth among Pacific Rim countries.

These trade initiatives were part of a **globalization** trend sweeping the world by the end of the 20th century. Globalization was partly the result of rapid changes in communications technology and the fall of communism. Goods could be shipped easily around the world, and the Internet made it possible to do business online from almost anywhere on the planet.

- What contributed to Canada's world presence?

KEY TERM

globalization a process by which the regions and countries of the world are becoming economically and culturally interconnected

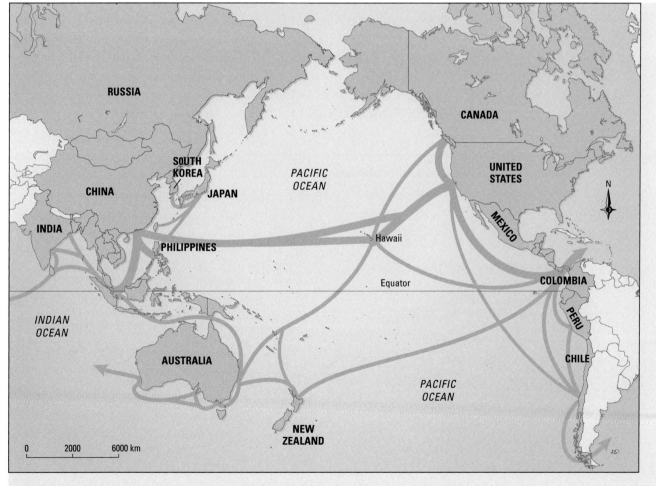

FIGURE 8–34 The APEC trading area, including major ocean trading routes

- How does globalization affect living standards?

HISTORICAL INQUIRY

Communicate

What was the Liberal government's position on the Kyoto Accord? Why did the Conservative government withdraw from the Kyoto Accord in 2011? Write a brief opinion piece to support your thinking.

Globalization as an Issue

People have strong views on globalization and there have been fierce protests against it. Supporters believe that globalization is a powerful trend that will raise living standards for everyone, rich and poor. They argue that when large corporations invest in less-industrialized countries, jobs and economic opportunities are created for people. This, in turn, raises standards of living, which benefits everyone.

Opponents say that globalization makes businesses rich at the cost of workers everywhere. For example, in the 1990s, many multinational corporations moved production away from North America, Europe, and Japan to countries that had lower labour costs and fewer environmental regulations. As the 21st century began, China became the world's leading producer of manufactured goods of all kinds—and this trend continues. Meanwhile, thousands of Canadian factories have closed.

Globalization also raises ethical questions. For example, although no country has a perfect human rights record, should Canada build trade relationships with countries that consistently disregard human rights? Canada has introduced human rights as a topic in some of its trade talks, a move critics believe does little to change conditions in countries with poor human rights records.

Environmental Action on a Global Scale

Globalization has created strong economic links around the world. At the same time, the global community has come together to work on environmental issues. The Kyoto Protocol is an international agreement that sets targets for reducing greenhouse gas emissions. It was an important step in the fight against climate change. Unfortunately, Canada has not met the goals of the Kyoto Protocol. You will learn more about this in Chapter 9.

CHECKPOINT

1. What caused the debt crisis of the 1990s? How did Conservative and Liberal governments deal with debt?

2. How did the Liberals deal with the deficit?

3. Why did Jean Chrétien organize "Team Canada" trade missions?

4. What is globalization? What are its benefits? What are its disadvantages?

5. Find out why the Ontario government made a deal with Samsung to generate more green energy and pay green energy producers a premium.

6. What economic reasons might the Canadian government give for not reducing greenhouse gas emissions?

A New Era of International Action

Canada's international role shifted over the decades as world events and government priorities changed. It became increasingly difficult for Canada to maintain its role as a middle power that gave it the prestige to mediate international disputes. Canadian governments have always been aware of the consequences of close adherence to American foreign policy and of how important it is that Canada pursue its own goals on the world stage.

Canada's relationship with its closest neighbour continued to complicate its foreign policy. The extent of Canada's support for American decisions remained an issue for Canadian leaders. For example, Prime Minister Mulroney generally supported U.S. foreign policy while Prime Ministers Trudeau and Chrétien were much less inclined to do so.

- What was Canada's involvement in the Cold War and its end?

- What measures did Canada take to promote a distinct Canadian identity?
- What contributed to Canada's world presence?

The Cold War Continues: Canada's Concerns

The Cold War continued to define international relationships throughout the 1980s. In 1981, the United States government announced a massive increase in its defence budget, with most of the money to be spent on modernizing its nuclear arsenal. The U.S. also continued its policy of fighting communism in the Americas and elsewhere. As a result, the U.S. supported numerous right-wing movements and governments that disregarded human rights. The U.S.S.R., on its side, supported pro-communist struggles.

In September 1983, Soviet jets shot down a Korean passenger jet that had strayed into Soviet air space. The next month, U.S. forces invaded the Caribbean nation of Grenada and deposed the pro-Soviet, left-wing government. The two superpowers accused one another of provoking hostilities.

Prime Minister Trudeau appealed to the United States and the Soviet Union to show more restraint. He visited a number of countries to enlist other political leaders in his campaign to mediate between the superpowers. Unfortunately, Trudeau's initiative had little effect.

> *Let it be said of Canada and of Canadians, that we saw the crisis; that we did act; that we took risks; that we were loyal to our friends and open with our adversaries; that we have lived up to our ideals; and that we have done what we could to lift the shadow of war.*
>
> *–Prime Minister Trudeau's summary of his peace initiative, delivered to Parliament in February 1984*

FIGURE 8–35 In 1978–1979, there was a revolution in Nicaragua against a repressive military government. After a left-wing government was established, the U.S. gave support to right-wing, anti-government rebels called Contras. This support undermined American prestige around the world. In this photo, an 87-year-old man of the first Sandino rebellion, armed with a double-barrelled shotgun, stands with an 18-year-old guerrilla holding an assault rifle in Leon, Nicaragua, June 19, 1979. "I fought against the Yankee invasion in the thirties and I'd like to fight today, but I'm too old," said the old man.

1945	Second World War ends United Nations established Gouzenko Affair
1949	NATO formed
1950– 1953	Korean War
1955	Warsaw Pact established
1956	Suez crisis
1957	Canada and U.S. sign NORAD agreement
1962	Cuban Missile Crisis
1963	Canada accepts Bomarc missiles
1966	190 000 U.S. troops in South Vietnam
1973	Last U.S. combat forces leave Vietnam
1983	Soviet jet shoots down Korean passenger jet U.S. announces "Star Wars" defence shield
1989	Fall of the Berlin Wall
1991	Collapse of Soviet Union

GO ONLINE
Visit the Berlin Wall Memorial and select English to learn more about the history of the wall and its demolition.

The End of the Cold War

By the mid-1980s, Soviet leader Mikhail Gorbachev realized that the Soviet Union could no longer afford its costly arms race with the United States. He proposed massive cuts in the arsenal of both superpowers. Gorbachev then began a series of sweeping economic, social, and political reforms that would help the communist countries run more efficiently and create better conditions for their citizens. He also loosened censorship and allowed greater freedom of speech. These policies, called *perestroika* (reconstruction) and *glasnost* (openness), encouraged the people of East Germany, Poland, Czechoslovakia, Hungary, and Romania to demand similar reforms in their countries. By 1991, the Soviet Union had collapsed, and the Cold War was over. The various member republics of the Soviet Union regained their independence and a new Russia emerged under the leadership of Boris Yeltsin, an ex-communist who now supported democracy.

FIGURE 8–36 The Berlin Wall, a powerful symbol of Cold War tensions, fell in November 1989. A few days before this picture was taken, guards would have machine-gunned anyone who tried to cross the Wall. Dismantling the wall that had divided Germany for 28 years was an operation that lasted weeks. Many Germans and visitors from other countries chipped off souvenirs and cheered the reuniting of long-lost relatives and friends.

Evaluate and Draw Conclusions Why do you think some historians called the end of the Cold War "the end of history"?

Communist China, too, experimented with a kind of *perestroika*, allowing capitalism to flourish in some areas of the economy. However, Chinese citizens' hopes for political freedom were brutally dashed in Tiananmen Square in June 1989. Red Army soldiers and tanks attacked students involved in the democracy movement, killing hundreds, perhaps thousands, of protesters.

FIGURE 8–37 A protester stands in front of tanks approaching Tiananmen Square in Beijing, China, in June 1989.

FAST FORWARD

The Air India Tragedy

Canada's place in the world and international tensions were emphasized by the Air India tragedy. In 1985, a bomb exploded in the cargo hold of Air India Flight 182, causing it to crash into the Atlantic Ocean off the coast of Ireland. The flight was on its way from Montréal to London, England, en route to Delhi and Bombay. All 329 people on board died, including 280 Canadians. At the time, this was the largest number of people killed in an act of air terrorism. The plot to destroy the aircraft was hatched and planned on Canadian soil. The investigation and prosecution of the bomber suspects went on for 20 years, but only one person, Inderjit Singh Reyat, was convicted and imprisoned for five years on the lesser charge of manslaughter. It was not until 2005 that Ripudaman Singh Malik and Ajaib Singh Bagri, the final suspects who were arrested in connection with the bombing, were found not guilty of all charges. There were allegations that the case was mishandled by the RCMP and the Canadian Security Intelligence Service (CSIS).

FIGURE 8–38 The Air India memorial in Ireland, unveiled on the first anniversary of the tragedy

1. Why was Flight 182 the target of a terrorist attack?
2. Why did the investigation take so long?
3. In what ways did the RCMP and CSIS mishandle the case?
4. Do you think justice was served in this case?

GO ONLINE
Delve into reports on the Air India disaster.

CHECKPOINT

1. Contrast Prime Minister Brian Mulroney's approach to foreign affairs with that of Prime Minister Pierre Trudeau. Present your information in the form of a diagram, chart, paragraph, poem, or other representation.

2. What brought about the end of the Cold War?

3. What actions did the Canadian government take during the last years of the Cold War?

4. Use the Cold War timeline on page 280. Make a list of the events in which Canada participated. Was Canada's involvement small, medium, or large?

- What was Canada's response to modern world conflicts?

- How did Canada participate in UN initiatives?

- What contributed to Canada's world presence?

Canada's Role in Peacekeeping

Many thought the end of the Cold War might bring a new era of world peace. Instead, regional conflicts and ethnic rivalries erupted, most notably in the Persian Gulf, the former Yugoslavia, and Africa. The United Nations looked for ways to solve these problems using its standard methods: negotiation, peacekeeping, and sanctions.

With the end of the Soviet Union, the United States was left as the only world superpower. Now unrivalled, it could enforce its will anywhere on the planet. It was not long before this new reality played out in the Persian Gulf, in the first international crisis of the post–Cold War era.

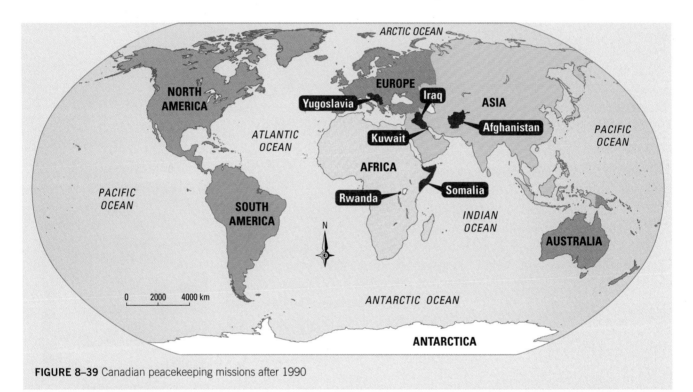

FIGURE 8–39 Canadian peacekeeping missions after 1990

FIGURE 8–40 American marines near a burning oil well in Kuwait during the First Gulf War

The Persian Gulf War

In August 1990, Iraqi forces under the leadership of Saddam Hussein invaded the oil-rich country of Kuwait. Almost immediately, the United Nations demanded that Iraq withdraw and threatened economic sanctions if it refused. The United States insisted that military force be used to oust Iraqi forces.

For the first time since the Korean War, the United Nations authorized a multinational force against an aggressor nation. As in Korea, the United States would take the lead. The U.S. was joined by a coalition of forces from 35 other countries. Canada contributed two destroyers, a supply ship, a squadron of CF-18 fighter jets, a field hospital, and hundreds of military personnel.

Although the Canadian contribution was modest, there was considerable debate in Parliament before forces were sent into combat. Prime Minister Mulroney emphasized that Canada made its commitment to enforce United Nations resolutions against Iraq, not merely to support the United States. Critics argued that sanctions had not been given enough time to work.

In January 1991, U.S. and coalition forces began bombarding targets in an effort to drive Iraqi troops from Kuwait. The use of "smart" weapons, such as laser-guided bombs and cruise missiles launched many kilometres from their targets, significantly changed the nature of the war. By February 27, the Iraqis were overcome by the forces massed against them. The coalition had won a stunning victory, with only a few casualties. Not a single Canadian soldier was killed or injured in the fighting. In the end, the Gulf War destroyed the Iraqi fighting force and much of the country's infrastructure.

After victory in the Gulf War, U.S. President George H. W. Bush proclaimed a "new world order," one in which the United Nations would take a much more active role as a global police force. In the past, the UN had been dedicated to peacekeeping—negotiating settlements and keeping warring factions apart. Now it would have more of a peacemaking role: it would, where necessary, use military force to preserve long-term peace and security. As the only superpower remaining after the collapse of the Soviet Union, the United States would take the lead in this peacemaking role.

KEY TERM

Rwandan genocide the 1994 mass murder of nearly one million Tutsis in Rwanda

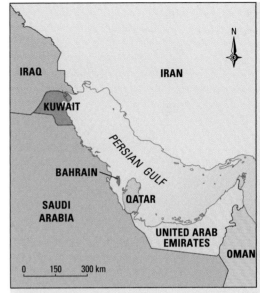

FIGURE 8–41 The Persian Gulf

Genocide in Rwanda

The population of the central African country of Rwanda is divided into two major groups—Tutsis and Hutus. Tutsis occupied a position of economic and political dominance in the country. In 1994, after an incident in which a prominent Hutu was killed, the Hutus overthrew the Tutsi-led government and began murdering Tutsis and their supporters. France and Belgium, the former colonial powers in the area, sent troops to try to control the slaughter and the UN sent a small detachment of peacekeepers under the command of Canadian Lieutenant General Roméo Dallaire.

Dallaire sent a series of urgent appeals to United Nations headquarters and outlined an ambitious military plan to halt the killing. As he saw it, the UN needed to send a large multinational force to disarm the warring factions. His plan required two things: speed and the support of the United States, the only country that could provide enough troops on short notice. Unfortunately, the response from the UN and Washington was unenthusiastic. The U.S. feared a defeat similar to that in Somalia. Dallaire watched helplessly as close to a million people were murdered in the **Rwandan genocide**.

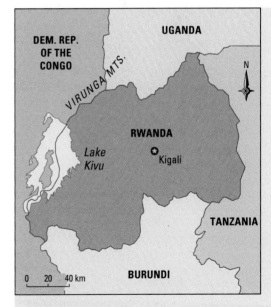

FIGURE 8–42 Rwanda

Crisis in Somalia

Until 1991, Canadians tended to see their soldiers as peacekeepers. Although Canada was a member of NATO, which had military bases in Europe, Canadian soldiers were most often involved in peacekeeping. Peacekeeping is similar to policing in many ways. It rarely involves fierce fighting, since its purpose is to prevent conflict. Peacekeeping cannot work unless warring parties agree to the presence of the peacekeeping forces.

Canada's role in military conflicts changed with the Persian Gulf War, when Canadian troops were part of a large coalition against Saddam Hussein. Since then, Canadian soldiers have been involved in other conflicts and are sometimes called upon to fight and die in military operations. Changing the mission of the military has changed the way Canadians view themselves and the way the world sees Canada.

Canada's more aggressive stance has had other consequences, some of which have hurt our international reputation. In 1992, the UN launched "Operation Restore Hope" in Somalia. Somalia, an East African nation, was ravaged by a civil war that broke out in 1991. By 1992, many Somalis were starving. Canadian forces joined those from other countries in distributing food and other essential supplies to the desperate local population. The mission was directed by the U.S. which has important strategic interests in the "Horn of Africa."

One night, members of the Canadian Airborne Regiment arrested a Somali teenager found wandering in the Canadian base camp. During the night, the teen was tortured and beaten to death. At first, a military inquiry found that only a few low-ranking soldiers had committed this terrible, racist crime. As more evidence came to light, however, it became clear that there had been a high-level attempt to cover up the incident.

Canadians were shocked by the brutality of these events and, in 1995, the federal government disbanded the Airborne Regiment.

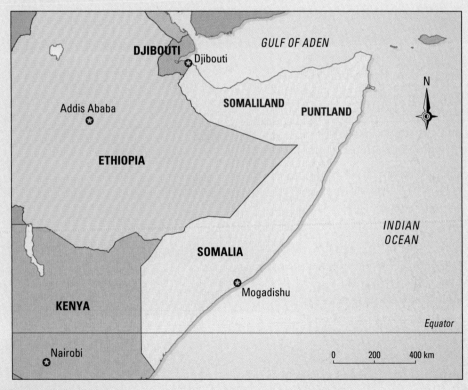

FIGURE 8–43 Somalia

Thinking It Through

1. How is peacekeeping different from combat? How would you describe the operation in Somalia?

2. How does the way Canada uses its military reflect on Canadians? On Canadian identity?

3. What kind of international operations do you think Canada's military should be involved in?

Civil War in Yugoslavia

After the Second World War, a communist nation called the Federal People's Republic of Yugoslavia was created in Eastern Europe. It was made up of six small republics: Serbia, Croatia, Bosnia-Herzegovina, Macedonia, Slovenia, and Montenegro, as well as two autonomous regions, Kosovo and Vojvodina. Until 1980, Yugoslavia was run by political strongman Prime Minister Josip Tito, but after his death, internal divisions began to appear.

When Slobodan Milosevic became president of Serbia in 1989, tensions among the republics broke out into ethnic conflict. United Nations peacekeeping missions, which included Canadian forces, were sent into the area, but they were unable to control the situation. Eventually, the member countries of NATO threatened to take steps to end the fighting.

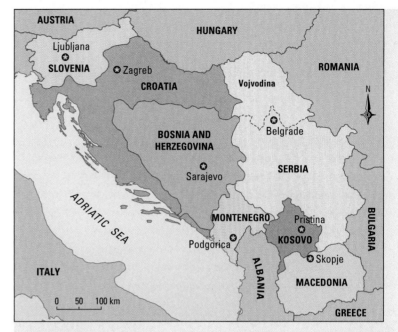

FIGURE 8–44 This map of the Balkans shows the political divisions of the former Yugoslavia after the civil war in the 1990s. Although still contested by Serbia, Kosovo has been recognized as an independent nation since 2008.

In May 1995, NATO forces launched a series of air strikes against the mainly Serbian forces of the Yugoslav army, which was perceived as the aggressor. The warring factions eventually agreed to a ceasefire, and American troops were sent to bolster the UN peacekeeping forces.

In 1998, Serbian forces moved into the province of Kosovo to ensure it would remain under Serbian control. The Albanian Muslims who made up the majority of the population in Kosovo were persecuted, murdered, and displaced. In spring 1999, after diplomatic efforts failed to stop the Serbian operations, the U.S.-dominated NATO alliance launched new military operations against Serbian forces. Canada, as a NATO member, engaged in the controversial air strikes on the Federal Republic of Yugoslavia.

Canada's participation in the bombings was the subject of heated debate at home. Some Canadians supported NATO's bombings, insisting that NATO was obligated to prevent the Serbian-Albanian conflict from spreading to neighbouring countries. Critics of the bombing argued that NATO should never have interfered in the domestic affairs of a sovereign nation, and that its involvement escalated the conflict. Some Canadians began to question NATO's role in the "new world order" and Canada's role in NATO.

Throughout the developments in the Persian Gulf, Africa, and the former Yugoslavia, the world watched with concern. The failure of UN efforts to keep the peace brought grave doubts as to the effectiveness of the organization.

❓ HISTORICAL INQUIRY

Gather and Organize

How did participation in peacekeeping and peacemaking missions in Rwanda and Yugoslavia encourage Canadian support for the development of the UN "Responsibility to Protect" and the Ottawa Land Mines Treaty?

FIGURE 8–45 A young Muslim girl pats a Canadian peacekeeper on the head as he walks by the front gate of the Canadian base in Visoco, Bosnia, in 1994.

Interpret and Analyze What impression of the UN mission does this image convey?

CHAPTER FOCUS QUESTION   How did Canada and Canadian identity change as a consequence of social, economic, and cultural trends at the end of the millennium?

Canada experienced severe political and economic shocks in the final decades of the 20th century. Our Constitution finally came home, but attempts to bring Québec onside failed—Canadian unity barely survived two referenda on Québec sovereignty. The national debt rose and Canada experienced a severe recession. Gradually, our economy became more integrated with that of the United States, particularly after the signing of NAFTA. Globalization also became a fact of life and manufacturing moved increasingly offshore. At home, women continued to enter the workforce in increasing numbers and Aboriginal peoples began to make significant progress in securing rights that had previously been denied or resisted by governments.

1. Create an organizer such as the one below. Provide as many examples as possible from the text for each category.

Social Trends	Consequences for Canadian Identity
·	
·	
·	
·	
·	
Economic Trends	**Consequences for Canadian Identity**
·	
·	
·	
·	
·	
Cultural Trends	**Consequences for Canadian Identity**
·	
·	
·	
·	
·	

Knowledge and Understanding

2. This chapter covers the final steps to Canadian autonomy. Complete the timeline by writing the name and date of each event and explaining how the event contributed to Canadian independence.

3. Why do you think the Canadian government has not made more progress in responding to the issues of Aboriginal peoples?

4. When the Assembly of First Nations released its "report card" on the progress that had been made for Aboriginal peoples since 1991, it highlighted issues of poverty, high school completion, unemployment, and life expectancy (see page 272). What solutions would you propose to improve the standard of living of Aboriginal peoples?

5. Do you think Canada should have signed NAFTA? Provide support for your opinion.

6. Compare how governments in the 1980s and 1990s dealt with economic crises versus governments during the Great Depression. Which do you think were most effective? Why?

7. How did the UN involvement in the Gulf War, Somalia, Yugoslavia, and Rwanda affect its reputation in the eyes of the world? Why do you think the traditional role of peacekeepers no longer seems to apply?

Apply Your Thinking

Historical Significance

8. Use the organizer from Question 1 to help you complete the following task.

Select five different trends and rank them from most impact on Canadian identity to least impact. Provide an explanation for each ranking.

For your top two selections (most impact), explain the long-lasting consequences of each for Canada.

9. "Canadian politicians should make every effort to have Québec sign the Constitution." Create arguments for and against this statement. Prepare to discuss your position with the class.

10. Compare the 1980 (from Chapter 7) and 1995 Québec referendum questions and results. Your teacher will give you copies of the questions. To analyze the results, you will need to do additional research. Why do you think the Parti Québécois government changed the question? What were the results in 1995? How important was Lucien Bouchard's role in the campaign? Why did Bouchard eventually abandon the idea of a completely independent Québec?

Communicate

Ethical Dimension

11. Some people say that individuals cannot make a difference in our world and there is no point in being active in social organizations or politics. Do you agree? How did Terry Fox make a difference? Why was he successful? How did he inspire the athletes who came after him? How have social media made it easier for individuals to make a difference?

? HISTORICAL INQUIRY

Evaluate and Draw Conclusions

12. Consider the following copy of a primary source document.

Canada MUST redefine its independence on the world stage, and in particular set a course in foreign policy independent of the United States. There are already welcome signs of this, including... Canada's advocacy role in trying to establish a world ban on the use of land mines.... There is much to recommend the long-standing relationship between Americans and Canadians across the longest undefended border in the world, but lock-step adherence to U.S. foreign (military) policy is not one of them. (A recent example of this kind of concern was provided on the CBC National News..., when the Minister of Defence, Mr. Art Eggleton, ...opined that Canada should consider contributing to the resurgent, ultimately destabilizing and doomed-to-failure U.S. "Star Wars" missile defence program.)

In this way [by redefining its independence on the world stage], Canada will recover the world respect it deserves from an earlier time, and rediscover its mandate to provide a much needed forum of sober second thought, a necessary counter-measure to those "great powers" too often inebriated by their own self-righteous views....

–Professor Donald Fleming

- When and why was this document produced?

- What is the nature of the document? For example, is it an official government document, a statement of personal opinion, or something else? Does the nature of the document influence how it can be used?

- What is Professor Fleming's thesis and how effectively does he support it?

- Comment on the effectiveness of the language used. Does the professor state his case well? Explain.

- In your opinion, could a historian use this document to assess Canadian public opinion for the years leading up to 2000? Explain.

9

Facing the Future:
Canada in the Post-9/11 World

Social, Economic, and Political Context

- In what ways did Canadian society change after 2001?
- In what ways did the world change after 2001?
- How did the Canadian government respond to economic challenges after 2001?

Communities, Conflict, and Cooperation

- How are Aboriginal peoples responding to challenges in the 21st century?
- What was Canada's involvement in the war in Afghanistan and other world conflicts?
- How does the government of Canada respond to terrorism and other world crises?

Identity, Citizenship, and Heritage

- How have artists and performers contributed to Canadian culture in the 21st century?
- How involved should government be in promoting the arts in Canada?
- What factors affect Canadian citizens in the 21st century?

A young boy protests on a national day of action in 2015 against Bill C-51, the government's proposed anti-terrorism legislation.

Evaluate and Draw Conclusions Does anti-terrorism legislation ensure that Canada will remain a safe and secure society? Or does it infringe on personal rights?

TIMELINE

2001

Terrorist attack on New York's World Trade Center (9/11)

Canadian Forces at war in Afghanistan

2003

U.S. Government invades Iraq; Canada does not take part

2004

Haida v. British Columbia establishes the "duty to consult" Aboriginal peoples before infringing on their rights or land

2006

Stephen Harper becomes Canada's twenty-second prime minister

CHAPTER FOCUS QUESTION

Which events, people, and organizations have had the most impact on Canadians since September 11, 2001?

KEY TERMS

terrorism

Taliban

weapons of mass destruction (WMD)

ISIS/ISIL

greenhouse gas

commodity

Truth and Reconciliation Commission (TRC)

Idle No More

super-diversity

cyberbullying

privacy

surveillance

The years after September 11, 2001 are partly defined by a world-changing terrorist act—the destruction of the World Trade Center Towers in New York City. This attack raised important questions. What is terrorism? What are the goals of terrorists? How should the world respond?

In the years that followed 9/11, security became a priority. Entire regions were disrupted by war, and millions fled to refugee camps. Canada, long a peacekeeper nation, found itself at war again. Canadians debated the country's place in the "war on terror." An attack on Ottawa's Parliament Hill in 2014 shook the nation and prompted new laws on terror.

Terrorism was not the only agent forcing change around the world and in Canada. Rapid technological change revolutionized Canadian society. Technology transformed many everyday activities, such as entertainment and shopping, but it also created new issues surrounding privacy, identity, security, and bullying.

Vast demographic, economic, and social changes are also remaking the world. Canada is part of a global community. Earth's human population continues to grow rapidly, but in some countries services cannot keep pace. Despite new medical discoveries, deadly diseases such as the Ebola virus appear and spread quickly, straining the resources of the international community.

At home, Canada's political landscape shifted as the new millennium progressed. The Liberal Party was swept from office, and the Conservative Party came to power in 2006. For the first time in Canada, the New Democratic Party achieved Official Opposition status in Parliament. Aboriginal peoples fought for recognition of their rights, and the Canadian government apologized for the treatment of Aboriginal people in residential schools.

As the 21st century unfolded, Canada faced many challenges on political, social, and cultural levels. What do Canadians need to know and understand if we are to deal effectively with these challenges? How should we adapt and respond to change so that our society continues to be safe, democratic, and prosperous?

? HISTORICAL INQUIRY

Formulate Questions

Scan the headings in the chapter and then make a list and convert them into questions. Which historical thinking concepts may be addressed in these sections of the chapter?

2008	2010	2012	2013	2014
Global financial crisis causes the collapse of major financial institutions	Vancouver hosts the 2010 Winter Olympics	Idle No More movement is founded	A Federal Appeals Court confirms that Métis and non-status Indians have the same rights as those enjoyed by status Indians living on reserves	Ebola outbreak threatens healthcare workers

Terrorist attack on the Canadian National War Memorial and Parliament of Canada |

FIGURE 9–1 On September 11, 2001, terrorists attacked the World Trade Center in New York City. Six months after the attack, two blue beams were projected into the night sky to memorialize the twin towers and the lives lost.

KEY TERMS

terrorism the use of violence, threats, and intimidation to frighten people to try to achieve a political goal

preventive arrest arrest and detention of suspected terrorists without warrant in order to prevent a terrorist attack

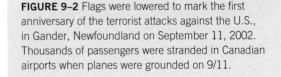

FIGURE 9–2 Flags were lowered to mark the first anniversary of the terrorist attacks against the U.S., in Gander, Newfoundland on September 11, 2002. Thousands of passengers were stranded in Canadian airports when planes were grounded on 9/11.

A New Era of Terror: The Attacks of 9/11

On September 11, 2001, members of a fundamentalist Islamic group called al-Qaeda hijacked four passenger jets. They flew two passenger planes into the Twin Towers of the World Trade Center in New York City, destroying both buildings. They crashed another plane into the Pentagon, the headquarters of the United States Department of Defense in Virginia. The fourth plane crashed into a field in Pennsylvania after passengers attacked its hijackers. The 9/11 attacks killed nearly 3000 people, including at least 24 Canadians. They also destroyed or damaged billions of dollars' worth of property.

The fact that terrorists could strike at the heart of such a powerful country came as a shock to many. President George W. Bush declared a "war on terror" and promised to strike back. Leaders of NATO countries and others rushed to show their support for the United States and its people. American security agencies went to work to learn as much as possible about the perpetrators and the organization that had dispatched them. President Bush stated that he personally made "no distinction between those who committed these acts and those who harbour them."

Canada's Response to 9/11

The 9/11 attacks shocked Canadians, and Canada responded with expressions of outrage and moral support. Commercial flights across North America were quickly grounded when the attacks happened. Gander International Airport in Gander, Newfoundland, received and assisted more than 6000 passengers and 473 flight crew from planes that could no longer land in the United States.

Many Canadians wondered how our relationship with the United States might change. Although Prime Minister Jean Chrétien said that Canada stood "shoulder to shoulder" with its neighbour, some Americans saw Canadian security as weak and its open border as a way for terrorists to enter the United States. Canada responded with the *Anti-Terrorism Act*—its first anti-terror legislation ever. Enacted in December 2001, the Act accomplished the following:

- defined **terrorism**
- established crimes of terrorism, including facilitating and financing them
- gave the government broad powers to seize the assets of terrorists without trial and imprison terrorists for life
- allowed for **preventive arrest**, whereby individuals could be arrested if there was a belief the arrest could prevent terrorist activity

As the United States imposed new restrictions and requirements on cross-border travel, Canada did likewise. By 2009, both Americans and Canadians needed a passport or other approved documentation to cross the border between Canada and the United States.

Canada's Role in the War in Afghanistan

A month after the 9/11 attacks, the United States, with the support of the United Kingdom, attacked Afghanistan. The **Taliban** government in Afghanistan was shielding al-Qaeda and its leader, Osama bin Laden. The Canadian government promised that Canada's military would participate.

The Taliban was quickly driven out, and members of al-Qaeda were either killed or forced to flee the country. Canada's special forces took part in this first phase of the war. The fighting in Kandahar province, where Canadians were stationed for five years, was especially fierce as the Taliban and al-Qaeda launched attacks to try to regain power. Canadian forces would remain in Afghanistan until March 2014, although combat duty ended in 2011. More than 40 000 Canadian personnel participated in the campaign, and 158 died as a result of fighting in Afghanistan.

- What was Canada's involvement in the war in Afghanistan and other world conflicts?

KEY TERMS

Taliban fundamentalist political movement originating in Afghanistan, which enforces Sharia law and strict dress codes, and opposes education for women and western influences

weapons of mass destruction (WMD) chemical, biological, or radioactive weapons capable of causing widespread death and destruction

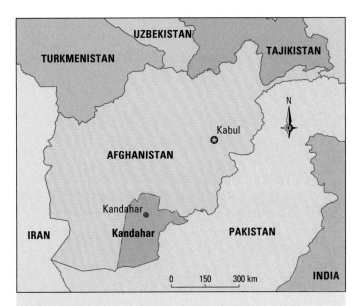

FIGURE 9–3 Kandahar province is close to Taliban strongholds in Western Pakistan. For NATO forces, it was one of the most dangerous parts of Afghanistan. What might happen to Afghanistan if the Canadian military failed to secure this area?

FIGURE 9–4 In August 2007, the stretch of Highway 401 between Trenton and Toronto was renamed the Highway of Heroes, to honour Canadians killed in Afghanistan. During the war, many Canadians would line the overpasses and wave flags as motorcades carrying the bodies of fallen soldiers were transported to Toronto for autopsy.

Historical Significance What does this picture reveal about Canadian values? Why do citizens and countries remember their fallen soldiers?

The War in Iraq

In 2003, the United States and its allies invaded Iraq, charging that the Iraqis had **weapons of mass destruction (WMD)** and were prepared to use them. This time, Canada did not participate directly. The United States and Britain, with several contingents from other countries, defeated Iraq and occupied the country.

CHECKPOINT

1. The 9/11 attack highlighted—some might say, strained—the relationship between Canada and the United States. Examine this relationship from at least two different perspectives, and state why you think it was mostly cooperative or mostly conflicted. Explain your reasoning.

Should Canada have participated in the War in Iraq?

When the United States invaded Iraq in 2003, Canada was once again forced to react. The U.S. invaders planned to topple the country's government and destroy weapons of mass destruction (WMD). American intelligence provided "clear evidence" to the media that Iraq had such weapons and was planning to develop more.

The governments of Britain, Australia, and Poland were persuaded by the data and joined the American-led invasion. Other countries, including Canada, declined to participate. Prime Minister Jean Chrétien reinforced Canada's independence by not automatically following the American lead.

The Canadian government was not at all convinced that the Iraqis had WMD ready to use. True, the Iraqi dictator, Saddam Hussein, had made threats and seemed dangerous. His forces had invaded the neighbouring country of Kuwait in 1990–1991 but had been soundly defeated. Did the fact that Hussein was a brutal tyrant justify an invasion of Iraq? Many people thought not. In addition, Iraq is a major oil-producing nation. Could these oil resources be worth a war?

FIGURE 9–5 What do you see? A simple aluminum tube? It may not be so simple. During the lead-up to war, this picture was described in the media as a tube used to develop nuclear weapons in Iraq. It was later revealed that the tubes were most likely used to develop conventional explosives, not WMD. However, to the American government, these tubes seemed to confirm the existence of WMD in Iraq.

Historical Significance What is the historical significance of the discovery that evidence used to justify the war in Iraq was largely fabricated? What lessons should historians take from this event?

As it turned out, no WMD were found. The United States and its allies in the war defeated Saddam Hussein's forces and occupied the country. Sometime later, Hussein was captured, tried, and executed. Since the invasion, Iraq has endured a weak and corrupt government, suffered through a civil war between warring religious factions, and has almost disintegrated. Radical Islamist groups took advantage of the situation and gained control of large parts of the country. They represent a grave threat to other Arabs and the rest of the world.

In a speech to Parliament in 2003, Prime Minister Jean Chrétien explained the government's position on the war in Iraq:

> Canada took a principled stand against participating in military intervention in Iraq. From the beginning our position has been very clear: to work through the United Nations to achieve the goals we share with our friends and allies; disarming Saddam Hussein; strengthening the international rule of law and human rights; and working toward enduring peace in the region.
> ...
> The decision on whether or not to send troops into battle must always be a decision of principle, not a decision of economics, not even a decision of friendship, alone.

The decision not to follow the American lead reinforced Canada's independence in foreign policy and contributed to our sense of nationhood.

Thinking It Through

1. Explain why you think Canada would go to war in Afghanistan and not in Iraq.

2. In your opinion, is it important to support allies no matter what they propose to do? Explain your answer by referring to the Iraq War.

In 2002, American forces fighting in Afghanistan severely wounded and captured Omar Khadr, two months shy of his sixteenth birthday. Khadr, a Canadian citizen, was allegedly fighting with al-Qaeda. American authorities accused him of killing an American medic, Christopher Speer. He was imprisoned at the U.S. detention camp in Guantánamo Bay, Cuba. Khadr was held in maximum-security conditions with adults.

Khadr was still at Guantanamo in 2010 when he decided to plead guilty to the American charges—a plea bargain, not an admission of guilt. He was sentenced to eight years of further imprisonment, some of which could be served in Canadian detention. In 2012, Khadr was moved to a Canadian prison, even though the Canadian government had long resisted the transfer. He was released on parole from a prison in Alberta in May 2015.

The case of Omar Khadr is about more than guilt or innocence. Khadr was tortured, held without trial, and presumed guilty in defiance of Canadian and American law. Also, Khadr was a child soldier at the time of his arrest.

Canada claims it is in "full compliance" with international standards on detention of juvenile offenders. These standards are as follows:

- arrest and detention only as a last resort, followed by speedy resolution of the case
- prompt access to legal assistance
- separation from adult prisoners
- the right to maintain contact with family
- right to special care and assistance, including the right to education and recreation
- access to juvenile justice systems

1. What rights was Omar Khadr denied as a child soldier and juvenile offender?

2. In Afghanistan and in other conflicts, teenagers often fight in battles. Would the fact that Omar Khadr was a teenager at the time excuse participation in the firefight in 2002? What risks might Canadian soldiers fighting in Afghanistan and other places face when confronted by teenage soldiers?

What If...

Imagine if the standards of justice applied in the Khadr case were used in all juvenile criminal cases in Canada. Should Canada's standards of justice be relaxed in terrorism-related cases involving juveniles?

FIGURE 9–6 Omar Khadr spent years in prison without trial, often in solitary confinement.

Ethical Dimension Why is the right to a speedy trial and the right to know the reasons for imprisonment important to basic justice?

[I] call upon the Egyptian government to reverse the actions that they've taken to interfere with access to the Internet, to cell phone service, and to social networks that do so much to connect people in the 21st century. At the same time, those protesting in the streets have a responsibility to express themselves peacefully. Violence and destruction will not lead to the reforms that they seek.

–President Barack Obama, speaking at the height of the Arab Spring protests

GO ONLINE

Read more about the Muslim Brotherhood.

Upheaval in the Middle East and North Africa

In 2011, a number of dictators in the Arab world were deposed. Citizens took to the streets to protest the governments they were living under, often led by corrupt, brutal leaders. The protests took the form of peaceful and non-peaceful demonstrations. While authorities allowed some protests to continue, others were met with a violent response.

Arab Spring and Social Media

Ordinary people accomplished this feat, often using social media to organize protests. Some Western reporters called the events the Arab Spring, and they looked forward to a new era of democracy and freedom. Young people dominated the protests, which often focused on high youth unemployment, censorship, and human rights violations.

Tunisia's autocratic president was the first to go. After a month of protest, he fled the country for Saudi Arabia. Soon there were new campaigns to depose or remove corrupt leaders in other Arab countries (see the timeline below). Many other Arab governments promised to reform, but the gains were, for the most part, short lived. Today, the military is once again in power in Egypt, fighting continues in Libya, and civil war continues in Syria. The future of the Middle East remains unclear.

FIGURE 9–7 In 2011, these Egyptians marched to protest against the government of Hosni Mubarak, who was deposed as a result of actions like this. After a brief period of democracy, followed by government by the Muslim Brotherhood—an organization founded in 1928 to promote governance through Islamic law—the military took control of the country.

TIMELINE

Regime Challenges in the Arab World, 2011–12

January 14, 2011	Tunisian leader Zine el-Abidine Ben Ali is deposed.
February 14, 2011 to March 2012	Bahraini regime crushes an uprising and arrests almost 3000 people.
March to October 2011	Syrian leader Bashar al-Assad's regime cracks down on peaceful protests and arrests more than 10 000 people.
October 20, 2011	Libyan leader Muammar al-Qaddafi is captured and killed.
November 2, 2011	Egyptian leader Hosni Mubarak is deposed.
February 27, 2012	Yemeni leader Ali Abdullah Saleh resigns.

Canada's Return to Combat

KEY TERM

ISIS/ISIL Islamic State in Iraq and Syria/Islamic State in Iraq and the Levant; Islamic fundamentalists who attempt to establish a caliphate, or religious state, in Iraq and Syria through violent means

What happens when national governments lose control or fail to provide their citizens with justice, peace, and security? Sometimes these failures provide terrorist organizations with opportunities to seize power. The groups and the governments they oppose may try to drag the rest of the world into their regional struggles. Should the rest of the world get involved? This important question continues to confront Canada and the world community.

The demand for democracy that swept North Africa and the Middle East also reached Syria. Syrian dictator Bashar al-Assad responded to peaceful demonstrations with violent repression, but his opponents fought back. As the country deteriorated into civil war, different factions tried to gain power. The fundamentalist group **ISIS/ISIL** (also known as the Islamic State) emerged as the most powerful force in the region, and its influence spread quickly to neighbouring Iraq. It killed hundreds, perhaps thousands, of Muslims, Christians, and Yazidis (a religious minority). Cultural heritage sites in the region were vandalized or destroyed.

FIGURE 9–8 An Iraqi family fleeing attacks by the Islamic State on the city of Mosul arrives at a refugee camp in June 2014.

Cause and Consequence Conditions at most refugee camps are primitive. What might the consequences be for young people growing up in a camp rather than at home?

ISIS grew quickly into a major threat, not only to peace and security in the Middle East, but also to the world, since the group has been accused of recruiting citizens of Western countries to commit terrorist acts. (Some intelligence sources believe that at least 130 Canadians were fighting with ISIS in 2014.) Few countries wanted to send troops back into the area, but one option favoured by many was air support and army training. The Canadian government decided to send warplanes to strike at Islamic State targets, just as the Americans and other countries were doing.

Although the Stephen Harper government strongly defended such measures, others were critical, noting that bombing targets does not protect civilians and that such efforts would not destroy ISIS. However, Canada also sent money and supplies to help Syrian refugees, many of whom were driven from their homes by ISIS.

• In what ways did Canadian society change after 2001?

Terror at Home

On October 22, 2014, Michael Zehaf-Bibeau, a 32-year-old Canadian with a criminal record, shot and killed Corporal Nathan Cirillo, a soldier on duty at the National War Memorial. When the attacker entered the Parliament buildings and continued shooting, he was cornered by four RCMP officers and Sergeant-at-Arms Kevin Vickers, and was quickly brought down. Although the shooter had no links to any terrorist organization, the RCMP classified the attack as terrorism.

FIGURE 9–9 Many people placed flowers and other tributes at the cenotaph in Ottawa where Corporal Nathan Cirillo was killed.

Cause and Consequence Could anything have been done to prevent this tragedy?

Only days before the attack in Ottawa, two Canadian Forces members were deliberately hit by a car in Québec. These attacks added to the losses Canadians felt after 9/11 and the Air India bombing of 1985. Canadians began to realize that they were not immune to terrorism.

In 2015, largely in response to the Ottawa attack, the Conservative government introduced stricter security laws with Bill C-51, some of which, critics said, eroded the civil and legal rights of citizens. Law enforcement agencies now have the power to arrest someone if they suspect a terrorist act "may" be carried out. It is also now illegal to "promote" terrorism.

The measures raised many fundamental questions for Canadians. Are new laws the best way to deal with a domestic terrorist threat? Should courts override the basic legal rights of Canadians to make them feel safer?

CHECKPOINT

1. Write a paragraph explaining what you think the limits of free speech ought to be and why.

2. Social media were used effectively as a rallying cry and information tool during the Arab protests.

How can social media shape a protest? Share your ideas in a group.

3. Summarize the debate over security and civil rights in Canada.

©P

Political Upheaval After 2001

War and terror may dominate headlines, but Canadian governments must balance their response to international events with their primary task, which is to govern the country well. Canadian democracy allows governments to change when they lose the confidence of the people. Sometimes parties lose elections because of shifts that occur in society. Sometimes they are voted out because citizens no longer think they are governing well—or are fit to govern.

• What factors affect Canadian citizens in the 21st century?

The Fall of the Liberals

For much of the 20th century, the Liberal Party governed Canada, and many came to see the party as the "Natural Governing Party." They seemed poised to continue that leadership into the new century. The Liberals ruled the country for two-thirds of the century, winning 17 elections between 1911 and 2011. The Conservatives formed the government only 10 times; it seemed voters turned to the PCs when they were fed up with the Liberals—for example, in 1930 at the height of the Great Depression or in the 1980s in the post-Trudeau era.

FIGURE 9–10 Paul Martin succeeded Liberal leader Jean Chrétien and was prime minister from 2003 to 2006.

The Québec Factor

The Liberals had dominated politics in large part because of their base in Québec, which had generally voted Liberal since the days of Wilfrid Laurier. That changed with Québec-born Brian Mulroney, who carried the province for the Conservatives in two elections in the 1980s. However, his falling out with Lucien Bouchard led to the latter's founding of the separatist Bloc Québécois in 1991, which held most of the seats in the province for the next two decades. Both the Liberals and the Conservatives were denied a base of seats in that province.

Although Mulroney and the Conservatives won two elections in 1984 and 1988 and formed majority governments, the Liberals were back in power in less than a decade. In 1993, Jean Chrétien led the Liberals into the new millennium. He stepped down as PM after a 10-year reign, and his rival and former finance minister, Paul Martin, replaced him. Martin, also from Québec, became prime minister in 2003. Chrétien, Martin, and their Liberals held power for 13 years.

Three Minority Governments

In 2003, the Liberals' hold on power was slipping. Paul Martin suddenly had to deal with an embarrassing incident, known as the Sponsorship Scandal, when the media revealed that key party members in Québec misused government funds—a form of corruption. Many Canadians were disgusted and thought it was time for a change. In the 2004 election, Martin was returned with a minority government. The fallout from the Sponsorship Scandal spread, and in December 2005, the Conservative, New Democratic, and Bloc Québécois MPs defeated Martin and the Liberals in a non-confidence motion (a vote of no confidence in the government). Martin called an election for January 23, 2006, but he came second to the Conservatives and resigned as leader of the Liberal Party.

In 2006, Stéphane Dion was elected leader of the Liberal Party to replace Paul Martin. The Conservatives immediately launched negative advertising that attacked Dion as a weak leader and questioned his record as Minister of the Environment. In the next election called by Prime Minister Harper during the 2008 economic crisis, the Conservatives won another minority government, but they still received less than 38 percent of the people's votes. When Stéphane Dion and Jack Layton—the leader of the federal NDP—saw the Conservative budget, they planned to form a new coalition government with the support of Gilles Duceppe and the Bloc. Harper persuaded Governor General Michaëlle Jean to suspend Parliament and avoid a defeat in the House of Commons. The Conservatives launched attack ads against the idea of a coalition government even though it had the support of MPs from parties that had received over 56 percent of people's votes.

In late January 2008, Harper presented a new budget that was much more attractive to the Liberal Party, and they decided to support it instead of proceeding with the coalition. Stéphane Dion was forced by his party to step down as leader and was replaced by Michael Ignatieff. The Conservatives launched more attack ads on the new leader. They managed to turn strengths, such as intelligence, into negatives, implying that Ignatieff was "just visiting" Canada because he had a teaching career in the UK and the United States. Many of these tactics copied those used by American political parties and made political contests far less civil.

Harper called another election in 2011. Voters seemed to have tired of minority governments and frequent elections, and the Conservatives elected 166 MPs and formed a majority government. The Liberals came third in seats, and Michael Ignatieff lost his own seat in the House of Commons. He stepped down, and in 2013, Justin Trudeau was elected as the new Liberal Party Leader.

HISTORICAL INQUIRY

Formulate Questions

What questions would you like to ask Stéphane Dion and Michael Ignatieff on their experiences as leaders of the Liberal Party?

The Rise of the NDP

The Bloc Québécois vote collapsed in 2011, and Jack Layton and the NDP won 103 seats, 59 of them in Québec. The NDP became the Official Opposition for the first time in their history. Layton was a Toronto MP who had grown up in Québec. He appealed to the nationalist voters in Québec who were less interested in independence from Canada and were tired of the old political parties. Unfortunately, Layton had been diagnosed with cancer just prior to the election. He died in August 2011, only months after leading the NDP through its most successful federal election. The following year, the NDP elected Montréal lawyer Thomas Mulcair as their new leader. Mulcair had been a member of the Québec National Assembly and a member of the cabinet of Liberal Premier Jean Charest.

FIGURE 9–11 Thomas Mulcair (left), leader of the NDP, and former leader Jack Layton (1950–2011) campaign during the 2011 election.

Throughout Canada's history, a total of 12 women have served as first ministers—11 as provincial or territorial premiers, and one as prime minister. Two-thirds of them gained office in the 21st century.

Today, an average of 23.8 percent of provincial and territorial legislatures are women. In British Columbia, the number is 36 percent.

Why so many more female politicians now?

The rise of women to leadership roles in government is evidence of a major shift in Canadian society over the past few decades. While women were often politically active in the past, they rarely achieved high office. Partly this was because powerful forces within political parties worked against women candidates. Politics was a "men's club" where women were rarely encouraged to participate or lead. In addition, some voters would not support female candidates.

Presented here are a few of the Canadian women who have broken those barriers since 2001.

Kathleen Wynne (Liberal) is the 25th premier of Ontario. Her introduction to politics came in the 1990s when she helped found Citizens for Local Democracy, which opposed the amalgamation of the City of Toronto. Wynne became a school trustee in Toronto's Ward 8 in 2000. Within six years, she was promoted to minister of education. Between 2006 and 2014, Wynne held numerous portfolios, including transportation, municipal affairs and housing, and Aboriginal affairs. She became leader of the Liberal Party of Ontario and premier of Ontario in 2013, and was re-elected in 2014.

Eva Qamaniq Aariak was the second premier of Nunavut, a post she held from 2008 to 2013. Aariak was elected as a member of the Legislative Assembly to represent the district of Iqaluit East. Prior to running for office, Aariak was a reporter for CBC Radio and Nunavut's first languages commissioner, charged with the responsibility of protecting the language

rights of all residents of Nunavut. Aariuak has also served as chair of the Nunavut Film Development Corporation and coordinator for the Baffin Divisional Council's publishing program for children.

Kathy Dunderdale (Conservative) was the 10th premier of Newfoundland and Labrador, from 2010 to 2014, when she opted to resign from provincial politics. Dunderdale was active in the 1980s in the fight to save a fish-processing plant in her home town of Burin, Newfoundland. In the 1990s, she became president of the Progressive Conservative Party of Newfoundland, and ran in her first provincial election in 1993. Dunderdale won a seat in the Newfoundland and Labrador House of Assembly in 2003 and became acting premier in 2010, after holding several cabinet portfolios.

Christy Clark (Liberal) is the 35th premier of British Columbia. She was a member of the British Columbia Legislature from 1996 to 2005, and served as deputy premier from 2001 to 2005. After a break from politics during which she hosted her own radio talk show and wrote a column for the *Vancouver Province,* Clark decided to seek the leadership of the BC Liberal Party. She became Premier of British Columbia in March 2011 and was re-elected in 2013.

FIGURE 9–12 Prime Minister
Stephen Harper

Prime Minister
Stephen Joseph Harper

- born April 30, 1959, Toronto,
  Ontario
- computer systems operator,
  Imperial Oil

Domestic Record

- first prime minister to lead the new
  Conservative Party, formed in 2004
  after merger of the Progressive
  Conservatives and the Canadian
  Alliance
- won the 2006, 2008, and 2011
  elections
- responsible for Canada having the
  lowest debt-to-GDP ratio of the G7
  economies
- scrapped the Canadian Firearms
  Registry

International Record

- ended dispute with the United
  States over softwood lumber
- increased Canada's border security
  following 9/11
- sent Canadian troops to
  Afghanistan to fight the Taliban
- withdrew Canada from the Kyoto
  Protocol
- declared sovereignty over the
  Arctic waters between Nunavut
  and the Northwest Territories

The Harper Years

Canadian politics changed dramatically when Stephen Harper and the
Conservatives took power. The party won the federal election of 2006 and
formed a minority government. It increased its support in 2008 and won a
majority in 2011. Majority government meant that the Conservatives had complete control of Parliament and did not have to compromise with other parties.

Building a New Conservative Party

Steven Harper's rise to power was remarkable. Based in Alberta, he helped
form the Reform Party, which later became the Canadian Alliance. Harper
took over as leader in 2002. Like many other western protest parties, the
Alliance was strong in the West but weak in the East, and that seemed
unlikely to change. Unless Harper could create a national party, he would
never achieve his goals, which were very different from those of the Liberals.
His solution was to merge his party with the once mighty Progressive
Conservative Party, which had several seats in the East.

The Alliance was much larger and even more conservative than the old
Conservative Party. Many party loyalists resisted, but the merger took place
in 2003. Harper and the Conservatives won the federal election of 2006—a
stunning rise to power. The Conservatives could have lost control of the government in 2010 when the opposition parties threatened to join in a coalition,
which would have given them more seats than the Conservatives. However,
because Harper prorogued (suspended) Parliament, the threat ended.

FIGURE 9–13 This cartoon mocks Prime Minister Harper's proroguing of Parliament in
January 2010. The government claimed it needed time to consult with Canadians on its
economic action plan. Opposition parties claimed the measure was undemocratic.

©P

Moving Canada to the Right Politically, Harper's Conservative government is "right of centre." This means that the Conservatives want lower taxes, a smaller bureaucracy, and less government spending. They want more focus on law and order, strict punishment for crimes, and a stronger and more active military. The Conservatives have also decided not to fund universal day care, giving money instead, in the form of tax credits and other programs, directly to individual families.

Once in power, the Conservative government lowered taxes while at the same time cutting government jobs and services. Internationally, the government largely rejected Canada's traditional peacekeeper role and sent troops to Afghanistan and Syria.

Economy vs. the Environment The Conservatives have tended to favour the economy over the environment. The vast Athabasca Oil Sands, in northern Alberta, hold the world's largest supply of crude bitumen, a form of petroleum. Getting 1.98 million barrels of oil out of the sands each day is a major carbon-producing activity. Although the sands have been in operation for decades, the Conservative government has supported their expansion. In practice, this has meant reversing the environmental goals of past governments.

Critics charge that environmental restrictions on oil sands development and on other carbon-producing industries are weak or ineffective. Environmental reviews on large-scale economic projects such as pipelines have been shortened or cut. In fact, the government strongly supports the Keystone XL Pipeline Project. If completed, it would carry oil from the oil sands to refineries in the southern United States. In 2015, President Obama vetoed this project because of environmental concerns.

The government has also distanced itself from environmental goals laid out by past governments. For example, Canada signed the Kyoto Protocol in 1997, which was designed to limit **greenhouse gases** and the effects of global warming. The Protocol went into force in 2005, but Canada withdrew from it in 2011. At that time, the government claimed it could not meet Kyoto targets and pointed to the withdrawal of the United States and others as its reason for dropping out.

- How did the Canadian government respond to economic challenges after 2001?

KEY TERM

greenhouse gas gas, such as CO_2 produced by industry and agriculture, that contributes to global warming

FIGURE 9–14 Canada's oil sands are a major source of pollution. But they also produce wealth.

Evaluate and Draw Conclusions Why would the government loosen environmental protection for this industry? Explain why you think this is a positive, a negative, or a neutral policy.

CHECKPOINT

1. Examine the fall of the Liberal Party and the rise of the NDP prior to and including the election of 2011. What caused the Liberal decline, and what were its consequences?

2. Research the life and legacy of Jack Layton. Identify two policies you believe he will be remembered for. Explain your response.

3. **Continuity and Change** Do you think Canada's legislatures will one day include an equal number of male and female representatives? Give reasons for your response. Note: In the whole world, only one legislature is made up of at least 50 percent women.

4. Explain what you think is meant by the term "moving Canada to the right." What other issues are Conservatives interested in?

What does a resource boom in Alberta mean for different regions of Canada?

Did you know that the value of the Canadian dollar is strongly linked to the price of oil? For example, when the price of a barrel of oil plummeted between September 2014 and February 2015, the value of the Canadian dollar also dropped dramatically.

Oil price and the dollar are what economists call "highly correlated," which means they rise and fall together. During the first years of the 21st century, the price of oil skyrocketed because of demand from the rapidly growing economies of China and other countries. When there is a big demand for a product or service, companies can charge more for it.

Starting in the 1990s, China was in the middle of an economic boom. It was becoming rapidly industrialized and needed oil and natural gas to power its machines and make the products consumers wanted—products that are usually made of petrochemicals. In 2004, China alone accounted for 31 percent of the worldwide growth in demand for oil.

Boom in Alberta

In Canada, the result was that the oil sands industry in northern Alberta boomed. Oil companies also drilled new wells all over the West and began fracking to produce more oil and natural gas. (Fracking involves using water and chemicals at high pressure to crack layers of rock to release the oil and gas.) Soon, a large part of Canada's Gross Domestic Product (GDP)—the wealth the country generates—was coming from the petroleum industry. One consequence was that the Canadian dollar rapidly increased in value.

Bust in Ontario and Québec

However, the resource boom in Alberta wasn't good for everyone in Canada. The rise in the price of oil, and of the Canadian dollar, hit Ontario and Québec manufacturing very hard. There are several reasons for this. Manufacturing needs factories. Factories need a great deal of fuel, oil, and gas byproducts such as plastics. When the price of these goes up, the cost of manufacturing also rises. So factories must charge more for what they produce.

In addition, when the Canadian dollar goes up, the price of anything made in Canada rises as well. We sell our products to other countries, mostly to the United States. Products that cost more than those from other countries are not purchased by consumers. The result is that the factories lay off workers, close down, or relocate to other countries where labour is cheaper, leaving Canadians out of work. Between 2007 and 2012, Statistics Canada data showed that 182 900 manufacturing jobs had been lost in central Canada. Many economists tie the loss to oil.

FIGURE 9–15 A 30-year-employee holds one of the last boxes of cereal produced at the Kellogg's plant in London, Ontario. The plant closed in 2015 after a 107-year history of producing cereal. It was one of many factory closures in Ontario in the 21st century.

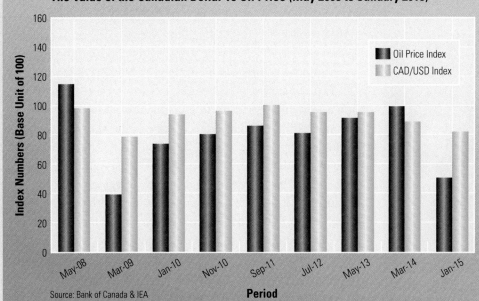

The Value of the Canadian Dollar vs Oil Price (May 2008 to January 2015)

Oil Price Index
CAD/USD Index

Index Numbers (Base Unit of 100)

Source: Bank of Canada & IEA   Period

FIGURE 9–16 Oil prices are one factor affecting the value of the Canadian dollar. In the first half of 2014, the oil industry accounted for 30 percent of Canada's economic growth, but then oil prices fell by 25 percent. The loss of taxes on the commodity hurt government revenues and weakened the overall economy.

Prices Rise and Fall

Oil and gas are **commodities**, which means they sell for whatever the market is willing to pay. When commodities are in demand, their price is high. But when they are not, as in late 2014 and 2015, the price drops.

So why did the price of oil suddenly fall? There were many factors. One reason is that lots of countries now produce oil, including the United States, Russia, Saudi Arabia, Nigeria, Algeria, and Iraq. Because there was so much oil on the international market, the price of oil dropped. In addition, the economies of the importing countries weakened somewhat and their vehicles became more energy-efficient. They simply needed less oil.

This sudden turnaround has happened with many of the resources Canada exports, not just oil. The price

of copper, for example, dropped significantly between 2011 and 2015. Perhaps the important message is: Even when the dollar is high, focusing on one resource means that less attention is being paid to other industries that could one day make money.

Thinking It Through

1. Describe how the economic activities of western and central Canada are linked. What is the role of the federal government in balancing economic activities across Canada?

2. Why do high oil prices help make the Canadian dollar stronger?

3. Why are high prices for oil bad for manufacturing?

4. What are the positive and negative consequences of resource boom?

KEY TERM

commodity a raw material that is mined or grown and then sold to industry, including oil, natural gas, coal, soybeans, corn, beef, copper, and many others

KEY TERM

duty to consult the principle of requiring resource companies to consult Aboriginal peoples affected by a proposed development

FIGURE 9–18 Haida gather to celebrate their Supreme Court victory in 2004.

Evaluate and Draw Conclusions What is the purpose of organizing public demonstrations and protests, and when are they most effective?

First Nations peoples will oppose any development which deprives our children of the legacy of our ancestors. We will no longer accept poverty and hopelessness while resource companies and governments grow fat off our lands and territories and resources. If our lands and resources are to be developed, it will be done only with our fair share of the royalties, with our ownership of the resources and jobs for our people. It will be done on our own terms and our timeline.

–National Chief Perry Bellegarde, Assembly of First Nations, December 2014

Aboriginal Peoples in the 21st Century

In 1996, the Royal Commission on Aboriginal Peoples in Canada published its final report. However, ten years had gone by with few of its recommendations implemented.

In 2005, Prime Minister Paul Martin struck what became called the Kelowna Accord with Aboriginal leaders. It was an agreement worth $5 billion to provide economic development and improve Aboriginal education, housing, and health and water services. However, three days after the deal was struck, the Martin government fell. The new Conservative government agreed to allocate only $450 million over two years. Aboriginal leaders such as Phil Fontaine were highly critical of the Harper government's failure to honour the Kelowna Accord.

There were some successes. A 2004 Supreme Court decision establishing the **duty to consult** Aboriginal peoples before infringing on their treaty rights changed the way companies could develop resources on Aboriginal land. *Haida v. British Columbia* stated that the Haida Nation had a right to object to the transfer of tree farm licences to a logging company because the transfer would have interfered with their right to harvest red cedar in the area. In this unanimous decision, the court found that the duty of the government to consult prior to taking action was "grounded in the principle of the honour of the Crown," and applied even if Aboriginal title to land had not been proven. The Nisga'a Nation also settled once and for all the issue of its territory in British Columbia. The 2011 Supreme Court decision is known as the Nisga'a Final Agreement. And in 2013, a Federal Appeals Court upheld an earlier ruling that Métis and non-status Indians could be granted the same recognition and rights as those enjoyed by status Indians living on reserves. According to National Chief Betty Ann Lavallée, this marked the first time that Métis and non-status Indians could be certain "where they fit within Canadian society."

Still, Aboriginal leaders continued to draw national attention to goals still to be achieved:

- better health care for Aboriginal peoples, who are often at higher-than-average risk for disease or early death

- a reduction of child mortality

- the study and prevention of suicide among communities where the risk is high

- better educational opportunities and more control over education by Aboriginal peoples

- improvements in housing

- better access to clean drinking water

- more opportunities for employment

The Truth and Reconciliation Commission

In 2008, Prime Minister Harper apologized, on behalf of the people of Canada, to the survivors of the residential school system. Residential schools, run by churches, once dominated Aboriginal education in Canada. The apology acknowledged the harm the system did to generations of Aboriginal children, forcibly removing them from their homes and attempting to destroy the cultures from which they came. Apologizing was an important first step. That same year, the **Truth and Reconciliation Commission (TRC)** was established with a mandate to travel across Canada and hear the testimony of witnesses forced into the residential school system. More than 7000 witnesses came forward over a period of seven years.

But was it enough?

KEY TERM

Truth and Reconciliation Commission (TRC)
a commission that reveals and documents prior wrongdoing by governments

GO ONLINE • • • • • • • • • • • • • •

Read more about the Truth and Reconciliation Commission.

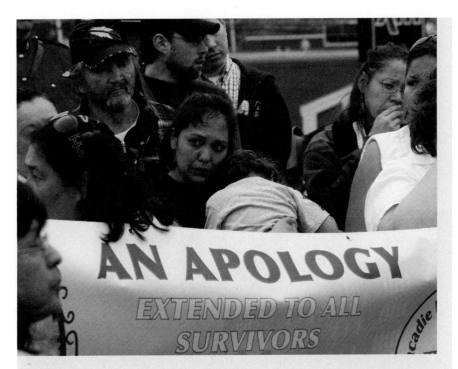

FIGURE 9–17 A "Letting Go" ceremony in Shubenacadie, Nova Scotia after Prime Minister Harper's apology

? HISTORICAL INQUIRY

Gather and Organize

Research the apologies offered by the Anglican Church, Presbyterian Church, and United Church of Canada. What was the initial response of the Roman Catholic Church? Why did the head of the commission, Justice Sinclair, recommend that the Pope be invited to come to Canada to offer an apology to survivors of the residential schools and their families?

Two primary objectives of the Residential Schools system were to remove and isolate children from the influence of their homes, families, traditions, and cultures, and to assimilate them into the dominant culture. These objectives were based on the assumption Aboriginal cultures and spiritual beliefs were inferior and unequal. Indeed, some sought, as it was infamously said, "to kill the Indian in the child." Today, we recognize that this policy of assimilation was wrong, has caused great harm, and has no place in our country.

—Prime Minister Stephen Harper: Statement of Apology, June 11, 2008

We believe the current government is not willing to make good on its claim that it wishes to join with Aboriginal people in Canada in a "relationship based on the knowledge of our shared history, a respect for each other and a desire to move forward together," as promised nine years ago. Words are not enough.

—Justice Murray Sinclair, head of the TRC

Is today's government responsible for injustices of the past?

In the early 1980s, Prime Minister Pierre Trudeau refused to apologize for past injustices committed by Canadian governments. He claimed that we cannot rewrite history; we can only try to be just in our time. Those calling for apologies say it is not about rewriting history. They feel acknowledging that the government and its institutions took wrong turns in the past shows that we are on the right road today.

Since 1988, federal and provincial governments have recognized and tried to compensate for past wrongs by issuing official apologies. In 1988, the Conservative government apologized to Japanese Canadians for their internment during the Second World War (see Chapter 5) and again in 1990 to Italian Canadians for similar reasons. Perhaps the most significant event to date has been Prime Minister Stephen Harper's 2008 formal apology to Canada's Aboriginal peoples, acknowledging that "...the treatment of children in Indian residential schools is a sad chapter in our history" (see page 10 and Chapter 8). Supporters of this approach hope that such apologies offer closure to a hurtful past. Opponents say that no matter how sincere an apology, it cannot undo what has been done.

The following Canadian immigration case studies examine two apologies and corresponding responses.

The Chinese

As you read in Chapter 1, the federal government tried to discourage Chinese people from coming to Canada by imposing a head tax in 1885. The tax was increased from $50 to $100 in 1900, and to $500 in 1903. On July 1, 1923, the federal government introduced the Chinese Exclusion Act—an Act that tried to halt Chinese immigration altogether. Chinese Canadians refer to this day as Humiliation Day. The Act was in place for more than 20 years; it was repealed in 1947.

In 1984, the Chinese Canadian National Council (CCNC) began a campaign for an apology from the federal government. They also asked for a repayment of $23 million, the amount collected from 81 000 Chinese immigrants who were forced to pay the tax.

In 1994, the Canadian government rejected the redress claim stating that it was more important to erase inequality in the future than to compensate people for past mistakes. Dr. Alan Li, then president of the CCNC, disagreed. He stated:

> *Returning the money is only basic justice. It is a strong statement of principle that a government cannot, and should not, and must not, benefit from racism.*
>
> *–Alan Li, Speech, 1994*

HISTORICAL INQUIRY

Evaluate and Draw Conclusions

Why were only the Chinese immigrants required to pay this fee? What conclusions does this suggest about Canada's immigration policy in 1918?

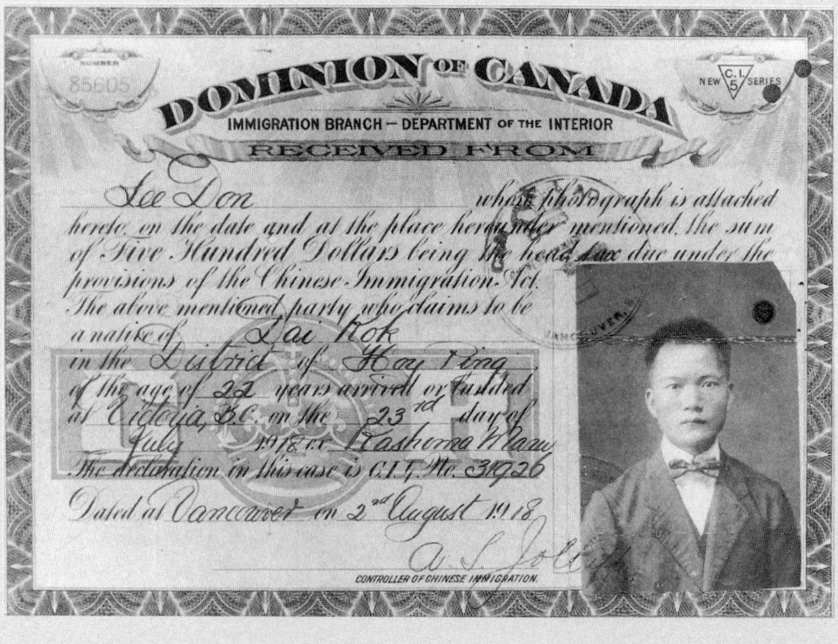
DOMINION OF CANADA
NUMBER 85605
NEW C.I. 5 SERIES
IMMIGRATION BRANCH — DEPARTMENT OF THE INTERIOR
RECEIVED FROM
Lee Don whose photograph is attached hereto on the date and at the place hereunder mentioned, the sum of Five Hundred Dollars being the head tax due under the provisions of the Chinese Immigration Act.
The above mentioned party who claims to be a native of Lai Kok in the District of Hoy Ping of the age of 22 years arrived or landed at Victoria, B.C. on the 23rd day of July 1918 ex Kashima Maru
The declaration in this case is C.I. 4 No. 31926
Dated at Vancouver on 2nd August 1918
CONTROLLER OF CHINESE IMMIGRATION.

FIGURE 9–19 Immigration certificate for Lee Don, 1918

Gather Evidence How old was Lee Don when he was admitted to Canada? How much was the head tax he had to pay?

In 1995, the CCNC approached the United Nations Human Rights Commission to ask for their help with this issue. In 2006, the Canadian government agreed to address the claim and offered a parliamentary apology for the head tax and exclusion of Chinese immigrants from 1923 to 1947. The federal government promised financial redress of $20 000 to each of the surviving head tax payers or their spouses.

> *For over six decades, these malicious measures, aimed solely at the Chinese, were implemented with deliberation by the Canadian state. This was a grave injustice, and one we are morally obligated to acknowledge.*
>
> *–Prime Minister Stephen Harper, June 22, 2006*

For Sid Chow Tan, national chairperson of the CCNC and president of the Head Tax Families Society of Canada, the apologies must not distract us from present-day problems. He stated:

> *The historical injustices of the Chinese Head Tax are being replicated today through Canada's exploitative guest-worker programs and restrictive immigration policies. The descendants of these policies will be demanding apologies in future decades. We should deal with this present reality and not just dwell on the past, especially if a history that we are supposed to have learnt from is repeating itself.*
>
> *–Sid Chow Tan*

The *Komagata Maru*

In 1908, the federal government passed an order-in-council that required all immigrants to come to Canada by a "continuous journey," or non-stop route. This effectively made immigration from countries such as India impossible, as no steamship companies offered direct routes to Canada at that time. This law was challenged in 1914, when the passengers on the *Komagata Maru*, a steamer chartered to carry Sikh immigrants from Hong Kong to Vancouver, were refused entry to Canada.

In May 2008, the British Columbia legislature extended an apology for the *Komagata Maru* incident.

FIGURE 9–20 The *Komagata Maru* was docked for two months in Vancouver while the Canadian government decided the fate of its 340 passengers. In the end, the ship was forced to depart.

A few months later, at a Sikh festival in B.C., Prime Minister Harper also offered an apology for the incident. Sikh organizations have rejected the prime minister's apology, comparing it to the formal apology to Chinese Canadians in 2006. The Sikh community requested a formal apology in the House of Commons, but the Conservative government said there will be no further apology. However, on May 1, 2014, a stamp commemorating the 100th anniversary of the arrival of the *Komagata Maru* was released by Canada Post.

Historical Perspectives

1. Compare the responses of Prime Minister Trudeau to those of Prime Minister Harper. What might explain the differences in their opinions?

2. Official apologies for past wrongs have happened increasingly since 1988. Why do you think this is so? Would you support treating all claims for redress for past wrongs equally? Why or why not?

3. Organize a debate on the topic: Should we try to right the wrongs of past generations?

Idle No More

In the winter of 2012–13, thousands of Canadians, Aboriginal and non-Aboriginal, joined together in flash mobs to dance in public places such as the intersection of Dundas and Yonge streets in Toronto. These round dances were just one facet of the unusual protest movement **Idle No More**, which sought to protect Aboriginal rights and lands across Canada.

The Idle No More movement began as a protest against Bill C-45, but grew into a wider fight for Aboriginal rights. The movement, initiated by three Aboriginal and one non-Aboriginal women—Jessica Gordon, Sylvia McAdam, Nina Wilson, and Sheelah McLean—used social media to call on all Canadians "to join in a revolution which honours and fulfils Indigenous sovereignty which protects the land and water."

The movement's organizers argued that Bill C-45 would reduce environmental protection and make it easier for companies to develop projects that would pollute rivers, streams, and lakes. They argued that such changes would affect treaty rights and so could not be done without the consent of Aboriginal people.

At the same time, Chief Theresa Spence of Attawapiskat, Ontario, went on a hunger strike in Ottawa to draw attention to the dangerous housing problem on her reserve. She said that many members of her community were forced to live in substandard housing and called for a meeting with the prime minister and the governor general. Her hunger strike dragged on for six weeks and ended only in response to requests from her community and First Nations leaders. The prime minister refused to meet with her, although he did meet with other chiefs, and the federal government alleged that the reserve had misspent government funds which could have been spent on housing.

The novel forms of protest used by the Idle No More movement drew national and international attention to the ongoing social and treaty issues facing Aboriginal people in Canada today. While round dances may have stopped for now, the issues remained unresolved and the government passed Bill C-45 into law.

FIGURE 9–21 Idle No More protesters assembled and marched across the nation. This demonstration took place at Dundas Square in Toronto in 2013.

CHECKPOINT

1. Discuss the importance of the 2008 apology on behalf of the Canadian people to the Aboriginal peoples.

2. What are some of the issues that affect Aboriginal peoples today?

3. What is the Idle No More movement? What are its goals? How have organizers used social media in their campaign?

The Trappers' Case of Grassy Narrows

Grassy Narrows is small Aboriginal community near Kenora in northwestern Ontario. Home to the Asubpeeschoseewagong (a-sub-ee-shko-see-wa-gong) First Nation, its people share many concerns of other First Nations across the country—and more. The Asubpeeschoseewagong receive few benefits from the extensive timber industry that has taken place on their ancestral lands.

The lands around Grassy Narrows have been heavily logged, and rivers and streams are dammed. Pulp mills have polluted the air and the waters. Rivers and streams are contaminated with mercury, a metal used in the papermaking process. The poisonous metal is now in the flesh of the fish the Asubpeeschoseewagong eat. The loss of fishing and tourism revenues devastated the community.

Governments and companies have tended to ignore or downplay the concerns of the Asubpeeschoseewagong Nation, in spite of a history of protest. In the 1980s, the Asubpeeschoseewagong received an out-of-court settlement. However, the pulp and paper mill that contaminated the water admitted no guilt, and the mercury remains in the water.

In 2005, three trappers from Grassy Narrows launched a lawsuit to prevent a company from clear-cutting the forest that provided their livelihood. Removing the trees would end their ability to trap, hunt, and fish— rights that were recognized in Treaty 3. As the lawsuit went on, the people of Grassy Narrows blockaded the area in an attempt to prevent logging.

In 2011, the Ontario Superior Court ruled that the province could not authorize logging in Grassy Narrows, but did not issue an injunction to stop the logging. In 2014, the Supreme Court of Canada decided that Ontario did have the right to permit logging. However, the court also ruled that the province was still required to consult and accommodate the people of Grassy Narrows.

Thinking It Through

1. How can logging and other activities interfere with traditional ways of relating to the land?

2. How do Aboriginal peoples and European immigrants differ in their perspectives regarding ownership and use of land? Why must these conflicts often be resolved in the courts?

FIGURE 9–22 Signs point the way to the Grassy Narrows First Nation road block. Clear-cutting a forest might provide jobs, but these jobs often vanish when the cutting ends. The forest may take decades to regenerate. Is it possible to harvest forests and other natural resources in ways that benefit Aboriginal peoples and resource companies?

- In what ways did Canadian society change after 2001?

- What factors affect Canadians in the 21st century?

FIGURE 9–23 New Canadian citizens take the citizenship oath during the Citizenship and Immigration ceremony.

Can Canada Be a Cultural Model for Other Nations?

For much of the 20th century, discrimination was woven into the fabric of our nation. Changing a socially repressive, bilingual nation, where a majority of its people had European ancestors, to an open, inclusive, and multicultural society did not happen quickly. It was a long process of changing social attitudes and laws that has continued into the 21st century. How did we get this way? How successful have we been? Should other countries try to be like Canada?

Urbanization and Canadian Culture

The urbanization of Canada was a phenomenon of the 20th century. Between 1911 and 2011, the rural population of the country declined from 55 percent of the total population to just 19 percent. Major cities such as Toronto, Vancouver, and Montréal grew very quickly as industry, transportation, and services developed at these centres. While jobs attracted people to the city factories, the mechanization of agriculture and forestry meant fewer workers were needed in the rural areas. As a result, rural populations declined.

In many ways, the culturally diverse country we enjoy today is a product of this urbanization. As cities grew and prospered, immigrants were drawn by employment opportunities and the advantages of city life. Successive waves of immigrants discovered vibrant ethnic communities flourishing within those urban centres. In fact, today, the most cited reason for immigrants settling in Canada's "big three" cities is the opportunity to join an existing network of family and friends who share a similar ethnicity and culture.

FIGURE 9–24
Today, 80 percent of Canada's population lives in cities and towns.

Interpret and Analyze
On this map, the areas of provinces and cities are drawn in proportion to their population. What pattern do you see?

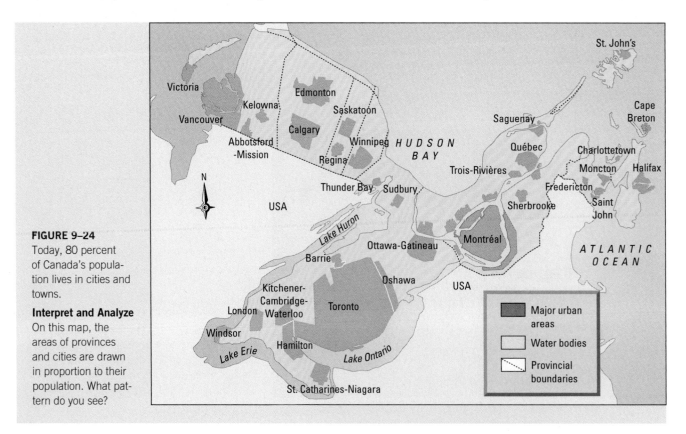

©P

Multiculturalism in Canada in the 21st Century

Canadian society has changed a great deal since the passage of the Multiculturalism Act in 1988. Even 30 years ago, few Canadians were visible minorities. Today, approximately 200 different ethnicities are represented across the country, and 20.6 percent of Canadians report being born outside the country—the highest percentage since 1931.

Compared to other Western democracies, Canada's policy of multiculturalism has been successful. According to *The Current State of Multiculturalism in Canada*, a report by Citizenship and Immigration Canada, "there is growing evidence that immigrants to Canada and visible or religious minorities fare better than most, if not all, other Western democracies." One measure of this success is the high level of mutual acceptance between immigrants and native-born Canadians. In addition, Statistics Canada reports that 98 percent of Canadians speak one or both official languages, and most immigrants are able to participate in all aspects of Canadian life. Canada's immigration point system continues to award the most points for bilingualism and a high level of education.

In the 21st century, Canada entered an era of **super-diversity**—mostly in its large urban centres. Super-diversity is the term social scientists have given to areas where multiculturalism is pervasive. It calls into question standard terminology about majority and minority cultures. For example, Statistics Canada estimates that by the year 2030, visible minorities will make up most of Toronto's population, and notions such as "visible minority" will have to be re-defined. In situations of super-diversity, long-time immigration from varied places of origin also leads to exposure to many cultural, religious, and linguistic traditions. Such exposure has influenced what it means to be a Canadian by encouraging everybody's differences as a way of belonging.

KEY TERM

super-diversity a situation in which more than 100 nationalities are represented in one area, usually a city; the term may also describe diversity in other conditions, such as the way people choose to define themselves

Canadians view immigrants and demographic diversity as key parts of their own Canadian identity. Compared to every other Western democracy, Canadians are more likely to say that immigration is beneficial ... and more likely to support multiculturalism and to view it as a source of pride.

–Will Kymlicka, "The Current State of Multiculturalism in Canada," 2010

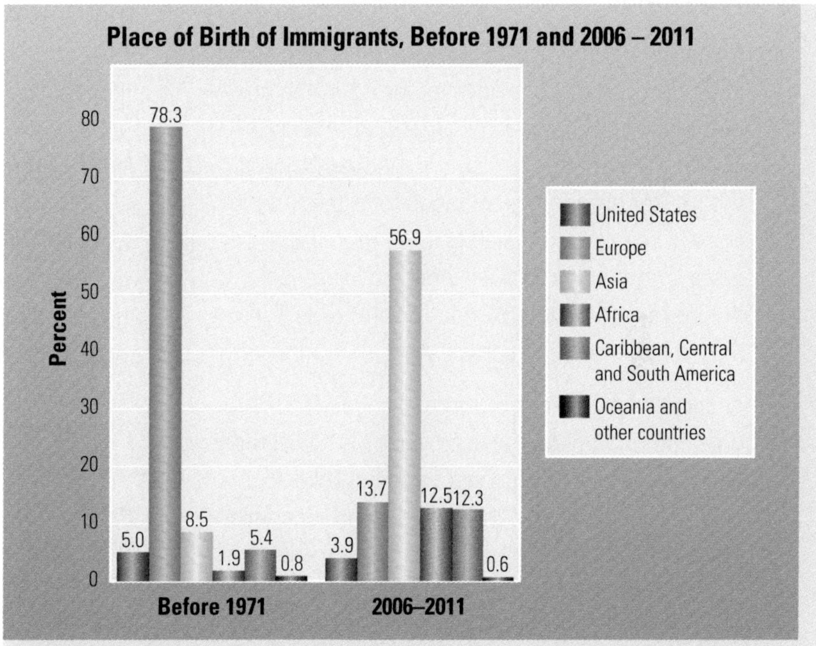

Place of Birth of Immigrants, Before 1971 and 2006 – 2011

Legend:
- United States
- Europe
- Asia
- Africa
- Caribbean, Central and South America
- Oceania and other countries

Before 1971: 5.0, 78.3, 8.5, 1.9, 5.4, 0.8
2006–2011: 3.9, 13.7, 56.9, 12.5, 12.3, 0.6

(y-axis: Percent)

FIGURE 9–25 Between the 1960s and 2011, the source of Canadian immigration shifted dramatically. What were some of the greatest changes?

CHECKPOINT

1. Discuss the link between urbanization and multiculturalism in Canada.

2. In 2010, Angela Merkel, the German Chancellor, said that multiculturalism had failed in Germany. She criticized some immigrants for not learning German and said they should speak German at home. Compose an e-mail to Chancellor Merkel on Canada's experience with multiculturalism. Make one recommendation to her on multicultural policy.

3. **Gather Evidence** Compare Figure 9–25 (above) with Figure 8–5 on page 252. What trends have continued since 2001? What has changed since 2001?

Until recently, researchers could not easily access accurate and up-to-date data on population and urbanization. Although the Internet makes finding and gathering such information much easier than in the past, online sources must be used with care. Sites can easily track and capture data on the researcher and use it, for example, to target advertising. The Internet is not monitored. In most cases, no one is overseeing the content that appears there. Some sites may be unreliable sources of information. Some may even deliberately spread misinformation. The 7-Step Online Research Evaluation Guide below will help you better evaluate the online sources you use.

7-Step Online Research Evaluation Guide

1. **Authority** Are those who produce content clearly identified and do they have expertise in the content area? Is the person or organization responsible for a site or page clearly identified? Check the site for credentials and look for a track record. Know if the site is official. Is it the product of a government agency, a university, a legitimate business, or a reputable media source? Is it from a preferred domain such as .gov, .edu, or .org?

2. **Accuracy** Are sources of information credited? Are data current and are dates provided? Is bibliographic information provided, such as external links, journals, or books? Is the data accurate and complete? If something is measured, how is this done and what exactly is being measured? Is the purpose of the site clear? Does the domain name reflect the site's purpose? Is the information verifiable? Can information be confirmed on other unrelated sites?

3. **Confirmation** Can you confirm the accuracy of information on other sites? Use other reliable sites to cross-check your findings.

4. **Bias** Does the author or producer have a particular point of view that might colour the data presented? Does it appear that the author or producer has been selective in the data or information provided? Are multiple perspectives presented? Are facts clearly distinguished from opinions?

Use external links and statements of purpose to help determine the target audience for a site.

5. **Coverage** Are all the topics you need to research covered by the sites you choose?

6. **Currency** Is the information up to date? Many websites have a copyright date. Almost all show their last publication date. How current are the links the site contains?

7. **Usability** Do you understand the material? Is the data easy to read and use? Has the data been well organized, sorted, and presented? How much advertising, if any, is on the site?

Using the Guide

What should you do when information on different sites on the same topic is different, perhaps even contradictory? For example, three reliable sources give different figures for worldwide deaths from influenza from 1918–1919. Stanford University estimates 20 to 40 million deaths. The U.S. Department of Health and Human Services estimates 21.5 million deaths. And the Centers for Disease Control (CDC) estimates more than 50 million deaths. All three organizations are highly reliable, so which figure would you use and why? Start with the 7-Step Online Research Evaluation Guide. Step 3 might be most useful here. Likely, you would focus on what was being measured, and how and when. Some figures, for example, may be estimates. If any of the data are sourced, you could also follow up with the original sources.

Gather and Organize

1. Search the Internet to find five websites that give information about one of the topic areas you covered in this unit.

2. With a partner, create a chart based on the 7-Step method described above. Put the sites you have found along the vertical side of the chart and the 7 Steps along the top. Rate each site Excellent (E), Good (G), Fair (F), or Poor (P).

The Internet Age

The Internet did not exist when the Canadian Radio-television and Telecommunications Commission (CRTC) was formed in 1968. Since then, the CRTC had mostly concerned itself with protecting Canadian content on radio and television, and in publishing.

In the past, the CRTC required that at least 60 percent of Canadian television programming be Canadian in origin. However, in 2015, the CRTC announced that it would reduce the number of hours each day when Canadian programs must be broadcast. The CRTC said that it did not want to "force" Canadians into watching Canadian programming, but merely wanted to foster an environment in which they would choose to do so.

This new attitude results from the digital environment we currently live in. In 2006, for example, the CRTC did not impose any Canadian-content rules on television programming delivered through cellphones. In 1999, it decided not to regulate the Internet at all.

The Power of the Internet

The Internet provides access to more content than ever before and enables anyone to have a voice or be a content creator. In this sense, it is the most democratic medium in the world. The Internet also brings people together. The success of online petition platforms demonstrates the power of the Internet to help citizens make a difference locally and globally. Successful petitions have challenged retailers, governments, schools, and companies.

But the Internet is not all positive. It has created problems in certain areas, such as breaches of personal information and personal security, **cyberbullying**, and child pornography.

- How involved should government be in promoting the arts in Canada?

- In what ways did the world change after 2001?

KEY TERM

cyberbullying bullying through electronic means, either by use of threats or intimidation, or by invasion of privacy

GO ONLINE •·································

Find out more about successful online petitions and the people who launched them.

FASTFORWARD

Rehtaeh Parsons

Since 2003, there have been 41 cases of cyberbullying involving suicide in Canada, the United States, Australia, and the United Kingdom. The vast majority of the victims were bulled online and in person before committing suicide.

In 2013, 17-year-old Rehtaeh Parsons of Dartmouth, Nova Scotia, attempted suicide. Two years earlier, another student had taken a cellphone photo of Parsons allegedly being raped and circulated it widely throughout her school population. No one was charged for the assault, and Parsons endured vicious bullying and degrading personal comments. She died after being removed from life support on April 7, 2013.

After Parson's death, the RCMP re-opened the case. Two boys were charged—one with making child pornography and the other with distributing it.

FIGURE 9–26
Rehtaeh Parsons

(An image of a minor being sexually assaulted is considered child pornography.)

In 2014, Justice Minister and Attorney General of Canada Peter MacKay announced Canada's anti-cyberbullying campaign, "Stop Hating Online." Its goal is to raise awareness of cyberbullying and related criminal activity. Canada has also introduced legislation that forbids the distribution of intimate images without the consent of the person depicted.

privacy the right to be free of secret surveillance or observation or intrusion by
others

surveillance spying, using electronic and
other methods to gather information about
people who are generally unaware they
are targets of secret information-gathering

HISTORICAL INQUIRY

Gather and Organize

Who was Edward Snowden? Why
did he become world famous on
the issues of privacy and security?
What happened to him?

Privacy and Security Issues

Accessing the Internet and social media means that **privacy** becomes an
issue. It is not a coincidence, for example, that soon after you search for a
particular item, all the websites you visit later feature advertisements for
that product or service.

But privacy and security are more serious than the inconvenience of too
many ads. Giving up our privacy is something we ought to think about very
carefully. Receiving targeted advertising is one thing, but having an anonymous entity using our personal data in order to create a profile of our interests,
buying habits, or political views without our consent is unacceptable to many
Canadians. We have learned that spy agencies routinely collect information
about us. Often they do this to prevent terrorism and increase our nation's security. Most Canadians understand this. They also expect and hope that our courts
and government will ensure our rights as Canadians are protected.

In June 2014, the Supreme Court of Canada confirmed Canadians' right to
privacy by stating that Internet users have the right to remain anonymous. If
police need to uncover someone's online identity, they must do it by obtaining a warrant. This ruling addressed a situation that had been unfolding for
several years whereby Internet service providers would reveal customer
names if requested by law enforcement. In 2011, the Canadian Wireless
Telecommunications Association said nine of its twelve companies had
received a total of more than a million such requests in one year.

The proliferation of drone use in Canada
is another privacy issue. Across the country, a
number of police forces have begun using drones,
or pilotless aircraft. Operators fly drones using
remote control, sometimes from long distances
away from the place they are deployed. In Canada,
police use drones to take aerial footage of accident
scenes, search for missing persons, or investigate
crimes. However, the fact that drones can fly
almost undetected and, with their cameras, look
in windows, has raised concerns with the Office
of the Privacy Commissioner of Canada (OPC).
The agency is concerned that the few regulations
related to the operation of drones relate only to
safety and that drone use could, under certain
circumstances, amount to illegal **surveillance** of
Canadians going about their business.

FIGURE 9–27 A small drone equipped with a camera

Ethical Dimension How would you balance the need to search for
missing persons against the privacy concerns of ordinary citizens? If
drone technology is available for one purpose, ought it be used for
any purpose?

CHECKPOINT

1. Create a web diagram on the digital age and its
influence on the lives of you, your family, and your
friends. Use colour to indicate whether you think
an element (such as drones, for example) has or
will have positive, negative, or uncertain results.

2. Why do you think the CRTC decided not to regulate the Internet? What would happen if it did? Do
you know of any countries where the Internet is
regulated?

Developments in Science and Technology in the 21st Century

The 21st century is the beginning of a new age for technology. Digitization, smart phones, nanotechnology, and many other developments are transforming the way people do things. Many argue that such advances also change the ways people relate to each other. In other words, our technology is changing society in the most basic way.

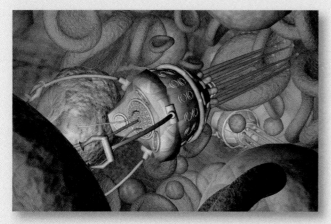

Nano-medicine Nano means small, incredibly small—about one-billionth of a metre. One of the newest trends in medicine is to develop nano-robots to go inside the human body to repair injuries and target diseased organs. Techniques are also being developed to use nanotechnology to deliver drugs to cancer cells and infection sites.

Smart phones Smart phones are part of everyday life, so much so that we scarcely think about how remarkable this technology is. *The Economist* magazine calls them "super-computers," and they have thousands of uses. The use of smart phones is skyrocketing around the world. Today, more than 2 billion people have the devices, and likely 6.1 billion people will have them by 2020.

Private space travel The desire to travel in space is a fantasy for most people. Until now, space travel has been under government control. Several companies are now developing commercial spacecraft that will take paying passengers into orbit—even to Mars to start the first human colony!

3-D printers are nothing short of amazing. They can create almost anything in much finer detail than most machines. Need a new part for that one-of-a kind bicycle? Today it can be printed. The same technologies are already being applied to create replacement body parts and even food.

- How have artists and performers contributed to Canadian culture in the 21st century?

KEY TERMS

G8 an organization of the eight most highly industrialized nations in the world, including Canada

advanced economy countries with well-developed industries, educated workers, superior technological advantages, and high GDP per capita

FIGURE 9–28 Author Alice Munro

Canada's Place in the Modern World

Most Canadians likely entered the 21st century with optimism. An economic recession in the United States that began in 2001 and ended in 2003 had only minor effects on Canada—an indication that our economy was becoming ever more independent from that of the United States. Old worries about Canada's international status based on our colonial past faded away. Canada belongs to the **G8**, which includes the world's leading **advanced economies**. The Canadian government hosted meetings of the G8 in 2002 and then again in 2008.

Culturally, Canadians were also making a mark on the world. Canadian authors, filmmakers, musicians, and other entertainers showcased a diverse, progressive, and inclusive culture, winning international acclaim and awards.

In spite our best hopes and successes, however, the 21st century did not bring an era of safety and peace to the world. Civil wars raged in Europe, Africa, and Asia. Civilians, including children, were often casualties. A financial crisis in 2008 affected Canada and other nations. Natural disasters and epidemics, including devastating earthquakes in Haiti in 2010 and in Nepal in 2015, threatened the lives of millions. Across the globe, the rights of women to be educated and live without violence still seemed like an elusive goal. How would Canada respond to these crises? Could Canada make a difference?

Canada's Cultural Ambassadors in the 21st Century

At the 2010 Winter Olympics in Vancouver, Canada won fourteen gold medals, breaking the record for the number of gold medals won at a single Winter Olympics. Canadian ice dancers Tessa Virtue and Scott Moir also became the first ice dancing team outside Europe to win gold and later toured the United States, Korea, and Japan.

In the field of literature, Canadian writer Alice Munro, whose short stories had long been admired at home, won the prestigious Nobel Prize for Literature in December 2013. When Munro was announced as the winner, the Nobel academy commented on her ability to portray Canadian life "with almost anthropological precision" and her use of the local landscape as setting for her fiction. The award introduced Munro to new audiences throughout Europe and re-introduced her to readers in Canada, where sales of her books spiked 4424 percent.

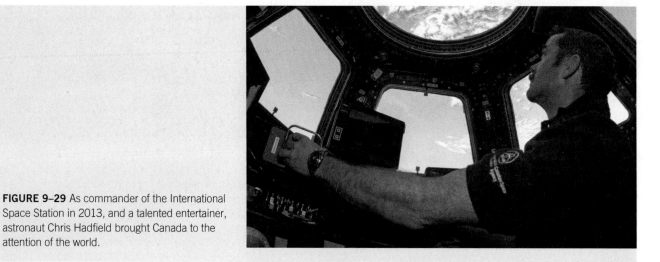

FIGURE 9–29 As commander of the International Space Station in 2013, and a talented entertainer, astronaut Chris Hadfield brought Canada to the attention of the world.

Canadian filmmakers, many of whom turned to their original cultures for inspiration, also received increased international exposure to their work. Toronto director Atom Egoyan, born to Armenian parents in Egypt, explored the 1915 genocide of Armenians in Turkey in his 2002 film *Ararat*. It was awarded Best Picture at the 2003 Genies, and three of Egoyan's films later went on to be nominated for a *Palme d'Or* at the Cannes Film Festival in France. Director Deepa Mehta, whose films often deal with the tension between modern identity and traditional culture, received an Academy Award nomination for her 2005 film *Water*, about a group of widows in rural India in the 1940s.

In music, Canadian artists continued to be well represented in a variety of genres, including pop, hip hop, and jazz. Canadian rapper, songwriter, and producer Drake produced a string of successful, award-winning albums beginning in 2010, including *Thank Me Later* and *Take Care*. By 2015, he was a best-selling recording artist, beaten only by Taylor Swift. Drake launched the record label OVO Sound in 2012 and became the "Global Ambassador" for the Toronto Raptors in 2013.

FIGURE 9–30 Canadian film director Deepa Mehta was born in Amritsar, India, and came to Canada in the early 1970s.

FIGURE 9–31 Tanya Tagaq is a throat singer from Nunavut and Polaris Prize winner. Tagaq's collaborations with the Iclandic experimental singer Björk have made her known in Canada and around the world.

FIGURE 9–32 International superstar Drake has always proclaimed his Canadian roots. Toronto's CN Tower and the Rogers Centre are featured in the video for his single "Headlines."

● How did the Canadian government respond to economic challenges after 2001?

The Financial Crisis of 2008

While Canada had largely avoided the recession that hit the United States in the early 2000s, another financial collapse in 2008 threatened to destroy much of the global economy. How did this happen, and what was its effect on Canada?

The crisis began suddenly when a huge stock trading company and bank called Lehman Brothers went bankrupt. This almost triggered the collapse of other banking houses and companies all over the world.

Why did this happen? Mostly it was because bankers lent out more money than they held as assets (value) to cover the debt. Many borrowers could never hope to pay their debts, especially when, in the case of mortgages, the value of the homes plummeted. Also, in their race to lend money, many financial institutions gave loans to people who were poor risks and would not or could not pay their debts when times got tough.

The amounts were huge—trillions of dollars lent all over the world, which created short-term financial gain for only a few. Lenders got nervous and tried to sign as many loans as they could before the scheme collapsed. Soon billions more were owed than could be collected. The situation was almost catastrophic.

In a desperate bid to save the world economy, governments, including Canada, pumped billions of dollars into the system. Without this infusion of cash, there is little doubt that the world would have seen another Great Depression.

The Great Recession of 2008 did not affect Canada as badly as it did the United States. One reason is that Canadian banks are much more tightly regulated than American banks. In practice, this means they will not offer loans or credit as freely. In the late 1990s, Canadian banks wanted to merge and become more like American banks. At that time, Prime Minister Chrétien and Finance Minister Martin refused to let that happen. Because Canadian banks remained strong during the crisis, the Canadian economy did not suffer from the collapse of credit.

FIGURE 9–33 Armed police guard the New York Stock Exchange in September 2008. Why might banks need protection in a major financial crisis?

©P

Population Trends and World Stability

The world's population, which reached 6 billion in 1999, continues to soar. But some experts predict that growth will peak at 10.9 billion in 2100. By 2015, it stood at over 7 billion, an increase of a billion people in 16 or so years. Canada's population has also risen steadily and now stands at around 35.7 million. The rate of growth has increased by an average of 1.1 percent per year for the past 30 years, much faster than other countries in the G8. Statistics Canada estimates that Canada will have a population of 35.7 million in 2056—mostly due to immigration. Canada is a huge country with large areas with low population density, but most of us live within a few hundred kilometres of the American border.

Population growth can have serious consequences, as more people consume more energy, food, and water resources. Is there a point, many wonder, when the number of people will exceed the carrying capacity of the Earth? Population projections are just that—projections based on current data. In some heavily populated countries such as Bangladesh and Iran, the birthrate has been declining steadily since the 1980s, from approximately six children per woman to two.

While 7 billion people seems like a high number for our planet, the issue is also complex. Consumption of resources, for instance, is not consistent across the world. People in the developed world consume four to ten times as many minerals, ores, fossil fuels, and renewable organic materials as the average person in India today.

• In what ways did the world change after 2001?

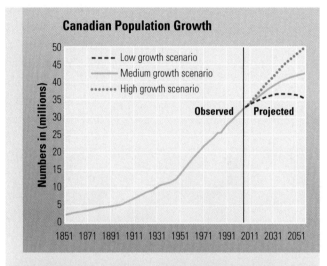

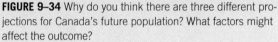

FIGURE 9–34 Why do you think there are three different projections for Canada's future population? What factors might affect the outcome?

World Population	When Reached?	How Long to Reach?
1 billion	1804	Human history to this date
2 billion	1927	123 years
3 billion	1960	33 years
4 billion	1974	14 years
5 billion	1987	13 years
6 billion	1999	12 years
United Nations' Estimates of Future Growth		
7 billion	2013	14 years
8 billion	2028	15 years
9 billion	2054	26 years
10 billion	2200	146 years

FIGURE 9–35 The world population will continue to increase in the 21st century, testing humanity's ability to deal with the problems such growth can create. Why is international cooperation on matters such as pollution and water conservation important?

- How does the government of Canada respond to terrorism and other world crises?

KEY TERM

child soldier a person under the age of 18 who is forced or otherwise persuaded to fight in an official or unofficial army

FIGURE 9–36 These child soldiers escaped from a rebel army in the Democratic Republic of the Congo in 2009.

Humanitarian Assistance

Children at War

The United Nations Children's Fund (UNICEF) and other groups estimate that **child soldiers** are involved in armed conflicts in most parts of the world. Some of the participants are as young as eight or nine. They are used in many roles—as fighters, couriers, spies, or bombers—and may also be sexually abused.

Canada has a long-standing reputation as an advocate for children caught up in armed conflict. In 2000, Canada led the international community in hosting the first international conference on children affected by armed conflict. Since 2006, it has chaired the Group of Friends on Children and Armed Conflict, a group comprising nearly 40 member countries.

At issue is the need to address lives of millions of children caught up in civil war. Many who cannot flee the violence are forced to become child soldiers, attacking civilians and participating in bloody atrocities. Some are forced or persuaded to become suicide bombers, blowing up themselves and others in attacks planned by adults. It has been estimated by War Child International that children are employed in nearly 75 percent of all armed conflicts worldwide, both by regular armies and rebel groups. As many as 80 percent of these children may be younger than 13.

Some human rights organizations, such as Amnesty International, would like to outlaw the practice of using children as soldiers. They want the UN Convention on the Rights of the Child to forbid military recruitment before age 18. Countries that have 16-year-old soldiers in their armies oppose this proposal. Other critics point out that in some African societies, a 16- or 17-year-old is not considered a child. The key issue, critics argue, is that military service should be voluntary.

Canada's role is currently focused on contributing to development projects that can help reintegrate children caught up in armed conflict. It also supported the United Nations resolution adopted in 2006 to improve monitoring and reporting on the use of child soldiers and punishing those who violate international law.

CHECKPOINT

1. Why is it important for Canada to have cultural ambassadors—people who represent Canada to the world in the areas of sport, literature, film, and music? Name one contribution from pages 316–317 that you think is especially noteworthy, and give a reason for your choice.

2. What caused the financial crisis of 2008? Why did Canada escape its worst effects?

3. As a modern industrialized nation, Canada consumes a larger portion of the world's resources than underdeveloped countries with much larger populations. What responsibility do you think Canadians have with regard to consumption and pollution?

4. How are children convinced or forced to become soldiers? Why is it difficult to end the practice of using children as soldiers?

Responding to Disasters

As a developed nation with many resources, Canada has a responsibility to help other nations when natural disasters occur. Canadians often help with initial rescue efforts, providing food, shelter, warm clothing, disease control, and clean drinking water, and by staying in the country to rebuild infrastructure.

The Earthquake in Haiti Haiti is one of the world's poorest countries, with a history of dictatorship and corruption. On January 12, 2010, a massive earthquake rocked the capital, Port-au-Prince, almost instantly destroying 250 000 homes and 30 000 commercial buildings. The shocks also devastated the education system, hospitals, prisons, and sewage disposal systems, and broke water pipes. Collapsing buildings and falling debris killed tens of thousands of people and left an estimated 1.5 million people homeless. A **cholera** epidemic caused by bacteria in polluted water subsequently killed thousands more.

Canada sent 2000 Canadian Forces personnel, meals, safe drinking water, and millions of dollars in financial aid to Haiti. The government also sent the RCMP to help with security. The Canadian International Development Agency (CIDA) has provided an additional $150 million in aid to provide emergency shelter and supplies. In all, Canada has contributed about $850 million in aid since the disaster occurred.

The Ebola Epidemic As a member of the international community, Canada is not isolated from easily transmittable diseases. When a serious outbreak of Ebola virus disease occurred in West Africa, many Canadians worried that the disease would come to Canada. Ebola spreads by means of contact with bodily fluids, such as blood or sweat, and can rapidly infect others who are not properly protected. An often-fatal illness, Ebola kills an average of 50 percent of those infected.

The first cases of Ebola appeared in Guinea and quickly spread to Sierra Leone and Liberia. Relatives who cared for the sick and those who helped bury the dead became infected, and the disease spread further. Medical services in countries most impacted were unable to cope with the disaster. The Centers for Disease Control estimates that out of over 25 000 cases, more than 10 000 people died from Ebola—a **mortality rate** of 40 percent.

The Canadian chapter of Médecins Sans Frontières/Doctors Without Borders participated in the international organization's Ebola response, which began in March 2014. Doctors such as Windsor-based Tim Jagatic travelled to Guinea before facilities were even set up "so the team was quite literally building the hospital around us as we were taking patients."

Canada made another important contribution: its experimental vaccine, VSV-EBOV, was made available to the World Health Organization. Experts are cautiously optimistic about its long-term impact on the Ebola virus.

FIGURE 9–37 A man picks his way through collapsed buildings and debris left by the 2010 earthquake in Haiti. Why is polluted, standing water a potential hazard?

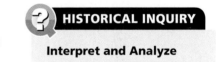

HISTORICAL INQUIRY

Interpret and Analyze

What was the SARS epidemic? What did Canadians learn that they could apply in the Ebola epidemic?

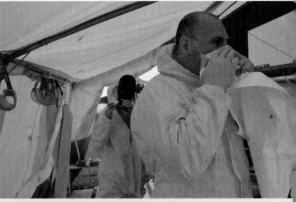

FIGURE 9–38 Canadian physician Tim Jagatic of Médecins Sans Frontières/Doctors Without Borders suits up before caring for patients with Ebola virus.

Violence Against Women

In many parts of the world, women are still fighting for respect—whether the right to go to school or the right not to be attacked or even killed in the name of honour. (In some cultures, a woman is valuable only insofar as she brings her family "honour." Honour killings are the most extreme form of punishment for dishonouring the family.) Canada is a leader in recognizing the rights of women and the need for gender equality. Since 1948, Canada has been a signatory to the United Nations' Universal Declaration of Human Rights (UDHR). In 1980, it ratified the Convention on the Elimination of All Forms of Discrimination Against Women (CEDAW).

Canada strengthened its commitment to CEDAW in 2002 by approving a mechanism whereby individual women, or groups of women who could find no justice in their own countries, could submit their complaints directly to the United Nations.

Malala Yousafzai: Youngest Nobel Peace Prize Winner In 2012, after 15-year-old Malala Yousafzai had boarded her school bus in Pakistan, a man called out her name and shot her. She had been attacked for openly criticizing the Taliban for its restriction of girls' education. After recovering from her injuries, Yousafzai insisted on continuing her education even after more threats. In 2014, she became co-recipient of the Nobel Peace Prize—the youngest person to receive the award.

Canada announced its intention to bestow honorary Canadian citizenship on Yousafzai for courageously advocating for "human rights and freedom against the backdrop of Taliban extremism and oppression." However, on the day Yousafzai was to receive her honorary citizenship, a terrorist attack on the National War Memorial and the Parliament buildings occurred and the ceremony was cancelled.

GO ONLINE

Visit Malala's website to find out what she is doing today about education for all girls.

The terrorists thought they would change our aims and stop our ambitions, but nothing changed in my life except this: weakness, fear and hopelessness died. Strength, power and courage were born...

–Malala Yousafzai

FIGURE 9–39 Malala Yousafzai speaks at a news conference in Washington, D.C., in 2013. Following her attack, a group of Islamic clerics denounced anyone trying to justify killing Yousafzai based on religious reasons.

CHECKPOINT

1. Why is important that Canada respond to international crises such as the Haiti earthquake and the Ebola epidemic?

2. In what ways are young activists such as Malala Yousafzai an inspiration to all peoples who battle for human rights?

The Missing and Murdered Aboriginal Women

In the summer of 2014, 15-year-old Tina Fontaine from Manitoba's Sagkeeng First Nation was murdered in Winnipeg. Less than two months earlier, she had left her great aunt's home where she had been living since the murder of her father three years before. While in Winnipeg, Fontaine had been in the care of child services, but had run away from several foster homes. She had been housed in a hotel because there were too many Aboriginal children in need of temporary housing. One night she went missing. A week later, her body was found in a bag near the Red River in Winnipeg.

Tina Fontaine was just one of at least 1181 Aboriginal women who have been murdered or gone missing during the previous three decades. That number emerged from an RCMP report issued later in 2014 in response to calls from Aboriginal people for an investigation into murdered and missing Aboriginal women in Canada. The RCMP study showed that Aboriginal women are murdered at three times the rate of other Canadian women.

In fact, Fontaine is one of six women from the Sagkeeng First Nation alone who have been murdered or gone missing since 1991. And a few months after her murder, another Aboriginal teenager from Winnipeg, Rinelle Harper, was attacked and left for dead.

In response to the RCMP report and Tina Fontaine's murder, Aboriginal people and other Canadians, including provincial and federal politicians, have called on the federal government to launch an inquiry into the murder or disappearance of Aboriginal women. Despite these calls for action and criticism from the United Nations, Prime Minister Harper resisted setting up such an inquiry and stated that the police should continue to investigate these matters.

FIGURE 9–40 Canadians gather for a vigil on Parliament Hill in Ottawa to call for a national inquiry into missing and murdered Aboriginal women.

©P

CHAPTER FOCUS QUESTION   Which events, people, and organizations have had the most impact on Canadians since September 11, 2001?

The attack on the World Trade Center in 2001 set the tone for the beginning of the 21st century. The world became increasingly security-conscious. New wars broke out, disasters struck, and millions of civilians had to survive as best they could. The world suffered financial shocks and almost fell into another Great Depression. At the same time, computer technology transformed the way many of us do things and communicate with one another. Courageous citizens around the world stepped forward to advocate for human rights and peace.

1. Complete the following organizer to summarize the most important influences on Canadian society in the early years of the 21st century. Indicate whether you think the event's significance and effects are short or long term.

Influence	Description	Significance	Consequences

Knowledge and Understanding

2. Create a timeline of important world events, beginning with the 9/11 attacks and ending with the Ebola crisis of 2014–15. Write the name and date of each event on the timeline.

3. What was the financial crisis of 2008? What were its causes?

4. Describe how digital technology has transformed society.

5. Explain the significance of each of the following:

   a) The Sponsorship Scandal

   b) The Iraq War

   c) The attack on the National War Memorial

   d) ISIS/ISIL

   e) The oil resource boom

6. Explain how and why you think Stephen Harper and the Conservatives rose to power.

7. Explain what generated the Idle No More movement.

Apply Your Thinking

8. On January 7, 2015, two gunmen—brothers—assaulted the Paris offices of the satirical magazine *Charlie Hebdo*. The magazine, which publishes controversial jokes, cartoons, and editorials, had a long history of targeting religious institutions. In 2007, Muslim organizations unsuccessfully sued the magazine because it published offensive cartoons featuring the prophet Muhammad.

    a) Do you think that free speech extends to making comments deemed offensive about someone's religion? Why or why not?

    b) Twelve staff cartoonists were killed during the *Charlie Hebdo* attack. In response, the surviving cartoonists produced another cartoon of the prophet Muhammad holding a sign saying *je suis Charlie* (I am Charlie). Would you have made the decision to publish this cartoon? Give reasons for your response.

Historical Significance

9. Pick three events, persons, or technological advances that you think have benefited Canadian society in the past 15 years. Assess and rank them according to their importance to Canadian society. Give reasons for your ranking.

10. Explain how the approach of Stephen Harper's government to world conflict has differed from that of earlier governments. What, in your opinion, is the long-term significance of this change, if any?

Continuity and Change

11. Create a report card on the success of Canadian multiculturalism since 1988. Grade the country based on such factors as freedom to express ethnicity, protection of ethnicity in laws, and lack of discrimination.

12. Prepare a presentation on a topic you and a partner identify as the most important Canadian or international social issue of the past 15 years. In your presentation, show how the problem has developed over the time period and/or how it has always existed but has only recently entered the consciousness of Canadians.

Communicate

Ethical Dimension

13. "*The government needs to tighten security and must override the law to protect us.*" Present a reasoned argument for or against this statement.

HISTORICAL INQUIRY

Evaluate and Draw Conclusions

14. Analyze the cartoon using the following questions to guide you.

- What is the cartoon's message?
- Whose perspective does it reflect?
- In your opinion, is the perspective represented one that is tied to the present and a particular worldview, or is it timeless and universal? Explain your response.
- Is the cartoon optimistic or pessimistic? Explain your response.
- What developments does the cartoon overlook?

Thinking It Through

Use this study guide to continue synthesizing your learning about Canada's history since September 11, 2001. Referring back to the focus questions for chapters in this unit will help you review your understanding.

STEP 1 Unpacking Knowledge

Use a chart to record concepts and terms you learned in Unit 4. Classify them under the following categories. Highlight items that you feel you need to understand better or cannot define so that you can prioritize what you need to study.

Canada and the World	Canadian Politics and Government	Aboriginal Peoples	Social Change and Innovation

STEP 2 Organizing Your Understanding

Create a mind map titled Canada at the Dawn of the 21st Century. Map important events, persons, and trends you have learned about in Unit 4. Use larger and smaller bubbles to signify importance.

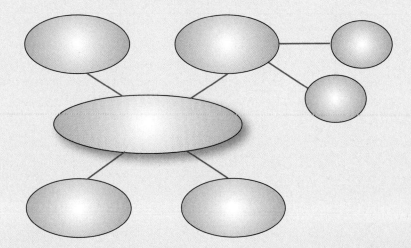

STEP 3   Making Connections

Select a Canadian or international newspaper, blog, or other legitimate news source dealing with national, international, and provincial news. Find and identify as many examples of the following as possible:

- political opinions or government policy—summarize what you find.
- stories about world issues. Describe how each world issue affects, or does not affect, Canadians.

STEP 4   Applying Your Skills

Examine the following images taken during the Arab Spring. Write a caption for each and identify the point you think the photojournalist was trying to capture and convey. In your opinion, has the photographer presented the viewer with a neutral or a biased point of view? Explain. How might these images become dated? What can we learn from such images, even when they no longer show current events? What are the dangers of using images as historical evidence?

◀ **SOURCE 1:** A woman snaps a photo during an election rally in Tunisia.

▲ **SOURCE 2:** Young Egyptians in Tahrir Square in Cairo

▶ **SOURCE 3:** A Syrian protester displays a picture of President Bashar al-Assad.

▲ **SOURCE 4:** Riot gas in Egypt

▲ **SOURCE 5:** Following the capture of Muammar al-Qaddafi, various militia members try to seize control of Libya.

STEP 5   Thinking Critically

Evidence

Ethical Dimension

Ethics is about proper behaviour, about doing the right thing in a certain situation. We know from experience that people have different ideas about what this means. Some government decisions and policies have a definite ethical dimension. In other words, they highlight a situation in which an action or policy seems morally right or morally wrong.

Choose an event from Chapters 8 and 9 that you think highlights the ethical dimension in government decision-making. The decision can, in your opinion, highlight ethics or disregard them. Write a blog post in which you explain to others why you think an important historical decision or policy was ethically right or ethically wrong. Offer specific reasons and details for your evaluation.

▲ **SOURCE 6:** Some critics thought Brian Mulroney had made a mistake in reopening the Constitution debate. What might have been behind his decision to do so? What point of view about Mulroney and the Meech Lake Accord is this cartoon expressing?

GLOSSARY

abdicate to give up a position of authority

ace a fighter pilot who has shot down five enemy aircraft

advanced economy countries with well-developed industries, educated workers, superior technological advantages, and high GDP per capita

allegiance loyalty or faithfulness

alliance a union or agreement among groups working toward a common goal

Allies countries fighting against Germany during the Second World War, including Britain, France, Canada, Australia, New Zealand, and after 1941, the United States and the U.S.S.R.

amending formula the process by which changes can legally be made to the Canadian Constitution

Anti-Ballistic Missile Treaty (ABMT) an agreement between the U.S. and the U.S.S.R. limiting strategic offensive weapons and defensive systems

anti-Semitism discrimination or hostility toward Jewish people

armistice an agreement by warring parties to end hostilities

arsenal of democracy a slogan coined by President Franklin D. Roosevelt in December 1940 promising to help the Allies fight the Germans by providing military supplies while staying out of the actual fighting

artillery large guns used to fire shells

assimilation adoption of the customs and language of another cultural group so that the original culture disappears

atomic bomb a bomb containing radioactive material, capable of destroying an entire city or region

autonomy the power to govern oneself and make one's own decisions

Axis alliance between Germany, Italy, and Japan

baby boom the increase in the birth rate that occurred after the Second World War

Balfour Report the conclusions of the 1926 Imperial Conference that acknowledged Canada as an autonomous community within the British Empire

Battle of Britain an air campaign launched in 1940 by the Royal Air Force to stop the Germans from achieving air superiority

Battle of Hong Kong Japan's attack on the British colony of Hong Kong in which there were heavy Canadian losses

Battle of the Atlantic the struggle between the Allies and the Axis powers to control the Allies' shipping route across the Atlantic Ocean

Bill 22 provincial legislation that made French the official language of Québec

Bill 101 also called the "Charter of the French Language," Bill 101 strengthened the position of the French language in Québec

biplane an airplane with two sets of wings, one on top of the body and one underneath

Black Christmas December 25, 1941, the date Hong Kong fell to the Japanese

Black Hand a terrorist group of Bosnian Serbs that was determined to free Bosnia from Austria-Hungary

Black Tuesday October 29, 1929, when the New York Stock Exchange collapsed

blitzkrieg German war tactic of surprise attacks by tanks and fighter planes

Bloc Québécois a federal party dedicated to Québec separation from Canada

Bloody Saturday June 21, 1919, when the Royal North-West Mounted Police charged a crowd of protesters during the Winnipeg General Strike

Bomarc missiles nuclear missiles that Canada agreed to accept from the U.S. During the Cold War; led to a rift in Canada–U.S. relations

Bomber Command the section of the RAF that directed the strategic bombing of Germany

boom town a town that enjoys sudden prosperity or develops quickly

boom-and-bust cycle a term used to describe a healthy (booming) economy and/or one that is failing (bust)

branch plants factories, offices, or other operations set up in Canada but owned or controlled by U.S. or other foreign companies

British Commonwealth an association of nations that were formerly colonies of the British Empire

British Commonwealth Air Training Plan (BCATP) a program to train pilots and aircrew during the Second World War; it produced half of all Commonwealth aircrew and is the largest air training program in history

Canada Act an Act of the Parliament of the United Kingdom passed in 1982 at the request of the Canadian government to patriate Canada's constitution

Canada Council for the Arts the group that funds Canadian artists and supports the arts in Canada

Canadian Bill of Rights a federal document that set out the rights and freedoms of Canadians; it was enacted in 1960 under the leadership of Prime Minister John Diefenbaker

Canadian Charter of Rights and Freedoms the bill identifying human rights that are guaranteed to everyone in Canada; enacted in 1982 and embedded in the Constitution of Canada

Canadian Constitution the document that describes the powers and responsibilities of the government and its parts, and the rights of citizens

Canadian Radio-television and Telecommunications Commission (CRTC) the agency that regulates the amount of foreign material broadcast over the airwaves in Canada and imposes rules requiring Canadian content

Canadiens French descendants of the original settlers of New France

capitalism an economic system in which the production and distribution of goods are owned privately or by shareholders in corporations who have invested their money in the hope of making a profit

capitalist one who believes in an economic system in which the production and distribution of goods are owned privately or by shareholders in corporations that have invested money in the hope of making a profit

casualties those injured, killed, captured, or missing in action

Central Powers the German Empire, the Austro-Hungarian Empire, the Ottoman Empire, and the Kingdom of Bulgaria

Chanak Crisis the Canadian government's refusal in 1922, led by King, to support British troops in defending the Turkish port of Chanak; the first time the Canadian government did not support the British military

child soldier a person under the age of 18 who is forced or otherwise persuaded to fight in an official or unofficial army

cholera a deadly disease caused by bacteria in contaminated water or food, causing severe diarrhea, vomiting, and dehydration; it can kill even healthy people within a matter of hours

civil liberties basic individual rights protected by law, such as freedom of speech

Clarity Act (Bill C-20) legislation passed by the Chrétien government requiring separatist referendums to pass with a "clear majority" rather than 50 percent plus 1, before Québec could negotiate separation

coalition a formal alliance of political parties

Cold War a period lasting approximately from 1945 to 1989 when there was tension and hostility between the communist Soviet Union and its allies and the capitalist United States and its allies

collective bargaining negotiation of a contract between unions and management regarding such things as wages and working conditions

commodity a raw material that is mined or grown and then sold to industry, including oil, natural gas, coal, soybeans, corn, beef, copper, and many others

communism a social and economic theory that property, production, and distribution of goods and services should be owned by the public, and the labour force organized for the benefit of all members of society

communist one who believes that property and the production and distribution of goods and services should be owned by the public and that the labour force should be organized for the benefit of all; the application of the theory in the Soviet Union, China, Cuba, and other countries resulted in dictatorships by leaders of communist parties

comprehensive claims the assertion of the right of Aboriginal nations to large tracts of land because their ancestors were the original inhabitants

confidence in politics, it means support

conscientious objector a person who opposes war for religious or moral reasons

conscription forced enlistment in the armed forces of all fit men of certain ages

convoy a group of ships travelling together protected by an armed force

Co-operative Commonwealth Federation (CCF) Canada's first socialist party, founded in the Prairies in 1932; advocated government control of the economy

corporate tax a tax charged to businesses based on their total revenues

corvettes small, fast warships built in Canada to help protect convoys in the Atlantic Ocean

counterculture a subculture, especially of young people, with values or lifestyles that are in opposition to those of the dominant, established culture

"cradle to grave" social security social assistance provided by the government, from birth to death

credit the ability or power to obtain goods before paying for them

crimes against humanity widespread attacks against civilians, including murder, enslavement, deportation, and torture

Crown corporations businesses and industries owned by the Canadian government

cyberbullying bullying through electronic means, either by use of threats or intimidation, or by invasion of privacy

D-Day June 6, 1944; the day Allied armies, including Canada, invaded France; the biggest Allied invasion of the Second World War

deficit the amount of money a government owes when it takes in less money than it spends

deflation the opposite of inflation, deflation occurs when the price of goods and services falls

deport to send back to one's country of origin

deportation the act of sending someone back to his or her native land

depression a long period of severe economic and social hardship, massive unemployment, and suffering

dictator a ruler with unrestricted power, without any democratic restrictions

Dieppe Raid the 1942 trial raid by Canadian troops against Germany's occupation of Dieppe; Canada suffered heavy losses

disenfranchised to be deprived of basic legal rights

displaced persons those who are forced to leave their native home because of war or for political reasons

Distant Early Warning (DEW) Line radar stations in northern Canada set up between 1958 and 1960 to detect Soviet activity over the North Pole

distinct society a phrase that refers to the recognition of the unique nature of Québec within Canada; it often has the sense that Québec should have special powers and privileges to protect its language and culture

dogfight aerial duel between aircraft

draft resisters citizens who refuse to join the army to fight in a war during conscription

Dunkirk port town in France from which a massive Allied evacuation took place in May 1940, when German forces conquered France

duty to consult the principle of requiring resource companies to consult Aboriginal peoples affected by a proposed development

embargo the prohibition by a government or organization that prevents certain goods from being shipped in or out of a country

enemy alien a national living in a country that is at war with his/her homeland

enfranchisement historically, the process by which an Aboriginal person lost his or her Indian status and became a Canadian citizen

equalization payments a federal transfer of funds from richer to poorer provinces

ethnocentric the belief that one's own culture is superior, and that other cultures should be judged by its values

Famous Five five Alberta women who fought for the political status of women

fascist a form of authoritarian government that is totalitarian and nationalistic

federalism a political system that divides power between federal and provincial legislatures

feminist a person who supports the idea that women are equal to men and deserve equal rights and opportunities

Final Solution the Nazis' plan to systematically kill all European Jews

five-year plans Stalin's plans for economic development in the Soviet Union over five years

FLQ (Front de libération du Québec) a revolutionary movement founded to work for an independent, socialist Québec

free trade trade between countries without tariffs, export subsidies, or other government intervention

Free Trade Agreement (FTA) the agreement that came into effect in 1989 between Canada and the United States to allow goods produced in each country to cross the border tariff-free

G8 an organization of the eight most highly industrialized nations in the world, including Canada

genocide the systematic extermination of a religious or ethnic group

globalization a process by which the regions and countries of the world are becoming economically and culturally interconnected

governor general the person who represents the British crown in Canada

Great Depression a severe economic downturn in the global economy in the 1930s

greenhouse gas gas, such as CO_2 produced by industry and agriculture, that contributes to global warming

Group of Seven group of Canadian landscape painters in the 1920s

habeas corpus the right of a detained person to be brought before a judge or other official to decide whether the detention is lawful

Halibut Treaty a 1923 treaty between Canada and the U.S. to protect halibut along the Pacific Coast; the first treaty negotiated and signed independently by the Canadian government

head tax the fee that Chinese immigrants were required to pay after 1885 in order to enter Canada

Holocaust the Nazi imprisonment and murder of 6 million Jewish people and 5 million other people during the Second World War

homesteaders newcomers who claimed and settled land

honour rationing a civilian effort to consume less and conserve supplies on the home front

Hundred Days Campaign the final Allied offensive against the Central Powers on the Western Front, from August 8 to November 11, 1918

hydroelectric power electricity produced from the energy of falling water

Idle No More an Aboriginal protest movement in Canada founded by women that seeks to "develop community and Indigenous nationhood, protect the environment, and establish connections with non-Aboriginal people who recognize the nation-to-nation relationship established in the treaties"

immigration policy a nation's regulations surrounding immigration

Imperial Conference a meeting of the leaders of the countries in the British Empire

imperialism the policy of one nation acquiring, controlling, or dominating another country or region

imperialists people who support imperialism, the policy of one nation acquiring, controlling, or dominating another

income tax a tax on personal income

Indian Act an Act created to regulate the lives of the First Nations of Canada

industrialization change in production systems to large-scale mechanized factories

inflation the rise in prices for goods and services that increases the cost of living and triggers demand for higher wages

intercontinental ballistic missiles missiles equipped with nuclear warheads that have a range of 5500 kilometres

internment camp a government-run camp where people who are considered a threat are detained

ISIS/ISIL Islamic State in Iraq and Syria/Islamic State in Iraq and the Levant; Islamic fundamentalists who attempt to establish a caliphate, or religious state, in Iraq and Syria through violent means

isolationism the policy of remaining apart from the affairs of other countries

Italian Campaign 1943 Allied battles to recapture Europe from the south, through Sicily and Italy

Juno Beach the nine-kilometre stretch of beach in France where Canadian troops landed on D-Day

Keynesian economics an economic theory named for John Maynard Keynes (1883–1946), who advocated government intervention in the economy, especially during economic downturns

khaki election the name given to the 1917 federal election because of Borden's efforts to win the military vote

King-Byng Crisis a situation that occurred in 1926 when Governor General Byng refused Prime Minister King's request to dissolve Parliament and call an election

Kristallnacht a coordinated attack against Jewish people and their property carried out by Nazis in Germany on November 9, 1938

laissez-faire an economic condition in which industry is free of government intervention

lobby to try to influence the opinions and votes of public officials for or against a cause

Luftwaffe the German air force

majority government a government in which the ruling party has more seats in the House of Commons than all other parties combined

Manhattan Project the code name during the Second World War for the American plan to develop the first atomic bomb

marginalized to be pushed aside and made less important in terms of social standing and power

market economy an economic system in which individuals produce goods and prices are determined by supply and demand

Massey Commission a body set up by the federal government to study the state of Canadian culture

Medical Care Act an Act passed by Parliament in 1966 that provided free access to physician services for Canadians

Meech Lake Accord a package of constitutional amendments that would define Québec as a distinct society within Canada

megaprojects large-scale construction projects that require a huge capital investment; the construction of the St. Lawrence Seaway is an example

merchant marine civilian ships and sailors that transported food, weapons, and munitions

middle power a nation that is not a superpower but has international influence

militarism a nation's policy of enlisting, training, equipping, and maintaining armed forces ready for war

Military Service Act a 1917 Act that made conscription compulsory for all Canadian men between the ages of 20 and 45, calling up the younger men first

Military Voters Act an Act that allowed men and women serving overseas to vote

minority government a government in which the ruling party has less than half the total number of seats in the legislature

mixed economy an economic system in which both individuals and the government produce and sell goods

mortality rate a ratio of how many people die out of a given population over a given period of time for a given reason

multiculturalism a policy of encouraging the expression of the cultures of many ethnic groups that make up a country's population

Multiculturalism Act or Bill C-93, adopted in 1988 to provide a legal framework for multiculturalism in Canada

national debt the amount of money owed by a federal government; most of Canada's national debt money is owed to Canadians who hold Government of Canada savings bonds, treasury bills, and so on

National Resources Mobilization Act an Act passed in 1940 enabling the government to do whatever was necessary for the war effort; it was amended in 1942 to allow conscription

nationalism devotion to and support of one's culture and nation, sometimes resulting in the promotion of independence

nationalists people who have a strong attachment to their culture or nation

nationalize move from private to government ownership

Nazis members of the National Socialist German Workers' Party; the Nazis were extreme nationalists who took power in 1933 and controlled every aspect of German life through a police state

New Deal a series of programs, such as social assistance for the aged and unemployed, introduced by U.S. President Roosevelt in the 1930s to deal with the Depression

no man's land the area between the trenches of two opposing forces

non-aggression pact an agreement between two countries not to attack each other

North American Aerospace Defence Command (NORAD) a defence agreement signed in 1958 between Canada and the United States (known as the North American Air Defence Agreement until 1981)

North American Free Trade Agreement (NAFTA) the agreement signed in 1992 and implemented in 1994 between the United States, Mexico, and Canada to create a free trade zone among the countries

North Atlantic Treaty Organization (NATO) the mutual defence organization set up to protect several Western European countries, Canada, and the U.S. from possible aggression from the U.S.S.R. after the Second World War

notwithstanding clause a clause in the Canadian Constitution (Section 33[1]) that enables Parliament or the legislature of a province to allow an Act to stand even though it contravenes the Charter of Rights and Freedoms

Official Languages Act the Act that states that French and English are Canada's official languages, and that all federal institutions must provide services in English and French

Old Age Pension Act an Act passed in 1927 to provide social assistance to people over 70

On-to-Ottawa Trek a 1935 rail trip from Vancouver to Ottawa (stopped at Regina) by unemployed men to protest conditions at employment relief camps

Operation Barbarossa Germany's unsuccessful invasion of the Soviet Union in 1941–1942, which broke the non-aggression pact and ultimately led to the Soviet Union joining the Allies

overproduction more goods being produced than being sold; leads to a decrease in production, which leads to increased unemployment

paratroopers soldiers trained to parachute from airplanes onto combat areas

Paris Peace Conference a meeting in Paris in 1919 to discuss the terms of a peace agreement after the First World War

Parti Québécois (PQ) a Québec provincial party that advocates separation from Canada

patriate to take control of a document from a former colonial government

Pearl Harbor the Japanese bombing of the U.S. naval base in Hawaii

persecution to oppress or ill-treat because of race, religion, gender, sexual orientation, or beliefs

Persons Case a court case in which the Famous Five successfully fought to have women declared "persons" under Canadian law in 1929

plebiscite a direct vote by electors on an issue of public importance; the outcome of the vote may not be binding on the government

pogey relief payments by a government, sometimes in the form of vouchers for food and other essentials

policy of appeasement giving in to an aggressor's demands in the hopes that no more demands will be made

populist someone who appeals to the concerns of ordinary citizens

pressure group a group of people who get together around a particular issue to try to influence government policy

preventive arrest arrest and detention of suspected terrorists without warrant in order to prevent a terrorist attack

primary industry an industry that deals with the extraction or collection of raw materials, such as mining or forestry

privacy the right to be free of secret surveillance or observation or intrusion by others

profiteering making a profit by raising prices on needed goods or producing poor-quality materials

prohibition the banning of the sale and consumption of alcohol

propaganda information, usually produced by governments, presented in such a way as to inspire and spread particular beliefs or opinions

prorogue to postpone or suspend, as in Parliament

prosperity in the economic cycle, the period of economic growth and expansion

protectionism a system of using tariffs to raise the price of imported goods in order to protect domestic producers

Québec nationalism a movement advocating for the protection and development of Québécois culture and language

Quiet Revolution a period of rapid change and reform that modernized Québec society during the years 1960 to 1966 under the Liberal provincial government of Jean Lesage

recession a decline in the economy, resulting in lower levels of employment and production

reconnaissance military search or exploration

recovery in the economic cycle, the period following a recession during which the value of goods and services rises

Red Paper Aboriginal response to the federal government's White Paper of 1969; the Red Paper caused the government to change its policies

Red Scare the fear that communism would spread to Canada

referendum the process of referring a political question to the people for a direct vote

refugee a person displaced from his or her home and territory by war and other acts of aggression

Regina Manifesto platform of the Cooperative Commonwealth Federation party; it supported public ownership of industry and social programs to assist those in need

Regina Riot a riot that occurred when police attempted to clear On-to-Ottawa trekkers from a stadium in Regina

regional disparity differences in income, wages, and jobs in one area compared with another

regionalism a concern for the affairs of one's own region over those of one's country

reparations compensation from a defeated enemy for damages caused by war

reserves land set aside by the government for the use of First Nations

residential schools government-authorized schools, run by the churches, in which Aboriginal children lived apart from their families and were educated in Canadian culture

Rowell-Sirois Report report of the Royal Commission on Dominion–Provincial Relations, a commission set up in 1937 to examine the Canadian economy and federal–provincial relations

Royal Commission on Bilingualism and Biculturalism a commission created by the federal government to recommend ways of enhancing and promoting the historically bilingual nature of Canada

Rwandan genocide the 1994 mass murder of nearly one million Tutsis in Rwanda

Schlieffen Plan Germany's plan to stage a two-front war with Russia in the east and France in the west

secondary industry an industry that deals with manufacturing or construction

self-determination the freedom for a group to form its own government

self-government the right of a colony or cultural group to define the structure, laws, and policies that will govern its affairs

sharpshooter a person skilled in shooting

Slavic relating to peoples in eastern, southeastern, and central Europe, including Russians, Serbians, Croatians, Poles, Czechs, and so forth

Social Credit Party political party founded in Western Canada; opposed to capitalism

socialist a believer in a political and economic system in which the means of production and distribution in a country are publicly owned and controlled for the benefit of all members of a society

sovereignty-association a proposal by Québec nationalists that Québec have political independence yet retain close economic ties or association with Canada

specific claims First Nations' claims to land based on the belief that the government did not fulfill its obligations under a treaty or other agreement related to money, land, or other assets

speculation buying shares "on margin" with the expectation that the value of the shares will increase enough to pay back the loan and make a profit

status the specific legal identity of an Aboriginal person in Canada, accompanied by rights and benefits; loss of status (non-status) refers to the absence of status, rights, and benefits

Statute of Westminster the law that changed the British Empire into the British Commonwealth; all commonwealth countries to be considered equal in status with Britain and able to make their own laws

suffragist a person who advocates that women should have the right to vote

super-diversity a situation in which more than 100 nationalities are represented in one area, usually a city; the term may also describe diversity in other conditions, such as the way people choose to define themselves

superpowers the term used to refer to the United States and Soviet Union in the post–Second World War period when both were engaged in building up powerful arsenals of weapons of mass destruction as deterrents against aggression

supply and demand the quantity of a product that is available and the market's desire for that product; the price of the product varies based on supply and demand

surveillance spying, using electronic and other methods to gather information about people who are generally unaware they are targets of secret information-gathering

Taliban fundamentalist political movement originating in Afghanistan, which enforces Sharia law and strict dress codes, and opposes education for women and western influences

tariffs taxes on imported goods

terrorism the use of violence, threats, and intimidation to frighten people to try to achieve a political goal

the Blitz the heavy, frequent bombing attacks on London and other British cities by Nazi Germany

tied aid aid given to a foreign country with conditions attached

total war the mobilization of the entire resources of a nation for war

totalitarian state a dictatorship in which the government uses intimidation, violence, and propaganda to rule all aspects of the social and political life of its citizens

trade and aid the process of stimulating the economies of developing countries with aid so that they can access global markets and trade with developed nations

trade union a group of workers who unite to achieve common goals in discussions with owners and management of businesses and industries

transient an unemployed person who moves from place to place in search of work

Treaty of Versailles one of the treaties that ended the First World War; it imposed strict sanctions on Germany

tribunal court of justice

Triple Alliance the alliance of Germany, Austria-Hungary, and Italy prior to the First World War

Triple Entente the alliance of France, Britain, and Russia prior to the First World War

Truth and Reconciliation Commission (TRC) a commission that reveals and documents prior wrongdoing by governments

Union Government the coalition government formed by Conservatives and some Liberals and independents that governed Canada from 1917 to 1920

Union nationale nationalist French Canadian political party led by Maurice Duplessis

unionization the formation of labour unions

United Nations (UN) an organization established in 1945 to bring peace and security to the world

United Nations Children's Fund (UNICEF) a UN organization that works to protect children's rights, to make sure the basic needs of children are met, and to help children reach their full potential; originally called United Nations International Children's Emergency Fund

Victorian of or pertaining to the reign of Queen Victoria; also someone who shares the values of that period

Victory Bonds bonds issued by the Canadian government to support the war effort

war brides foreign women who married Canadian troops serving overseas and then immigrated to Canada after the war

war crimes the killing, torture, and hostage-taking of civilian populations, or the deliberate and extensive destruction of their property

War Guilt Clause an article in the Treaty of Versailles that made Germany responsible for starting the First World War

War Measures Act an Act that gives the federal government emergency powers during wartime, including the right to detain people without laying charges

war of attrition a military strategy based on exhausting the enemy's manpower and resources before yours are exhausted, usually involving great losses on both sides

Warsaw Pact a post–Second World War military alliance established in 1955 involving the Soviet Union and the Soviet-bloc countries of Albania, Bulgaria, Czechoslovakia, East Germany, Hungary, Poland, and Romania

Wartime Elections Act an Act that gave the vote to Canadian women related to servicemen, but cancelled the vote for conscientious objectors and immigrants from enemy countries

Wartime Information Board board established in 1942 to coordinate wartime propaganda in Canada

weapons of mass destruction (WMD) chemical, biological, or radioactive weapons capable of causing widespread death and destruction

Weimar Republic the democratic government in Germany after the First World War

welfare state a state in which the government actively looks after the well-being of its citizens

Western alienation the feeling on the part of Western Canada that federal policies favour Central Canada; it has led to the rise of several regional parties

Western Front the area of fighting in western Europe during the First World War, characterized by trench warfare and inconclusive battles with heavy casualties on both sides

White Paper of 1969 the government report proposing dramatic changes to the lives of Aboriginal peoples, including the elimination of the Indian Act

Winnipeg General Strike massive strike by workers in Winnipeg in 1919

World Health Organization (WHO) the United Nations health organization responsible for providing leadership for global health

INDEX

CREDITS

bg/i: background/inset
t/c/b/l/r: top/centre/bottom/left/right

Photo Credits

viii tl © James Davies/Alamy; **viii bl** Archives of Manitoba Foote 1491 (N2438); **viii bc** *The Globe*, October 25, 1929; **viii tr, br** © CBW/Alamy; **xii bl, br** © Raiford Guins; **xiii bl** © Tim Duarte and Scott Stilphen of The 2600 Connection; **xiii br** © Huguette Roe/Shutterstock; **Unit 1 Opener 2tr** Woodruff/Library and Archives Canada/C-004745; **2tc** © Veterans Affairs Canada; **2b** © Lordprice Collection/Alamy; **3t** © THE CANADIAN PRESS/National Archives of Canada/William Ivor Castle; **Chapter 1 3b** Library and Archives Canada © Canada Post Corporation; **4-5** City of Vancouver Archives CVA 371-917, W.J. Cairns; **6** Glenbow Archives NA-3509-8; **8** Library and Archives Canada © Canada Post Corporation; **9** © First Light/All Canada Photos; **10** NAC/PA-48475; **11** Charles A. Aylett/Library and Archives Canada/C-014090; **13** Woodruff/Library and Archives Canada/C-004745; **14bl** TRL T11245; **14br** Archives of Manitoba Foote 1491 (N2438); **15tl** © D. Hurst/Alamy; **15c** © Pictorial Press Ltd/Alamy; **15tr** © INTERFOTO/Alamy; **15bl** © CP Images; **15br** Glenbow Archives NA-2685-61; **16** Archives of Ontario I0003361; **17b** CTA #SC244-136A; **17i** © David J. Green - Lifestyle/Alamy; **Chapter 2 21-22** © CANADIAN PRESS IMAGES/National Archives of Canada/William Ivor Castle; **22** © Popperfoto/Getty Images; 23 © Mary Evans Picture Library/Alamy; **25** © The Granger Collection, New York; **27** Source unknown; **28** Canada. Dept. of National Defence/NAC/PA-022759; **29bl** Library and Archives Canada, Acc. No. 1983-28-854; **29bc** NAC/95378; **30** © McCord Museum; **32** NAC/PA-2468; **33** © Hulton-Deutsch Collection/CORBIS; **34** © charistoone-travel/Alamy; **35tr** William Rider-Rider/Canada Dept. of National Defence/NAC/PA-002165; **35br** © Veterans Affairs Canada; **36t** CWM 19920044-674 George Metcalf Archival Collection © Canadian War Museum; **36c, b** © Bettmann/CORBIS; **37tl** Reproduced with the permission of the Department of National Defence, 2015; **37tr** International Film Service/The New York Times Company 1919; **37c** Tony Bryan, British Mark I Tank 1916 © Osprey Publishing Ltd. www.osprey-publishing.com; **37br** © Classic Image/Alamy; **38** Canada Dept. of National Defence/NAC/PA-002826; **39** Library and Archives Canada © Canada Post Corporation; **40** © Popperfoto/Getty Images; **41** NAC/C-57358; **42tl** Archives of Ontario 7606-9024; **42bl** Canada Dept. of National Defence/NAC/PA-024435; **43** NAC/C-019944; **44tc** Portrait by Irma Coucill. Courtesy of the Woodland Cultural Centre; **44tr** © Veterans Affairs Canada; **45** © Roberto Herrett/Alamy; **46** William Rider-Rider/Canada Dept. of National Defence/NAC/PA-002279; **Chapter 3 52-53** © Lordprice Collection/Alamy; **54** © Bettmann/CORBIS; **57** GA, Calgary NA3452.2; **58** © Pictorial Press Ltd/Alamy; **59** © Wave/All Canada Photos; **60** Archives of Manitoba #N2762; **61** NAC/e000008187; **62** Glenbow Archives NA-3217-2; **63** Reprinted with permission from Denny May; **64tl** Library and Archives Canada © Canada Post Corporation; **64tr** Glenbow Archives NA-4179-9; **64bl** © Bettmann/CORBIS; **64br** Source unknown; **65cl** Whyte Museum of Canadian Rockies #NA 33-882; **65br** Library and Archives Canada © Canada Post Corporation; **66** NAC/PA-151007; **67** Lake Superior, c.1924 (oil on canvas), Harris, Lawren Stewart (1885-1970)/Art Gallery of Ontario, Toronto, Canada/Bequest of Charles S. Band, 1970/Bridgeman Images; **68** © The Granger Collection, New York; **69** Balfour Photo; **70** National Film Board/Library and Archives Canada/PA-048574; **72** VPL #8956-D; **73** © CANADIAN PRESS IMAGES/*Winnipeg Free Press*/Ken Gigliotti; **74** Glenbow Archives NA-3055-24; **75** Glenbow Archives NC-6-11899; **77** © Michael de Adder/Arizans.com; **81** *The Globe*, October 25, 1929; **83** © Michael Eddenden; **Unit 1 Study Guide 85** Library and Archives Canada/c148K; **86t** City of Toronto Archives, Fonds 1244, Item 1155; **86b** Glenbow Archives NA-1497-69; **Unit 2 Opener 88t** Glenbow Archives NA-2496-1; **88b** NAC; **89tl** NAC/C-29397; **89tr** © CORBIS; **89bl** © CORBIS; **Chapter 4 90-91** Glenbow Archives ND-3-6742; **92** © Hulton-Deutsch Collection/CORBIS; **95b** Pearson Education Ltd; **96** Glenbow Archives NA-2496-1; **97** City of Toronto Archives, Fonds 1244, Item 1683; **98** NAC/C-29397; **99** Courtesy of Ontario Jewish Archives. Reproduced with the permission of the Archives.nlc-10915; **100c** NAC Acc. No. 1990-119-1; **100r** Yukon Archives #8533; **103** NAC/C-087860; **104** On to Ottawa Historical Society Vancouver, British Columbia, Canada; **105** CTA #SC244-1682; **106tl** Source unknown; **106br** Courtesy of CBC, cbc.ca; **108** Glenbow Archives NA-2377-1; **109** © Vic Davidson/Montréal Gazette. Reprinted by permission; **110** Glenbow Archives NA-3622-20; **111t** NAC/C-31058; **111b** © CHRIS ROUSSAKIS/Reuters/Landov; **113t** © Lucien Aigner/CORBIS; **113bl** © CANADIAN PRESS IMAGES/Stf/Files; **113br** Parks Canada; **114** Dale/*Winnipeg Free Press*/19 Jan 1931; **115** Dale/*Winnipeg Free Press*; **116** © Bettmann/CORBIS; **Chapter 5 120-121** City of Vancouver Archives CVA LP 109, Claude Dettloff; **122** © Paul Almasy/CORBIS; **123** © AP Photo; **124tl** Star of David cloth patch, printed "Jood", as compulsorily worn by Jews in Nazi Europe/Private Collection/Bridgeman Images; **124b** © CORBIS; **125tr** © Bettmann/CORBIS; **125br** © AP Photo; **129** NAC/PA-119013; **130** © AP Photo; **131** City of Toronto Archives, *Globe and Mail* fonds, Fonds 1266, Item 30791; **132** City of Toronto Archives, Fond 1244, Item 826; **133** Christopher J. Woods/Canada Dept. of National Defence/Library and Archives Canada/PA-142289; **134tl** NAC, Acc. No. 1987-72-105 The Hubert Rogers Collection, Gift of Mrs. Helen Priest Rogers; **134r** *Maintenance Jobs in the Hangar* by Paraskeva Clark, #14085 © Canadian War Museum; **136** © CORBIS; 139 Remember Hong Kong poster #19700036-024 © Canadian War Museum; **140** NAC/PA-112993; **141** © AP Photo; **142t** © INTERFOTO/Alamy; **142cl** © Hulton Archive/Getty Images; **142cr** Library of Congress Prints and Photographs Division [LC-USZ62-101012]; **142b** © Skip Higgins of Raskal Photography/Alamy; **143tl** © Tim Scrivener/Alamy; **143tr** © SSPL/Getty Images; **143b** NAC/a144981; **144** National Archives of Canada C 14160; **145** © CP Photo; **146** NAC/PA-163938; **150tl** Alexander Mackenzie Stirton/Canada. Dept. of National Defence/NAC/PA-134376; **150b** © AP Photo; **151** © Hulton Archive/Getty Images; **152** Library of Congress, cph 3c13495; **153** Library of Congress, cph 3c13494; **154tl** © CORBIS; **154i** © Reuters/Bettmann/CORBIS; **155, 156bl** National Film Board of Canada. Photothèque/NAC; **156br** © The Art Archive/Alamy; **157** TRL BDS 1939-45 Espionage #5; **158** McCord Museum M965.199.3242; **159** NAC; **161** City of Toronto Archives, *Globe and Mail* fonds, Fonds 1266, Item 104988; **163** © AP Photo; **Unit 2 Study Guide 165** © Sueddeutsche Zeitung Photo/Alamy; **166t** © Sueddeutsche Zeitung Photo/Alamy; **166b** © Sueddeutsche Zeitung Photo/Alamy; **167** Library and Archives Canada, Acc. No. 1983-30-680; **Unit 3 Opener 168t** © Michael Ochs Archives/Getty Images; **168tc** NAC/PA-129625; **168bc** © Bettmann/CORBIS; **168b** © CP PHOTO; **169tl** © CP PICTURE ARCHIVE/Fred Chartrand; **169tr** © CP/AP Images; **Chapter 6 170-171** York University Libraries, Clara Thomas Archives & Special Collections, *Toronto Telegram* fonds, ASC00832; **172** Public Archives of NS #G1066-2; **173** © Lambert/Getty Images; **174b** © Allan Cash Picture Library/Alamy; **174i** © DeBrocke/ClassicStock/Corbis; **175tr** © Mondadori Portfolio/Getty Images; **175b** © Michael Ochs Archives/Getty Images; **176** © CBS/Getty Images; **177bl** © Hulton Archives/Getty Images; **177br** © CANADIAN PRESS IMAGES/Wisconsin Historical Society/Courtesy Everett Collection; **178** Photo courtesy National Ballet of Canada; **179** Rev. William Maurice fonds, at the Shingwauk Residential Schools Centre; **180** Gar Lunney/National Film Board of Canada. Photothèque/NAC/PA-191422; **181** NAC/C-123991; **182** NAC/PA-112693; **183** Bob Brooks/National Film Board fonds/e010975948; **184t** Centre d'archives de la région de Thetford, Fonds Syndicat des travailleurs horaires de L'Amiante CSN Inc.; **184l** Public domain; **184r** © Nicolas Raymond/Shutterstock; **185** CWM 20010129-0543 © Canadian War Museum; **186tr** © CP PHOTO 1999/NAC C-071095; **186b** © Greg Taylor/Alamy; **187cl** © AP Photo/NASA; **187bl** © SSPL/Getty Images; **187b** © Wire_man/Shutterstock; **187br** © Maxx-Studio/Shutterstock; **187cr** © Dario Sabljak/Shutterstock; **187tr** © Phant/Shutterstock; **188** © Pavel Cheiko/Alamy; **189** © Hulton Archives/Getty Images; **190** NAC/PA-129625; **191** © American Stock/Getty Images; **192** © Getty Images; **193** Public domain; **195tr** NORAD; **196** © *Washington Post*/Getty Images; **197tr** Avro Aviation; **197bl** © Canada Aviation and Space Museum, 1967.0387; **197br** © Malcolm Fife/Getty Images; **198** © Spencer Platt/Getty Images; **200** © CP/AP Images; **Chapter 7 204** *The Globe and Mail*, October 17, 1970; **206** © Harvey Lloyd/Getty Images; **207tr** © Michael Ochs Archives/Getty Images; **207br** © MARK BLINCH/Reuters/Landov; **208** © Bettmann/CORBIS; **209tc** Cover from SILENT SPRING by Rachel Carson (Boston: Houghton Mifflin Harcourt Publishing Company, 1962). Used by permission of Houghton Mifflin Harcourt Publishing Company. All rights reserved; **209br** © Greenpeace/Robert Keziere; **210** © The Canadian Press, Jacques Boissinot; **211** © Rick Madonik/GetStock.com; **212br** © Bettmann/CORBIS; **213** © CP PHOTO/*Halifax Chronicle Herald*; **214** © CP PHOTO; **215cr** © Jason Pineau/All Canada Photos; **216t, c** © Pearson Education Archives; **216b** © P. Uzunova/Shutterstock; **217** © CP Photo; **218** © CP Photo/Peter Bregg; **219** © The Canadian Press Images/*Montreal Gazette*; **220** © Artizans/Roy Peterson; **221tr** © CP Photo; **221bl** © AP Photo; **222** © CP Photo; **224** © Joseph Heller; **226** © Firefoxfoto/Alamy; **227tl** © AP Photo/NASA; **227bl** © Archive Holdings Inc./Getty Images; **227br** © AP Photo/rw/bd; **227cr, tr** © SSPL/Getty Images; **228tl** © Piero Oliosi/Polaris/Newscom; **228b** © Hulton Archive/Getty Images; **229, 230** © AP Photo; **231** © Dick Darrell/*Toronto Star*/GetStock; **232bg** © Bernard Weil/GetStock.com; **232i** © CP/Daniel Morel; **234** © CP PICTURE ARCHIVE/Fred Chartrand; **235tr** © CP PICTURE ARCHIVE/*Toronto Star*/Frank Lennon; **235br** © MAECD-DFATD/David Barbour; **239l** Duncan Cameron/Library and Archives Canada/PA-209888; **239c, r** © Bettmann/CORBIS; **239bl** © CP PHOTO/Carl Bigras; **239br** © Greenpeace/Robert Keziere; **Unit 3 Study Guide 241** © The Granger Collection, New York; **242** © CP PHOTO; **Unit 4 Opener 244tl** © ZUMA Press, Inc./Alamy; **244tr** © CP PHOTO/Kevin Frayer; **244b** © Terry Prekas Photography/Alamy; **245tl** © Mary Crandall; **245tr** © THE CANADIAN PRESS/Stf-Ron Poling; **245b** © CP/Tom Hanson; **Chapter 8 246-247** © CP PHOTO/str-Shaney Komulainen; **248t** © David Cooper/GetStock.com; **248b** *The Simpsons*; **250l** © kkong/Alamy; **250tr** © Stocktrek Images, Inc./Alamy; **250bl, b** © Chris Willson/Alamy; **250b** © Sergio Azenha/Alamy; **250br** © Hugh Threlfall/Alamy; **251tr** © DJC/Alamy; **251cl, c** © Shutterstock markos86; **251bl** © Richard A. McGuirk/Shutterstock; **251bc** © ZUMA Press, Inc./Alamy; **251br** © Press Association/AP Photo; **251i** © Fedor Bobkov/Shutterstock; **253r** Courtesy of CBC, cbc.ca; **253b** © Cindy Ord/WireImage/Getty Images; **254** © WENN Ltd/Alamy; **255** © Boris Spremo/GetStock.com; **256i** © TheStoreGuy/Alamy; **256bl** © Images Distribution/Agence Quebec Presse/Newscom; **256tr** © Steve Russell/ZUMA Press/Newscom; **256br** © Canadian Press Images/Frank Arcuri; **257tl** © Alex Waterhouse-Hayward;

Literary and Source Credits

Castellano, Linda Archibald, and Mike DeGagne, p 126. Ottawa, ON: Aboriginal Healing Foundation, 2008. With permission from the Legacy of Hope Foundation; **180** From *Naniiliqpita*, Fall 2009, p. 35. A Publication of Nunavut Tunngavik Inc.; **182** Source unknown; **188** Mackenzie King, House of Commons Debates, Spring 1941; **192** © Government of Canada. Reproduced with the permission of the Minister of Public Works and Government Services Canada. Source: Library and Archives Canada/Clifford W. Harvison fonds/MG31-E119, Vol. 1, File 1-6, «What Communists Have Achieved,» Page 6; **192** "Anti-Communist Ballot Cuts Out All but Two," *The Globe and Mail*, January 2, 1948; **192** "The Red Scare: Canada Searches for Communists During the Height of Cold War Tensions." 2001. http://www.cbc.ca/history/EPISCONTENTSE1EP15CH1PA2LE. html Last accessed Apr. 20, 2010; **192** House of Commons, Oct. 16, 1970; **Chapter 7 205** FLQ, "Revolution by the People for the People," March 1963; **210** CBC television clip, first broadcast on Dec. 21, 1967. http://archives.cbc.ca/politics/rights_freedoms/topics/538/ Last accessed Apr. 20, 2010; **212** House of Commons Debates, 3rd Session, 28th Parliament, Vol. 8, Oct. 8, 1971; **214** Statement of Government of Canada on Indian Policy, 1969 (The White Paper), presented to the first session of the twenty-eighth Parliament by the Honourable Jean Chretien, Minister of Indian Affairs and Northern Development. Ottawa: Indian and Northern Affairs Canada, 1969. http://www.ainc-inac. gc.ca/ai/arp/ls/pubs/cp1969/cp1969-eng.asp. Reproduced with the permission of the Minister of Public Works and Government Services Canada, 2010; **214** Harold Cardinal, *The Unjust Society: The Tragedy of Canada's Indians* (Mel Hurtig Publishers, 1969); **221** CBC television clip, first broadcast on Oct. 13, 1970. http://archives.cbc.ca/war_conflict/civil_ unrest/clips/610/ Last accessed Apr. 20, 2010; **223** Pierre Trudeau, *Memoirs* (Toronto: McClelland & Stewart, 1993), 136; **223** René Lévesque, *Memoirs* (Toronto: McClelland & Stewart, 1986), 247; **223** J.L. Finlay and D.N. Sprague, *The Structure of Canadian History* (Toronto: Prentice Hall, 1984), 444; **223** Robert Bothwell, Ian Drummond, and John English, "Quebec and the Constitution: Phase One," *Canada Since 1945: Power, Politics, and Provincialism* (Toronto: University of Toronto Press, 1989), 373. © University of Toronto Press 1981, 1989. Reprinted with permission of the publisher; **225** Peter Lougheed, Federal-Provincial Conference on Energy, Ottawa, January 22, 1974; **225** "Catalogue F1-21/1982E," Department of Finance. Reproduced with the permission of the Minister of Public Works and Government Services, 2010; **233** Michael Byers, "Afghanistan: Wrong Mission for Canada," *The Tyee*, Oct. 6, 2006. http://thetyee.ca/Views/2006/10/06/ Afghanistan/ Last accessed Apr. 20, 2010; **233** Andrew Coyne and Paul Wells, "Afghanistan: Noble fight or Lost Cause?" *Macleans*, Nov. 1, 2009. http://www2.macleans. ca/2009/11/01/afghanistan-noble-fight-or-lost-cause/3/ Last accessed Apr. 20, 2010; **234** © Government of Canada. Reproduced with the permission of the Minister of Public Works and Government Services Canada (2010). Source: Library and Archives Canada/ Pierre Elliott Trudeau fonds/Series 011, Vol. 63, file 13; **237** Paul Kaludjak, "Sovereignty and Inuit in the Canadian Arctic," *Arctic Peoples*, Nov. 18, 2006. http://www.arcticpeoples. org/news/item/83-sovereignty-and-inuit-in-the-canadian-arctic Last accessed Apr. 20, 2010; **Unit 3 Study Guide 241, 242, 243** Sources unknown; **254** Source: http://www. hrcr.org/safrica/equality/egan_canada.html; **Chapter 8 265** *CBC Sunday Morning*, broadcast on March 4, 1990. Michel Cormier, reporter. http://archives.cbc.ca/pro-grams/682-5323/page/2/ Last accessed Apr. 20, 2010; **267** © Catherine Rolfsen/*Vancouver Sun*; **269** Source unknown; **270** Excerpted from *Three Day Road* by Joseph Boyden. Copyright © 2005 Joseph Boyden. Reprinted by permission of Penguin Canada, a division of Penguin Random House Canada Limited, a Penguin Random House Company; **272** Canada Mortgage and Housing Corporation (CMHC). Census-based housing indicators and data, 2004. http://www.cbc.ca/news/background/aboriginals/status-report2006.

html All rights reserved. Reproduced with the consent of CMHC. All other uses and reproductions of this material are expressly prohibited; **278** Liyu Guo, Program Assistant, Campaign 2000, Family Service Toronto; **279** "Initiatives for peace and security." Remarks in the House of Commons, Ottawa, Feb. 9, 1984. Ottawa: Department of External Affairs, Statements and Speeches No. 84/2; **287** Prof. Donald Fleming, University of British Columbia, "Kosovo and Canada's participation in NATO's war." Letter to Bill Graham, Chair, Standing Committee on Foreign Affairs and International Trade, April 21, 2000. Found at http://www.balkanpeace.org/index.php?index=/content/background_studies/ lan/lan01.incl Last accessed Apr. 20, 2010; **Chapter 9 290** Television broadcast of President George W. Bush, Address to the Nation, September 11, 2001; **292** "Source: *Hansard*, April, 8, 2003 http://www.parl.gc.ca/HousePublications/Publication. aspx?DocId=824069#T1015. With permission from the Office of the Law Clerk and Parliamentary Counsel. Avec la permission du Bureau de Légiste et Couseiller Parlementaire"; Source: https://ca.news.yahoo.com/blogs/canada-politics/10-years-later-jean-chr%C3%A9tien-talks-decision-not-065718393.html Adapted from http://www.law. utoronto.ca/documents/Mackin/Khadr_ChildSoldier.pdf; **294** Source: http://www. whitehouse.gov/blog/2011/01/28/president-obama-situation-egypt-all-governments-must-maintain-power-through-consent-; **304** National Chief Perry Bellegarde, Assembly of First Nations, December 2014. http://norj.ca/2014/12/new-afn-chief-puts-focus-on-resource-ownership; **305** © Office of the Prime Minister (2015). Bureau du Premier Ministre (2015); **305** © *Eagle Feather News*; **306** © Office of the Prime Minister (2015). Bureau du Premier Ministre (2015); **306** Speech by Alan Li, Then President of the Chinese Canadian National Council, 1994; **307** © Office of the Prime Minister (2015). Bureau du Premier Ministre (2015); **307** Harsha Walia, "Komagata Maru and the Politics of Apologies," Aug. 25, 2008 © Harsha Walia; **311** *The Current State of Multiculturalism in Canada, 2010* http://www.cic.gc.ca/english/pdf/pub/multi-state.pdf; **311** Source: Statistics Canada, http://www4.hrsdc.gc.ca/.3ndic.1t.4r@-eng.jsp?iid=38; **319** Source: http://www.statcan.gc.ca/pub/91-003-x/2007001/4129907-eng.htm#1; **319** United Nations, "The World at Six Billion," p. 3. http://www.un.org/esa/population/publica-tions/sixbillion/sixbilpart1.pdf Last accessed Apr. 20, 2010. © United Nations. Reproduced with permission. The United Nations is the author of the original material; **321** www.msf.ca; **322** CBC; **322** Source: http://www.reuters.com/article/2013/07/12/us-malala-un-idUSBRE96B0IC20130712.

Art Credits

Deborah Crowle Art Group: *Chapter 1:* 2–3, 7, 9; *Chapter 2:* 23, 24, 31, 33, 47; *Chapter 3:* 55, *Chapter 4:* 96; *Chapter 5:* 126, 128, 135, 137, 138, 147, 148, 149, 160; *Chapter 6:* 168–169, 172, 180, 190, 195, 200, 201, 203; *Chapter 7:* 225, 229, 230, 233, 237; *Chapter 8:* 249, 252, 272, 277, 282, 283, 284, 285; *Chapter 9:* 291.

Donna Guilfoyle: *Prelims:* ix; *Chapter 4:* 88–89, 108, *Chapter 8:* 244–245, 268; *Chapter 9:* 303, 310, 311, 319.

Steve MacEachern: *Chapter 3:* 77, 78, *Chapter 4:* 93, 95.

Key Events in History

Aboriginal Peoples	Women	Minorities and Immigration

1960 — 1960 • Aboriginal peoples win right to vote in federal elections

1963 • Betty Friedan's book *The Feminine Mystique* launches the women's movement

1962 • Most racial discrimination is eliminated from Canada's immigration policies

1965 — 1965 • Aboriginal peoples win the right to vote in Alberta

1969 • Aboriginal peoples win the right to vote in Québec

1967 • Royal Commission on the Status of Women

1969 • Bill C-150 recognizes the right to abortion and gives women access to contraception

1970 — 1969 • Bill C-150 decriminalizes homosexuality

1971 • Official policy of multiculturalism introduced

• White Paper proposes changes for Aboriginal peoples, including eliminating the Indian Act

1971 • National Action Committee on the Status of Women established

1970s

• Provinces across Canada change family law to gradually eliminate gender bias

1975 — 1970 • "Red Paper" demands Aboriginal self-government

1973 • Supreme Court recognizes Aboriginal land title in *Calder* case

1980 — 1977 • Aboriginal peoples halt Mackenzie Valley Pipeline

1978 • Assembly of First Nations formed

1985 —

1990 — 1990 • Oka land dispute

• *Sparrow* case establishes that Aboriginal rights, such as hunting and fishing, in existence in 1982 are protected under the Constitution

1988 • Svend Robinson becomes first openly gay federal MP

• Canadian Multiculturalism Act (Bill C-93)

1993 • Kim Campbell becomes Canada's first female prime minister

1992 • Canadian military bans discrimination on the basis of sexual orientation

1995 — 1991 • Royal Commission on Aboriginal Peoples

1993 • B.C. Treaty Commission established

2000 — 1996 • Last federally funded residential school closes

1997 • *Delgamuukw* decision

2000 • Nisga'a Treaty

2002 • Canada renews commitment to UN Convention on the Elimination of All Forms of Discrimination Against Women (CEDAW)

2005 — 2004 • Supreme Court affirms principle of "duty to consult" in *Haida v. British Columbia*

2005 • Civil Marriage Act legalizes gay marriage throughout Canada

2006 • Federal government apologizes for Chinese Head Tax

2010 — 2006 • Residential school settlement agreement

2008 • Prime Minister Harper apologizes to former residential school students

2008 • Prime Minister Harper apologizes for *Komagata Maru* incident

2012 • Malala Yousafzai awarded Nobel Peace Prize

2015 — 2011 • Nisga'a Final Agreement

2012 • Founding of Idle No More

2015 • 20.6 percent of Canadians are born outside the country

2015 • Truth and Reconciliation Commission issues final report